The Judgment of the Trojan Prince Paris
in Medieval Literature

Margaret J. Ehrhart

The Judgment of the Trojan Prince Paris in Medieval Literature

upp   *Philadelphia · 1987*

UNIVERSITY OF PENNSYLVANIA PRESS

University of Pennsylvania Press

MIDDLE AGES SERIES

Edited by
EDWARD PETERS
Henry Charles Lea Professor
of Medieval History
University of Pennsylvania

A complete listing of the books in this series
appears at the back of this volume

Library of Congress Cataloging-in-Publication Data

Ehrhart, Margaret J.
   The judgment of the Trojan prince Paris in medieval literature.

   (The Middle Ages)
   Bibliography: p.
   Includes index.
      1. Literature, Medieval—History and criticism. 2. Paris (Greek
mythology) in literature. I. Title. II. Series.
PN687.P27E39   1987   809'.93351   87-10894
ISBN 0-8122-8068-7

To my aunt Rosemary Pellegrini-Quarantotti

Contents

Illustrations

Preface and Acknowledgments

That tales of the pagan gods were adopted and put to use by the Christian Middle Ages is a testimony to the medieval genius for assimilation. That the effort seemed worthwhile is a tribute to the powerful seduction of classical culture. One tale that was adapted to almost every category of literature was the story of how the Trojan prince Paris judged the rival goddesses. When he chose Aphrodite as the most beautiful and accepted the Greek queen Helen as her gift of thanks, the war he caused lasted ten years, and his notoriety much longer. The Judgment of Paris was rehandled time and again between the fall of ancient civilization and the Renaissance. To follow its adaptations to its medieval audiences is the purpose of this study.

Chapter 1, "The Judgment of Paris in the Ancient World," sets out the origins of the three traditions through which the Middle Ages knew the Judgment: the classical, the allegorical, and the rationalizing. In the classical tradition, the story is presented as a true event, an encounter between a mortal and the gods. It appeared thus, for example, in the *Cypria*, the *Krisis* of Sophocles, and the plays of Euripides, and it was passed on to the Middle Ages by the *Fabulae* of Hyginus, Ovid's *Heroides*, and two medieval compilations which derive from a handbook produced during the late-classical period.

In the allegorical tradition, the story is important not because it is true, but because it stands for truths. The Stoics, in particular, developed the story's allegorical dimension, introducing the theme of the three lives—contemplative, active, and voluptuous—which was to become almost inseparable from the Judgment for two millennia. The most important allegorical treatment of the Judgment from the ancient world was that of Fulgentius, and his analysis was to dominate medieval allegorical interpretations of the story.

In the rationalizing tradition, Paris's judgment of the goddesses is debunked in some way, usually by the premise that he dreamed it. The Judgment was first presented as a dream by the Greek Sophist and rhetorician Dio Chrysostom, but the most important example of the dream-Judgment appears in the *De Excidio Troiae Historia* of "Dares the Phrygian," a work accepted for centuries as the literal truth of the Trojan War.

The Middle Ages regarded the Trojan War as history, and the Judgment was considered a key historical episode because it explained how the conflict between the Greeks and the Trojans began. Chapter 2, "The Judgment as History," considers the treatment of the Judgment in histories of Troy, histories of individual European nations (who emulated the *Aeneid* by tracing their origins to fleeing Trojan heroes), and histories of the world. For the most part, these works followed the rationalizing tradition of Dares, in which Paris's judgment of the goddesses is only a dream, because they sought to give the episode a historical justification.

Certain stories seem destined for allegorical interpretation. Already in fifth-century Athens, the story of the Judgment, in which a young man makes a choice that leads to his own downfall, may have had an allegorical dimension. Within a few centuries, the allegorical significance of the Judgment became explicit, and thus began a tradition which was never completely abandoned. Chapter 3, "The Judgment as Allegory," considers medieval allegorizations of the Judgment, imposed allegories in which an interpreter saw in the Judgment ideas which really originated in his own mind. Most of these interpretations follow Fulgentius's scheme, which saw Paris's choice among the goddesses as a choice among contemplative, active, and voluptuous lives, and which condemned all but the contemplative life. Medieval interpretations reflected the aims of the interpreters, but the Fulgentian scheme underlay nearly every approach.

The Judgment's exemplary character was most effectively exploited with the rise of the allegorical dream vision in fourteenth-century France. Guillaume de Machaut, Jean Froissart, and the anonymous author of the *Echecs amoureux* all saw in the Judgment of Paris the inspiration for extended allegorical narratives. In Chapter 4, "The Choice of Paris," the early development of the Judgment in histories and collections of allegorized fable helps interpret these three important dream visions. The Judgment and its long allegorical tradition helped fashion these narratives which invite the reader to look beneath the surface for the play of ideas which is their *raison d'être*.

Chapter 5, "The Meaning of the Judgment," considers a group of works which, like the dream visions considered in Chapter 4, use the Judgment for some purpose other than its supposed historical truth or the explicit allegorical interpretations that can be imposed on it, but which, unlike the dream visions, are not allegories. This chapter asks when a story's traditional allegorization is relevant to the meaning of a work in which it is used, and demonstrates that the moral force of the Judgment varies greatly from century to century. Graeco-Byzantine romances like *Floire et Blancheflor* and *Athis et Prophilias*, for example, used the Judgment because it echoed their own plots, but there was no suggestion that a character whose actions parallel those of Paris is to be condemned. By the middle of the fourteenth century, however, the Italian humanist Convenevole da Prato flattered his patron Robert of Naples by showing Robert's awareness that Paris fell when he submitted to Venus. Yet a late work like William Nevill's *Castell of Pleasure* saw Paris as an exemplary lover who rightly avoids the lure of money and worthily pursues love.

The Epilogue, "The Judgment and the Meaning of History," shows how the classical, allegorical, and rationalizing traditions came together in a Renaissance treatment of the Judgment: *Les Illustrations de Gaule et singularitez de Troye* by Jean Lemaire de Belges. The work is a history purportedly based on authoritative new sources and intended to show that Troy and Gaul can trace their origins to founders who share descent from Noah. In the midst of his history, however, Lemaire inserted the classical version of the Judgment. He then supplied a detailed allegorical interpretation not only of the goddesses and their attributes but of the story itself, completely blurring the distinction between history and allegorized fable. His handling of the Judgment and its allegorical tradition demonstrates that in the Renaissance the Judgment's allegorical significance was no longer deeply felt.

An appendix, "The Judgment of Paris in Medieval Art," shows how the variations which characterize the different versions of the Judgment in medieval literature are reflected in artistic depictions of the episode.

Working with the wide variety of texts in which the many Judgments I studied are contained, I have relied for most Greek and some Latin sources on the Loeb Classical Library; elsewhere, translations are my own unless otherwise indicated. Latin biblical quotations are from the Vulgate; English translations, from the Douay-Rheims Bible. In referring to classical deities, I use their Greek names when discussing Greek texts and their Latin names when discussing Latin texts. In the texts I studied, Paris is infrequently called Alexander. I call him Paris throughout.

It is a pleasure to thank the people and institutions who have helped me with this project. As my advisor in graduate school, Jackson J. Campbell encouraged my interest in Guillaume de Machaut, whose poetry led me to the Judgment of Paris. My debt to John Block Friedman will be obvious to anyone who has read his *Orpheus in the Middle Ages.* I thank him further for his detailed commentary on an earlier draft of this work. Charles Dahlberg, a former colleague, has been more than generous in encouraging my study of the Judgment. I owe debts of gratitude to Dr. J. B. Trapp, who corresponded with me in the early days of my project and graciously welcomed me to the Warburg Institute; to Professor Jürgen Stohlmann, who responded with extreme generosity to my query about the Judgment's occurrence in medieval Latin literature; to Professor Siegfried Wenzel, who has kindly supplied me with a number of references and with a transcription from his microfilm of Harley 7322; and to Professor Bruno Roy, who responded to several inquiries about the *Echecs amoureux* and its commentary. I would also like to thank the two anonymous readers who reviewed my manuscript for the University of Pennsylvania Press. Their comments managed both to encourage me and to spur me on to further effort.

The project would have been impossible without the staffs of the various libraries whose holdings I consulted: the New York Public Library, the British Museum, the Warburg Institute, and the libraries of Columbia University, Princeton University, Ohio State University, and the University of Illinois. At the Weiner Library of Fairleigh Dickinson University, librarians Judith Katz and Laila Rogers gave invaluable assistance in obtaining interlibrary loans.

The American Council of Learned Societies funded the early stages of my research and writing with a generous grant; more recently Fairleigh Dickinson University awarded me a grant-in-aid to assist with the completion of the project.

The discussion of Machaut's *Dit de la fonteinne amoureuse* which appears in Chapter 4 was published in somewhat different form in *Philological Quarterly* 59 (1980). Some of my material on Christine de Pisan's use of the Judgment will appear in a collection of essays being edited by Jane Chance.

My final thanks go to my family. Though Paris has made our marriage a *ménage à trois* for the past seven years, my husband, Norman Smith, responded generously to requests for help, reading the entire manuscript and making valuable suggestions for its improvement. To my son, Matthew, who has never known life without the Judgment of Paris, I owe my thanks as well.

I

The Judgment of Paris
in the Ancient World

One of the ancient Greeks' most appealing myths is that of the Judgment of Paris. The Trojan prince who declared that Aphrodite's beauty outshone that of Hera or Athena, thus winning the wife of the Spartan king Menelaus and bringing about the destruction of his city by the angry Greeks, still fascinates us. The Middle Ages was fascinated by the myth as well, but to collect versions of the Judgment from the pages of medieval literature is to assemble a bewildering variety of tales. Medieval fancy embroidered the story in countless ways, yet the versions of the Judgment known to the Middle Ages derive clearly from traditions already existing in ancient times. The complex skein we must unravel when we study the Judgment of Paris in medieval literature is composed of separate strands which lead us back to classical tradition. We can understand neither the Middle Ages' originality nor its debt to tradition unless we base our study of the Judgment firmly in the classical period. We must accordingly begin with the Judgment's earliest forms in ancient Greece.[1]

Paris was a son of Priam, king of Troy. As he pastured his beasts in the field one day, a Greek bull came and fought one of his own. When the intruder won, Paris crowned it. His justice impressed three goddesses, Hera, Athena, and Aphrodite, who needed a judge to settle their dispute about who was most beautiful, and they entrusted the decision to Paris. Each offered him a gift in exchange for decision in her favor, but Paris chose Aphrodite, who had offered him the fairest lady alive.

Paris was a handsome prince of Troy. It was said that he judged Aphrodite more beautiful than Hera or Athena—but this is only a story told by poets, who meant to suggest that young men are swayed by beauty and give their lives over to pleasure.

Paris was a prince of the Trojan house. As he hunted one day with his men, he pursued a great stag which led him away from his companions. Tired out by the chase, he lay down and slept. He dreamed that three goddesses asked him to choose one of them most beautiful. Spurning the bribes offered by Hera and Athena, he awarded the prize to Aphrodite, who had promised him the loveliest woman in Greece.

Each of these versions of the Judgment is well represented in the Middle Ages, yet each exemplifies a tradition already established in Greek literature. I call the three traditions the classical, the allegorical, and the rationalizing. My first example above represents the classical tradition. In this tradition, Paris's encounter with the goddesses is real, and the Trojan prince is herding animals when he meets the divine embassy. My second example represents the allegorical tradition. The Judgment is regarded as a conceit of poets, significant for its inner truth rather than its historical validity. My third example represents the rationalizing tradition. Paris's encounter with the goddesses is a dream or vision rather than a true event, making it an acceptable prelude to the Trojan War even for those skeptical that gods would bother with the opinions of men.

The oldest version of the Judgment is the classical one; this was the version known to the authors of the earliest Greek literature. The only surviving Greek epics presuppose the Judgment as a condition of their plots, since in claiming the prize Aphrodite promised him, Paris caused the Trojan War. When Homer refers in book 24 of the *Iliad* to "the delusion of Paris / who insulted the goddesses when they came to him in his courtyard / and favoured her who supplied the lust that led to disaster,"[2] he knows that the allusion is sufficient to evoke the whole story of the war's origin.

A later epic, however, one of those that filled in the complex story which the *Iliad* and the *Odyssey* narrate only in part, included a detailed treatment of the Judgment. The *Cypria*, which dates from the seventh or sixth century B.C., is now known only through summaries which survive in the *Chrestomathy* of Proclus and the Epitome of the *Library* of Apollodorus.³ The two summaries include complementary versions of the Judgment.

As the *Chrestomathy* has it:

> Strife arrives while the gods are feasting at the marriage of Peleus and starts a dispute between Hera, Athena, and Aphrodite as to which of them is fairest. The three are led by Hermes at the command of Zeus to Alexandrus on Mount Ida for his decision, and Alexandrus, lured by his promised marriage with Helen, decides in favour of Aphrodite.⁴

The Epitome of the *Library* omits the context of Peleus's wedding feast, but it specifies the gifts offered by the other two goddesses. The apple is probably a later interpolation and not to be traced to the *Cypria*:

> Strife threw an apple as a prize of beauty to be contended for by Hera, Athena, and Aphrodite; and Zeus commanded Hermes to lead them to Alexander on Ida in order to be judged by him. And they promised to give Alexander gifts. Hera said that if she were preferred to all women, she would give him the kingdom over all men; and Athena promised victory in war, and Aphrodite the hand of Helen. And he decided in favour of Aphrodite.⁵

From the *Cypria*, the Judgment of Paris was transmitted to the dramatists of fifth-century Athens, where it provided the theme for Sophocles' satyr-play, the *Krisis*.⁶ Though this work is extant only in fragments, it is important to the Judgment's history because in it Sophocles appears to have given the episode an allegorical dimension. At least this was the impression of Athenaeus, whose *Deipnosophists*, written six hundred years later, is a transcript of an imaginary dinner-table conversation which preserves hundreds of fragments of now-lost works. Athenaeus recalls Sophocles' drama thus:

> the poet Sophocles in the play called *The Judgement* brings on Aphrodite as goddess of Pleasure ['Hδονήν], anointing herself with perfume and toying with a mirror, whereas Athena, who is Wisdom [Φρόνησιν] and Reason [Νοῦν] and Virtue ['Αρετήν] besides, anoints herself with olive oil and plays the gymnast.⁷

A fragment of the *Krisis*, "and indeed I am covered by this cloak as by my own,"[8] suggests that Sophocles had Aphrodite appear to Paris nude.[9]

Sophocles may have omitted Hera from the *Krisis*; perhaps the play considered the claims of only Aphrodite and Athena, thus making a neat contrast between pleasure and virtue, as in the already-popular apologue of Hercules at the crossroads.[10] The two goddesses' distinctive natures were certainly emphasized. Aphrodite's nudity, scent, and mirror imply her role as goddess of love, while Athena's oil and gymnastics suggest her link with physical prowess and *aretē*. Whether the play featured two goddesses or three, however, the Judgment was well on its way to becoming a moral choice.

Euripides too used the Judgment of Paris. Though he based no known play on the theme, his is the most complete handling of the story extant in Greek drama. Euripides includes the Judgment in five of his Trojan plays: *Andromache*, *Hecuba*, *The Daughters of Troy*, *Helen*, and *Iphigeneia at Aulis*,[11] and his treatment of the story probably derives from the *Cypria*.[12]

In Euripides' version, Paris, the king's son,[13] is herding his flocks on Ida[14] when the three goddesses, led by Hermes,[15] come to him so that he can resolve their dispute about who is most beautiful.[16] The outcome of the Judgment is determined not by the goddesses' beauty, but by their promised gifts. The promises are most explicit in *The Daughters of Troy*:

> This guerdon Pallas offered unto him—
> "Troy's hosts to vanquish Hellas shalt thou lead."
> Lordship o'er Asia, and o'er Europe's bounds,
> If Paris judged her fairest, Hera proffered.
> Cypris, with rapturous praising of [Helen's] beauty,
> Cried, "Thine she shall be if I stand preferred
> As fairest." (925–31)

Our final source from the ancient Greek period is the *Encomium on Helen* (c. 370 B.C.), a *tour de force* of rhetoric in which the Attic orator Isocrates takes on the challenge of vindicating Helen.[17] The similarity of his version of the Judgment to the others we have considered shows how influential the *Cypria* was in standardizing the story. His treatment also confirms that, as suggested by Sophocles' *Krisis*, the Judgment early acquired a moral dimension.

To summarize Isocrates' version of the story: Paris, son of Priam, is appointed arbitrator of the three goddesses' quarrel. To bribe him, Athena offers victory and Aphrodite Helen, while Hera offers sovereignty over Asia. Paris, of course, chooses Aphrodite.[18] Isocrates must have known a tradition which criticized Paris as a seeker of pleasure, for in telling the story of the Judgment, his main purpose is to absolve the young man of blame. He first tries to clarify the inherent confusion of motives in the story—whether Paris was swayed by Aphrodite's beauty or her gift.[19] According to him, overwhelmed by the sight of the goddesses, Paris could not judge their beauty and thus had to consider their gifts instead. He chose Helen not for pleasure but for her worth, beauty being esteemed even by the gods. "He was eager to become a son of Zeus by marriage" (83–85) and to pass this heritage on to his children. Isocrates thus disposes of the argument that Paris foolishly let a weakness for pleasure cause the downfall of Troy. He was swayed by neither Aphrodite's beauty nor Helen's, and in choosing among the gifts offered by the goddesses was led by the highest of motives—a desire that his heirs should be the descendants of Zeus.

We now reach a crucial stage in the transmission of the story. This version of the Judgment known to the ancient Greeks was included in that collection of mythographic material which has come down to us under the name of Hyginus's *Fabulae*. Because the *Fabulae* were an important source for medieval knowledge of classical myth, this work was one of the key means by which the story of the Judgment was transmitted to the Middle Ages.

Fable 92 tells the story of the Judgment:

> When Jove married Thetis to Peleus, he is said to have invited all the gods to the banquet except Eris, that is, Discord, who when she later arrived was not admitted to the banquet. From the door she threw in the midst an apple; she said the most beautiful should pick it up. Juno, Venus, and Minerva began to champion their own beauty. When great discord arose among them, Jove ordered Mercury to lead them to Mount Ida to Paris Alexander and order him to judge. Juno promised him, if he chose her, that he should rule in all lands and be distinguished before all in riches; Minerva, if she departed victorious,

[promised] that he would be strongest among all mortals and know every science; Venus, however, promised to give him in marriage the daughter of Tyndareus, Helen, most beautiful of all women. Paris placed the last gift first and judged Venus to be the most beautiful, whence Juno and Minerva were angry with the Trojans.[20]

Hyginus's version of the story is clearly one with which we are already familiar. The goddesses' argument begins, as in Proclus's summary of the *Cypria*, at the Wedding of Peleus and Thetis, where Eris, or Discord, provokes them. As in the *Cypria*, Jove orders Mercury to lead the goddesses to Ida so that Paris can judge their beauty. With respect to the promises, Fable 92 retains material that was probably in the *Cypria:* Juno offers sovereignty, Minerva strength (i.e., victory), and Venus Helen.

Hyginus also includes unfamiliar details—details which were probably not in the *Cypria*. The implied motive for Eris's starting the quarrel among the goddesses seems the very human one of personal pique and strikes us almost as a motif from folklore.[21] The apple—Hyginus's fable is the earliest extant reference to it—was probably added to the story during the Alexandrian period[22] and thus made its way into the Epitome of the *Library* as well. Fable 92 supplements the traditional three promises with two more. Juno offers sovereignty *and* riches; Minerva offers strength—or victory—*and* knowledge. This link between Juno and riches is the first literary occurrence of a motif which was to become increasingly important in the allegorical interpretation of the Judgment. Perhaps derived from the natural association of wealth with royal power, Juno's connection with riches becomes an important aspect of her identification with the active life. Equally important in the allegorical tradition but easier to explain is Minerva's association here with knowledge. As early as Homer and Hesiod, Athena was associated with wisdom.[23]

Except for compilations like the *Fabulae* of Hyginus, no surviving literature after Isocrates treats the Judgment of Paris for over two centuries. When the story again appears, it is still recognizable as the Judgment of the *Cypria*, Euripides, and Isocrates, but striking new features have been added: Paris is an aesthete who makes his judgment on the basis of feminine beauty, and the apple has become

a common feature of the story. Overall, the appearance of the goddesses to the Trojan prince is no longer an awe-inspiring epiphany.
The Judgment has become a pretty vision in which three nude
beauties pose for their unlikely judge, a shepherd-aesthete.[24]

For our purposes, the most significant treatment of this new,
Alexandrian-influenced Judgment is Ovid's, which was widely
known in the Middle Ages. Ovid treats the Judgment in the
Heroides, Letter 16, Paris to Helen, and Letter 17, Helen to Paris.
The Judgment is part of Paris's argument in his epistolary seduction
of Helen:

> There is a place in the woody vales of midmost Ida. . . . From here,
> reclining against a tree, I was looking forth . . . when lo! it seemed to
> me that the earth trembled beneath the tread of feet . . . and there
> appeared and stood before my eyes, propelled on pinions swift, the
> grandchild of mighty Atlas and Pleione . . . and in the fingers of the
> god was a golden wand. And at the self-same time, three goddesses—
> Venus, and Pallas, and with her Juno—set tender feet upon the sward.
> I was mute, and chill tremors had raised my hair on end, when "Lay
> aside thy fear!" the winged herald said to me; "thou art the arbiter of
> beauty; put an end to the strivings of the goddesses; pronounce
> which one deserves for her beauty to vanquish the other two!" And,
> lest I should refuse, he laid command on me in the name of Jove, and
> forthwith through the paths of ether betook him toward the stars.
>
> My heart was reassured, and on a sudden I was bold, nor feared to
> turn my face and observe them each. Of winning all were worthy, and
> I who was to judge lamented that not all could win. But, none the
> less, already then one of them pleased me more, and you might know
> it was she by whom love is inspired. Great is their desire to win; they
> burn to sway my verdict with wondrous gifts. Jove's consort loudly
> offers thrones, his daughter, might in war; I myself waver, and can
> make no choice between power and the valorous heart. Sweetly
> Venus smiled: "Paris, let not these gifts move thee, both of them full
> of anxious fear!" she says; "my gift shall be of love, and beautiful
> Leda's daughter, more beautiful than her mother, shall come to thy
> embrace." She said, and with her gift and beauty equally approved,
> retraced her way victorious to the skies.[25]

The setting of the Judgment is, as it was in every version we
have considered, Mount Ida, where Paris leads the simple life of a

shepherd. As always, Mercury is the divine herald who brings the three goddesses into his presence; as the *Cypria* specified, it is Jove's will that Paris judge.

With the appearance of Venus, Pallas, and Juno, the Alexandrian influence becomes apparent, but we only learn of the goddesses' nudity from Helen's letter: "You say . . . that in the vales of Ida three goddesses presented themselves unclad before you" (233). It is appropriate that the goddesses show themselves nude to their judge because their beauty has become an issue in this contest. Two traditions are uneasily fused in the Judgment of Paris: the beauty contest and the choice of good things. In early versions of the story, we are never really certain whether Paris chooses Aphrodite because he is won over by her beauty or by the gifts she offers. Isocrates solved the problem by making Paris so astonished by the goddesses' beauty that he had to rely on their gifts to make his choice, and he made Paris coolly choose the benefits of divine ancestry for his heirs. Ovid, influenced by the Alexandrian approach, solves the problem another way. The goddesses' gifts are the traditional ones— Juno offers "thrones," Pallas "might in war," and Venus Helen—but Paris judges on a new basis. He is a man easily swayed by beauty. Ovid's Paris, handsome himself, is a born lover. Helen writes, "As for your loud vaunting and talk of brave deeds, that face belies your words. Your parts are better suited for Venus than for Mars. Be the waging of wars for the valiant; for you, Paris, ever to love!" (243). Once Paris has gathered the courage to inspect the goddesses, he is immediately moved by Venus's beauty, and it is his nature as a lover and connoisseur of beauty, shown by his attraction to Venus, that explains his choice of her gift: "beautiful Leda's daughter." Ovid's Venus wins on two counts—"her gift and beauty equally approved"—but it is beauty in both goddess and gift that has moved the judge.

Two other writers of the Hellenistic period fuse the story of the Judgment from the *Cypria* with Alexandrian motifs: Apuleius and Lucian. In *The Golden Ass*, Apuleius (born c. 125 A.D.) describes a pantomime representation of the Judgment which is close to the *Cypria* in its details.[26] The Judgment takes place on a hill intended to represent Mount Ida. Mercury indicates to Paris Jupiter's command that he judge the goddesses. Juno offers the young man lordship over Asia, while Minerva will make him "the most strong and victorious man alive" (531), but Paris, of course, chooses Venus.

Apuleius adds to this basic outline certain details characteristic of the story by this period. He includes the apple, which in his version is gold. Mercury hands it to Paris as he gives him instructions from Jupiter. Apuleius also implies that Paris makes his choice on the basis of beauty. That Venus promises "the fairest spouse of all the world and one like to herself in every part" (533) suggests that Paris has an aesthete's eye for women. That he chooses on the basis of beauty is also indicated when he awards to Venus the golden apple, "which was the victory of beauty" (533).

Apuleius elaborates upon the Judgment in other ways. Probably to serve the needs of dramatic spectacle, Paris is dressed more like a Trojan prince than like a shepherd; he is "richly arrayed with vestments of barbary" (527). Probably for the same reason, Mercury and the three goddesses are rendered with particular attention to their traditional iconography. Mercury is nude except for a cloak, has golden wings on his head, and carries a caduceus and a wand (527). Juno wears a diadem and carries a scepter; Minerva wears a helmet decorated with an olive-branch garland and carries a shield and spear; and Venus wears only a thin smock (524). Each goddess is accompanied by an entourage of demigods and personifications.

The other Hellenistic writer to treat the Judgment is Lucian, an important source for the Middle Ages, though he wrote in Greek, because his Judgment includes features passed on to the Middle Ages by compilers and summarizers. His version is that of the *Cypria*, with the addition of the now-familiar Alexandrian material and some details that may be his own elaborations.

Dialogues of the Sea-Gods describes the Wedding of Peleus and Thetis;[27] the story is completed in the *Judgment of the Goddesses*.[28] As in Proclus's summary of the *Cypria*, the Judgment is linked to the Wedding of Peleus and Thetis, where the goddesses are roused by Eris to argue about their beauty. We recognize the influence of the *Cypria* too when Zeus dispatches Hermes to lead the goddesses to Paris on Mount Ida. Lucian is also conservative with respect to the promises. He uses the tradition of the *Cypria*—sovereignty, victory, and Helen—and his promises are precisely those of Isocrates.

Lucian adds to the *Cypria* the three motifs usually attributed to Alexandrian influence: the apple, Paris's taste for beauty, and the goddesses' nudity, and he elaborates upon them in distinctive ways. He makes Eris raise the quarrel among the goddesses by means of an apple, which, as in Apuleius, is gold. For the first time in extant literature, however, the apple has an inscription indicating that it is intended for the most beautiful. It is in Lucian, too, that we clearly see for the first time the identity between the apple of Discord, or Eris, and the apple that Paris awards: in Hyginus, the apple does not figure explicitly in the Judgment, and the pantomime which Apuleius describes does not include the Wedding of Peleus and Thetis.

Lucian's Paris is the Paris with whom we are familiar from Ovid. Zeus chooses him as judge in the dialogue of Panope and Galene because he is "a connoisseur of beauty" (205). In the *Judgment of the Goddesses*, he is handsome and "well-schooled in all that concerns love" (385). That he intends to conduct the contest on the basis of beauty—though he is later swayed by Aphrodite's gift—is shown by his request that the goddesses disrobe (397); that he is a man susceptible to beauty is shown by his rapturous praises when he sees the goddesses' revealed charms (401).

After Lucian, the Judgment becomes for several centuries the property of scholars, scholiasts, and compilers.[29] It is largely through their commentaries and handbooks that details of the story pass to the Middle Ages. The Judgment, with golden apple included, figures in a commentary on *Aeneid* 1.27 (necessary because Vergil, like Homer, merely alluded to the story) attributed to Servius and dating from the end of the fourth century.[30] A version of the story which passes on the golden apple and its inscription is included in another fourth-century commentary on the *Aeneid*, that of Tiberius Donatus.[31] A Greek scholion on Euripides' *Hecuba* 637 includes a very complete Judgment whose form is that of the *Cypria* with elaborations.[32] Most significant, however, are two compilations which derive ultimately from a handbook produced during this period.

These works, the *Excidium Troiae* and the *Compendium Historiae Troianae-Romanae*, are extremely important because they were the means by which a distinctive classical version of the Trojan story was transmitted to the Middle Ages.[33] Both are thought to derive from an exemplar produced between the fourth and sixth centuries A.D.[34] and based ultimately on Greek materials.[35] The earliest manuscript of the *Excidium Troiae* dates from the ninth century;[36] the *Compendium* is thought to date from the tenth century.[37]

Though the version of the Judgment included in the *Excidium Troiae* is for the most part the familiar classical one, it introduces certain novel details.[38] Discord, excluded from the wedding feast, makes a golden apple inscribed "a gift for the most beautiful goddess" (3). When Juno, Minerva, and Venus argue over it, Jove sends them to the shepherd Paris on Mount Ida, a just judge. Paris is the son of Priam, king of Troy. His mother ordered that he be exposed at birth because she had dreamed that she bore a firebrand which destroyed the city. The baby was rescued and raised among shepherds, becoming a shepherd himself. In Paris's herd was a large bull, which conquered bulls of the neighboring herds, and Paris always crowned it with a golden crown. One day Mars changed himself into a bull, fought Paris's bull, and conquered it. When Paris rewarded him with the crown, the young shepherd became known for his justice. Thus Jupiter designates him judge of the goddesses. When they ask him to award the golden apple, he tells them to return in two days. Each comes to him secretly to offer a bribe in return for the prize. Minerva promises victory, Juno increase of his herds, and Venus, disrobing, a beautiful wife. The youthful Paris is inflamed with love and declares her the most beautiful of the three.

The *Compendium* begins with Hecuba's dream, rather than inserting that episode between the Wedding and the Judgment.[39] The decision to destroy the child is Priam's, rather than his wife's. Hecuba, in contrast to the version in the *Excidium*, rescues the infant by handing him over to a herdsman to be raised. Paris grows up to become a herdsman, gains a reputation for right judgment when he rewards a victorious neighbor bull with a flower wreath, and, in an added detail, saves his herd from twelve robbers.

It is at this point in the narrative that the *Compendium* inserts the goddesses' quarrel, but the episode is somewhat garbled. Peleus and Thetis have become Proserpina and Perithoy—a substitution perhaps deriving from the tradition that, like Peleus and Thetis, Proserpina and Perithoy were united by Zeus.[40] Aside from this confusion, the scene of the wedding is close to that in the *Excidium* and clearly dependent on classical tradition. It even includes an additional detail which may be very old. Discord throws the golden apple from the ceiling of the house as she does in the scholion to *Hecuba* 637.

Most distinctive in the *Excidium*'s Judgment was the fact that, rather than rendering judgment immediately, Paris told the goddesses to go away and return later. The *Compendium* includes this version of the episode as well. The detail was probably in the late-classical exemplar to which both these works have been traced, and it may have been a feature of early literary or dramatic versions of the story. Perhaps it was an early attempt to accommodate the mechanical difficulties of getting the promises made. Each goddess must, of course, make her promise privately; yet if they all arrive together, how can each get a separate audience with the judge?

Only the *Excidium* includes the gifts offered by all three goddesses. Minerva promises victory, a promise with which we are already familiar. Juno's promise is, however, completely novel—that Paris's herd shall increase as his beasts all give birth to twins. This most likely does not go back even to the Latin exemplar of the *Excidium*, but represents an innovation of later date and unique to this particular work. Though the Roman Juno is traditionally the goddess of childbirth,[41] and even the Greek Hera was associated with birth,[42] fertility is not usually an attribute of Juno in the Judgment of Paris, where, as far back as Euripides, she is "Queen of the Sky"—Zeus's consort—and thus offers the gift associated with herself, sovereignty. The innovation here is a clever twist, though; if Paris is a herdsman, and if each goddess's gift is linked with some area of her patronage, Juno could offer no more appropriate gift than twin beasts.

Both works agree too in the novel detail of having Venus show herself to Paris nude and thus inflame his desire. The tradition of a nude Venus is actually older than what we see in Ovid and Lucian, where all three goddesses disrobe so that Paris may better judge them: it may go back to Sophocles' *Krisis*. Paris's reaction is consistent with the love of beauty and pleasure attributed to him by, for example, Ovid. That it combines oddly with the tradition of Paris as a just judge is probably the result of a separate development of judgment and exposure materials. As in the pantomime which

Apuleius describes in the *Golden Ass,* Venus offers not specifically Helen but a beautiful wife. The Paris who is influenced by the sight of the nude Venus is likely to be moved more by the beauty of the promised wife than by her identity. The Venus episode in the *Compendium* is a logical development of the story's handling in the *Excidium.* If the sight of the nude Venus inflames the youthful shepherd with love, it is reasonable that he should desire Venus herself as his reward, as he does in the *Compendium.* The themes of beauty contest and gifts are ingeniously merged when Venus offers Paris Helen as a substitute for herself.

The *Excidium Troiae* and the *Compendium Historiae Troianae-Romanae* are the first works we have seen which combine with the Judgment in one narrative material relating to the birth and early life of Paris. This material is so inextricably connected with the Judgment here and in later works that we must take it into account in studying the transmission of the Judgment.

The material relating to Paris's birth and early life is very old, though probably not as old as the Judgment.[43] The story of Paris's exposure as a baby and his rescue by shepherds may, in fact, have developed in order to explain his presence on Ida when he encounters the goddesses.[44] The first extant literary reference to Hecuba's dream occurs in Pindar's fragmentary Eighth Paean,[45] and both Sophocles and Euripides wrote plays, now lost, dealing with Paris's birth and early life;[46] extant plays of Euripides refer to Hecuba's dream, the exposure, and Paris's rescue by shepherds.[47] Though details of the story as it can be reconstructed in these early sources vary,[48] Hyginus's Fable 91 is a useful example of the theme's oldest form.

As Hyginus tells the story, when Priam had had several children by his wife, Hecuba, she dreamed while pregnant that she bore a burning torch from which serpents issued. Told of the dream, the dream interpreters recommended that the expected infant be destroyed, lest it cause the ruin of the country. When Hecuba gave birth to Alexander, he was handed over to be killed, but, moved by pity, the servants exposed him instead. He was adopted and raised by shepherds, who named him Paris, and when he grew up, he had a favorite bull.[49]

This chapter began with three versions of the Judgment. The

first, as we have seen, can be traced back to the epic period of Greek literature; its survival into the Middle Ages is accounted for by Hyginus, Ovid, and various late-classical compendia. The second version of the Judgment is the allegorical. This approach considers the story significant chiefly for the truths which can be shown to lie hidden beneath its surface. The allegorical approach to the Judgment was extremely important in the Middle Ages. Yet this quintessentially medieval tendency—to see truths of moral import beneath the story's surface—derives directly from a tradition already well established in ancient times and is nearly as old as the classical version of the Judgment.

The Greeks themselves found an allegorical dimension in the fables of the poets, and the allegorical interpretation of Greek mythology is nearly contemporary with the Judgment's first literary appearances.[50] So pervasive was the Greek tendency to see myth as allegory that even in early literary treatments of mythological subjects, allegory, particularly moral, may be implicit. Already in the *Iliad*, the contrast between Athena and Aphrodite is a contrast between action and passion,[51] and Sophocles may have intended the *Krisis* as a moral allegory. Whether he meant his play allegorically or not, we owe our knowledge of much of its content to a writer who interpreted Paris's choice as a moral allegory. In the *Deipnosophists*, Athenaeus declares, "I for one affirm . . . that the Judgment of Paris . . . is really a trial of pleasure against virtue. Aphrodite, for example—and she represents pleasure—was given the preference, and so everything was thrown into turmoil."[52] He also compares the story to that of Hercules at the crossroads (12.510c).

Euripides too seems to have seen moral significance in the Judgment of Paris. Two speeches in *The Daughters of Troy* show that he regards Aphrodite herself as a personification of love and passion.[53] The speech at 840ff. is an address to the goddess as the personification of love, and a conception of Aphrodite as a personification of sensual pleasure may underlie Hecuba's speech to Helen (especially 987–92). Hecuba argues against Helen's claim that she succumbed to Paris because Aphrodite accompanied him to Sparta; this only signifies, says Hecuba, that Helen was carried away by passion on account of Paris's beauty. The Judgment itself functions as an "exemplum" in *Iphigeneia at Aulis*; it is placed strategically after a

choral ode condemning excessive sexual passion and recommend-
ing the pursuit of *aretē* or virtue.[54]

Isocrates' oration *Helen* also implies a tradition of moral interpretation for the Judgment. "Overwhelmed by the sight of the goddesses," Paris was "compelled to make a choice of their proffered
gifts"—and chose Helen (83). But he did not choose her on account
of the pleasure to be gained, "although even this is thought by the
wise to be preferable to many things" (83). He chose Helen, as we
have noted, rather because he wished to ally his family with the
Olympians by marrying the daughter of Zeus, a nobler choice than
those offered by Hera and Athena (83–85). That Isocrates considers
it necessary to clear Paris of blame by insisting that he was not seeking pleasure suggests that there was a tradition which attributed his
choice to the pursuit of pleasure and which criticized him for his
choice.

In the late fourth century B.C., the Stoics elaborated and sys-
tematized existing methods of allegorical interpretation. Their
writings are lost, but their ideas survive in a students' manual
produced by Cornutus during the reign of Nero,[55] in the *De Natura
Deorum* of Cicero, and in later commentaries which drew on Stoic
thought.[56] The Stoics were eclectic, using all the approaches to
myth which had been developed in the past. In support of their interpretations, they used ingenious etymologies developed by earlier interpreters.[57]

Two Stoic interpretations of the Judgment have survived. One
represents a psychological or moral approach, which was to become
the dominant approach to the Judgment in the Middle Ages; the
other represents a physical or cosmological approach, important
too as a tradition which was never entirely lost, even up to the
fifteenth century. The early psychological-moral interpretation is
the first extant application to the Judgment of the ancient theme of
the three lives, an interpretation which was to become almost inseparable from the story for nearly two millennia.

Preserved in a scholion to Euripides' *Andromache* 276 is an interpretation of the Judgment from the *Ethika* of the Stoic Chrysippos,
who lived in the third century B.C.[58] The myth means only, he says,
that when Paris determined what direction his life should take, he
preferred a life of love [ἐρωτικῆς] to one that was warlike [πολεμικῆς]

or royal [βασιλείας].⁵⁹ For Chrysippos, Paris's choice among the three goddesses signifies his choice among three modes of life, that of a lover, warrior, or ruler. The life represented by each goddess reflects her own essential nature and the gift which she has traditionally offered.

A physical or cosmological approach to the Judgment, thought to derive from the Stoics, has been preserved in a commentary on the *Iliad* produced by the twelfth-century Byzantine John Tzetzes.⁶⁰ According to this analysis, Athena represents fire, Hera moist air, and Aphrodite σύγχρασις, or mixture. The argument of the goddesses signifies a time when, after the earth and sea had appeared, the elements were still in conflict, with sometimes fire, sometimes water, predominating. The apple for which the goddesses contend represents the universe, which, like an apple, is round. At the urging of Jupiter, divine intelligence, the world is awarded to Aphrodite, that mixture which unifies and creates harmony.⁶¹

This allegory includes unexpected elements. Though we have not yet considered many allegorical interpretations of the Judgment, we are used to literature which implies criticism of Paris's choice because of its implications for Troy, and which links Aphrodite with excessive sexual passion. The story here is so far from being an allegory of the Trojan shepherd's fatal choice that Paris is not even mentioned, and Zeus, who usually refuses to judge, urges and supports the decision for Aphrodite. In keeping with Stoic cosmological allegory, Hera and Athena represent elements, Hera's identification with air supported by an ancient etymology traceable to Theagenes of Rhegium.⁶² What is surprising, though, is Aphrodite's positive role in the story: she is the harmony which benefits the world by reconciling the warring forces in the cosmos.

Aphrodite, and her Roman counterpart Venus, were complex figures. Venus's twofold nature, as Venus *celestis* and Venus *scelestis*, was a medieval commonplace, but the tradition of a "good" and "bad" Aphrodite is very old. Philosophers early seized on Aphrodite for her possibilities in betokening a positive love as well as a destructive one. Plato separated the heavenly Aphrodite (Aphrodite Urania, motherless offspring of Uranus) from the common Aphrodite (Aphrodite Pandemos, daughter of Zeus and Dione).⁶³ Both Zeno and Heraclitus took up Empedocles' identification of Aphrodite with *philia*, that love which, in opposition to *neikos*, or hate, unites diverse elements.[64] Aphrodite thus represents a harmony or concord in the universe, like the divine love which rules the universe later in the *Consolation of Philosophy*. As a vicar of Zeus, the divine intelligence, she is responsible for keeping the warring elements within their bounds. This interpretation of the goddess, and its application to the Judgment of Paris, gives a very different cast to its allegorical possibilities, though the interpretation of the Judgment which predominates is that which sees Paris's choice of Aphrodite as a blameworthy descent into sensual pleasure.

The allegorical interpretation of mythology became even more important in the late-classical period as the traditional religion, which for its adherents represented civilization itself, struggled against the onslaughts of Christianity.[65] Charges of frivolity and immorality leveled at the gods, and charges of superstition leveled at those who still honored them, could be countered by showing the wealth of significance to be found in the myths. These interpretations were not new, but derived from Stoic and earlier approaches to Greek mythology. The choice-of-lives theme, which had seemed almost inherent in the Judgment of Paris from its first appearance in literature, came to dominate allegorical interpretation of the story, as seen in the pseudo-Clementine *Recognitions* and *Homilies*, Sallust's *Concerning the Gods and the Universe*, Proclus's commentary on Plato's *Republic*, and the *Mythologies* of Fulgentius.

The pseudo-Clementine *Recognitions* and *Homilies* deal with the adventures of the Apostle Peter and his disciple Clement of Rome. Both works date from the fourth century A.D., though both derive from a source produced a century earlier.[66] The interpretations of the Judgment appear in a disputation, shared by both works and probably present in their common source, concerning the uses of heathen mythology.[67]

In the *Recognitions*, the Judgment is explained by Niceta, a Christian who argues that pagan myths have value when their meaning is understood:

> The affair of the supper of the gods stands in this wise. They say that the banquet is the world, that the order of the gods sitting at table

is the position of the heavenly bodies. Those whom Hesiod calls the first children of heaven and earth, of whom six were males and six females—they refer to the number of the twelve signs, which go round all the world. They say that the dishes of the banquet are the reasons and causes of things, sweet and desirable, which, just as this world is ruled and governed, are checked by the position of the signs and the courses of the stars. Yet they say these things exist after the free manner of a banquet, inasmuch as the mind of everyone has the option whether he shall taste aught of this sort of knowledge, or whether he shall refrain; and as in a banquet no one is compelled, but everyone is at liberty to eat, so also the manner of philosophizing depends upon the choice of the will. They say that discord is the lust of the flesh, which rises up against the purpose of the mind, and hinders the desire of philosophizing; and therefore they say that the time was that in which the marriage was celebrated. Thus they make Peleus and the nymph Thetis to be the dry and the moist element, by the admixture of which the substance of bodies is composed. They hold that Mercury is speech, by which instruction is conveyed to the mind, that Juno is chastity [*pudicitiam*], Minerva courage [*fortitudinem*], Venus lust [*libidinem*], Paris the understanding. If therefore, they say, it happens that there is in a man a barbarous and uncultivated understanding, and ignorant of right judgment, he will despise chastity and valor, and will give the prize, which is the apple, to lust; and thereby ruin and destruction will come not only upon himself, but also upon his countrymen and the whole race. . . . if anyone has a pastoral and rustic and uncultivated understanding, and does not wish to be instructed, when the heat of his body shall make suggestions concerning the pleasure of lust, straightway he despises the virtues of studies and the blessings of knowledge, and turns his mind to bodily pleasures.[68]

The allegory, clearly in the Stoic tradition, is both cosmological and moral.[69] The connection between the Wedding of Peleus and Thetis and the Judgment of Paris, which has existed since the *Cypria*, is ingeniously exploited on the allegorical level, as the cosmological interpretation of the Wedding gives way to the moral interpretation of the Judgment. The wedding feast itself is made to represent the world. The twelve Olympians of Hesiodic tradition, who sit around the table, represent the twelve signs of the Zodiac, which encircles the earth. Alongside the older Stoic material, there is a newer astrological element: the dishes of the banquet, which represent the natural laws of the universe, are said to be under the control of the gods—the signs of the Zodiac and the stars.[70] A long tradition in which the heavenly bodies were identified with the gods makes gods as Zodiac a natural interpretation.[71] By late-classical times, however, a separate tradition with oriental origins had fused with this one; it gave the stars power over human destiny and natural law.[72]

The moral allegory of the Judgment develops from the cosmological allegory of the Wedding by the implicit equation of virtue with philosophy. The traditional subject for the philosopher is, of course, "the reasons and causes of things." Sampling the dishes of the banquet, that is, engaging in philosophical speculation, is available to all; each may choose, having free will, whether to taste. Discord, however, is the lust of the flesh that hinders one from the pursuit of wisdom; since lust always strives against wisdom, Discord is said to have been present at the Wedding. Paris represents the human understanding, to which are available "the virtues of studies and the blessings of knowledge." With the opportunity to be instructed by Mercury, who represents, as always, speech,[73] and offered the *pudicitia* of Juno and the *fortitudo* of Minerva, he chooses instead the lust of Venus. The *Recognitions* thus interprets Paris's choice among the goddesses as a choice of lives. We have already seen him choose between lust and virtue, and we have seen him choose among the lives of lover, warrior, and ruler. Here he chooses among *pudicitia, fortitudo,* and *libido.*

In this philosophically oriented allegory, however, we are interested less in the specific virtues that Paris eschews than in a simpler dichotomy reminiscent of Sophocles. By choosing lust, Paris shuns virtue, and the implicit link between virtue and speculative philosophy recalls the Aristotelian ideal expressed, for example, in the *Nicomachean Ethics.* This interpretation anticipates that of Fulgentius, in which Minerva herself becomes associated with the contemplative life and the three goddesses are ranked in a clear hierarchy. Here Venus is rejected, but the other two goddesses are regarded with equal favor. Perhaps Juno's traditional association with sovereignty has been put aside because *pudicitia* and *fortitudo* would be useful in fostering Paris's pursuit of wisdom—man's ultimate goal.

Though based on the same source, the passage on the Wedding of

Peleus and Thetis and the Judgment of Paris in the *Homilies* is quite different from that in the *Recognitions*. Where the interpretation in the *Recognitions* is philosophical, that in the *Homilies* is more specifically moral, and it lacks the brilliant link between the allegory of the Wedding and that of the Judgment which we find in the *Recognitions*.

In the *Homilies*, it is Clement who provides the allegorical meaning of the Wedding and Judgment:

> The banquet, then, is the world, and the twelve [divine guests] are these heavenly props of the Fates, called the Zodiac. Prometheus is foresight, by which all things arose; Peleus is clay, namely, that which was collected from the earth and mixed with Nereis, or water, to produce man; and from the mixing of the two, i.e., water and earth, the first offspring was not begotten, but fashioned complete, and called Achilles. . . . Then Hera, and Athena, and Aphrodite, and Eris, and the apple, and Hermes, and the judgment, and the shepherd, have some such hidden meaning as the following: Hera is dignity [σεμνότης]; Athena, manliness ['ανδρεία]; Aphrodite, pleasure ['ηδοναί]; Hermes, language, which interprets thought; the shepherd Paris, unreasoned and brutish passion. Now if, in the prime of life, reason, that shepherd of the soul, is brutish, does not regard its own advantage, will have nothing to do with manliness and temperance, chooses only pleasure, and gives the prize to lust alone, bargaining that it is to receive in return from lust what may delight it,—he who thus judges incorrectly will choose pleasure to his own destruction and that of his friends. And Eris is jealous spite; and the golden apples of the Hesperides are perhaps riches, by which occasionally even temperate [σώφρονας] persons like Hera are seduced, and manly ['ανδρείους] ones like Athena are made jealous, so that they do things which do not become them, and the soul's beauty like Aphrodite is destroyed under the guise of refinement. To speak briefly, in all men riches provoke evil discord.[74]

The allegory which the author of the *Homilies* derives from the Wedding and Judgment is considerably less interesting than that which the *Recognitions* drew from the same story.[75] As before, the Wedding is taken as a cosmological allegory, with the banquet representing the world and the twelve Olympians the twelve signs of the Zodiac. That they are called "heavenly props of the Fates" again suggests belief in an astrologically determined world. The discussion of the banquet is much shorter, and there is no identification of the cosmos as the subject matter of philosophical speculation. The interest in the Wedding derives less from its cosmological significance than from the meaning of the union it celebrates. As before, the marriage of Peleus, or clay, with Thetis, or water, is taken as the union of the elements in the composition of the human body, but a new episode is included, the birth of Thetis's son, Achilles, identified as the first man.[76]

The episodes of the apple and the quarrel of the goddesses are elaborated too. Eris—or Discord—has become identified with "jealous spite," probably because, as the tradition had developed in classical literature, she introduced the apple into the feast in order to gain revenge for being excluded. The apple itself has become assimilated to the golden apples in the garden of the Hesperides,[77] and, in a connection doubtless suggested by its golden color, has come to represent riches—and this identification explains why it causes the goddesses to quarrel. All three goddesses long for the apple, since riches tempt even the temperate and manly and have completely destroyed Aphrodite.

The Judgment, interpreted as a moral allegory, follows, and it deals less with philosophy than with the sinful condition of man.[78] The basic framework—choice of lives—is emphasized more than it was in the *Recognitions*. Paris still represents the human understanding or reason, but here there is a nice turn on his traditional identification as a shepherd; he represents the human reason, "that shepherd of the soul." Reason, however, makes the wrong choice, rejecting manliness and dignity or temperance, the virtues represented by Athena and Hera, for the lust represented by Aphrodite.

A third late-classical interpretation of the Judgment appears in Sallust's *Concerning the Gods and the Universe*, written about 363 A.D. This work, an apologia for the traditional religion and a defense against the attacks of Christianity, uses the riches discovered by allegorical interpretation to justify the old myths.[79] Its author is believed to have been an intimate of the Emperor Julian and to have written his treatise as a statement of the beliefs which Julian sought to protect.[80] Characteristic of the period is the work's strong Neoplatonic bent;[81] thus Sallust's interpretation of the Judgment reflects Neoplatonic beliefs about the universe and the soul.

Sallust sees the Wedding of Peleus and Thetis and the Judgment of Paris as a "blended" myth. In his system, myths can reveal truths concerning the physical universe, the human soul, material reality, or the true natures of the gods; blended myths embrace more than one of these areas. He interprets the story thus:

> the banquet signifies the supramundane powers of the gods, and that is why they are together, the golden apple signifies the universe, which, as it is made of opposites, is rightly said to be thrown by Strife, and as the various gods give various gifts to the universe they are thought to vie with one another for the possession of the apple; further, the soul that lives in accordance with sense-perception (for that is Paris), seeing beauty alone and not the other powers in the universe, says that the apple is Aphrodite's.[82]

The myth conceals, first, a theological element, since it expresses something about the essential natures of the gods. Gods do not literally feast at banquets, but the figure of the banquet signifies that they exist together in a realm removed from physical reality. The myth also conceals a physical or cosmological element, since it shows by means of allegory that the universe is composed of elements in contention with one another, and that each element, signified by a god, seeks to gain control. Finally, the myth conceals a psychological element, since it shows that the soul that follows only its senses, signified by Paris, wishes the universe to be governed by Aphrodite alone.[83]

Though Sallust's interpretation is related to that in the *Homilies* and *Recognitions*, it differs from them too in certain respects, and the differences are partly due to the influence of late-classical Neoplatonism.[84] Instead of representing the Zodiac, a part of the cosmos, as they did in the Pseudo-Clementines, the gods now signify a supramundane divine power—a clear reference to the Neoplatonic concept of transcendence. The apple, which now stands for the cosmos, and the goddesses' striving show that the elements contend for mastery of the universe. This allegory is based on traditional Stoic etymologies such as ‘Ηρα = ’αήρ, and is reminiscent of the interpretation preserved by Tzetzes.

In the psychological allegory of the Judgment, the choice-of-lives theme is viewed from a Neoplatonic perspective. Paris represents the soul who cannot transcend sense perception and is thus blind to all but beauty, represented by Aphrodite. In the usual choice-of-lives interpretation, the life represented by Aphrodite is to be rejected in favor of Athena's or Hera's, both of which are regarded with favor. Here each of the three goddesses is necessary in order to form a complete whole, and Paris's mistake lies in choosing only one. Were he able to go beyond sense perception, he would understand that what appears to be conflict is actually harmony.[85]

That the interpretation of the Judgment as a choice of lives was a late-classical commonplace is shown in its use by the fifth-century Neoplatonic philosopher Proclus in his commentary on Plato's *Republic:*

> Three ways of life are offered to someone, the life of a king, the life of a lover, and the life of a warrior, just as the myths say that to Alexander Hera offered the life of a king, Aphrodite the life of a lover, and Athena the masculine life, the life of a warrior.[86]

Of crucial importance to medieval understanding of the Judgment is its treatment in the *Mythologies* of Fabius Planciades Fulgentius, a Latin Christian writer of the fifth and sixth centuries.[87] Though his materials derive primarily from Stoic tradition, Fulgentius's approach is eclectic.[88] His interpretation of the Judgment, compounded largely out of materials already in existence, carries on the choice-of-lives theme which has been an explicit or implicit feature in most of the interpretations we have seen. He is, however, the first to identify the three lives represented by the goddesses with the three modes of life described by the philosophers of ancient Greece, and he is also the first to condemn the life represented by Juno, regarding only that of Minerva as praiseworthy.

The Judgment of Paris opens book 2 of the *Mythologies.* Since Fulgentius's aim is to illustrate philosophical or moral truths with the fables of the poets, he begins, not by telling the story of the Judgment, but by listing and defining the three modes of life, or "threefold life," which "philosophers have distinguished . . . for mankind." The first, the meditative or contemplative life, "has to do with the search for knowledge and truth." Fulgentius describes it as "the life led in our days by bishops, priests, and monks, in olden days by philosophers." The second, the practical or active life, "covets what it can get rather than seeks after knowledge."

The third, the sensual or voluptuary life, is "entirely given up to lust" or other vices. Fulgentius then relates the three lives to the Judgment of Paris: "The poets explain in such terms as these the contest of the three goddesses." When Paris was given the choice, he was attracted to lust, rather than virtue or wealth (64–65).[89]

Most of Fulgentius's discussion of the Judgment is devoted to establishing each goddess's association with the life that she represents. He summarizes the traditions concerning each one's nature and attributes, then allegorizes each detail. The material dealing with the goddesses is for the most part standard, whereas the allegorizations may be Fulgentius's own.

Minerva represents the intellectual life, "born from the head of Jove, because the intellect is situated in the brain." Each of her attributes is fraught with meaning: the head of Medusa which she wears on her breast signifies fear because "the wise man bears awe in his breast to guard against his enemies." Her plumed helmet shows that "the mind of the wise man is both armed and noble." That her robe has three folds shows that wisdom is "many-sided," that it is "kept hidden," or that it is "concealed from without." Her long spear shows that "wisdom strikes at long range with its pronouncements." The owl with which she is traditionally associated means that "wisdom has its flashes of lightning even in the dark." Finally he etymologizes her name: "Minerva in Greek is called Athene, for *athanate parthene*, that is, immortal virgin, because wisdom cannot die or be seduced" (65).[90]

Juno represents the active life. That she "rule[s] over dominions" and carries a scepter shows the relationship between the active life and riches. That her head is veiled shows that "riches are always hidden." She is the goddess of birth to show that riches are both "productive" and "abortive." Her traditional attribute of a peacock is appropriate "because the whole acquisitive life of power is always looking to adorn its appearance," yet as the peacock exposes its hind quarters when it spreads out its tail, so the pursuit of wealth and fame seems appealing but eventually exposes itself. Iris, the rainbow, is connected with her because fortune, "though at first glance brightly colored, soon after fades away" (65–66).[91]

Venus, whose name was interpreted by the Epicureans to refer to "the good things of life," by the Stoics to refer to the empty things,[92] represents the life of pleasure. She is also called Aphrodite, from Greek *afros,* or foam, either from the transient nature of lust, or "because the ejaculation of seed is foamy." That Venus is said to have been born from Saturn's genitals when they were cut off and thrown into the sea is only "a piece of poetic folly." Since Saturn is Chronos, or 'time,' in Greek, this means that "the powers of the seasons, that is, crops, are totally cut off by the scythe and, cast into the liquids of the belly, as it were into the sea, needs must produce lust." She is often shown naked "either because she sends out her devotees naked or because the sin of lust is never cloaked or because it only suits the naked." She is also sometimes shown swimming in the sea "because all lust suffers shipwreck of its affairs."

Among Venus's attributes are roses, doves, the three Graces or *Carites,* and the conch. As lust blushes, pricks with sin, and soon fades, so roses are red, thorny, and transient. Doves are appropriate because of their lechery. The Graces, "naked because no grace has any part of subtle adornment," are always depicted with only two facing the viewer "because all grace sets off alone but returns two-fold." The conch is an attribute of Venus because such a creature "is always linked in open coupling through its entire body" (66–67).[93]

As Fulgentius's reference to the "threefold life" of the philosophers implies, he is drawing on tradition when he divides human life into the contemplative, active, and voluptuary spheres.[94] Plato distinguished the three parts of the human soul in the *Republic:* "that with which a man learns," "that with which he feels anger," and "the appetitive part." The first always strains "towards knowledge of the truth of things" and so is a "lover of learning and lover of wisdom." The second "is wholly set on predominance and victory and good repute," and so is "ambitious . . . and covetous of honour." The third desires "food, drink, sex, and other things which follow from these." It could accordingly be called "the money-loving part, because money is the chief instrument for the gratification of such desires."[95]

For Plato, only the life of learning derives from the reasonable part of the soul, while the pursuit of victory and honor is an activity of the "spirited" part. These two parts, however, easily exist in harmony with one another; together they rule the third, or lower, part and defend the entire man (4.15 [Loeb 1.401–5]). In pleasantness, Plato ranks the activities of these two parts of the soul near one another, and far above the activities of the third part (9.8 [Loeb 2.381]).

Aristotle, too, distinguishes three parts of the soul, and he makes them correspond to three modes of life.[96] For him, the three lives are those of contemplation, politics, and enjoyment.[97] Those who pursue the first are governed by the speculative intellect (6.2 [p. 329]); they seek wisdom, and their contemplation is an end in itself (10.7 [pp. 613–15]). Those who pursue the second seek to live in accord with practical wisdom, which is "a truth-attaining rational quality, concerned with action in relation to things that are good and bad for human beings" (6.5 [p. 337]). This is the life of political activity, which works toward some practical end (10.7 [pp. 615–17]). Those who pursue the third mode of life seek the same sort of existence as does an animal (1.5 [p. 15]).[98]

For Aristotle, both the intellectual and the practical lives are activities of the rational part of the soul.[99] By its nature, then, the practical life has value, and it is governed by its own set of virtues, the moral virtues. Yet for Aristotle the life of contemplation is superior to the practical life[100] because its goal is the pursuit of wisdom, and wisdom produces happiness.[101]

Plato and Aristotle, then, arranged the three lives in a hierarchy, with contemplative first, practical second, and voluptuary third, though the practical life was also considered virtuous. But let us return to Fulgentius, who draws on this classical tradition of the three lives, combining it with traditional interpretations of the Judgment of Paris to create a distinctive new approach to the theme.[102]

Venus's role in the Judgment of Paris is by far the most consistent. As soon as the Judgment implied a choice of lives, the opposition was clear: *aretē* opposed pleasure. Venus had always offered love and represented lust, and Fulgentius only picked up the tradition when he made her represent the sensual or voluptuary life condemned by the philosophers.

Athena, or Minerva, traditionally represented the life of the warrior, and her usual promise to Paris was victory or courage. Now Fulgentius associates her with the intellectual or contemplative life—an eminently appropriate connection. Athena's association with wisdom is very old,[103] and Hyginus had already made her offer Paris both strength and knowledge.[104]

Juno's role has fluctuated the most; in his view of the life she represents, Fulgentius departs strikingly from the classical hierarchy of the three lives. Hera may have been absent from the Judgment when Paris's choice was between virtue and pleasure; later she offered sovereignty. Yet when the Pseudo-Clementines first linked her explicitly with a life, it was one of chastity, dignity, or temperance. In Fulgentius's scheme, however, the practical or active life of Juno is a life devoted to the pursuit of riches. Juno's only other association with riches occurred in Hyginus, who made her offer both riches and rule. Her old link with sovereignty could easily foster a connection with the active life of the philosophers, Aristotle's life of the political man, but Fulgentius mentions nothing of this connection.

Most striking here, though, is Fulgentius's evaluation of the life represented by Juno: he condemns it. Traditionally only the life assigned Venus has been condemned. The *Recognitions*, for example, implied that both Juno's chastity and Minerva's virtue could help Paris reach the goals of a philosopher. In the tradition of the three lives, too, only the voluptuous life has been castigated, while the active life has been ranked close to, equal with, or even above the contemplative. For Fulgentius, the active life is almost as reprehensible as the voluptuous. Indeed, it has absorbed much of Plato's appetitive part, which, as he said, could also be called "money-loving," or Aristotle's life of pleasure, which, he claimed, is led by many "of high position [who] share the feelings of Sardanapallus."[105] Fulgentius's active life seeks and covets the enjoyable things of existence as did the tyrants of old. Fulgentius clearly represents a variation on the classical tradition, yet because of his popularity in the Middle Ages, it was his version of the three lives which held the stage, almost without exception, for nearly a thousand years.

The allegorical approach to myth, exemplified by Fulgentius's treatment of the Judgment, views the tales of the gods as integuments under which psychological or cosmological truths have been hidden by poets, or at least may be discerned there by the perceptive. Competing with this interpretation of myth in the ancient world was another which sought not to save the stories of the poets but rather to expose them as lies. This is the rationalizing approach, represented by the third version of the Judgment with which I opened this chapter. The rationalizing approach to myth springs from an impulse similar to that which created the allegorical tradition: a questioning spirit which asks, what are the myths if they are not true stories of gods and heroes? Unlike the allegorical approach, however, it does not view the myths as receptacles for deeper truths. It views them rather as exaggerations and distortions of events which actually occurred, events to which the passage of time, human credulity, or the machinations of poets have given a fabulous form.[106] Allegorical interpretation was partly responsible for the Judgment's popularity in the Middle Ages; equally responsible was the rationalizing tradition.

Because it seeks in myth a kernel of truth which can be located in the past, the rationalizing approach is profoundly different from the allegorical. The aim of the analysis is to discover the literal meaning—the datable events which underlie the fanciful story. There is never any sense, as is the case with allegorical interpretation, that the poet has hidden a timeless truth within his allegory.[107]

The rationalizing approach is as ancient as the allegorical: already in the sixth and fifth centuries B.C., Hecatus of Miletus attempted a rational interpretation of myth.[108] Slightly later, the Sophists and others sought various rationalizing explanations for the traditional religion;[109] the skeptical spirit of the time is reflected in Euripides' *The Daughters of Troy* 971–81. Even the Stoics in the next century accepted certain rational or historical explanations of the gods, seeing them as heroes or great men deified for their services to the human race.[110] Whereas the Stoics, however, respected the gods, and used their interpretations to explain aspects of the traditional religion which might otherwise be criticized, one particularly influential development of the rationalizing approach was intended rather to discredit the gods and to show that there was no reason to serve them.[111] This was the approach of Euhemerus, who lived in the third century B.C.[112]

The work in which Euhemerus set out his theories was the Ἱερὰ Ἀναγραφή, or "Sacred Inscription," a geographical romance in which the author describes his journey to the imaginary island of the "Panchaïe," where he finds a column supposedly inscribed by

Zeus with the truth about the gods.[113] This truth is that they are ordinary men and women whose "divinity" is due only to the ignorance of their worshippers. Euhemerus had a number of followers, and euhemerism was a long-lived phenomenon in the mythographical tradition.[114] Most important for our purposes is the effect of euhemerism, and the rationalizing approach in general, on the relationship between mythology and history. At the outset, of course, mythology *was* history, as the work of a poet such as Hesiod shows. With skepticism toward mythology developing as early as the sixth century B.C., however, it was essential, if mythology was to be regarded as a record of the past, that an explanation be found for the fabulous aspects of myth. This is precisely what Euhemerus and the other less radical rationalists provided. The effect of the rational tradition on the treatment of history persisted well into the Middle Ages and beyond.[115] The rationalizing tendency was partly responsible for the incorporation of the Trojan War into histories of the world and for the acceptance of the Judgment of Paris as a historical episode.

Versions of the historical truth behind the myth of the Judgment are many and varied, but each is based on a fundamental objection to the idea that goddesses would submit themselves, particularly in a matter so petty as the question of beauty, to the arbitration of a shepherd. Preserved in a scholion to *Andromache* 276 is the opinion of Antikleides: "the Judgment of the goddesses was untrue. . . . For three cheap local girls were selected for the contest of beauty."[116] Antikleides rationalizes the story by changing the goddesses to ordinary women, thus removing the major source of objection.

The anonymous *De Incredibilibus,* a work in the tradition of the Alexandrian Palaephatos, who lived in the second century B.C. or earlier,[117] explains the Judgment thus:

> It should be known that Alexander, who is called by another name Paris, did not judge goddesses, but, since he excelled in wisdom, he wrote in praise of them. Thus has been given occasion for the fable that he pronounced judgment among Pallas, Juno, and Venus.[118]

The *De Incredibilibus* disposes of the chief objection to the Judgment in another way. The goddesses did not submit themselves to Paris for judgment; he merely wrote an unsolicited poem in their praise.

Dio Chrysostom, the Greek sophist and rhetorician who flourished in the first century A.D., takes a rationalizing approach to the Judgment in two orations.[119] In the *Trojan Discourse,* the premise of his argument is that gods are superior to men and that, therefore, if a goddess seems petty or does things which even men would not do, such as punishing an arbitrator whose decision she has agreed to accept, the story must be a lie.[120]

In the other oration, *Retirement,*[121] Dio provides an explanation for the myth of the Judgment. Since the story could not be literally true, Paris must have imagined the visit of the goddesses. In Dio's view, Paris invented the Judgment in his isolation on Ida, as he longed for marriage with a beautiful woman:

> he is appointed by Zeus, he fancies, umpire over the goddesses; and as to the other goddesses [Hera and Athena], he disregarded both their persons and their gifts, and chose the third in return for the bribe and gift of winning that woman as wife who had been the object of his thoughts and for whom he had prayed. (265)

Had he not been a prince, Dio continues, the daydream would have been harmless. But his royal status made it possible for him to carry out the remainder of the fantasy "just as if the first part had actually happened" (265). Building ships, he sailed to Sparta and took Helen from the home of Menelaus, his host (265–67).

Dio has rationalized the myth by one simple expedient: the Judgment, which nevertheless incorporates all the standard details, is a daydream which Paris fabricates in his long days and nights among the herds. Thus the Judgment is preserved as the cause of the war, but, to credit its role in history, one need only believe in the power of solitude to call forth strange imaginings.

According to the *Strange History* of the Alexandrian Ptolemy Chennos, who lived in the second century A.D., the fable of the Judgment arose when Alexander awarded Mēlos, the beautiful son of the river Scamander, to Aphrodite. She, Hera, and Athena had quarreled over the boy, each wanting him for her priest.[122] Ptolemy has made the noun *melos* 'apple' the point of departure for his rationalization, interpreting the fable's origin as a case of confusion between two similar words.[123]

Such treatments of the Trojan War, which made even marvelous events into history by finding rational explanations for them, assured that not only the war itself, but every detail associated with it, could be incorporated into world histories. Accordingly, the Judgment of Paris was included in the *Chronicon* of the influential Greek historian Eusebius, Bishop of Caesarea (c. 260–339 A.D.). This work synchronized secular history with Old and New Testament history. The Greek text of the *Chronicon* now exists only in fragments, but its Latin translation, made by Jerome, preserves the contents of the original.[124]

According to Eusebius, the Judgment of Paris occurred in the eight hundred and twentieth year after Abraham: "Alexander stole Helen. The Trojan War, of ten years' duration, arose: the cause of the evil was the argument of three women for the prize of beauty, one of them promising Helen to the shepherd judge."[125] Eusebius traces the war's origin to the familiar quarrel, bribe, and judgment. Yet the contenders in the beauty contest are not goddesses, but three ordinary women, like the three cheap local girls in Antikleides' version of the story. Such an interpretation indeed reduces the myth to history, yet in a sense the story becomes less plausible rather than more so, since one might inquire how one of these ordinary women was able to command Helen of Sparta as a bribe to offer her judge.

To the climate of thought which tried to find the kernel of truth in the *Iliad* belongs the document which was to dominate medieval understanding of the Trojan War as history, the *De Excidio Troiae Historia* of "Dares of Phrygia." This influential work and a similar one, the *Ephemeridos Belli Troiani Libri* of "Dictys of Crete," claim to be Latin translations of chronicles written by actual participants in the war, Dares purportedly fighting on the side of the Trojans and Dictys on that of the Greeks. Like Dio Chrysostom, they reject the lies of Homer. Both claim to tell the truth about the events they narrate, and both generally avoid the marvelous, restricting their narratives for the most part to things which could have actually been seen first hand.[126]

These works were accepted at face value for centuries, almost completely supplanting the version of the war found in the *Iliad*.[127] Dares was particularly influential in the West, since many European countries traced their origins to Trojan heroes who, like Aeneas, fled Troy when the city fell.[128] It was not until the eighteenth century that the putative authors' claims to have written at the time of the Trojan War were finally repudiated.[129] Since then, there has been considerable controversy about the true dates and provenance of these works, but it is now generally agreed that both works were originally written in Greek in the first or second century A.D.[130]

The date and provenance are supported by the fact that these works are congenial to what is known of Greek culture in the first few centuries A.D. The post-Alexandrian period appears to have given rise to a large number of similar forged accounts of the Trojan War, and there once existed other such histories under names like Sisyphos of Cos, Korinonos the Ilian, Phaidalos of Corinth, and Antipater the Acanthian.[131]

Though the chronicles of Dares and Dictys, and their now-lost counterparts, cannot have been produced as anything other than patent forgeries, as false as the lies which they purported to correct, and though they are probably to be attributed to the ingenuity of the Sophist rhetoricians—of whom Dio Chrysostom is a good example—they nevertheless could not have come into existence except as a culmination of the rationalizing tradition. Only a long tradition of skepticism concerning the Trojan War, and Homeric myth in general, could make the compositon of completely invented chronicles conscionable, and only a well-developed public taste for the supposed truth behind myths could permit an account of the war clearly devoid of the marvelous and purportedly based on first-hand experience to gain such ascendancy over the version of Homer.[132]

Though much in the early chapters of the Latin *De Excidio Troiae Historia* (the version that has come down to us) is borrowed from the *De Raptu Helenae* of Dracontius[133]—a circumstance which complicated identification of its original date and provenance—the version of the Judgment which it includes is notably original. Dracontius's treatment of the Judgment was brief and allusive, but it was clearly the familiar story in which the shepherd tending his flocks on Ida rejects Juno and Minerva in favor of Venus.[134] In the *De Excidio Troiae Historia*, the Judgment has acquired striking new features:

While hunting in the woods on Mount Ida, [Paris] had fallen asleep and dreamt as follows:

Mercury brought Juno, Venus, and Minerva to him to judge of their beauty. Then Venus promised, if he judged her most beautiful, to give him in marriage whoever was deemed the loveliest woman in Greece. Thus, finally, on hearing Venus's promise, he judged her most beautiful.[135]

Most noteworthy is the fact that the Judgment has now become a dream. It is impossible to know whether the original Greek Dares included a version of this episode; the Judgment in the Latin Dares, however, whether supplied by the translator or suggested by something in the original Greek text, is very much in keeping with the rationalizing spirit of the rest of the work. The only previous example we have seen in which the beauty contest is an imagined rather than real occurrence is the Twentieth Oration of Dio Chrysostom, in which the Judgment is a fantasy resulting from Paris's isolation as he herds his sheep.

A second significant difference is that Paris is no longer a shepherd. In the most ancient versions of the story, Paris herds cattle on Mount Ida as a Trojan prince, and the Judgment is also frequently linked with a tradition in which the infant Paris, exposed at birth and then rescued by a shepherd, grows up in obscurity, thus explaining his existence as a shepherd. Here, however, all reference to the shepherd motif has been dropped, and Paris's presence on Mount Ida is explained by his being on a hunting expedition.

Third, the *De Excidio Troiae Historia* differs from most previous versions of the Judgment with respect to the goddesses' promises. The promises of Juno and Pallas are not identified, and, as in Apuleius, Venus does not offer Helen specifically, but rather "whoever was deemed the loveliest woman in Greece." In medieval rehandlings of Dares, this sketchy treatment of the Judgment was to invite—even demand—elaboration, and medieval authors turned to a wide variety of sources in their attempts to supplement Dares's bare outline.

The fourth difference is the placement of the Judgment in the story, and this difference is important because the *De Excidio*'s version of the preliminaries to the war was to influence nearly every medieval version of the tale of Troy. The *De Excidio Troiae Historia* begins with what is known as "the first destruction of Troy." Sailing with the Argonauts in quest of the Golden Fleece, Hercules is insulted by the Trojan king, Laomedon—Priam's father. Hercules later revisits Troy, conquers the city, kills Laomedon, and rewards his companion Telemon with Hesione, Laomedon's daughter. Hearing what has happened, Priam, who has been away at the head of an army, returns to Troy and rebuilds the city. He is willing to forget the injuries done Laomedon if the Greeks return Hesione, and he accordingly sends an embassy to Greece. When the embassy is unsuccessful, Priam calls a council to announce his plans for war. It is at this council that Paris relates his dream of the Judgment, arguing that he should lead the army against Greece because the gods intend his success.

Though no specific extant source exists for the section in Dares on the first destruction of Troy,[136] this tradition is very old. References to Hercules' destruction of the city occur in the *Iliad*,[137] and the *Library* of Apollodorus preserves a tradition according to which Troy's destruction is linked with the theft of Hesione (2.5.9). The first destruction of Troy and the capture of Hesione may have been associated with the Argonautic expedition by Dionysius of Mitylene in the now-lost *Kyklos* (second century B.C.).[138] The first extant source in which these two great cycles are connected is the *Library of History* by Diodorus Siculus (first century B.C.),[139] and the version in Hyginus's Fable 89 is very similar to this one. In his commentary on *Aeneid* 1.619, Servius too brings together the first destruction of Troy, the theft of Hesione, and the Argonautic expedition.[140]

With the *De Excidio Troiae Historia*, we have followed the rationalizing interpretation of the Judgment to the threshold of the Middle Ages. Dares's treatment of the Judgment and of the war itself was to dominate the medieval understanding of the Trojan legend, yet Dares's insufficiency was to encourage borrowings from works which preserved the classical version of the story. Eventually, too, with the rise of the fourteenth-century dream vision, the tradition represented by Dares was to find a natural application to allegory, as Paris's dream became assimilated to the dreams which set the stage for allegorical adventures.

2

The Judgment as History

To study the Judgment of Paris in the Middle Ages is to study in microcosm the process by which medieval Europe made the classics its own. The allegorical tradition, in which the fables of the ancients were viewed as repositories of moral lessons or Christian doctrine, represents the most striking assimilation. Some classical stories were valued too, however, because they were regarded as history. In this tradition, the Trojan saga enjoyed particular esteem. Inspired by Vergil's *Aeneid*, the nations of Western Europe magnified themselves by tracing their origins to fleeing Trojan heroes. Thus the Trojan War came to be considered a crucial episode in the history of Europe.[1]

But the line between history and literature was blurred in the Middle Ages. Before the Trojan saga was history, it was literature and, by the eleventh century, an important theme for medieval Latin poets. Writers like Godfrey of Reims and Baudri of Bourgueil drew from the saga separate episodes for literary application.[2] By the early twelfth century, however, entire narratives were based on the tale of Troy. The *Pergama Flere Uolo* was the first,[3] and it inspired at least four subsequent poems.[4] Two of them include references to the Judgment. In the *Viribus, Arte, Minis*, Petrus Sanctonensis writes:

> Paris is the country's torch, by which judge of divine beauty, you, Troy, capital of Phrygia and flower of Asia, lie dead! When the shepherd obeyed Venus he offended Juno; when he sat as judge, he gave you so many harms![5]

Simon Aurea Capra describes the Judgment thus in his *Ylias,* written after 1155:

> to [Paris] came Juno, Minerva, and Venus. They sought judgment which among them was the most beautiful; each also promised him gifts: Juno honor, Pallas strength, and Venus a girl. But he allowed Venus to conquer, conquered by her.[6]

These works encompass the whole tale of Troy, from the Judgment of Paris to the wanderings of Aeneas, yet their purpose is not primarily narrative. They are aimed at cultured audiences who already know the story, and the plot serves as the framework for a display of rhetoric. The story has not yet acquired a vitality and life of its own in its new surroundings. The authors of these works wished to establish that medieval culture was not inferior to classical, but literary forms that were vital for Homer's and Virgil's audiences reflected world views other than those of the Middle Ages. Classical themes could achieve the same currency in medieval culture that they had enjoyed in the ancient world only when the forms that embodied them ceased to be classical.[7] The literary application of this principle is nowhere more relevant than in the case of the medieval *romans d'antiquité,* which accomplished what the learned Latin tradition had not: they made classical themes at home on medieval soil.

That medieval romance reflected a new sensibility is a commonplace.[8] The earliest romances were based on classical materials—Alexander, Aeneas, Thebes, Troy—yet few genres are more quintessentially medieval. That the poems were written in the vernacular rather than in Latin is only one aspect of their novelty and not the most significant. In the romances, ideals of chivalry have replaced the heroic ethic, and romantic love has become an important motivation for the characters' actions. Classical heroes and heroines have been transformed into medieval knights and ladies, and the old stories have been accommodated to a medieval world view. The loves, hates, fears, and desires of a Paris or an Aeneas have become the loves, hates, fears, and desires of a twelfth-century man.

The Judgment of Paris, with its origin in the divine wedding feast and its Olympian cast of characters, presented problems for the medieval writer. A classical hero could become a medieval knight, but how, outside the allegorical tradition, did one integrate a classical divinity into a Christian culture? Dares's rationalization—that Paris dreamed his adventure—was ultimately the solution. It was only because of Dares that the Judgment was able to take its place in those narratives of a war which, as prose succeeded verse, became regarded more and more firmly as historical fact. It was Benoît de Sainte-Maure who, by adopting the *De Excidio Troiae Historia* as the framework for the *Roman de Troie*, introduced into the vernacular the useful tradition that Paris's judgment of the goddesses was only a dream. Benoît was not, however, the first to introduce the Judgment into a romance. That distinction belongs to the anonymous author of the *Eneas*, a *roman d'antiquité* based on Vergil's *Aeneid*.

The *Eneas* was probably written about 1160, perhaps as early as 1158.[9] Its author medievalized Vergil's hero,[10] but some impulse, probably scholarly, drove him to add additional classical materials. The *Aeneid* itself refers to the Judgment of Paris in only a glancing way. As Aeneas and his companions leave the burning Troy, Vergil explains why Juno is angry with them: "deep in her heart lie stored the judgment of Paris and her slighted beauty's wrong."[11] At the corresponding spot in the medieval poem, the whole story of the Judgment unfolds.

Juno, Pallas, and Venus were at a "parlemant" when suddenly Discord threw among them a golden apple. Greek words on the apple identified it as a gift for the most beautiful goddess. A great conflict arose, since each wanted the apple for herself. Determined to ask for an outside opinion, they approached Paris, who had a reputation for justice. They showed him the writing on the apple, trusting his knowledge of the law to make his judgment just. Paris told them to return in three days for his decision, supposing that he could thus profit by the bribes they would have a chance to offer him in the meantime. They departed, but he had been correct in his assumption. Juno returned and promised him that if he gave her the apple she would make him a richer man than his father. Next came Pallas, goddess of battle, and promised that if he decided for her she would give him courage and make him invincible. Finally came Venus, lady and goddess of love. She promised that if he chose her, she would give him the most beautiful woman in the world. When

Venus left, Paris contemplated what he had been offered. Riches and strength appealed to him, but the woman promised by Venus appealed more. The goddesses returned at the appointed time and demanded their judgment. Paris gave the apple to Venus, who rewarded him with Helen.[12]

There seems little question that the author of the *Eneas* had access to a text related to the *Excidium Troiae* and the *Compendium Historiae Troianae-Romanae*.[13] The tradition represented in these sources includes many of the details which make the Judgment in the *Eneas* distinctive. We recognize the familiar Discord with her inscribed golden apple. Paris's reputation for justice is emphasized. Furthermore, as in the *Excidium Troiae* and the *Compendium Historiae Troianae-Romanae*, Mercury is absent. Most noteworthy, however, is Paris's postponing the judgment for three days, which gives the goddesses the opportunity to return separately with their bribes. Indeed, the *Excidium Troiae* even implied that bribery was in Paris's mind: "Because when a judgment is postponed, it is common to ask: 'What would you give to win?'"[14]

Vergil and Homer could allude to the Judgment. Their audiences, with classical culture their native element, already knew the story and its relationship to Troy's fall and Aeneas's wanderings. The audience for whom the author of the *Eneas* wrote had to be educated to its knowledge of the classics; he could not count on it to know the story of the Judgment. Further, his own pride as a classicist was at stake, and his audience looked to its literature for profit as well as delight. Thus, in the tradition of countless commentaries on the *Aeneid* or the *Iliad*, he expanded the allusion of his source into a full-blown narrative. Vergil's reference to the Judgment in connection with Juno's anger is precisely the spot at which Servius and Donatus tell the story in their commentaries. The Judgment which the author of the *Eneas* knows and uses, however, is not that of Servius or Donatus but one which must have been equally widespread.[15]

Though the Wedding of Peleus and Thetis has become simply a "parlemant," and Jove is not mentioned, nothing in the Judgment of Paris as it appears in the *Eneas* is distinctively medieval. The author lets pass without comment Juno's, Pallas's, and Venus's identity as goddesses and the premise, at which even classical authors had balked, that goddesses would come to earth and request judgment of a mortal. Perhaps, though, it is the function of this episode within the scheme of the poem which makes the version of the story from the tradition of the *Excidium Troiae* and the *Compendium Historiae Troianae-Romanae* acceptable: it functions only as a commentary, and its inspiration is the scholar's handbook, not the poet's muse.

The Judgment of Paris from the tradition of the *Excidium Troiae* and the *Compendium Historiae Troianae-Romanae* was appropriate for the purpose to which it was put in the *Eneas*. When the whole Trojan saga was turned into a vernacular romance, however, the source its author chose was not a version of the *Excidium Troiae* or the *Compendium Historiae Troianae-Romanae* but rather the *De Excidio Troiae Historia* of Dares. Benoît de Sainte-Maure, whose *Roman de Troie* is usually dated between 1155 and 1160,[16] openly repudiates the lies of Homer, who made gods and goddesses mingle in the affairs of men (57–70), preferring what he regards as the more historically accurate version of Dares.[17] Though his dependence on Dares is clear—the *Roman de Troiae* starts, for example, with the quest for the Golden Fleece and the first destruction of Troy—Benoît transforms his source into a four-volume medieval romance. The Greeks and Trojans become medieval knights, and Benoît adds battles, pageantry, marvels, psychological analysis, and love interest, all of which made the *Roman de Troie* immensely popular.[18] Its very success as a romance led to its influence as history. Benoît is, in the words of one critic, the "eigentliche Stammvater" of the medieval Trojan saga.[19] Because he activated classical themes by putting them in contemporary garb, the story seemed to his contemporaries an all the more faithful reflection of the classical past. He was accordingly responsible for the fact that, for centuries, Dares's version of the Trojan legend, rather than that of Homer—or even the *Excidium Troiae* and the *Compendium Historiae Troianae-Romanae*—dominated European letters and came to be regarded as the authentic, historical account of the war.[20]

That Benoît used the *De Excidio Troiae Historia* had crucial implications for the Judgment of Paris. For Dares, of course, Paris only dreamed that he judged the goddesses. Benoît picked up this tradition, and the influence of the *Roman de Troie* made the dream-Judgment, after about the middle of the twelfth century, the prevailing version of the episode. This transformation of the story was to have far-reaching effects. Not only did it aid the tradition which viewed the Trojan War as history, but it also set the Judgment up for allegorical treatments, as the dream which had been for Dares a rationalizing device merged with the dreams essential to the developing genre of the love vision. But I am getting ahead of myself. Let us see what Benoît does with Dares's bare three-sentence summary of the event which caused the fall of Troy.

Paris describes his judgment of the goddesses in the assembly which Priam has called to discuss his projected war against the Greeks. On the first of May, he hunted a stag in India Minor. All day his dogs chased the animal, but he could not catch it. The day was strangely hot and windless, and in the "vaus Cithariiens" he became separated from his companions and his dogs. Next to a fountain from which no animal drank, beneath the shade of a juniper, he slept. In his dream, he saw before him Mercury, leading Juno, Venus, and Minerva. Mercury called him three times, then told him that the goddesses had come to him for judgment. A golden apple had been thrown among them, with a Greek inscription indicating that it was a prize for the most beautiful of the three. Since each goddess wanted the apple, but they could not agree among themselves who deserved it, Mercury suggested that they put the question to Paris, and they agreed. Each came to Paris privately, and had he accepted the gifts they offered, he could have had anything he wanted. Venus, however, promised him the most beautiful woman in Greece, and he awarded her the apple.[21]

As in the *De Excidio Troiae Historia*, Paris's dream of the Judgment takes place while he is hunting; Benoît's "Inde la Menor"—India Minor—for Dares's Mount Ida is doubtless to be traced, as Léopold Constans suggests, to Benoît's use of a manuscript which abbreviated the *monte* in *Ida monte* in such a way that it could be read as *minore*;[22] there may also have been a misplaced suspension mark over the *i* in *Ida*. Mercury leads the three goddesses to Paris in the same order in which they appear in the *De Excidio Troiae Historia*. Venus's promise is, as in Dares, the most beautiful woman in Greece. Benoît also follows Dares in leaving the promises of the other two goddesses unspecified.

Benoît has, however, considerably amplified Dares's Judgment of Paris.[23] Two details come from the *Eneas:* the fact that the Judgment includes a golden apple with a Greek inscription and the fact that the goddesses approach Paris individually with their bribes.[24] The author of the *Eneas* took this material from a source related to the *Excidium Troiae* and the *Compendium Historiae Troianae-Romanae,* and thus it is ultimately classical in its inspiration. Remote both from the classical story of the Judgment and from Dares, however, are the details with which Benoît creates the setting of Paris's dream.

Benoît specifies that Paris's adventure occurred on the first of May ("es calendes de mai": 3860). As he unsuccessfully pursued a stag ("cerf"), the day grew hot and windless. Finally he became separated from the other hunters and his dogs in the valley of Venus ("vaus Cithariiens": 3868). He lay down to sleep beside a fountain in the shade of a tree. It was then that he had his dream.

In the setting which he creates for the dream, Benoît seems to anticipate the dream visions of the thirteenth and fourteenth centuries. He uses several motifs which were later associated with the idealized landscape of love in this genre: the spring day, the symbolic topography ("the valley of Venus"), the fountain. The *Roman de la Rose,* which established the fashion for the dream vision, was not, however, begun until 1236;[25] even the *Fablel dou dieu d'amours,* the first medieval poem to combine a dream of love with an idealized landscape, appeared well over a century later than the *Roman de Troie.*[26] Benoît's inspiration for Paris's dream came, of course, from the rationalizing approach of his late-classical source, and he may simply have *invented* the valley of Venus as an appropriate landscape for Paris's adventure. For the other motifs with which he set the stage for the divine embassy, however—the hunt, the date of May 1, the fountain, and the tree—he turned to Celtic tradition, finding there a useful analogue to the Greek supernaturalism of the story's mythological origins.

In the *Roman de Troie,* Paris is led to the site of his adventure by a stag which eludes him, leaving him separated from his dogs and the other hunters. This motif corresponds to an episode, found in early Irish literature, which Rachel Bromwich has identified as a dynasty myth:

> the intended ruler was set apart from his companions (in the stories he is separated from them in the hunt, either by nightfall or by a magic mist), and would inevitably and in spite of deceptive appearances, come together with the goddess representing his appointed territory.[27]

The motif of a hunter who is led by a stag, doe, or other animal to the scene of a supernatural adventure has been preserved in several Breton lays, such as *Graelent, Guigemar,* and *Tyolet,*[28] and in Arthurian literature, the chase of the white stag appears, according to Bromwich, "as an opening gambit which can form a prelude to almost any kind of magical adventure."[29] These sources are, of course, later than the *Roman de Troie,* but, as Bromwich has shown, the theme itself is very old.

The fountain next to which Paris has his vision of the goddesses may also be traceable to Celtic sources. In *Graelent,* the hero is led by a white hind to a fountain in which a beautiful lady is bathing. *Graelent* was written thirty or forty years later than the *Roman de Troie,*[30] and the Celtic source on which it was based is lost, but Tom Peete Cross cites examples from pre-twelfth-century Irish literature in which there is a similar connection between fountains and beautiful ladies who turn out to be fairies. Cross concludes,

> the subaqueous fairy princess was perfectly familiar to the ancient Celts, and the appearance of beautiful women from fairyland to chosen mortals beside fountains or larger bodies of water is a stock feature of Celtic fairy-mistress stories.[31]

Benoît could also have taken from Celtic tradition the date on which he makes Paris's adventure occur. The first of May had a clear association with the other world in Celtic lore and was thus an appropriate date for a supernatural embassy. According to A. J. Bliss, "the Irish *Oíche Bealtaine* 'May Eve' . . . was a traditional date for fairy visitations,"[32] and Constance Davies recalls that in *Culhwch and Olwen,* Gwyn and Gwythyr fight over a maiden every May-calends.[33]

That Paris falls asleep under a tree may also be an attempt on

Benoît's part to create a scene which, in Celtic tradition, would invite contact with the other word. G. V. Smithers identifies "an optional but common feature" in which the hero "opens the way for contact with a fairy . . . by sitting or sleeping under a tree," a motif which is preserved in the Middle English *Sir Landavall*,[34] with a variant in *Sir Degaré*.[35] The lay of *Desiré* includes a scene in which the hero meets a damsel at a fountain under a tree. She leads him to her mistress, who turns out to be a fairy.[36]

Benoît has thus medievalized the Judgment of Paris and adapted it to the romance genre. By choosing Dares's version of the Trojan saga, he chose a Judgment of Paris which required no suspension of disbelief on the part of the audience. Yet Dares's Judgment is dry and uninteresting. Its terseness hardly befits an episode whose effects were so momentous, nor does Dares do justice to an adventure with so much literary potential. For a medieval audience familiar with literature based on Celtic themes, the non-Christian otherworld was lodged in a fairy mound, not Mount Olympus. In Paris's dream that three goddesses visited him and offered him gifts, Benoît saw an analogue to Celtic stories in which fairies present gifts to mortals.[37] That he knew of this tradition is clear from a passage in the *Roman de Troie* which refers to a wonderful horse given Hector by the fairy Morgan la Fee (8023–30).

Paris's judgment led to his theft of Helen and the destruction of his city; love, moreover, often has tragic consequences in the *Roman de Troie*. Yet Benoît does not condemn romance. He deals with love because it interests him and his audience, and Paris's love for Helen gives Benoît the opportunity to chronicle a love affair. Benoît creates other romances from bare hints in Dares, and he invents out of nothing the story of Troilus and Briseide, which was later to interest Boccaccio and Chaucer.[38] Since Benoît does not regard Paris's love for Helen as reprehensible, he does not try to make the Judgment of Paris foreshadow impending doom. The atmosphere which he creates is not threatening but marvelous. Medieval literature had already diluted the numinous quality of those powerful Celtic fees who beckoned their mortal lovers to the Isle of Apples, and in the *Roman de Troie*, a charming adventure, Celtic in its inspiration, sets the stage for 30,000 lines devoted to love and chivalry.

Remote from Homer and even Dares in its spirit, Benoît's *Roman de Troie* was perfectly calculated to appeal to its age. Its popularity was assured by its anachronism;[39] medieval audiences looked into the mirror of history and saw themselves. The Greek and Trojan heroes had become knights concerned with chivalry and love. Benoît translated Dares's Latin into French, but more important was his translation of Dares's substance into medieval terms. Benoît set the fashion for the Trojan War as vernacular romance, and henceforth no classicizer would be able to undo what he had done. Two writers who labored after Benoît told the story in imitation of classical models and won for their pains virtual obscurity, even though, like Benoît, they based their poems on Dares's *De Excidio Troiae Historia*.

Joseph of Exeter, who is probably Chaucer's "Dares,"[40] wrote the *Frigii Daretis Yliados* sometime before 1190.[41] The poem is a *tour de force* of rhetoric in which Joseph uses Dares's plot as a background against which to display his style and erudition. Like Benoît, he supplements Dares with a wealth of detail, but in his case the detail is drawn from classical lore. It is particularly in the Judgment of Paris that Joseph has put his erudition to work to flesh out the bare bones of his source.

Unlike Benoît, Joseph is more interested in the rhetorical possibilities of the goddesses' debate than he is in the outcome of the Judgment: he devotes four hundred lines to a scene in which the rivals match wits in a manner reminiscent of Lucian, but passes so quickly over the Judgment that one critic missed it completely.[42] He makes the goddesses taunt one another with episodes such as Minerva's birth from the head of Jove, Venus's birth from the severed genitals of Saturn, and the capture of Venus and Mars in the net of Vulcan. His scholarship is evident too in the gifts which he makes the goddesses offer: riches and realms from Juno (309–12); skill in household crafts, victory, and wisdom from Minerva (449–54); and a woman as beautiful as herself from Venus, who flings off her veil at the climax of her speech to reveal her breasts to Paris (602–9).

Albert von Stade produced his *Troïlus* in the year 1249.[43] His main source is Dares, to whom he refers more than once (e.g., 3.239ff., 6.697ff.), and whom he follows extremely closely.[44] His Judgment of Paris is precisely that of the *De Excidio Troiae Historia*, except for a few reflections on women's vanity, such as "A beautiful woman is concerned with her chin, not her mind" (Mentum non mentem femina pulchra colit": 358). Like Joseph, Albert was earnest and learned, but like him also, he was too late: Benoît's *Roman de Troie* had changed literary tastes, or met a taste already changed, and, as Jürgen Stohlmann eloquently puts it, "Für einen antiken Stoff im antikischen Gewand war um 1250 die Zeit vorüber."[45]

The fortunes of the Trojan War in the Middle Ages were accordingly the fortunes of the *Roman de Troie*. Benoît's poem formed the basis, directly or indirectly, for most treatments of the Trojan saga. By the thirteenth century, audiences had developed a taste for prose,[46] and four complete prose reworkings of the *Roman de Troie* survive: the so-called Southern version, written before 1270;[47] another version possibly written after 1287;[48] the *Roman de Troie en prose* in Codex Bodmer 147, recently edited by Françoise Vielliard;[49] and an unedited version preserved in Ms. Rouen Bibl. Mun. 1049 (0.33).[50] As far as can be determined, they follow Benoît closely, preserving the atmosphere and most details of the Judgment.[51] The Southern version is particularly significant because it is the source on which Guido de Columnis based his *Historia Destructionis Troiae*.[52]

Guido's *Historia*, written between 1270 and 1287,[53] became the source and model for nearly every subsequent version of the Trojan story in medieval European literature. Guido wrote in Latin, and he claimed Dares as his chief source. He won, at the expense of Benoît, whom he actually copied at one remove, a reputation as a scholarly and factual writer. Through him, however, Benoît's version of the story and ultimately that of Dares continued to possess the European mind, and Paris's judgment of the goddesses remained a figment of the Trojan prince's imagination.

As Paris tells the story of the Judgment in Guido's *Historia*, his adventure occurred while he was in "India Minor" at his father's command. It was the summer solstice, with the sun in the beginning of Cancer. At dawn on a Friday ("die Veneris"), he went to the woods with a group of hunters to hunt. By noon he had found no game, but then he saw a solitary stag. Leaving his companions behind, he pursued it into the woods called Ida, only to have it disappear. He and his horse were tired, and his horse was soaked with sweat, so he dismounted and tied the horse to a tree, then stretched himself out on the grass in the shade, pillowing his head on his bow and quiver. Almost immediately, he fell asleep, and in his sleep he saw a wonderful vision.

It seemed that Mercury came to him leading Venus, Pallas, and Juno and explained that they had agreed to let him settle a dispute. As they ate at a feast, a certain apple of precious material was cast among them. A Greek inscription indicated that it was to be given to the most beautiful goddess. Mercury told Paris that each of the three believed she deserved the apple and then relayed the promise each offered him in exchange for the prize. Juno would make him most magnificent of all magnificent men in the world; from Pallas, he should obtain all human knowledge; Venus would give him the most beautiful and noble woman of Greece. Paris answered that he could not give true judgment unless all the goddesses presented themselves to him nude. Mercury ordered it done, and Paris decided that Venus deserved the apple.[54]

Guido's version of the Judgment is obviously derived from the Judgment which Benoît created[55] and which was passed on in the Southern version of the *Roman de Troie*. The setting of Paris's dream is particularly close to the corresponding episode in the *Roman*. Guido preserves the substitution of India Minor (or Major: see n. 54) for Mount Ida, and, as in Benoît, Paris is led to the site of his vision by a stag. Guido, however, suppresses the other Celtic motifs with which Benoît had created the effect of a magical but benign adventure. Instead, he provides details which evoke an atmosphere in keeping with his negative view of the events he narrates. Guido moralizes throughout the *Historia*, lamenting the chain of events which led to the fall of Troy and often blaming the fates for the city's undoing (e.g., book 5 [pp. 43–44]). He thus wishes to stress the Judgment's role as the first step in Troy's destruction. It is for this reason, I am sure, that he makes Paris's adventure occur on the "die Veneris," or Friday. Probably because of its association with the Crucifixion, Friday was and still is widely regarded as a day of ill luck.[56] Guido goes even further to create a sinister atmosphere for the Judgment. He implies that demonic influences caused Paris to dream that he judged the goddesses.

It was a commonplace in medieval dream lore that certain dreams were caused by demons. Even in ancient times, some dreams were regarded as illusions in which men's evil desires surfaced.[57] The logical development of this notion in Christian thought was early expressed in the *Moralia in Job,* where Gregory the Great identified the *illusio* as a type of dream caused by the devil.[58] Isidore of Seville and others passed this concept along to the later Middle Ages.[59] Summarizing medieval dream lore in the *Policraticus,* John of Salisbury identifies certain dreams as the inspiration of demons,[60] and for this reason he warns against belief in dreams (2.16 [1.94–96]). John particularly links delusive dreams with witchcraft when he suggests that those who believe that they have taken part in witches' sabbaths have actually only dreamed the experience, but that these dreams are caused by demons (2.17 [1.100–101]). Thus there is ample precedent in dream lore for Guido to regard Paris's dream as an example of demonic inspiration. Its subject matter would make it particularly suspect.

A long medieval tradition viewed the gods of the ancients as demons in disguise.[61] A development of the Greek rationalizing tradition, this notion can be traced up through the church fathers into the later Middle Ages. A particularly striking example of it is found in a story which first appeared in William of Malmesbury's *Gesta Regum Anglorum.* A young man puts his wedding ring on the finger of a statue of Venus so that he can play ball unhindered and later discovers that he has betrothed himself to a beautiful demon.[62] The Tannhäuser legend, too, has behind it an identification of Venus as a she-devil.[63] That Guido knew and believed this interpretation of classical mythology is clear in the *Historia.* In a long digression on idolatry, he explains the oracle of Delphi as follows: "through the wiles of this demonic deception the god Apollo revealed his answers to the petitioners on the island of Delos" (97). It is thus highly likely that he would regard Paris's dream of the Judgment with suspicion. By specifying that Paris's adventure began at noon—it is then that Paris first catches sight of the stag that leads him to the site of his vision—he further confirms that the dream is an effect of demonic inspiration.

Noon was traditionally the time of day when demonic influence was at its greatest. Belief in the power of the *daemonium meridianum,* or noon-day demon, is well attested in both learned and popular tradition. In Psalm 90, the psalmist had declared that with trust in God, one should not fear "the plague that wanders about in the night, nor the calamity that destroys at noon" (6), and to more than one commentator, the noon-day demon was Satan.[64] The beautiful woman named Meridiana (= noon) who at midday appears in the woods to Gerbert of Aurillac in a story reported by Walter Map is doubtless a variation on the theme, and one with particular relevance to Guido's Judgment.[65] Thus Guido implies that Paris's dream of the goddesses is a manifestation of the noon-day demon.

That Paris's adventure occurs at the summer solstice is also relevant. Throughout Europe, the summer solstice was marked by the celebration of St. John the Baptist's Day on June 24. Witches were believed to come abroad on St. John's Eve to gather herbs rendered particularly efficacious by the holiday.[66] The basis of the witchcraft delusion, well established by the time that Guido wrote the *Historia Destructionis Troiae*,[67] was the belief that demons were the source of witches' powers.[68] The pagan gods had already been identified with demons, an idea which Guido knew and accepted. Thus, with an easy association between witches and the goddesses who supposedly appeared to Paris, the summer solstice becomes an eminently appropriate date for the vision.

Guido's Judgment itself is relatively traditional, though it is in many respects different from Benoît's. Benoît, it will be recalled, made each goddess come to Paris secretly to offer her bribe, but he did not specify Juno's or Minerva'a promises. Here, on the other hand, the goddesses do not speak, and Mercury relays their promises to Paris. Juno's gift is magnificence, Pallas's knowledge, and Venus's, as in Benoît, the most beautiful woman in Greece. Most importantly, in a detail which enhances the implication that the three beautiful women of Paris's vision are demons posing as gods, Guido departs from Benoît to have Paris request to see the goddesses naked.

Christianity had brought with it a suspicion of that nudity which, in classical art, had been the glory of both god and hero.[69] To the Middle Ages, nudity was a sign of impurity and sensuality. For Fulgentius, the nakedness of the pagan gods almost always represents allegorically some negative characteristic.[70] When the demon-Venus appears in William of Malmesbury's story of the statue-engagement, she is so lightly clad that she appears to be nude, and it is implied that nakedness is a state appropriate only to Greek gods and to demons.[71] The balance and proportion of a nude are not, as in classical culture, the outward signs of an inner nobility or divinity, but rather the signs of utter depravity. Therefore, when Paris asks the goddesses to disrobe before him, they stand revealed, though he does not realize this, as the demon-gods that they are. Doubtless Guido had in mind too the nudity traditionally associated with witches.[72]

That Paris asks the goddesses to disrobe reveals something of his nature too. In one tradition, passed on by Ovid, Paris was not a warrior but a sensualist. Thus he would be particularly susceptible to the appeal of the three beautiful women who appeared in his vision. Since demons were known to take the forms of beautiful women, as in Walter Map's story, and since Venus herself was traditionally identified as a demon, he should have been more careful. To ask these mysterious lovelies to disrobe is to play into the hands of Satanic forces. One of Guido's main interests in the *Historia*, however, is to examine the errors and idolatry of the pre-Christian Greeks and Trojans.

It would not be valid to argue that every dream in medieval literature should be interpreted as a delusion inspired by demons. Medieval dream theorists recognized many causes for dreams. Nevertheless, Guido's own statements that gods are demons, and the details with which he surrounds Paris's adventure, justify interpreting this dream as a product of Satanic influence. John of Salisbury had censured one classic dream in the *Policraticus*, that which guided Aeneas to found Rome: "Aeneas, guided by oracles, found the promised land he was seeking, and there by the will—we shall not say of divinity but of demons—fixed his abode and planted the seed of the Roman race. . . ."[73] In John's view, the founding of Rome had dire results ("from that seed a tainted race springs"),[74] and he accordingly discourages belief in dreams and omens. Paris, too, regards his dream as an omen; he believes that it means the gods will favor his voyage to Greece. Guido implies, however, that he places his trust in a devilish delusion, and thus the stage is set for the fall of Troy.

Guido's version of the Trojan saga was to be the basis for nearly every subsequent treatment of the story up into the fifteenth century and beyond, both on the continent and in England. Little would be subtracted from or added to Guido's Judgment, though the subtle details by which he had indicated that Paris's vision was caused by demons would be altered as times changed and new attitudes toward the ancients made the pagan gods less suspect. By the beginning of the Northern European Renaissance, for example, classical culture was far enough in the past to be regarded with some perspective, while the old idea that Europe traced its origins to the Trojans was more important than ever before. Though based on Guido's *Historia Destructionis Troiae,* a fifteenth-century treatment of the Trojan legend, *Lystoire de la destruction de Troye la grant,* reflects this new spirit. It was written between 1450 and 1452 by one Jacques Milet, of whom little is known save that he held the degree of *maistre ès arts.*[75]

Milet, who makes clear in his prologue that he is interested in the Trojan story because of its relevance to the history of France,[76] took the *Historia* and turned it into a drama. He thus put classical antiquity on stage for an era which knew only religious theater.[77] The Judgment of Paris fits easily into Milet's dramatic scheme because, ever since Dares, the episode has been narrated by Paris in his report to Priam's council. Milet's Judgment is almost identical with that in his immediate source, Guido, yet he eschews both Benoît's and Guido's supernaturalism.

In "India Minor" at Priam's command, Paris becomes separated from his companions while pursuing a stag. After the chase, his horse is covered with sweat. He fastens the animal's rein to the branch of a tree, and so on. Milet, however, changes the date of Paris's adventure because he has no wish to connect his goddesses with fairies, demons, or witches. The episode occurs at neither the calends of May nor the summer solstice, but rather on a day in spring: "This was at the time when every flower turns green as for renewal, and the nightingale teaches lovers to enjoy themselves, and by singing sweetly he wants to induce them to love."[78] Milet will not be the only rehandler of the Judgment to associate Paris's dream of the goddesses with a spring day and thoughts of love. The *Roman de la Rose* had made such an association almost inevitable.

Milet also changes the time of Paris's adventure. From Dares, through Benoît and Guido, Paris's dream vision has occurred in the afternoon. His unsuccessful morning in the woods, when game should be abroad, the great stag appearing just when the forest would normally become still, and the noon-day heat which provokes Paris's lassitude all combine to create an atmosphere conducive to the operation of the supernatural. Milet, however, makes Paris venture forth to hunt after noon, and it is evening by the time he encounters the stag. Paris's sleep thus becomes not the demon-haunted sleep of a sultry midday but an ordinary overnight repose.

Milet's dependence on Guido is also clear in the Judgment. Mercury relays to Paris all that the goddesses have to say, and Paris asks them to disrobe before he selects Venus. The episode is, however, streamlined. For example, Mercury does not explain the background of the quarrel, so that, in a subsequent reference, "the gift" which Paris is to award is unexplained by the context. Milet expands the story too, though, in ways that show a respect for his classical materials and an interest in the lore of the antique. He tries to evoke the splendor of the Olympians by making Mercury appear in a blaze of light—clearly an image borrowed from Christian notions of the numinous. He also provides the goddesses with identities in which there is no suggestion of opprobrium: Juno is "lady of wealth," Pallas "seemed of great prudence," and Venus is "goddess of joy." Thus a few changes make Guido's Judgment the worthy production of a fifteenth-century humanist.

Like Milet's *Lystoire de la destruction de Troye la grant*, other continental treatments of the Trojan theme produced in the fifteenth century were inspired by an interest in the supposed progenitors of European culture. The story of Troy was particularly popular in Burgundy, where Philip the Good added numerous volumes dealing with Trojan history to the ducal libraries.[79] In 1430 he founded the order of the Golden Fleece, attracted to the motif possibly because of its connection with Troy in the version of the Trojan saga which Benoît and Guido had made the standard.[80]

Still anachronistically pictured as identical with medieval men in habits, beliefs, and social organization, the ancients were regarded as models of chivalry; thus Jason became the patron of an order devoted to chivalric, religious, and political ends,[81] an honor which he shared with the Old Testament Gideon because of

Gideon's connection with another fleece.[82] The *Historia Destructionis Troiae* of Guido de Columnis was the basis for nearly all Burgundian knowledge of the Trojan saga, and at least three French translations of it were known at the ducal court.[83] A view of classical culture as the embodiment of every chivalric ideal scarcely harmonized, however, with Guido's condemnation of the ancients as idolators and worshippers of demons. How could Jason, co-sponsor (with Gideon) of Philip's knightly order, be regarded in this light? The answer is that Guido's *Historia* was used selectively, not slavishly. At least one French translation of Guido's work shows that with subtle omissions and shifts in emphasis, Guido's substance could remain while his spirit was made more congenial to an age that looked to the past for inspiration even in the moral sphere.

In 1464 Raoul Le Fèvre, chaplain of Philip the Good, undertook at the duke's command[84] an ambitious three-volume work which was to place the Trojans in world history, beginning with the reigns of Saturn and Jupiter, and to chronicle four successive destructions of Troy.[85] This work was to be known as the *Recueil des histoires de troyes.* Raoul completed only the first two books.[86] Sometime before 1469, however, it became customary to supplement Raoul's two books with a third book, already in existence, in order to carry the Trojan history up to the destruction of the city by the Greeks. That third book was one of the French translations of Guido's *Historia.*[87]

The only significant differences between the Judgment of Paris in the *Historia Destructionis Troiae* and the Judgment as it appears in the *Recueil des histoires de troyes* are the date and time of Paris's adventure. The date has been changed to the beginning of May, and the time is now afternoon.[88] Consciously or unconsciously, the anonymous translator has altered the two details by which Guido sought to establish that Paris's dream of the goddesses was inspired by demons. Benoît had specified the calends of May, or May first, a date noted in Celtic tradition for visits from the other world, but the Judgment of Paris in the *Recueil* is more akin to Jacques Milet's. Early May was chosen, I would suggest, because by this time several centuries of literary tradition had made spring the conventional setting for a visionary experience.

The legend of Troy was as popular in the English vernacular tradition as in the French; England too looked to Troy for its origins.[89] As early as the eighth century, Nennius, in the *Historia Brittonum,* had traced the founding of Britain, in the "third age of the world," to a grandson of Aeneas named Brutus.[90] The tradition was picked up by Geoffrey of Monmouth and through his influence became widespread.[91] The Trojan origin of Britain forms the basis for the *Brut* of Wace, the *Brut* of Layamon, and a now-lost *Brut* of Gaimar.[92] Five major English works dating from the fourteenth and fifteenth centuries retell for English-speaking audiences the tale of Troy; the earliest, the *Seege of Troy,* follows traditions which predate Guido, while the other four are based closely on Guido's *Historia.* The *"Gest Historiale" of the Destruction of Troy* and the *Laud Troy Book* follow Guido so closely that they are scarcely more than footnotes to the *Historia.* John Lydgate's *Troy Book* is likewise heavily indebted to Guido but reflects as well changes in literary taste created by the rise of the dream vision.[93] William Caxton's *Recuyell of the Historyes of Troye* is indebted to Guido by way of the *Recueil des histoires de troyes* of Raoul Le Fèvre.[94]

The *Seege of Troy* probably dates from the first quarter of the fourteenth century.[95] It is thought to have been composed by a minstrel for recitation to a popular audience,[96] and its Judgment of Paris, in spite of, or perhaps because of, a fine disregard for classical scholarship, is an episode with great charm and dramatic interest. Basing the *Seege of Troy* ultimately on Dares,[97] Benoît,[98] and versions of the *Excidium Troiae* or *Compendium Historiae Troianae-Romanae,*[99] the poet has interpreted his material in terms with which his medieval audience would be familiar from the popular literature of the day.

The poet knows a version of Paris's birth and youth which derives from the tradition of the *Excidium Troiae* and the *Compendium Historiae Troianae-Romanae;* reflecting the work's humbler audience, though, the dispossessed Paris has been raised as a swineherd.[100] As far as the Judgment itself is concerned, the poet seems to have relied on his memory of learned sources for the outlines of the episode,[101] calling on his imagination to dramatize the story and make it accessible to his audience. Unhampered by any scholarly impulse, he handled his material with almost complete freedom, and the result was doubtless more effective for his purposes than a more accurate version would have been.

As is usually the case in versions of the Trojan saga indebted to Dares or Benoît, the story of the Judgment is narrated by Paris when he rises in Priam's parliament to describe the adventure which has convinced him that he should lead the Trojan fleet to Greece. As he tells the story in most manuscripts of the *Seege*, he was hunting one day in the forest when the weather changed, and in a great mist he became separated from his hunting party.[102] He rode so far that he took a wrong turn and lost his way, finally dismounting and falling asleep under a tree. Meanwhile, four ladies from Elfenland, playing in the forest, found a golden ball with silver letters which read, "Þe faireste wommon of al / Schal haue t welde þis riche bal" (lines 519–20). As three of them, Saturnus, Jubiter, and Mercurius, argued about who should have the ball, the fourth, Venus, suggested that they ask the sleeping knight, Paris. They agreed and bade him wake up and bestow the ball on the lady who most deserved it. As Paris hesitated, Saturnus offered to make him the richest man in the world if he awarded her the ball. Paris, however, reflected that he had no need of more riches. Mercurius offered to make him the strongest man in the world, but Paris considered that he was strong enough. Jubiter offered to make him the fairest man in the world, but Paris decided that he needed no more beauty. Finally Venus spoke, offering him the love of all women. Paris was swayed by her promise and awarded her the ball. Then Venus instructed him to tell his father the king to send him to Greece, where he would win the fairest lady.

Benoît had already assimilated the Judgment to its nearest analogue in contemporary popular literature when he gave it the aura of a Celtic tale. The poet of the *Seege* seems to have recognized in Benoît's treatment something congenial to his own tastes and aims.[103] Like Benoît, he makes of Dares's relatively prosaic adventure an encounter with the other world. Like Benoît, he creates an atmosphere which prepares us to expect magic, substituting for Benoît's heat and lost companions a great mist[104] and a wrong turn. Like Benoît, he places Paris beneath a tree for the sleep which is the prelude to his wonderful adventure.

The poet of the *Seege* has, however, gone further than Benoît in his transformation of the episode. Benoît drew only the setting of Paris's adventure from the world of faerie; the poet of the *Seege* maintains this atmosphere throughout. Benoît preserved the "rational" explanation for Paris's encounter with the supernatural: it was only a dream. In the *Seege*, the sleeping Paris is awakened for the Judgment, but the author has found another way to rationalize the adventure. The contestants for the prize of beauty are no longer goddesses, but rather "ffoure ladies of eluene land" (508), and thus the treatment of the Judgment in the *Seege* resembles Guido's approach—but on a humbler level.

If the great gods of the ancient world were regarded in medieval thought as demons or witches, so too were the various supernatural beings of Northern mythology: elves, fairies, gnomes, and the like.[105] A passage dealing with magic and witchcraft in the *Fasciculus Morum* (1320), a work produced in England and roughly contemporary with the *Seege*, makes very clear the equation elves = witches = demons:

> But, I ask, what is to be said of those wretched and superstitious persons who say that by night they see most fair queens and other maidens tripping with the lady Diana and leading the dances with the goddess of the pagans, who (i.e. maidens?) in our vulgar tongue are called *Elves*, and believe that the latter transform men and women into other shapes and conduct them to *Elvelond* . . . ?[106]

Jeffrey Russell points out, however, that despite the association between elves, demons, and witches, "the assimilation was never complete, for the creatures preserved something of their original identity in folk tradition. Even as demons, they were never nearly as powerful or terrible as the Judeo-Christian fallen angels."[107] Thus the atmosphere of the Judgment in the *Seege* remains nonthreatening, though the association between the goddesses and these ladies from Elfenland has given the poet a useful rationalizing device for the episode.

So effective is this transposition of the Judgment to the terms of English folklore that we hardly mind the poet's ignorance of classical tradition, but garbled indeed is his tale. Rather than the usual three contestants in the beauty contest, we have four, named, with complete disregard for gender, Saturnus, Jubiter, Mercurius, and Venus. Rather than intercepting a golden apple, they find a golden ball. Finally, the extra lady offers Paris a reward which we have not previously encountered: *he* is to become the fairest.

The Harley manuscript of the *Seege*, however, contains a version of the Judgment strikingly different from that found in the other manuscripts of the poem. The Judgment occurs at the same point in the narrative, as Paris rises in his father's parliament, but the story which he tells has about it less of the fairy tale and more of the school text. Clearly, the *Seege* has at this point been rehandled by a man of more learning than its original poet. He recognized a bungled version of this well-known classical incident and determined to rescue the poem.[108]

The version of the Judgment in Harley is only about half as long as that in the other manuscripts of the *Seege*, and Paris launches precipitously into his tale with the finding of the apple: "Sir . . . listeneth a stounde: / Thre goddes an apull fonde—."[109] The "goddes" are Juno, Pallas, and Venus, and the apple, with gold engraving saying that it is a prize for the fairest, has been thrown by Fortune "Too makyn werre þat ere was pees" (line 404). The goddesses begin to argue about who should have the apple, but agree to ask Paris to judge. Venus offers the fairest "leman" ever born, but through some mishap in the transmission of the text or some error in his source, the rehandler omits Pallas's scene and makes Juno promise wisdom.

Clearly this is a much more "classical" version of the Judgment than that found in the other manuscripts of the *Seege*. That the rehandler based his revision directly on a document in which the Judgment is not related by Paris is shown by the fact that for much of his tale in the Harley *Seege* Paris refers to himself in the third person. The poet has also eschewed the contrivance of the dream, by which Dares had rationalized the old story's premise that gods would care to solicit the opinions of men. In addition, he has cut details with which the earlier version of the poem had created an atmosphere suitable for the occurrence of marvels: the hunt, the tree, and the mist. Finally, he has returned to the story an ancient motive for the disruption of the feast. In late-classical and medieval versions of the story, Discord's action in provoking the goddesses' quarrel is usually attributed to her anger at being excluded from the wedding celebration. In the *Cypria*, however, Eris causes contention among the goddesses in order to carry out the will of Zeus; in collaboration with Themis, he has planned the Trojan War. Medieval handlings of the Trojan legend often place the war's origin and outcome in the hands of Fortune. To make Fortune responsible for the apple and the goddesses' quarrel, then, is to translate into medieval terms the cosmic perspective with which the *Cypria* viewed the war when it made Eris the vicar of Zeus in working out his will. Though it is in many respects more faithful to classical tradition, however, the narrative of the Judgment which the rehandler substitutes is much less effective from an artistic point of view.

The *Seege of Troye*, which we have just considered, reflects the influence of Dares, Benoît, and the tradition preserved in the *Excidium Troiae* and the *Compendium Historiae Troianae-Romanae*— but not Guido's *Historia Destructionis Troiae*. Perhaps when the *Seege* was written in the first quarter of the fourteenth century, Guido's influence had not yet reached England. Subsequent English rehandlers of the Trojan saga, however, turned wholeheartedly to Guido's version. That he had written in Latin prose and referred directly to the arch-authorities Dares and Dictys conferred on his work an authority untouched by any other.

The *"Gest Historiale" of the Destruction of Troy*, produced in 1375 and written in a mixture of the Northern and Midland dialects,[110] is the first English version of Guido's history.[111] The poem proceeds through the familiar first destruction of Troy, the theft of Hesione, Priam's rebuilding of the city, and the unsuccessful attempt to regain Hesione, to the council in which Paris describes the adventure which has convinced him that the gods intend him to lead the Trojan army against the Greeks. Scarcely a detail of the Judgment itself departs from Guido's version; even Guido's moralizations are included, and there is no sign at all of material from any additional source.

A second English version of Guido is found in the *Laud Troy Book*, which has been dated as early as 1343 and as late as 1400.[112]

The poet names his source, "Maister Gy"—along with Dares and Dictys—in his opening lines (87–97). There is little likelihood that his use of Dares and Dictys is direct, however, and his Judgment of Paris departs from Guido's in no essential detail. The poet covers the familiar ground: the fleece, the first destruction of Troy, the rebuilding of the city, and the unsuccessful embassy of Antenor. Then, in a discussion with Priam about who should lead the Trojan army to Greece and steal a noblewoman to exchange for "Oxonie," Paris tells his familiar tale.

The *Troy Book*, John Lydgate's English version of Guido's *Historia Destructionis Troiae*, was begun in 1412 at the request of the man who was to become King Henry V. It was completed in 1420.[113] Lydgate acknowledges in his opening lines that he is basing his work on Guido,[114] and the sequence of events leading up to Paris's recital of his dream follows the *Historia* closely.

When he gets to the Judgment, Lydgate supplements Guido's version of the episode with material from other sources, but his reliance on the *Historia* for the episode's outlines is clear. As in Guido's version, Paris is in India at the command of Priam, and his adventure occurs in mid-June during a day of hunting. He hunts all morning, then catches sight of the stag, which he loses in the groves of Ida; he has become separated from his companions, and he and his horse are exhausted, so he fastens the animal's reins to a tree and lies down to sleep. As in Guido's version, Mercury leads the goddesses to him and explains the background of their quarrel. He relays their promises to Paris in the same order in which he relays them in the *Historia*. As in Guido, Paris does not judge until he has seen the goddesses nude (2.2369–2792).

Despite this close dependence on Guido, however, Lydgate has added considerable material. His Judgment itself is more scholarly than was Guido's;[115] he explains, for example, the origins of the apple over which the goddesses quarrel and he makes the goddesses promise additional gifts (e.g., riches, renown, and honor from Juno). Much more important, however, are additions which Lydgate has made to the setting of Paris's adventure and the descriptions of Mercury and the three goddesses.

Lydgate has transformed the setting of Paris's adventure into that of a dream vision. By the time the *Troy Book* was written in the first quarter of the fifteenth century, almost two hundred years had elapsed since Guillaume de Lorris began the *Roman de la Rose*. We saw that in France about the middle of the fifteenth century, Jacques Milet and the anonymous translator whose French version of Guido's *Historia* was inserted in the *Recueil des histoires de troyes* saw in Paris's dream an analogue to the dream-vision tradition; each gave the adventure a setting which recalled the spring-day opening of the *Roman de la Rose*. Lydgate responded to the same tradition when he described Paris's visionary experience with the goddesses, but his setting is an even more elaborate allusion to the setting of a vision poem—and his awareness of the dream-vision genre has also affected his treatment of the dream itself.

In Lydgate's version of the Judgment, Paris rises early on a spring morning to honor love and Venus. He wanders out into the countryside, hunts unsuccessfully, and eventually falls asleep beside a river and a crystal well on the soft green grass of a pleasant valley, where he has his marvelous dream. Paris's hunt has, since Benoît, begun early in the morning on a spring day; the time of day is thus one of the *données* that Lydgate received from Guido. It is Lydgate, however, who supplies from the conventions of the dream vision the motive of going abroad to celebrate love and Venus. Paris's sleep has always occurred in the forest, since this is the scene of his hunt; Lydgate received this detail of the story, too, from Guido. Yet Lydgate, through his description of the setting in which Paris finds himself as he wanders, exhausted, with his exhausted horse, tries to create the effect of a *locus amoenus,* a perfect spot set apart. Paris's sleep occurs in a pleasant, pretty dell, where the grass is soft as velvet (2.2448–50). Finally, Lydgate adds to Guido's scene a fountain, that convention without which scarcely a medieval dream vision occurs (2.2454–60). With its gravel and bright stones, the "cristal welle" is reminiscent of the fountain in the *Roman de la Rose;* the river, too, suggests the river which the dreamer followed to reach the garden of the Rose. Benoît, it is true, included a fountain in his Judgment, but Guido did not pick up this detail, and Lydgate, as far as is known, did not consult Benoît directly.[116] The fountain would have been readily available to him as a convention of the popular dream vision. The Judgment of Paris suggested to him a dream vision, and thus he added details to emphasize the parallel.

As far as Paris's vision of Mercury and the goddesses is concerned, Lydgate, again under the influence of the dream-vision genre, has combined Dares's rationalizing approach to the Judgment with Fulgentius's allegorizing approach. While not drawing his allegorizations precisely from Fulgentius, Lydgate has given the three goddesses—and Mercury as well—allegorized attributes that reveal their traditional areas of patronage. This approach clearly derives from a work like the *Roman de la Rose* in which personifications acquire their significance from their iconographical attributes. In Paris's dream Venus, for example, has snow-white doves, which Lydgate says signify the innocence of those who intend truth in love, and mean that lovers should always be pure (2.2521– 30). Pallas bears a shield, representing the strength of virtue against vice (2.2557–60). Juno is accompanied by her peacocks because just as peacocks lose their feathers, riches forsake those who pursue them (2.2606–10). Thus Paris's dream of the goddesses serves Lydgate not only as the episode which explains the origin of the war he chronicles in the *Troy Book*, but also provides him with the opportunity to offer moral improvement by allegorizing the attributes of classical deities.

The final English version of the Trojan saga we shall consider is William Caxton's *Recuyell of the Historyes of Troye*, which he translated from the French *Recueil* of Raoul Le Fèvre on the order of Margaret of York [117] and which became the first English printed book.[118] Caxton began his translation at Bruges on March 1, 1468, completed it at Cologne on September 19, 1471, and printed it about 1474.[119] His translation of the *Recueil* is for the most part extremely literal, but he appears to have also consulted a Latin text of Guido's *Historia*. He includes, for example, the detail that Paris's horse "swette on all sides" (2.521) after chasing the stag. This is not in the *Recueil* but goes back to Guido's "equs meus totus esset madidus pre sudore" ("my horse was all soaked with sweat": 61). He has also altered the date of Paris's adventure, changing it from the *Recueil*'s early May back to summer: "I was in the lasse ynde [= India Minor] at the begynnyng of the Sōmer" (2.520). Caxton's intention is not, I am sure, to recreate the diabolical atmosphere with which Guido had invested the Judgment. Rather, as his addition of the phrase describing the horse's sweaty condition shows, he was attempting to do scholarly justice to his story by consulting a more authoritative source for supplementary details. The significance of Guido's date and time is lost on him. He merely renders the date as early summer, not the solstice, and, like the *Recueil*, he makes Paris's adventure occur in the afternoon: "after myddaye y fonde a grete herte" (2.520–21).

Works which narrate the entire Trojan saga were not the only means by which the story of Troy passed to the Middle Ages. As the event which dispersed fleeing heroes to found the nations of Europe, the Trojan War formed an obligatory chapter in histories of larger scope, and the Judgment itself was important as the cause of the war. More than one historian lingered over the tale of Paris and the divine beauty contest. With its inherent drama and its potential for narrative development, the Judgment appealed to historians, but it posed certain problems as well. Most crucially, a historian would have to find a way to rationalize the story's fabulous elements.

The story of Troy forms part of the compilation which Paul Meyer has identified as the oldest history in French prose.[120] *L'histoire ancienne jusqu'à César* narrates the history of the world from the creation to the time of Julius Caesar. Produced between 1223 and 1230 for a court at Lille whose châtelain was one Roger IV, the *Histoire ancienne* was probably written by a well-read clerk and, Meyer conjectures, intended for oral presentation.[121] It was extremely popular; at least fifty-five manuscripts of its first redaction are known.[122]

The outline of the *Histoire ancienne* is that of Orosius's *Historia Adversos Paganos*,[123] but the work is a compilation made up of separate episodes, such as Genesis, Thebes, Troy, and Aeneas. As Guy Raynaud de Lage has pointed out, the bulk of the *Histoire ancienne* is devoted to those stories which formed the subjects of the chief *romans antiques* of the twelfth century.[124] The section on Troy depends, however, not on Benoît but on Dares, possibly because Dares's Latin prose seemed more authoritative than Benoît's French verse.[125] The passage dealing with the Judgment incorporates material from another source or sources as well; clearly, the author wished to offer his audience all the details known to him and to develop the episode as fully as possible. He kept, though, the dream framework which had rationalized the Judgment in Dares's *De Excidio Troiae Historia*.

After Priam has rebuilt Troy and sent Antenor on his unsuccessful embassy to the Greeks, he calls the council at which Paris recounts his familiar dream:

> Afterward Paris spoke and said to his father that he should have the navy prepared and he would go to Greece if he wished, and he had so much trust in the gods that if he went there he would conquer his enemies so that he would have praise and he would return back with complete victory. "Now hear, sir, why I say this. It was not long ago that I went to hunt in the forest, and there appeared to me in sleep Mercury, who is a great god and lord, and it seemed to me that he led with him three goddesses: Juno and Venus and Minerva. Then Mercury called to me and said that I should make judgment and say which of his three was the most beautiful, and you should know well that Juno and Minerva promised me wisdom and strength enough, and Venus, if I would name her the most beautiful, promised me the most beautiful woman in the world from Greece, and I coveted the beautiful woman and said that, before all the others, Venus was the most beautiful."[126]

Up to the point at which Mercury addresses Paris, the passage is an extremely close—almost literal—rendering of the *De Excidio Troiae Historia*. As is typical in rehandlings of Dares, however, the Judgment itself, which in the *De Excidio Troiae Historia* occupied only two lines and did not specify the promises of Juno and Minerva, has been amplified. Here Mercury, as in the *Roman de Troie*, calls to Paris and explains what is required of him. Here, also, other promises are mentioned: wisdom and strength (*sens* and *prouesce*), one from Juno and the other from Minerva, though both are traditionally associated with Minerva.[127] Venus's promise, the most beautiful woman in the world from Greece, conflates that in the *Excidium Troiae*, the most beautiful wife, with that in Dares and Benoît, the most beautiful woman in Greece.[128]

A second redaction of the *Histoire ancienne*, possibly dating from the mid-fourteenth century,[129] possibly later,[130] includes a much more elaborate Judgment, part of a lengthy narrative dealing with Paris in a much-expanded treatment of Troy.[131] The section on Paris begins with descriptions of Priam's sons. Paris was fair, pleasant to ladies, good in archery and hunting, but not so knightly as his brothers. On the night he was conceived, Hecuba dreamed that she gave birth to a torch which set fire to Troy. Diviners told Priam the dream meant that his wife had conceived a child through whom the city would be destroyed. The king ordered the queen to kill the child, but Hecuba had pity on the infant and secretly sent him to a vavasor who adopted him and named him Alexander. When he was grown, he married Cenona (Oenone). Once when he had gone to see his animals, an unfamilar bull fought one of his own and, after a long battle, conquered it. Paris crowned the strange bull with flowers in sign of its victory. The story of his action spread through the country, and Paris was praised for his justice.

One day Juno, Pallas, and Venus gathered to enjoy themselves; when the goddess of discord saw that she had not been invited to the fête, she was angry. Determined to disrupt their pleasure, she made a golden apple inscribed, "Let this apple be given to the most beautiful." When the ladies had feasted, they entered a *vergier* and sat around a fountain to converse. Then the goddess of discord came flying through the air and let the apple fall among them. When the ladies saw the apple, each said she ought to have it, and the discord was great. Finally all agreed to seek a judge. They went through the forest until by chance they came upon a fountain under an olive tree where Paris slept. They said to one another, here is Paris, son of King Priam; his honesty is shown by his crowning the strange bull. They awoke him and asked him to award the apple to the most beautiful. Juno promised that if he chose her she would help him whenever he had need and would bring to his assistance all the powers of heaven. Pallas told him that as goddess of sapience she would give him wisdom and knowledge (*sens* and *sauoir*) and would aid him whenever necessary. Venus promised him that all women would love him and that he would have the most beautiful woman in the world for his *amie*. At last he gave the apple to Venus, and the other goddesses were very angry.[132]

The expanded Trojan material contained in the second redaction of the *Histoire ancienne* is usually described as a prose paraphrase

of Benoît's *Roman de Troie*,[133] though the more elaborate Judgment
has been noted.[134] Unlike the first redaction of the *Histoire ancienne*, the second contains no material from the Bible or from
other epic cycles. After the section on Troy comes the story of
Aeneas, and the history ends with the founding of Rome. This structure sounds very much like that of the *Excidium Troiae* and the
Compendium Historiae Troianae-Romanae. Details of the Paris
episode likewise suggest the tradition represented by these two
texts, particularly the *Compendium*. The author seems to have
taken his material from a handbook like the *Compendium Historiae Troianae-Romanae* and expanded it into a narrative with a certain amount of literary interest.

The *Histoire ancienne* follows the order of events in the *Compendium* rather than the *Excidium Troiae*: the dream of Hecuba,
the rival bull, the goddesses' quarrel, the Judgment. The *Histoire
ancienne* is closer to the *Compendium* too in the details of Hecuba's dream. Hecuba tells her vision to Priam, who orders that the
child be killed, but the queen secretly sends him away to be raised.
The bullfight which gives Paris his reputation for justice is closer
to the version in the *Compendium*. As in both Latin sources, the
goddess of discord is angry at her exclusion from the divine festivities and therefore makes ("provides" in the *Excidium Troiae*)
the golden apple with the message that starts the goddesses' quarrel. As in the *Compendium*, where Discord climbs up to the ceiling
to cast the apple, the *Histoire ancienne* makes her fly over the goddesses and drop the apple among them. The *Compendium* further
agrees with the *Histoire ancienne* in making the goddesses themselves choose Paris as judge; in the *Excidium Troiae* they are sent
to Paris by Jove.

Though the author has chosen to use this classical version of the
Judgment in his history, he has added certain details which may be
intended to rationalize the episode. As in Dares, Benoît, and Guido,
Paris is asleep at the start of his adventure. Here, though, he is
awakened by the goddesses. In the *Roman de Troie*, Paris slept by a
fountain under a tree, and I suggested that the fountain derived
from Celtic tradition and was intended to create an atmosphere
ripe for marvels. By the time the second redaction of the *Histoire
ancienne* was written, however, a sleep beneath a tree by a fountain

would be read differently. The tradition of the *Roman de la Rose* would have made such a setting evoke a visionary experience in the dream-vision genre. Though Paris seems to awake and participate in the scene, the dream-vision tradition has blurred the line between vision and reality.

Paris is sleeping in the woods when the goddesses approach him; typically, though, a dream vision occurred in an enclosed garden or *vergier*. That the author knew the conventions of the genre is suggested by the setting he provides for the goddesses' quarrel. When he makes them relax in their garden after their feast, he gives the garden a fountain as a matter of course—as if he knew that a fountain was an obligatory feature of an enclosed garden. The enclosed garden and fountain are appropriate to this scene, too, in light of allegorical treatments of the story, such as that in the *Ovide moralisé*, which identified the apple over which the goddesses quarreled as that which caused Adam and Eve's fall in the Garden of Eden.

The Judgment of Paris in the second redaction of the *Histoire ancienne* bears the impress of its literary environment. If we compare it with the version of the Judgment in the first redaction of the *Histoire ancienne*, produced over a century earlier, the influence of the literary milieu is particularly striking. The earlier version followed Dares closely, adding only a few details to make the story more complete. The later version, influenced by the dream-vision tradition, interprets Paris's encounter with the goddesses as a dream vision and links the goddesses' fête with the dream-vision tradition as well. It hints, moreover, at an allegorical reading for the goddesses' quarrel over the apple.

The two histories which we have just considered purported to be histories of the world. The matter of Troy found its way into histories of more restricted scope as well. Robert Mannyng of Brunne devotes a substantial portion of *The Story of England*, written in 1338, to the Trojan War.[135] Since Britain traced its founding to the Trojan Brutus, as Wace's *Roman de Brut*—one of Mannyng's sources[136]—and numerous other histories had made clear,[137] the Trojans loomed large in English history. Among historians of England, though, Mannyng is alone in treating the ultimate origin of the Trojan War, the Judgment of Paris.

Beginning his history in biblical times, Mannyng explains that, with the sons of Noah, the world was divided into three parts, and he traces the founders of various lands back to this original division.[138] He then proceeds with the tale of Troy, briefly narrating the city's first destruction "þat cam þorow Iasan, Pelles sone" (444) and Priam's rebuilding. From here, he goes immediately to the story of Paris.

In Troy lived Priam's son, Duke Paris, who pastured beasts in the field, this being in ancient times a privilege accorded only to knights. One day there came a Greek bull who fought a bull of Paris's, returning day after day for renewed battle. Paris determined to crown the winner, and did so even though it was the Greek bull which conquered. Three witches, who "ladies were cald, & in þe eyr dide fare" (504), happened to observe the bullfight and were impressed with Paris's justice. The witches were Juno, giver of might, Pallas, giver of wisdom and right, and Venus, giver of love. They began to argue about their beauty and decided to make Paris their judge, determining to make a ball for him to award the one he chose.

Before the day of judgment, Juno came to Paris secretly, explained their plan, and promised that if he gave her the ball, he should have no equal in Troy. Pallas came secretly also and promised to make Paris wisest of all if he gave her the prize. Venus came last, offering the fairest lady alive in exchange for the ball. Paris reflected that, being a king's son and the wisest in Troy, he had no need of Juno's or Pallas's gifts. He was eager to love, however, and so promised the ball to Venus. The witches arrived for judgment on the appointed day; Venus won the prize, angering the other two.

As has been the case more often than not in medieval rehandlings of the Trojan saga, Mannyng combines the more classical tradition of the *Excidium Troiae* and the *Compendium Historiae Troianae-Romanae* with elements ultimately from Dares. He claims Dares as a source, but all he really owes him is a very general eleven-line summary of the first destruction of Troy (443–54).[139] He may not even have consulted the *De Excidio Troiae Historia* directly. His attributing Troy's destruction to Jason rather than Hercules suggests that he did not know Dares well and that this section of the history is based on general recollection and a knowledge that Jason led the Argonauts. Mannyng in fact uses so little of Dares's material that he has no problem harmonizing it with his more classical elements. Indeed, we might ask why he bothered with the first destruction of Troy at all. Usually it leads into the second destruction because the motive of regaining Hesione provides the reason for Paris's journey into Greece. Mannyng, however, omits the capture of Hesione from his version of the first destruction. His tale of Paris unrolls neatly from beginning to end. He does not bother to find a way to make Paris tell the story of his adventure as a dream he had while hunting, nor to get Paris back to Troy in time to speak at Priam's council.

There is no question that Mannyng was familiar with some version of the *Excidium Troiae* or the *Compendium Historiae Troianae-Romanae*. He includes the bullfight which gives Paris his reputation for justice, and as Atwood points out, he follows the tradition preserved in the *Compendium* in that the rival bull returns more than once.[140] As in both works, each goddess comes to Paris separately before the day fixed for judgment and offers him a reward in exchange for the prize.

Mannyng omits material from the classical version of the story too. He leaves out the dream of Hecuba and the exposure of Paris. He accounts for Paris's presence with his herds in the field by explaining that it was in those days the custom for knights to keep beasts, picking up by chance or through familiarity with a now-lost source an ancient motif which may predate the fusion of the exposure materials with the Judgment. Mannyng also omits— whether by choice or owing to the form of his source it is difficult to say—all explanation of how the quarrel over beauty is supposed to have arisen. Omitting any version of the Wedding of Peleus and Thetis does, however, have the good effect of keeping the episode self-contained. The link between Paris's crowning the rival bull and being chosen judge is neat, though, and since they are merely witches, the ladies' presence in the woods is amply accounted for. There is no need for the Wedding of Peleus and Thetis to explain their strife.

Mannyng changes details from the tradition of the *Excidium Troiae* and the *Compendium Historiae Troianae-Romanae* as well. The apple which was the prize of beauty has become, as in most manuscripts of the *Seege of Troye*, which predates Mannyng by at least a decade, a ball. There the ladies found it while they were playing in the woods; here it is created ad hoc for the prize.[141] Mannyng departs from tradition with the promises that the goddesses make to Paris.[142] Indeed, it could be said that he errs. Close to the *Excidium Troiae* is Venus's promise of the fairest lady alive, but Mannyng calls Juno the giver of might and makes her offer power, while Pallas will make Paris the wisest. Traditionally, Pallas's gifts are strength or power and/or wisdom, whereas Juno is associated with riches and rule. Mannyng has taken Pallas's two traditional gifts and assigned one to each of the two goddesses. A similar switch occurs in the first redaction of the *Histoire ancienne*, where Juno and Minerva are said to offer *sens* and *prouesce*.

If the second redaction of the *Histoire ancienne* looked to the literature of the court to rationalize the Judgment of Paris, creating the atmosphere of a dream vision to call into question the distinction between the real and the visionary, Mannyng instead bases his rationalization on a body of lore stemming ultimately from folk belief. His most important deviation from his sources is his decision to make the goddesses witches. The ladies are no longer goddesses; thus there is no need to worry about how or why Olympians would interact with mortals and no need to demand of a Christian audience belief in pagan deities. Guido had already implied that Paris's dream was due to demonic intervention. Mannyng, following a tradition which makes Paris's judgment of the goddesses a real event, must go a step further. Possibly influenced by the *Seege*, which made the rival ladies come from Elfenland, Mannyng has made them witches. He has, moreover, given them the traditional mark of the witch—power to fly.[143]

Witchcraft seemed an even more serious threat in the fourteenth century than it had in Guido's time.[144] According to George Lyman Kittredge, fourteenth-century England is "rich in evidence" for belief in witchcraft; in 1330, eight years before Mannyng wrote his history, Roger Mortimer had used a charge of witchcraft to condemn Edmond, Earl of Kent.[145] In Mannyng's translation of the French *Manuel des pechiez*, he reproduces from his source a condemnation of witchcraft ("If ever you have practiced nygromauncye . . . and have offered sacrifice to the devil through witchcraft . . . you have sinned. . . . Put not your trust in witchcraft"), then he substitutes an example of his own for the example provided by the

Manuel.[146] Clearly, he believed that witches existed and that their powers were real, and he saw witchcraft as a fitting analogue to the supernaturalism of the classical story. The traditional powers of witches would make believable the supernatural aid which these creatures offered Paris, yet Mannyng would still be able to rationalize the episode. Despite his kinship with Guido in attributing the Judgment to the powers of witches, however, Mannyng does not give his Judgment the sinister atmosphere of Guido's. On the Continent, a scholarly systematization of widely scattered lore, popular and learned, provided the rationale for persecuting witches, whereas the English, Kittredge says, did not accept this complicated system and thus did not see witchcraft as part of a theory or heresy.[147] The Inquisition, too, contributed to fear and hatred of witches on the Continent;[148] England, having no Inquisition, never experienced the hysteria which fear of witchcraft created elsewhere.

The line between history and literature was blurred in the Middle Ages, and the historians we have just considered sought to offer an authoritative version of their material and to develop its literary possibilities as well. Other historians took a more scholarly approach. In an effort to be complete, some recorded with no attempt at reconciliation the mutually contradictory versions of Dares and the classical authors.

Vincent of Beauvais included the Judgment of Paris in his universal history, the *Speculum Historiale*, part of his great *Speculum Mundi*, which reduced to system all the learning available to a man of the thirteenth century.[149] The *Speculum Historiale* starts with Genesis and synchronizes sacred and secular history. Such a scheme was not unusual. Eusebius had used it in his *Chronicon*, and, by way of Jerome's adaptation of that work, his plan had passed to the historians of the Middle Ages.[150]

Vincent is thorough; his sources, credited and uncredited, are many. He is also selective, though perhaps not critically so. The Trojan War is discussed in chapter 60 of book 3, which begins with the birth of Moses. Chapter 59 concerns Jephte, the judge of Israel, and Hercules; Paris raped Helen the same year Jephte and Hercules died. There follows a discussion, opposing the testimony of Augustine to that of Orosius, concerning how long before the founding of Rome the rape occurred. Dares is cited, but only for an opinion as to how many Greek leaders sailed against Troy, and with how many ships. Vincent rationalizes the Judgment, but he prefers the rationalization of Eusebius to that of Dares—and borrows Eusebius's words as well: "The cause of the war was, however, as Eusebius writes—that argument of three women for the prize of beauty, one of them promising Helen to the shepherd judge."[151]

Yet Vincent knows that there is more to the story than that. "Concerning which thing a fable has been made thus," he continues: When Jupiter was in love with Thetis, he was forbidden by Proteus to marry her lest he engender a son who would overthrow his father. He therefore gave her in marriage to Peleus, king of the Peloponnese, Aeson's brother and Jason's uncle. This confusion between Peleus and Pelias is an error that Dares had passed on, but the rest of the story is classical: Jupiter celebrated the nuptials with all the gods and goddesses except Discord, who was forbidden to attend. Angered, she threw in the midst of the three goddesses—Vincent does not give their names—a golden apple inscribed, "To be given to the most beautiful." Arguing about their beauty, the three chose Jove judge, but he sent them to Paris, who preferred Venus to the others. From Peleus and Thetis, Achilles was born.

Vincent has thus harmonized his sources by claiming to present both the truth of the story and the fable that sprang up concerning it. The truth is that three women approached Paris to settle their argument concerning a prize for beauty; the fable is that they were goddesses whose argument stemmed from a golden apple thrown in their midst at a divine wedding celebration.

A second universal history that takes a scholarly rather than literary approach to its materials is the *Polychronicon* of Ralph Higden, a Benedictine monk of St. Werburg's Abbey, Chester.[152] Compiled in the mid-fourteenth century,[153] and later translated into English by John Trevisa,[154] the *Polychronicon* narrates the history of the world from the creation to Higden's own time. Higden places Antenor's unsuccessful embassy to the Greeks in the second year of Abesan's judgeship, thus generally agreeing with the chronological system used by Vincent of Beauvais, who made Paris steal Helen the same year that Abesan's predecessor, Jephte, died. For the Judgment, Higden follows the version of Dares, and is nearly as brief,[155] departing from Dares only in the matter of the promises. As

Higden's text now stands, only a promise made by Minerva, *sapientiam*, is mentioned, but English translations of Higden show that the Latin text must once have been fuller.[156] The fact that Higden probably included a promise for each goddess emphasizes again an important point about Dares's reception in medieval histories: even in histories which follow the *De Excidio Troiae Historia* extremely closely, the desire for completeness is so strong that it drives rehandlers to another source for a fuller version of the promises.

A third scholarly universal history to include the Judgment is the fifteenth-century *Supplementum Chronicarum* of Jacopo da Bergamo.[157] Jacopo's general scheme is the historical synchronization of Eusebius, whom he often cites, but this scheme is fleshed out with much additional material, some of it classical. Typical of his all-inclusive method is the fact that he provides three mutually contradictory versions of the Judgment.

From Jacopo's crowded pages, we can pick out the main thread of the Trojan saga from among genealogies of the pagan gods, lists of famous men, biographies of relevant heroes, and the like. Jacopo traces the war to the expedition of the Argonauts, briefly narrating the story of Jason's adventure. He describes Priam's rebuilding of Troy and his marriage with Hecuba, then glances back at Hesione's capture by Telamon—inserting for good measure the classical account of her rescue from the sea monster. The first Judgment of Paris occurs in a section on the figures involved in the Trojan War. Sent to Greece by Priam, Paris steals the wife of Menelaus, but, Jacopo adds, Paris also had the reputation of being a just judge. Explaining that this is a story the poets tell—"vt poete tradunt"— Jacopo adds that as the fame of his justice spread, Paris was asked to judge the beauty of the goddesses, then briefly narrates the episode:

> he rose to greatest fame for justice, and so great (as the poets tell it) that when Pallas, Juno, and Venus were quarreling over beauty on account of the golden apple—thrown to them by Discord at the feast— on which had been written "let it be given to the most worthy," when they had fallen into the greatest quarrel, they were sent [to him] by Jove for a decision. Truly when on account of lust he had judged that it should be given to Venus, who had promised him the most beautiful woman in the world, he was judged as unjust by many.[158]

Having glanced ahead at the Trojan War several times in his description of the events leading to it, Jacopo at last specifies the date of 1185 B.C., the first year of the judgeship of Abesan, for its inception. Then he cites Eusebius for its cause—the argument of three women concerning a prize of beauty (f. 62r)—and goes on to recount how Priam sent Antenor to the Greeks, saying that he would forgive all injuries if they would return Hesione. When the Greeks refused, Priam anticipated war and put Hector in command. Paris urged war also, saying that once when he was hunting on the isle of Ida, he saw in a dream Mercury, who led him to Juno, Minerva, and Venus that he might judge the most beautiful. Minerva (as Jacopo has it) promised that if he preferred her, she would give him a wife from Greece, more beautiful than anyone. Eventually he stole Helen from the island of Cytherea (f. 62r).

It is obvious that Jacopo has consulted many sources preserving many different traditions. He is consistent in his desire to downplay the supernatural in his history, but he does not reconcile his various versions of the Judgment. His first version of the story is the classical one in which the judgment of the goddesses is not a dream. In order to justify including this version of the episode in his history, however, he identifies it, as Vincent of Beauvais had done in a similar circumstance, as a story which the poets tell. He probably took it from a source in the tradition of the *Excidium Troiae* and the *Compendium Historiae Troianae-Romanae*. The Judgment is introduced through its link with Paris's reputation for justice; it includes the inscribed apple thrown by Discord and Jove's sending the goddesses to Paris for judgment. We know that the classical version of the Judgment makes Paris a shepherd rather than a hunter. Jacopo omits the material on his background—how he gained his reputation for justice—perhaps to avoid overt conflict with Dares's version of the Judgment, which he knew his readers would encounter soon enough in his pages.

Jacopo's other two Judgments, two different rationalizations of the story, are more to be expected in a history such as his. Characteristic of such a history too is the fact that he synchronizes the start of the war with the events of the Old Testament, situating Antenor's embassy, as had the *Polychronicon*, in the judgeship of Abesan, whom Jacopo calls Esebon. To explain the cause of the war, he now cites Eusebius, possibly by way of Vincent of Beauvais: The ultimate cause of the war was an argument among three women over a prize to be awarded for beauty. This explanation follows the euhemerizing approach of Antikleides, reducing myths to the doings of ordinary mortals. Jacopo ignores the fact that by thus tracing the war to an apparently real argument among three mortal women, he sets himself up for a certain amount of confusion when, in his third version of the Judgment, the familiar version of Dares, the women seem to become goddesses whose only reality is in Paris's mind. Like Dares, Jacopo links the Trojan War to the Argonautic expedition; like him, he describes Priam's rebuilding of Troy and the unsuccessful embassy of Antenor; like him, he makes Paris's judgment of the goddesses a dream that the Trojan prince has while hunting. Jacopo's blunder in making Minerva rather than Venus promise a beautiful wife from Greece only confirms the relationship with Dares. We have seen before how Dares's inclusion of only Venus's promise drove his followers to supplementary sources and seemed to engender various sorts of confusion in the Judgment scene.

In these histories, we have seen historians make shifts one way or another to rationalize the Judgment. For most, the rationalizing device was that which the *De Excidio Troiae Historia* had made available to the Middle Ages: Paris only dreamed he judged the goddesses, but acting as if his dream were reality, he stole Helen and caused the Trojan War. The motif of the dream was so strongly associated with the Judgment that a few authors included a sleeping Paris who was then awakened to judge the goddesses. Dares's version of the Judgment was excessively brief, however, so most historians who made the episode a dream supplemented the *De Excidio Troiae Historia* with materials drawn from classical sources. Thus the Judgment is likely to include promises for Juno and Pallas, details concerning Paris's background, and references to the reputation for justice which made him the goddesses' choice for their judge.

A second rationalizing device, and one which was probably inspired by Guido's treatment of Dares, was to transform the ladies who sought Paris's judgment into witches. In a sense, this version of the story has its roots in another classical rationalizing theme: Paris did not judge goddesses but ordinary women. To the Middle

Ages, a witch was an ordinary woman whose special powers were to be explained by her alliance with Satan. Thus, whereas Guido makes Paris dream of the goddesses but implies that his dream was inspired by demons, the author of the English *Seege of Troye* makes Paris judge ladies from Elfenland, and Robert Mannyng uses the rationalizing device of turning the goddesses into witches.

The next medieval tradition we shall consider had no need to rationalize the story of the Judgment. In the allegorical tradition, a fable's utility lay in the truth to be discovered beneath its surface. The fables of the ancients, unlike the stories of the Bible, were never supposed to be literally true. Thus we shall see that those who allegorize the Judgment usually prefer the story's classical version.

3

The Judgment as Allegory

St. Jerome recounts a dream in which he is told by the heavenly judge, "You are a Ciceronian, not a Christian." His dream expresses the strife between the seductions with which the paganism of the late-classical period wooed the mind and those with which Christianity wooed the soul.[1] Because antique culture was founded on a system of belief in the pagan gods, the very civilization in which the early Christians lived was suspect. Yet classical culture could be harmonized with Christian by invoking an approach to myth which was itself rooted in the ancient world: the allegorical tradition.[2] Developed to explain the apparent immoralities of Homer's gods, the allegorical interpretation of classical myth is almost as old as Greek literature itself.[3] Particularly popular with the Stoics in the centuries immediately before Christ,[4] allegorical interpretation remained important in the Christian era. For pagans, it provided a way to justify to Christian detractors the tales of the gods without which classical literature and culture could scarcely exist.[5] For the Christians of the ancient world, it was even more important.[6]

If the tales of the gods were merely allegories—fabulous stories whose delightful surfaces cloaked ethical, moral, or cosmological truths—then their study was justified and even praiseworthy. Allegorical interpretation of the Bible had already created a climate congenial to the allegorical interpretation of literature.[7] To justify using classical culture in the service of the new religion, Augustine cites the Israelites' appropriation of Egyptian treasure as they fled from captivity:[8]

In the same way all the teachings of the pagans contain not only simulated and superstitious imaginings . . . which each one of us leaving the society of pagans under the leadership of Christ ought to abominate and avoid, but also liberal disciplines more suited to the uses of truth, and some most useful precepts concerning morals.[9]

Jerome makes a similar point, citing Deuteronomy 21.10–13, in which the beautiful Gentile captive is permitted to become the bride of an Israelite. "What wonder is it," he asks, "if I also wish to make a servant and captive for the Israelites of secular wisdom on account of the attractiveness of its eloquence and the beauty of its members?"[10]

The precedent of Egyptian gold and the beautiful Gentile captive, then, sanctioned the integration of pagan thought into the new religion. An effective way to assimilate to the Christian scheme the suspect fables of the ancients was to interpret them allegorically, thus applying them to the service of higher truths. The most influential late-classical practitioner of this allegorical interpretation was undoubtedly Fulgentius, who in his three books of *Mythologies* presented a collection of fables provided with moral, ethical, and cosmological interpretations taken largely from Stoic tradition. For the Middle Ages, Fulgentius was the mythographer *par excellence,* and the *Mythologies* was Christian Europe's most important source of allegorized myth for at least a thousand years.

Interpreting the Judgment of Paris, Fulgentius brought to bear on the fable the old tradition of the three lives, contemplative, active, and pleasure-seeking, which can be traced back through Aristotle to Plato's division of the soul into three parts: "that with which a man learns," "that with which he feels anger," and "the appetitive part." Fulgentius, however, reinterpreted the three lives from a Christian perspective. He linked the contemplative life with the spiritual life of a monk, bishop, or priest, while the life represented by Venus showed a Christian preoccupation with lust as the most appealing and thus most dangerous of all physical pleasures. Particularly striking, though, was his view of the active life. For Aristotle, the active or political life was the life of a man who defended his city and participated in its government. If it did not conduce to the highest wisdom, it was certainly necessary for the good of society. Fulgentius radically reevaluated the active life. No longer did it represent the necessary and even praiseworthy involvement in the life of the *polis*. Now the active life was characterized exclusively as a materialistic quest for money, power, and possessions. In fact, it became almost the life sought in Plato's scheme by the appetitive part of the soul. Not only was the life redefined, but, because Christianity emphasized poverty and humility, Fulgentius considered his newly defined active life almost as bad as the life represented by Venus. For the Greeks, only the life of pleasure was reprehensible; for Fulgentius, only the contemplative life was praiseworthy.

So influential was Fulgentius that there is scarcely a medieval interpretation of the Judgment which does not betray an acquaintance with the *Mythologies*. Sometimes a writer does little more than repeat the late-classical mythographer's scheme. In other cases an interpretation is strikingly original, with Fulgentian influence evident only in small details. The debt to Fulgentius is most noticeable in the *structure* of the medieval interpretations, since each goddess is usually assigned a mode of life or faculty of the soul. Fulgentian influence is also seen, however, in the moral evaluation of the goddesses and the lives they represent. Thus most medieval interpreters follow Fulgentius in making the active life reprehensible. For almost a thousand years, in fact, the Fulgentian condemnation of the active life, represented by Juno, is a theme in nearly every interpretation.

While the persistent Fulgentian tradition links interpretations separated by centuries, however, the interpretations also bear the impress of their own ages. Successive interpreters wrest from the ancient fable meanings congenial to their centuries, milieux, and purposes. For writers associated with the "school of Chartres," interpretations focus on the aims of the philosopher. Preachers' manuals stress everyday morals and the Christian drama of fall and redemption. For a noble audience, the myth reflects the chivalric code. Eventually, changes in the intellectual atmosphere even affect the evaluation of Juno and the life she represents. In the later Middle Ages, Aristotelian influence reasserts the classical view of the three lives, and the active or political life is once again identified as the life suitable to men. This new-old view of the three lives influences interpretations of the Judgment, and the life represented by Juno becomes again almost equal to the life of the mind. Yet even then Fulgentius is not shaken off. His evaluation of Juno and the life she represents is repudiated, but not the basic scheme which glosses the Judgment with the three lives.

We can pass quickly over the Judgment as it appears in the mythological handbooks of the Middle Ages. The authors of these works are direct heirs to the late-classical mythographers, and their purpose is to compile and conserve. Thus they deviate little from the authorities on which they depend, and they give their materials no new or distinctive applications. In the Carolingian period, an interpretation of the Judgment taken directly from Fulgentius appears in the work of the Second Vatican Mythographer, probably Remigius of Auxerre.[11] Over two centuries later, the much more learned and sophisticated Third Vatican Mythographer, probably Alberic of London, is almost equally dependent on Fulgentius for his interpretation of the Judgment.[12] Well into the thirteenth century, Vincent of Beauvais abbreviates Fulgentius's allegorization in the *Speculum Doctrinale*.[13] In the fourteenth century, a preachers' manual produced in England repeats Alberic of London's interpretation of Wedding and Judgment almost word for word,[14] whereas near the close of the Middle Ages Thomas of Walsingham passes on the same interpretation in his *De Archana Deorum*, probably written in the first decade of the fifteenth century.[15]

The authors of these handbooks are collectors whose aim is accuracy and completeness. They pass on almost verbatim Fulgentius's interpretation of the Judgment, and they subordinate the material to no distinctive purpose or design—other than the obvious one of arranging in some logical order a great many myths and their traditional interpretations. The treatment of the allegorized Judgment in these handbooks is not, however, typical of its use by medieval writers. More often, though the dependence on Fulgentius's scheme is obvious, the interpretation is varied in ways subtle and not so subtle, as a writer contemplates the myth and sees reflected there his own ideas. Nowhere is this truer than in the writings commonly associated with the "school of Chartres."[16]

William of Conches includes the Judgment and its interpretation in his commentary on the *Consolation of Philosophy*, written sometime between 1135 and 1144.[17] He uses the story to elucidate what he sees as one of the most important themes of Boethius's work—in Winthrop Wetherbee's words, "the tension between human frailty and the discipline necessary to philosophical contemplation."[18] William introduces the Judgment and its interpretation in his discussion of book 3, meter 12, of the *Consolation*, where Lady Philosophy tells the story of Orpheus's descent to hell in quest of his wife Euridice. In hell, Orpheus's music momentarily releases the damned from their torments—among them Ixion, doomed to revolve forever on a wheel. The Judgment, with its Fulgentian interpretation, explains Ixion's punishment.

William first provides a simple explanatory gloss for Boethius's reference to Ixion: Ixion wanted to take Juno by force, but she hid herself in a cloud, and his seed fell to earth, whence giants sprang up. Cast into hell, Ixion is now punished on the wheel for his sins. William then extracts the truth—or "veritas"—from the fable, and in order to do so, he uses Juno's traditional identification with the active life. It is Fulgentius's condemnation of that life which provides the rationale for William's explanation. An attempt to take Juno by force, like Ixion's, is an attempt to win happiness by pursuing the active life. The cloud which Juno interposed between Ixion and herself shows that the active life darkens man's reason. That Ixion's seed fell to earth, giving rise to giants, or centaurs, shows that the active life makes man put all his thought on earthly things, giants standing for "ge" or earth and centaurs for "cure terrenorum." These earthly cares are part rational and part irrational, like centaurs, which are (William writes) part man, part ox. Ixion revolves on a wheel in hell because the person who pursues the active life is now raised by prosperity, now cast down by adversity. The wheel revolves swiftly because riches are changeable, but it is stilled by Orpheus's music, because the wise and eloquent man teaches how a life full of change can be avoided, or how no one ought to submit to such a life.[19]

The Fulgentian interpretation of the Judgment, which William has adopted, complements his interpretation of Ixion's story.[20] Subtle changes and additions show, however, that he is adapting the material to his own purposes. He has added to the description of Juno the fact that she is the stepmother of Hercules. This relationship signifies, he explains, that the active life is the enemy of wisdom, Hercules being a traditional prototype of the wise man. Thus William's added detail echoes the theme of Ixion's story. He has also added to the Judgment itself the golden apple, which for Fulgentius figured only in the Wedding of Peleus and Thetis, and he has changed its significance. Fulgentius made the apple represent cupidity, but for William it represents happiness. He explains that the three goddesses compete for the apple because each mode of life seems to make man happy. Seeking happiness, Paris wrongly chose Venus, or the life of pleasure, while Ixion, equally misguided, pursued a life of activity when he wanted to couple with Juno.

Contrasting with Ixion and Paris, however, is the figure of Orpheus, central—according to Wetherbee—to William's understanding of the entire work. When Orpheus descends to hell in search of Euridice, he represents the wise man distracted by *temporalia*.[21] As William puts it, "He [Boethius] demonstrates that while the intention is on earthly things, the highest good cannot be known or enjoyed, and this through Orpheus."[22] Orpheus's music slows Ixion's wheel because wisdom shows how a life of change can be avoided.[23]

William of Conches saw in the Judgment and its relationship with the myth of Ixion one of his own chief concerns—the philosopher's need to escape the manifold seductions of the world and, unimpeded, seek the highest truth. The allegories which he drew from these stories reflect the intellectual sophistication of his milieu. Sometime between 1315 and 1382, however, a translator now known as the Anonymous of Meun incorporated material from William's gloss, including the Judgment of Paris, into his French version of the *Consolation*.[24] To compare Ixion and the Judgment of Paris in his work with the corresponding portions of William's commentary is to see these myths and their interpretations change shape and focus radically.

During the course of the Middle Ages, translations of Boethius's work showed an increased interest in story and a decreased interest in the *Consolation*'s subtleties.[25] Something similar has occurred with respect to the commentary material that the Anonymous of

Meun has integrated into Boethius's text. For him, the Judgment's interest lies in its value as a story, not its deeper significance. No interpretations retard the story's development.

The translator creates narrative interest through various techniques. Much of the episode is given over to realistic dialogue, and he attempts to give the characters' actions a psychological motivation. As Paris contemplates the goddesses, attempting to decide which deserves the apple, suddenly and dramatically the situation is complicated: "But Juno approaches Paris: 'Do you want to have sovereignty and wealth?'" (p. 105, lines 81–82). The promises make his task more complex, and the interplay among the goddesses as each offers her bribe makes the divinities seem amusingly human. No sooner has Juno finished her speech than Pallas cuts in scornfully, "That's nothing, Juno" (p. 106, lines 87–88), and when it is her turn to speak, Venus prefaces her response with complacent laughter (p. 106, lines 121–24). We can imagine her easy confidence that what she has to offer will sway Paris, and we can even divine the skill with which she has determined the likely interests of the young man who is to judge. That she has been correct in her assessment is clear at the end of her speech when Paris, conquered, throws himself at her feet as a vassal of love and presents her with the apple (p. 107, lines 154–62).

The Judgment has thus been developed into a successful and amusing narrative vignette. In contrast, the allegorical elements of William's gloss have been simplified considerably. The moral drawn from the Judgment is the obvious conclusion that the darts of Venus are often preferred to God's goods or the world's (p. 108, lines 167–70). All other moral interpretation is concentrated in the brief passage dealing with Ixion and Juno, before the narrative of the Judgment really begins.

Like William, the Anonymous of Meun identifies the three goddesses with the three lives and, because of her relevance to Ixion's story, focuses particularly on Juno and her attributes. As in William, for example, Juno is the stepmother of Hercules because the active life is inimical to the wise (p. 104, lines 19–22). In the interpretation of Ixion's attempt to lie with Juno, the debt to William is clear, but the allegorizations are less sophisticated. The Anonymous of Meun omits, for example, the explanation that the cloud which Venus interposed between herself and Ixion signifies that the active life darkens man's reason; rather, he makes the cloud signify how intangible are the joys of such a life: "But [Juno] is nothing but cloud" (p. 104, line 33). Correctly identifying centaurs as half man, half horse—unlike William's half man, half ox—the Anonymous of Meun omits William's allegorical interpretation of these beasts—that earthly cares are half rational, half irrational. Instead, he substitutes a simpler explanation—a medieval commonplace ultimately from Boethius: men who find their joy in the world are like beasts; thus the centaurs that spring from Ixion's seed are born without reason (p. 104, lines 37–42).

The Judgment of Paris in the Anonymous of Meun's "roman de philosophie," to use Richard Dwyer's term,[26] is William of Conches adapted to the tastes of an audience reading Boethius in the vernacular. Returning to William's own milieu, we find in the commentary on the *Aeneid* attributed to Bernard Silvestris an allegorized Judgment which is much more akin intellectually to William's and which functions similarly in its context.[27] The interpretation of the Judgment itself echoes the commentary's major thrust so that the Judgment reveals on a small scale what the *Aeneid* reveals on a large scale. Further, the theme which runs through the entire commentary is closely related to a key theme which William saw in the *Consolation:* the necessity of moving beyond *temporalia* if one is to attain true wisdom.

For Bernard, the *Aeneid* is about "what the human soul, placed for a time in a human body, achieves and undergoes."[28] Bernard thus takes the first five books of the *Aeneid* to represent the five stages of human development, from childhood to maturity, as the spirit struggles against the limitations of the flesh.[29] The crucial descent to the underworld, which occupies the sixth book, is, as Winthrop Wetherbee puts it, "the key to liberation from the dominion of sense, for it represents the penetration of *mundana* by reason, and leads to knowledge of God."[30] Just before he descends into the underworld, Aeneas meets the Sibyl, an episode which signifies for Bernard Aeneas's introduction to philosophy. It is during his explanation of this passage that Bernard relates and interprets the Judgment of Paris. The placement of the material at this point in the commentary is crucial. Aeneas is about to embark on the descent which will finally free him from his bondage to sense, while Paris, in his choice of Venus, represents the state which Aeneas is rapidly transcending.

As Aeneas prays at the cave of the Sibyl for success in his venture, he begs the Olympians to look kindly on the fleeing Trojans: "Ye, too, may now fitly spare the race of Pergamus, ye gods and goddesses all, to whom Troy and Dardania's great glory were an offence."[31] Obviously thinking of the tradition which made Paris's choice of Venus responsible for Juno's and Pallas's enmity to Troy, Bernard glosses the lemma *dii et dee* with the Judgment and its interpretation:

> we read that three goddesses, Juno, and Pallas, and Venus, approached Paris that he might be the judge which of them should have the golden apple. By Pallas, we understand the "theoric" life, by Juno the active, by Venus pleasure, by the golden apple truly the highest good, and this on account of matter or on account of form: on account of matter because just as gold exceeds other metals, thus this good [exceeds] others: on account of form, truly, because just as that form [i.e., round] lacks beginning and end, thus and [so does] that good. And rightly is it said [to be] an apple because fruit is expected for honest labor. Truly it is uncertain which of those goddesses should have the apple. For some, like philosophers, prefer the contemplative life to the others; some, like politicians, prefer the active; some, like the Epicureans, [prefer] the "philargic" life to the active and contemplative. Venus seemed more beautiful to Paris because sense disregards contemplation and action in the face of pleasure, and for this reason Pallas and Juno took revenge on Troy. Because it is more beautiful to the sense to wallow in pleasures, it is troublesome to the flesh to contemplate or act.[32]

A later gloss (on *Aeneid* 6.494–95) stresses Paris's association with sense: "For *paris* in Greek is 'sensus' in Latin."[33]

Underlying Bernard's interpretation is the familiar Fulgentian scheme of the three lives. Bernard has also obviously been influenced by the Judgment of William of Conches.[34] Like William, he has included the golden apple, which Fulgentius had not, and his interpretation of the apple could easily be an elaboration of William's. For William, the apple represented happiness, and the three goddesses competed for it because the life each represented seemed to make one happy. For Bernard, the apple represents the highest good because to its adherents each of the three lives offers the highest good. Bernard provides some justification for identifying the golden apple with the highest good. From medieval schemata of hierarchies comes gold as the metal which exceeds all others, and from the Platonism of Bernard's intellectual milieu comes the sphere as a perfect form without beginning or end (e.g., *Timaeus* 33b). That the prize is an apple—or fruit—is appropriate, he explains, because fruit is a fitting reward and the adherents of each life seek the highest good as the reward of their labors.

Most important, however, is Bernard's association of Paris with sense. This detail reveals his Platonism most strikingly, and it makes his interpretation of the Judgment reinforce his interpretation of Aeneas's journey. For Fulgentius, Paris represented man endowed with free will. For William, similarly, Paris was "any man at all." For Bernard, however, Paris is only one faculty of man: sense. Significantly, Bernard has omitted from his version of the Judgment Jove's refusal to judge the goddesses. This refusal, Fulgentius had explained, gave the choice to man and signified God's gift of free will. In Bernard's version, the Judgment is no longer a drama because there is no choice. Paris is that *sense* which always chooses pleasure. Thus, the allegory of the Judgment acquires Platonic overtones. As long as man is encumbered with a body, he will always be drawn by his senses to a life of pleasure. He must strive constantly, then, to transcend the demands of the flesh. Paris, as sense, can never succeed. On the other hand, Aeneas's journey and final descent to the underworld liberate him from his bondage to earthly concerns. His journey represents for Bernard that transcendence.

William of Conches and Bernard Silvestris wrote for learned and sophisticated audiences. They venerated classical thought, and their intellectual program fostered the discovery in classical literature of truths consonant with the Christian scheme. Thus they readily exploited the notion that beneath a delightful integument the fables of the ancients contained much of profit for the mind and soul. Their interpretations reflected the interests of their milieu, focusing on the concerns of the philosopher and revealing the influence of Platonic thought. Almost two centuries later, however, the pagan myths yielded up moral profit for a very different audience.

The monumental preachers' manuals of the fourteenth century made allegorized myth a staple of the preacher's repertoire.[35] The premise is the same as it was for William and Bernard. Beneath their surface delights, the stories hide truths which justify their study. These later interpretations, however, reflect the tastes of their audiences. Most importantly, for the first time the interpretations not only harmonize with Christian beliefs but deal with explicitly Christian themes,[36] particularly, in the case of the Judgment, the drama of man's creation, fall, and redemption. Two significant fourteenth-century collections of allegorized myth were based on Ovid's *Metamorphoses*; they are the *Ovide moralisé* and the *Ovidius Moralizatus*.[37]

For the anonymous Franciscan who, between 1316 and 1328, wrote the *Ovide moralisé*, "Everything is [written] for our instruction" (1.2).[38] He makes his interpretive purpose clear in his introduction: "these fables . . . seem completely false, but there is nothing there which is not true: to one who could know the sense of it, the truth, which lies covered beneath the fables, would be obvious" (1.41–45). The author of the *Ovide moralisé* is typical of the mendicant orders in his desire to marshal all available lore and learning for the service of God by making it available for use in preaching. His interest in the classics, however, makes him atypical among his French contemporaries.[39]

Though one medieval tradition made of Ovid a Christian, Paule Demats has argued persuasively that the author of the *Ovide moralisé* did not believe that he was discovering in Ovid's fables Christian allegories intended by the poet.[40] Rather, she argues, he used the *Metamorphoses* as his starting point because it was such a complete collection of myth. Thus each myth could be given multiple interpretations because there was no one true "meaning" to discover.[41] The allegorizations are probably taken in large part from glossed manuscripts of the *Metamorphoses*, which had incorporated commentaries such as those produced by Arnulf of Orleans and John of Garland.[42] The allegories can be euhemerizing, cosmological, or, in a general way, moral, but the author favors the Christian interpretations.[43]

Though he regarded the *Metamorphoses* as a storehouse of tales ideally suited to his purpose, the author of the *Ovide moralisé* was

not content with Ovid's collection. He added a considerable number of fables from other sources with the aim, Demats suggests, of
making his own original contribution as a compiler in the mythographic tradition.[44] That he did not limit himself to the stories
Ovid had told in the *Metamorphoses* is obvious from the very fact
that we include his work in our discussion here. The *Metamorphoses* does not include the Judgment of Paris; the *Ovide moralisé*
does. The Judgment figures there in what Demats has characterized
as the *Ovide moralisé*'s own *roman de Troie,* which occupies
books 11–13 of the work, pointing out that the *Ovide moralisé*'s
author has added about 3,900 lines to the Trojan material already in
the *Metamorphoses.*[45] The link between his Trojan cycle and the
Metamorphoses itself is the section in book 11 of Ovid's work
which describes the union of Peleus and Thetis. This episode, in
fact, is what allows the author of the *Ovide moralisé* to introduce
the Judgment.

Though he elsewhere uses a considerable amount of material
from Dares and Benoît,[46] his Judgment is the classical one; it begins
with Discord's disruption of Peleus and Thetis's wedding feast. His
interpretations of Wedding and Judgment are obviously indebted to
Fulgentius,[47] but Fulgentius treated the Wedding and Judgment in
separate books of the *Mythologies.* Other authorities, such as Hyginus and the Vatican Mythographers, had passed on the tradition
which the *Ovide moralisé* follows,[48] though some version of the
Excidium Troiae or the *Compendium Historiae Troianae-Romanae* is the likeliest possible influence. Like the *Ovide moralisé,*
the *Excidium Troiae* inserts the dream of Hecuba and the youth of
Paris between Wedding and Judgment, and the *Ovide moralisé*'s
Judgment includes a curious detail which might derive from a version of the *Excidium Troiae.* As the goddesses argue before Mercury prior to his escorting them to Paris, Venus suddenly offers him
her body in exchange for the apple (11.1545–46), as she does with
Paris in the *Excidium Troiae* and the *Compendium Historiae
Troianae-Romanae* but nowhere else.

Whatever his source or sources for the fables of Wedding and
Judgment, however, the author of the *Ovide moralisé* has elaborated his material considerably. He may aim in his compilation for
the completeness of a mythographic manual, but his is not the

brief, dry summary which experience with that type of work would lead us to expect. He devotes over 1,300 lines to the Wedding and the Judgment, and the allegories occupy only a tiny portion of the whole. Joseph Engels has pointed to the influence of rhetorical treatises on the *Ovide moralisé*'s style.[49] Clearly its author is a man aiming to provide his audience not only with *sentence* but also with *solace,* goals particularly characteristic of the mendicant orders.[50]

The description of the wedding feast is detailed and humorous. When we are told that the only deity absent besides Discord is Saturn, who is ill, surely we are to recall his castration at the hands of Jupiter and understand why he would be loath to attend a wedding. There is broad comedy in the description of Priapus's erection on seeing Galatea, so large it raises his cloak, and that of the drunken Silenus vomiting up the wine he has drunk. Also comical are the guests' reactions to these *faux pas*. Some laugh at Priapus; others criticize. Venus covers her eyes with her hands but looks through her fingers. The feast was most enjoyable, the poet concludes, but what pleased the guests most was "the large member which reared itself up" and "the old one who, full of drunkenness, vomited up what he had drunk" (11.1295–97).

Dialogue, too, gives the story narrative interest. The goddesses, for example, argue over the apple in language which is vivid, racy, and colloquial. Juno exclaims, "Do you think, then, that it should be given to you? . . . You have judged quickly!" Venus responds, "I don't give a crumb for your wisdom or riches" (11.1516–21).

The narrative also includes extended passages, doubtless meant both to entertain and to edify, which elaborate conventional *topoi.* Considerable space is, for example, devoted to the materials of courtly love, though no attempt is made to reconcile this delineation of love psychology with the chief point of the Judgment's allegorical interpretation: that Paris was wrong to choose the love of Helen. As the three goddesses argue before Jove, Venus devotes over a hundred lines to a description of her power: she makes sages fools and fools sages; she sickens the healthy and cures the sick; she humbles the powerful and raises the humble; and so on. A second passage devoted to the traditional *topoi* of courtly love is inserted after Paris has decided that Helen is the most desirable prize and awarded the apple to Venus. Here Venus devotes 169 lines to the rule of love (11.2203–2372). Interesting in its own right as the narrative is, however, it is the allegorizations which are the work's *raison d'être*.

Though obviously based on Fulgentius, the interpretations of Wedding and Judgment in the *Ovide moralisé* include much not found in the late-classical mythographer. Most strikingly, the allegories are explicitly Christian. In the marriage of Peleus and Thetis, the *Ovide moralisé* sees God's creation of man and his promise of a redeemer. God, says the poet, had three children: body, soul, and regenerated man. The body was created from earth joined with Thetis, that is, moist humor, because God gave human form to moist earth and mud. He also gave it a soul: thus was man created, and God married him to the woman drawn from his side. Then God gave them organs of reproduction. Of the woman it was prophesied that she would conceive a son who would surpass his father. This is the son of God, who is to surpass the first man (11.1316–50).

This interpretation must have seemed arbitrary to an audience which did not know the corresponding passage in the *Mythologies*. The *Ovide moralisé* omits the etymology and the cosmological material which provided its rationale for Fulgentius, but we know from Fulgentius that Peleus is earth because his name sounds like the Greek word for mud, and that Thetis signifies water because she is a water nymph. We also know from Fulgentius that the soul, which was essential if the two elements were to unite, was present only because Jupiter—fire, or soul—presided over the wedding feast.

The rest of the interpretation moves even farther afield. Fulgentius seemed to be speaking generally of human conception; the *Ovide moralisé* situates its allegory in salvation history. This man composed of earth, water, and soul is clearly Adam, and the woman drawn from his side must be Eve. Though the poet had already "used up" Peleus and Thetis as the components of the first man, Jupiter's role in bringing together Peleus and Thetis reminds him that God united Adam and Eve, and we realize that for authors like this the myths could yield a whole series of interpretations. The poet sees profound Christian significance in the old prophecy that if Jupiter married Thetis, she would bear a son who would expel his father from his realm. It was to counter this prediction that Jupiter arranged for Thetis to marry Peleus. But he applies the prophecy

not to Thetis, who cooperated in the generation of the first man or
Adam, but to Adam's wife. The son who is to be greater than his
father is, of course, Christ. True to the original prophecy, he will be
the son of Jupiter, or God, but the father he is to surpass is his
human forebear, Adam.

With this attempt to see in the Wedding of Peleus and Thetis an
allegory of the creation and God's promise of a redeemer, we have
the first example of an interpretation to which preachers' manuals
would revert again and again. The drama of creation-fall-redemp-
tion was of supreme importance in medieval Christian thought. It
had been crucial to Augustine's philosophy of history, and through
his writings it passed to the Middle Ages and beyond. Refuting the
view that the world had always existed and that human history was
cyclical, Augustine had written in *The City of God,* "Who is able
to discover the undiscoverable and scrutinize the inscrutable sub-
limity, according to which God made man subject to time—man
who previously did not exist? Without change of will He created
him in time."[51] Christ's role in man's salvation, too, was a historical
event: "For once Christ died for our sins."[52] Copleston summarizes
thus the importance of salvation history for St. Augustine: "St. Augustine's thought centred round God and the soul's relation to God,
and . . . the man who is related to God is the concrete and actual
man of history, who has fallen from grace and who has been redeemed by grace" (p. 243).[53] Though particularly associated with
the Augustinian tradition, this view of history in its broadest outlines permeated all of medieval thought, even serving as an organiz-
ing principle for the great systematizations of the scholastics, from
twelfth-century books of *Sentences,* to Aquinas's monumental
Summa.[54]

Thus the author of the *Ovide moralisé* stresses that God person-
ally intervened in history to make man. In explaining why all the
gods were present at the wedding, or the generation of Achilles,
Fulgentius had merely passed on an old interpretation without
vouching for its truth: "the heathen believed that in a human being
separate gods gained possession of separate parts."[55] The author of
the *Ovide moralisé* elaborates the idea considerably, linking specific gods with the four elements as well as parts of the body, but he
introduces the material with a disclaimer: "The poets of former

days, who deceived themselves and the world, did not believe in God the creator, and they believed in creatures, so they made the people believe such fiction that was not true" (11.1389–94). Thereafter he emphasizes that man was created through the will of the one true God: "Those four elements—separate and conflicting—came together in human combination, *when God pleased*" (11.1418–21; my italics). Those who lived before knew little of the Creator who made all things through His goodness (11.1443–47). Thus the author of the *Ovide moralisé* asserts, in opposition to the views of the pagans, a crucial truth of the Christian world view.

If the interpretation of the wedding feast developed themes of creation and the promise of a redeemer, the *Ovide moralisé* sees in Discord's disruption of the celebration the episode which makes the drama complete: man's fall from grace. Discord is Satan, and the apple which she throws into the wedding feast is the apple which destroyed Adam and Eve's contentment in the Garden of Eden:

> When God had first joined man and woman and given them natural power to engender, they were in the earthly paradise . . . but the chief of wrath and of discord, who hates peace and joy and concord, and was greatly vexed and envious of their delightful life, troubled their joy and their happiness and gave them lamentable sorrow on account of the beautiful and pleasant apple of which he made them a deadly present. (11.2403–20)

To connect the apple which disrupted the wedding feast and ultimately caused the Trojan War with the apple which destroyed Adam and Eve's bliss in the Garden of Eden and caused the fall of man seems natural and obvious. At some level of the human psyche, they are the same apple, and the only reason no interpreter made the connection sooner is, no doubt, that the *Ovide moralisé*'s author was the first to interpret the passage in light of salvation history.

When he turns to the Judgment itself, the author of the *Ovide moralisé* offers first an interpretation which is obviously derived from Fulgentius: Juno signifies the active life, Pallas the contemplative, and Venus the voluptuous (11.2425–27). Both the active life and the life of pleasure are condemned; only the contemplative is recommended. As in Fulgentius, the active life is not a life devoted to politics but rather a life devoted to possessions. In the *Ovide moralisé*, the active life is made to sound particularly bourgeois: "He who chooses the active life is caught up in many affairs. He has much to undertake and to complete" (11.2430–32). He who seeks this life is always busy, but no matter how much he works, destroying both his soul and his body in the process, he always has more to do. One is reminded of Chaucer's Merchant, with his *bargaynes* and his *chevyssaunce*, "sownynge alwey th'encrees of his wynnyng."[56] The life of pleasure, too, is that described by Fulgentius: a life completely given over to the passions. This life "is determined and eager to seek all fleshly delight" (11.2428–29). To satisfy the body, it kills the soul (11.2443–44). The contemplative life has been interpreted to reflect even more than it had for Fulgentius the Christian view of man's true purpose. For the late-classical mythographer, it was in earlier times the life of philosophers, and that of bishops, priests, and monks in his own. Its goal was the search for knowledge and truth.[57] Fulgentius was a Christian, but he wrote under the spell of classical philosophy, as can be seen from the nature of his interpretations throughout the *Mythologies*. For the author of the *Ovide moralisé*, a Franciscan friar, the ancient quest for knowledge and truth ended when Christ came into the world. His contemplative life is devoted solely to the knowledge, worship, and service of God (11.2449–52). Those who seek this life, he says, live humbly on earth to win eternity.

As had Fulgentius, the author of the *Ovide moralisé* sees Paris's choice among the goddesses as an allegory for man's exercise of his free will: "God put these three kinds of life directly before man, giving him free opportunity to choose and take the best or the worst—or that which pleased him most" (11.2459–63). The interpretation is, however, considerably elaborated. The golden apple becomes discretion, or reasonable understanding (*discretion:* 11.2482; *raisonable entendement:* 11.2498), which God gave man, not to interfere with his free choice, but to let him know what he ought to choose and what reject (11.2479–84). Then the poet takes Paris's awarding the apple to Venus as a classical analogue to the parable of the talents in Matthew 25. The golden apple is said to be "the treasure which God, in the Holy Scripture, commanded be given over for investment, in order to gain manifold profit, [but] which the foolish servant hid in the ground" (11.2492–96). Filling in this allusive sketch, we can see that reasonable understanding is like the talents with which the three servants in the parable were entrusted by their master. Each was to increase his store, but the third servant buried his talent in the earth rather than investing it. Paris was given reasonable understanding by God but rather than make the most of this gift, he wasted it by setting his mind on Venus. With Paris's opportunity, says the poet, man should have awarded his judgment to the best, but vain delight led him to choose the worst instead (11.2498–2506).

In contrast to the Wedding of Peleus and Thetis, with its clear Old Testament parallel in the Eden story, the Judgment, whose drama is internal, was frequently interpreted tropologically. The *Ovide moralisé* sees the story as an allegory for that most important decision: Where shall a man direct his will? The author sees Paris's action in terms of Augustinian moral psychology—not surprisingly, since material produced for preaching to a popular audience would by its very nature be conservative, and since Franciscan thought was characterized by Augustinianism.[58] For Augustine, "When . . . the will . . . cleaves to the immutable good . . . , man finds therein the blessed life."[59] But, as Copleston notes, "the will is free to turn away from the immutable Good and to attach itself to mutable goods, taking as its object either the goods of the soul, without reference to God, or the goods of the body."[60] God has placed in man, however, reason and understanding, which make him distinctively human.[61] The author of the *Ovide moralisé* seems to have had precisely these ideas in mind when he interpreted the Judgment. Paris ignored reasonable understanding, which could have shown him that he should direct his will toward Pallas, or the contemplation and love of God. Instead, he chose Venus, a mutable good of the body. The author of the *Ovide moralisé* sees in the Judgment not the fall of Adam and Eve but the fall of Everyman, the individual reenactment of our first parents' sin.

As the interpretation of Wedding and Judgment draws to a close, the poet applies his moral directly to his audience. On account of the abundant evils of the age, the end of the world and the last judgment are near (11.2531–33). Fulgentius had lamented that to his contemporaries the life of pleasure seemed the natural life.[62] The author of the *Ovide moralisé*, too, sees himself surrounded by *luxuria* (11.2516–20). After his excursus into the classics, the Franciscan dramatically turns to his audience of preachers to show the practical applications of the material he has just reviewed.

The *Ovide moralisé* passes on Fulgentian interpretations of Wedding and Judgment, and it adds new and specifically Christian ones. Preserved from Fulgentius is the cosmic allegory in which Peleus, Thetis, and Jupiter are the earth, water, and fire which cooperate in forming the first man, with Discord as the disruption of the harmony necessary to creation. Also taken from the influential sixth-century mythographer is the allegory of the three lives among which man chooses with his God-given free will. Explicitly Christian is the connection of Pallas and the contemplative life with the service of God, rather than with the pursuit of wisdom. Christian too is the Augustinian interpretation of Paris's misusing the apple, or reasonable understanding, and the assimilation of the Judgment to the parable of the talents in Matthew 25. Most distinctive is the new association of Wedding and Judgment with the drama of man's creation, fall, and redemption. The first man is Adam; the regenerated man is Christ, destined to surpass his father. Discord is Satan, and the golden apple is the instrument of man's fall.

The strong appeal of this allegorical interpretation, which fuses the centuries-old Fulgentian approach with themes from salvation history, is demonstrated in a prose rehandling of the *Ovide moralisé* produced about a century and a half later. The *Ovide moralisé en prose*, written for René of Anjou by an anonymous Norman clerk and completed in 1467,[63] expands the narrative of the Judgment considerably, though the author shortens most of the mythological episodes in his source. As far as his allegorization is concerned, the tradition he follows is ultimately Fulgentian, but he includes as well the *Ovide moralisé*'s more specifically Christian embellishments. Cosmic allegory is fused with salvation history as the union of Peleus and Thetis is made to represent the creation of the first man, and the offspring of their union is taken to represent Christ. The golden apple which disrupted the wedding feast is seen as the apple which disrupted Adam and Eve's bliss in the garden of Eden. The familiar allegory of the three lives is applied to Juno, Pallas, and Venus, and the traditional definitions for the lives are retained. The life of pleasure is of course a reprehensible pursuit of carnality; the active life is a damnable quest for possessions; and the contemplative life, the only choice that is acceptable, is service of God in quest of salvation (286–87).

With his glimpse of Christian mysteries in the Judgment, the author of the *Ovide moralisé* influenced one of his contemporaries as well. The fourteenth century's second important preachers' manual based on classical materials was the *Ovidius Moralizatus* of the Benedictine Pierre Bersuire.[64] Bersuire wrote a first version of the work at Avignon sometime around 1340; two years later at Paris he added material taken from the *Ovide moralisé* and other sources.[65] The *Ovidius Moralizatus* is the fifteenth book of Bersuire's monumental *Reductorium Morale*, which also includes thirteen books of moralized natural history, a book "de natura mirabilibus," and an allegorical exposition of the scriptures.[66] Like the author of the *Ovide moralisé*, Bersuire wanted a definite narrative structure for his moralized fables, on the analogy of an allegorized Bible. He found that form in Ovid's *Metamorphoses*, whose opening creation scene had already made it the "Bible of the Gentiles."[67] Though the *Ovidius Moralizatus* begins with a chapter on the forms and figures of the gods, probably inspired by the structure of the Third Vatican Mythographer's handbook, it then follows the structure of the *Metamorphoses* closely.[68] Bersuire has added considerable material to Ovid, however, including the Wedding of Peleus and Thetis and the Judgment of Paris.

Unlike the *Ovide moralisé* and many mythographic handbooks, Bersuire does not combine the Wedding of Peleus and Thetis and the Judgment of Paris into a single narrative. For Jove's plan to unite Peleus and Thetis, Bersuire found no obvious link with Ovid's text. It seems an afterthought in the earlier version of the *Ovidius Moralizatus*, placed at the end of the last chapter with another story and introduced thus: "The two following stories or fables are not contained in the text."[69] In the Paris version, it has been moved to the end of chapter 1, "On the Forms and Figures of the Gods."[70] Bersuire had better luck integrating the Judgment into his commentary structure. In both the early version and the later, the episode of the Judgment, including Discord's disruption of the wedding feast, appears in book 12, where it helps gloss the funeral of Aesacus: "Paris was not present at the sad rite."[71]

Like the author of the *Ovide moralisé*, Bersuire mines from ancient literature Egyptian gold for the service of God. In his prologue, he affirms that just as, according to St. Paul, the stories of scripture have allegorical significance, so too do the poets' fables.[72] He is, in fact, much more interested in the interpretations of his stories than in the stories themselves. His brief summaries smack of the handbook, but his interpretations crowd in upon one another, testifying to his invention. Multiple meanings—"literal," "moral," "historical"—are offered for each fable. "Vel dic . . . ," he often advises his audience of preachers, proffering an additional idea for using a story. As the variety of terms that Bersuire uses for his interpretations suggests, he does not regard his stories exclusively as allegories. Sometimes they are taken purely as cautionary tales, whose surface meaning points a moral. Nor is there any attempt to draw from each complete fable a unified interpretation. Bersuire explains his stories episode by episode. A succeeding interpretation can contradict a former, and the moral significance of a given character depends only on the particular context.

For the most part, his interpretations seem shaped by the needs of his audience, the preachers for whom the *Ovidius Moralizatus* was written. Most often the interpretations deal with the small lapses of daily life; that they are designed for use in sermons is suggested too by the biblical citation with which each closes, echoing in divine literature the lesson which literature inspired only by the muses has yielded. For the Wedding and Judgment, he offers a plentiful assortment of interpretations. Most are simple and homely moralizations that pertain to everyday conduct. It was only when Bersuire revised the *Ovidius Moralizatus* under the influence of the *Ovide moralisé* that he began to see in the material of the Wedding and Judgment the drama of salvation history. Thus the Paris version of the work tends to see biblical parallel where the earlier version does not. An example of this difference can be seen in the Wedding of Peleus and Thetis.

In the earlier version of the *Ovidius Moralizatus*, Bersuire offers two interpretations of the Wedding, a "literal" one and a "moral" one. As the story goes, Jupiter wanted to carry off Thetis, goddess of the waters, but it was fated that he would thus generate a son greater than himself who would drive him from his realm. He therefore gave her to Peleus, and of that union Achilles was born. The "literal" interpretation proves to be the familiar cosmic allegory from Fulgentius, but, as was the case in the *Ovide moralisé*, certain Fulgentian details are overlooked so that elements of the interpretation seem puzzling and arbitrary. Jove is fire, Thetis water, and Peleus earth, and although Bersuire seems to regard the reasons for Jove's and Thetis's cosmic alter egos as self-evident, he makes sure to explain that Peleus is earth because "peles" means mud. Were Jove to combine sexually with Thetis, her water would extinguish his fire, but when she combines with earth or clay, and Jove or fire presides, Achilles, or a whole man, is the result. Bersuire, however, omits a key element from Fulgentius: Thetis's water is moist humor, Peleus's earth is flesh, and Jove's fire is soul. As in Fulgentius, Discord is absent from the wedding because the concord of the elements is necessary to the generation of man, but all the other gods are present because all the planets and stars convened for the event. Bersuire, however, omits the Fulgentian detail that makes this last item relevant: in antiquity each god presided over a specific part of the body.

Bersuire's moral interpretation of Peleus and Thetis builds on the Fulgentian cosmic allegory. Jupiter is the just man, and Thetis is the goddess of waters or delights, that is, *voluptas*, with whom the just man ought not to consort. Were he to seek union with her, he would generate a son, that is, a vice of temptation and a bundle of concupiscence, which would distract him from virtue and spiritual matters. As water extinguishes fire, enjoyment of the world overcomes the just and virtuous. Thus Jupiter gives such a wife to Peleus, or mud, representing men who are voluptuous, fleshy, and dirty. As fire and water cannot combine, neither can the just and voluptuous live together. Bersuire offers two biblical citations which parallel the sense of the classical fable: "Thou shalt not take thee a wife, neither shalt thou have sons and daughters in this place" (Jeremias 16.2), and "If Jacob take a wife of the stock of this land, I choose not to live" (Genesis 27.46).[73]

In the Paris version, on the other hand, under the influence of the *Ovide moralisé*, Bersuire sees the Wedding of Peleus and Thetis as an allegory for the central Christian mystery, the coming of Christ into the world. He repeats his cosmic allegory from the earlier version, then adds, "Or if you want, say that Peleus and Thetis are Adam and Eve, who produced from his [Adam's] progeny a son greater than himself—Achilles, that is, Christ, and this Adam [produced] Christ."[74] The interpretation draws on the prophecy regarding the offspring of Jupiter and Thetis; here the prophecy is applied instead to Peleus, or Adam.

Bersuire's procedure with the Judgment of Paris and its related fables is similar. As was the case with the Wedding of Peleus and Thetis, it is only in the Paris version of the *Ovidius Moralizatus* that Bersuire sees an allegory related to salvation history. In the earlier version his interpretations offer lessons for daily life, as he scrutinizes every facet of the story for a possible application.

Bersuire is, for example, the first mythographer to interpret the dream of Hecuba and the youth of Paris. That he includes even the distinctive episode in which Paris crowns the rival bull—Mars in disguise—which has conquered his own suggests some influence from the *Excidium Troiae* and the *Compendium Historiae Troianae-Romanae*.[75] The dream of Hecuba is to be used, he advises his preachers, "historialiter." Hecuba is an example of indiscreet piety. Moved by mercy, she kept Priam from killing Paris, but because Paris was saved, all of Troy was subsequently destroyed. The nature of mercy, Bersuire explains, consists rather in killing evil. Priam is taken as God or law. Both can decide for a legitimate cause to kill or punish, especially if, as in the case of Paris, a death would save the country. Bersuire completes this section with a quotation from the Gospel of John (11.50): "it is expedient for us that one man die for the people, instead of the whole nation perishing." Bersuire also takes Paris's fair judgment of the bulls "historice." Paris has become the good judge who conducts himself fairly and equitably in judgments, and the lesson finds its scriptural analogue in Deuteronomy 25.1: "If there be a controversy between men, and they call upon the judges, they shall give the prize of justice to him whom they perceive to be just.[76]

Bersuire draws from Discord's interruption of the wedding feast warnings against envy and avarice:

> Through these three goddesses peacefully coming together I understand good and just [people] peacefully conversing. Through the goddess of discord I understand the envious who when they are not

invited become angry and like to sow discord among them. Such
ones have continued to throw the apple of discord among others. And
to say words of detraction.[77]

Ecclesiasticus 28.15 provides the biblical parallel: "The whisperer
and the double-tongued is accursed, for he hath troubled many that
were at peace."

> Or say that the apple of discord signifies goods of this world, for in-
> deed those who have these things are scarcely able to be peacemak-
> ing because anyone at all wants to have them. These are the things
> which Discord sows and which prepare controversy for those who
> pursue them, and finally prepare wars and destructions. The goddess
> and mistress of discord is avarice, than which nothing is better able
> to make dissension between men.[78]

The scriptural tag is Genesis 13.6: "for their substance was great,
and they could not dwell together."

Bersuire's first interpretation of the Judgment is the familiar
Fulgentian allegory of the three lives. Each goddess represents a different type of person: wise, rich, or pleasure-loving. Since each type
of person considers his way of life most beautiful and best, each
wants the golden apple, or glory and honor, for himself. When
Paris, or stupid youth, judged among the goddesses, he gave the
apple to Venus, thus choosing the voluptuous life and claiming that
a life of delight was more blessed. Bersuire's scriptural tag, though,
tends to undercut his condemnation of Paris's choice: "Is it not
better to eat and drink, and to show his soul good things of his labors?" (Ecclesiastes 2.24).[79]

The second interpretation of the Judgment makes the three goddesses three powers of the soul. Pallas is *ratio*, which has wisdom;
Juno is *memoria*, which has riches of knowledge; and Venus is *voluntas*, which is mistress of delights. Paris represents sinners and
fools, who obey the will and condemn the other powers of the soul,
refusing to follow memory and reason. Instead, they offer the apple
of the heart to concupiscence. When they obtain Helen, or beautiful women, they excite quarrels and wars. The biblical citation
picks up the motif of inner strife: "turn away from thy own will. If
thou give to thy soul her desires, she will make thee a joy to thy
enemies" (Ecclesiasticus 18.30–31).[80]

With this interpretation, Bersuire enters what is for him a new

territory: the landscape of the soul. Following the tradition of the
Psychomachia, Bersuire takes the story of the Judgment as personification allegory, making the struggle of the goddesses signify the
contest of forces within the self for control of the personality. Bersuire had ample warrant for such an approach to the Judgment. Behind Fulgentius's identification of the three goddesses with the
three lives, there lay the ancient division of human activity into
three spheres, each corresponding to a part of the soul. Plato, for
example, had distinguished "that with which a man learns," "that
with which he feels anger," and "the appetitive part." In Bersuire's
tropological allegory, each goddess represents a function of the soul
conceived in Augustinian terms, and Paris's decision to award the
apple to Venus represents the all too frequent human decision to let
the fallen will follow its own inclinations. Bersuire predictably as-
signs to Pallas, the goddess of wisdom, *ratio*, the reasonable activity of the soul. The will, fallen and thus subject to the pull of the
appetites, is appropriate to Venus, goddess of delight.[81] Bersuire
makes the apple represent the human heart—that is, the essence of
the personality. When Paris gives the apple to Venus, he thus succumbs to concupiscence, the pull of the fallen human will toward
love of the creature rather than the creator.[82]

The rationale for Bersuire's associating Juno with memory is less
obvious. Note first that the positive evaluation she receives here is
uncharacteristic in a work written under Fulgentian influence. Bersuire makes a play on Juno's traditional patronage of wealth by
observing that memory has "riches of knowledge," but his identification of the third goddess with memory does not depend solely on
an equivocation. Traceable to Augustine is a scheme that sees memory, intelligence, and will as three functions of the soul which parallel the three-in-one structure of the Trinity.[83] This analysis was
transmitted to the later Middle Ages in the *Sentences* of Peter
Lombard and, Etienne Gilson says, "became a required subject of
meditation and teaching for every professor of theology."[84] The
scheme could easily have influenced Bersuire when he chose functions of the soul to assign to the three goddesses. Not being a theo-
logian or a philosopher, he replaced the more technical concept of
intellegentia[85] with *ratio*. *Ratio*'s function in the soul's economy
had been sanctioned in the simpler schemes of popular literary allegories which saw, for example, reason and passion in conflict. Not

only was memory seen by philosophers and theologians as a key function of the soul, it had already been identified with Juno in the classicizing tradition. In the *Fulgentius Metaforalis*, a preachers' handbook like Bersuire's, John Ridwall had, sometime around 1330,[86] assigned the virtue of prudence to Saturn and prudence's traditional subdivisions, memory, intelligence, and providence, to his children, Juno, Neptune, and Pluto. Thus there was ample warrant for associating Juno with memory, and for seeing the other goddesses as other functions of the soul.

The Paris version of the *Ovidius Moralizatus* offers a significant parallel to this interpretation:

> say [Bersuire advises] that in man, who is called India Minor, the three goddesses, or three powers of the soul, were first in agreement, and because the spirit obeyed reason there was no discord among the parts. Man was in harmony with God, and between them there was such concord that not at all did the flesh oppose the spirit. Finally the goddess or god of discord, that is, the devil, with pride or concupiscence, threw him the forbidden apple; he weakened peace and concord and destroyed the rule [*regum?*] of the soul.[87]

Clearly, this interpretation is derived from that in the earlier version of the *Ovidius Moralizatus*, which made the three goddesses three powers of the soul. This time, however, the conflict is not the timeless struggle within every sinner, but rather an event precisely situated in human history. Doubtless under the influence of the *Ovide moralisé*, Bersuire has turned from moral interpretations to biblical parallels; he sees the disruption of the wedding feast as a figure for the fall of man. His recollection of Benoît's Judgment in the *Roman de Troie* probably accounts for the reference to India Minor as the locale of the goddesses' quarrel and thus as a figure for the man in whom the *psychomachia* represented by the quarrel will occur.

Though he specifies that the three goddesses represent three powers of the soul, as was the case in the earlier interpretation, Bersuire seems actually to have something broader in mind. He envisions a triad in which those old adversaries, reason and the flesh, fight for control of the third element, the spirit. This is not an interpretation of the Judgment, with each goddess, or power, seeking the allegiance of Paris, but rather an explanation of the goddesses' quarrel. It attempts to explain why the human personality is no longer ordered toward the highest good. Bersuire's analysis, in fact, virtually paraphrases a passage from the *City of God* in which Augustine, using the imagery of Galatians 5.17, delineates the psychological effects of the fall:

> The soul, which had taken perverse delight in its own liberty and disdained the service of God, was now deprived of its original mastery over the body; because it had deliberately deserted the Lord who was over it, it no longer bent to its will the servant below it, being unable to hold the flesh completely in subjection as would always have been the case, if only the soul had remained subject to God. From this moment, then, the flesh began to lust against the spirit.[88]

Elsewhere Augustine explains the role of reason in the relationship of flesh to spirit. The human personality is ordered when reason rather than the flesh rules the soul,[89] but the flesh now strives constantly for the upper hand because the fall weakened reason's power:

> For since man, placed in honor, afterwards sinned, he has become similar to the beasts [Psalm 48.13], and he procreates as beasts do; however, something like a spark of reason in him, by which he has been made in the image of God, has not been quite extinguished.[90]

It is this complex of ideas which lies behind Bersuire's allegorical interpretation of the goddesses' quarrel. At first the three elements of the personality were in accord because the spirit obeyed reason. Thus man was in harmony with God. When the devil tempted man, however, concupiscence began to pull man's spirit toward the delights of the flesh.[91] When man fell, the order that had characterized the relationship between his flesh and spirit was disrupted, as was his relationship with God. As Augustine put it, "because [the soul] had deliberately deserted the Lord who was over it, it no longer bent to its will the servant [flesh] below it."

Bersuire is primarily interested in teaching moral lessons rather than elucidating the Christian mysteries. For the Wedding of Peleus and Thetis he passes on the cosmic allegory of Fulgentius; he then uses the identifications of Jove, Peleus, and Thetis with fire, earth, and water to create a moral allegory in which Jove, the just man, fearing lest his fire be extinguished by Thetis, or *voluptas*, unites her with the unclean Peleus. It is only when Bersuire supplements the first version of the *Ovidius Moralizatus*, under the influence of the *Ovide moralisé*, that Peleus and Thetis become Adam and Eve, and Achilles Christ. Bersuire's moral thrust is evident too in his interpretation of the dream of Hecuba and Paris's judgment of the bulls. Each is taken at face value as a lesson: Hecuba's behavior in sparing Paris was wrong; Paris's behavior in judging the rival bull was right. For the first time, these particular episodes, passed from handbook to handbook for centuries, are turned to a purpose other than narrative. The details preserved in the *Excidium Troiae* and the *Compendium Historiae Troianae-Romanae* bear fruit at the hands of the moralizer.

Moral lessons are Bersuire's first interest too in his interpretation of Discord's interruption of the wedding feast. Discord becomes successively the discord of the envious, who create contention, and the discord of avarice, which uses the golden apple, representing the good things of the world, to sow dissension among men. It is only under the influence of the *Ovide moralisé* that Bersuire sees the golden apple as the apple which tempted Adam and Eve in the garden of Eden, while Discord becomes the devil, who proffers the forbidden fruit and, in an analysis based on Augustinian psychology, destroys the harmony that man knew before the fall. Finally, with the Judgment, Bersuire at first sticks close to the Fulgentian interpretation, with its ethical-moral thrust. He makes Paris represent stupid youth, whose choice of Venus is a choice of the voluptuous life. In his second interpretation, however, he sees the Judgment as a tropological allegory, with the goddesses as personifications of conflicting powers of the soul.

Detached from the tale of Troy and sometimes scarcely recognizable as a classical story, the Judgment of Paris made its way into exempla collections much more heterogeneous than the *Ovide moralisé* and the *Ovidius Moralizatus*. These collections mingle classical stories with animal tales, marvels, and bits of local color—all grist to the preacher's mill. The interpretations, of course, are markedly Christian, since the stories are intended to enliven sermons. Strange are the uses to which the Judgment is put, and stranger still the permutations of its narrative.

A version of the Judgment appears in a handbook for preachers produced in England in the fourteenth century and preserved in Ms. Harley 7322.[92] The fable is narrated in slightly garbled fashion, and then there is a brief allegorical interpretation:

> Three queens sat at a fountain arguing among themselves which was more beautiful. A fourth queen threw from afar a golden apple on which was carved, "The most beautiful of you will have me." Then together they approached the god Apollo that they might ask which of them was more beautiful. First was the goddess of love who claimed for herself beauty of form. Second was the goddess Vesta, who showed herself more beautiful in moral character. Third [was] [name illegible], goddess of movement, who represented the active life. Then Apollo said Venus ought to have the apple because she greatly exceeded the others in beauty of form [and] because many willingly met with death on account of her love. But since the other two did not yet agree to all of this, they ascended to the god Jove, who said that Pallas, that is, the goddess Vesta, ought to have the apple and not Venus, because Venus encourages and boasts of pleasures, nor [should] [name illegible], who rules over riches, [have it], but Pallas, who is concerned with divine matters.
>
> The apple is eternal life; the three queens are three kinds of man living three different kinds of life. The throwing of the apple is God offering His realm equally to all. The god Apollo is the will selfishly and foolishly choosing pleasure. The god Jove is reason, inflexible and most true, proceeding reasonably. He is well called god of gods because it is impossible for Him to lie.[93]

Though this is unquestionably a version of the Judgment, it features some startling departures from the classical story. It substitutes Apollo for Paris, changes the goddesses' names, and makes the two rejected ones press Jove for a repeal of their judge's decision. True to the traditional narrative, however, it includes the golden apple with its inscription, the argument over beauty, the three goddesses' traditional associations with love, virtue, and riches, and the appeal to an arbitrator from the outside. It also shows a definite, if sporadic, acquaintance with other medieval versions of the Judgment. As in the second redaction of the *Histoire ancienne,* the golden apple is thrown to the three goddesses not as they converse at the wedding of Peleus and Thetis but as they sit by themselves around a fountain. Like the *Histoire ancienne,* as well, this version makes the three goddesses seek their own arbitrator. As does the *Ovide moralisé,* it stresses Venus's great power as goddess of love.

The story reflects, too, a certain knowledge of classical mythology. Initially, the second goddess, noted for her moral character, is identified as Vesta, a logical substitution, since Vesta was anciently a virgin goddess like Pallas. The name of the third goddess is not completely legible in Harley 7322, but Siegfried Wenzel has suggested to me that it might possibly be a distortion of Lucina; the author may have known this name as one sometimes applied to Juno. The last line of the interpretation, "He is well called god of gods," indicates an awareness that Jove was chief of the Olympians.

In the interpretation, elements of the old Fulgentian allegory form the basis for a new, specifically Christian moralization, which follows the narrative twists of the modified fable. As in Fulgentius, the three goddesses represent three modes of life, and in the narrative, the third goddess is explicitly identified with the active life, though corresponding associations are not made for the other two. The interpretation goes beyond Fulgentius, however, to define the good life not in classical but in Christian terms. The prize is an eternity with God, and the exemplum answers the question, by what mode of life may a man gain salvation? As in Fulgentius, too, the choice of Venus represents a shortsighted preference for the life of pleasure over the active and contemplative lives, but the change in the fable's plot allows the exemplum to illustrate a wise choice as well as a foolish one. As the arbitrator who reverses the false judgment of Apollo and correctly chooses Pallas, Jove is interpreted as reason. Thus reason, which, the exemplum implies, should rule the soul as Jove rules the other gods, wisely sees that a life focused on the divine most surely leads to salvation, whereas the will erroneously believes that salvation lies in the pursuit of pleasure.

The interpretation uses what might be called the popular psychology of the Middle Ages. Greatly simplified from the complex and subtle schemes with which the pioneering Augustine analyzed the Christian's inner life, the strife between reason and the fallen will (or reason and passion, reason and the flesh, the soul and the body) provided the drama in much allegorical literature of the later Middle Ages and doubtless gave structure to the inner conflicts of many on whom the *De Libero Arbitrio* would have been lost. As was the case with some of Bersuire's analyses, then, this preachers' manual sees in the Judgment an allegory for the struggle between good and evil in the daily life of the Christian.

Two more versions of the Judgment appear in the *Scala Coeli* of the French Dominican Johannes Gobi. Produced between 1323 and 1330, the work arranges exempla under alphabetically ordered topics, such as *accidia*, *beneficia*, *crux*, and so on. Each topic is subdivided into sections, and each subdivision is usually the occasion for at least one exemplum.[94] The first version of the Judgment appears in the section on war, "De Bello." It illustrates the third "good condition" for undertaking war: "bellum debet esse pium":

> Helinandus reports that, wanting to bring war to the city of Troy, a certain person had a golden apple made, around whose circumference was written, "It is to be given to the most beautiful." When, however, all the most noble women had been assembled at a certain feast, the apple was thrown in their midst and, having read the writing, one of them said that it was hers, extolling her beauty. When, however, the ruler had been asked for justice and was contemplating the beauty of all of them, he saw, apart from the others, a poor woman of most excellent beauty. It had not been considered fitting that she should associate with the beautiful ones [but] she was given the apple to the confusion of the others.
>
> The apple is the Son of God. He who nominated [her is] the Spirit. [The women are] the virtues or talents of holy women who led the way in the Old Testament. The poor woman is the Blessed Virgin or humility.[95]

The second version of the Judgment appears in the section on charity, "De Charitate." It illustrates the sixth example of what charity does: "it honors":

> We read in the Trojan history that when a certain noble had invited a multitude of noble women to a solemn feast, a certain cleric threw in their midst a golden apple inscribed around its circumference. And the tenor of the writing was this: "It is to be given to the most beautiful." And when that golden apple had been picked up in the middle of the festivity and celebration, and the writing was read, a debate arose among the women for the reason that any one of them claimed

her own beauty to be most excellent and requested the apple. When it had come to the judgment of the king, and he had judged it should be given for having a face more beautiful and clothing more honest in virtue, someone was found, excellent and in most honest clothing, to whom the apple was given.

For this feast is the celestial court; that noble is the Holy Spirit, the women, however, virtues, the apple the Son of God. But more beautiful is charity, dressed in most precious robes, not from the hair of sheep or animals, but from the flesh of Christ, thus woven that it could not be divided, thus colored that all the goodness of God was represented in it, thus honored that it was venerated in the court of God and concealed a multitude of sins. And therefore, over all virtues He deservedly regarded this one for the incarnation of Christ and our salvation.[96]

In each case, the narrative is substantially the same, and the golden apple with its well-known inscription makes the tale recognizably the Judgment of Paris. In the first exemplum, the apple's purpose is to start a war. This detail goes back to Eris's motive in the *Cypria* for provoking the goddesses to quarrel. In other ways, however, the story is far removed from classical tradition. It has obviously been rationalized: the Wedding of Peleus and Thetis has become a noble feast, its host a nobleman, and its guests noblewomen. The second exemplum makes "a certain cleric" throw the apple. This detail may derive from a tradition in medieval illustrations of the Judgment which depicted Mercury as a monk or bishop.[97] A miniature depicting Mercury in clerical clothes and holding the apple could easily be construed as an illustration of "a certain cleric" taking aim to throw. The plot has been changed as well. Paris has vanished, and the decision among the quarreling women is made by the ruler-host. He corresponds to Jove in the original story, but Jove always refused to judge lest he offend the two goddesses who would inevitably lose. Finally, rather than choosing one of the noble contestants, the ruler selects a humble outsider with no part in the original quarrel.

The exemplum was probably inspired by the Wedding and Judgment in Vincent of Beauvais's *Speculum Historiale*. Gobi's first version attributes the story to Helinandus, his second to "hystoria troyana," but since the details are so similar, the source for both is probably the same. When Gobi lists his sources in his prologue, he refers neither to Helinandus nor to a Trojan history, but he does include the *Summa* of "Brother Vincent." Vincent names Helinandus as his major source when he narrates the causes of the Trojan War in the *Speculum Historiale.* Gobi would not be the first medieval author to borrow both material and attribution from an unacknowledged intermediary. Though Vincent is more faithful to classical tradition, his material could easily be transformed into Gobi's version. As the true explanation of the war, Vincent gives a bare summary ultimately traceable to Eusebius: "The cause of the war was, however, as Eusebius writes—that argument of three women for the prize of beauty, one of them promising Helen to the shepherd judge."[98] He goes on, however, to narrate the "fable" which has been "feigned" concerning this history: the Wedding of Peleus and Thetis and the Judgment of Paris. Vincent's version of the fable includes *mutatis mutandis* exactly what Gobi's does: the feast, the inscribed golden apple, and the quarreling beauties. Most significantly, its context is, as in Gobi's first exemplum, an explanation of the war's cause. The classical story as Vincent tells it, however, would not have supported the allegorical interpretations that Gobi draws from his version of the narrative.

Gobi's interpretations see in the Judgment an allegory of Christ's incarnation. That this central event of salvation history was ever present in the Christian mind, to the point that its seductive outlines could be discerned in nearly any story, is suggested by the fact that Gobi even sees it in the version of the Judgment with which he illustrates the third "good condition" for undertaking war. For this first interpretation of the Judgment, Gobi supplies a straightforward typological allegory. The apple awarded by the ruler to the poor woman sitting apart from the others is Christ, conceived by the power of the Holy Spirit in the womb of the Virgin Mary. In making the ruler the Holy Spirit, Gobi is of course thinking of the Holy Spirit's role in the Incarnation of Christ: "When Mary his mother had been betrothed to Joseph . . . she was found to be with child by the Holy Spirit."[99] We doubtless owe to a rising tide of interest in the Blessed Virgin, which even by the thirteenth century had spilled over into sermon literature,[100] the fact that Mary is here brought into the story at all. Indeed, Gobi has stressed her personal qualities—"a poor woman of most excellent beauty"—and made her in effect the heroine of the exemplum. In doing so, he has substituted for the queen of love a lady whose cult was, according to G. R. Owst, "fostered—by the Mendicant in particular—to counteract the popularity of the *trouvère's* secular love-themes."[101] So far Gobi's allegory and its rationale are clear. In order to understand what he means, however, when he identifies the women who were passed over for the prize as "the virtues or talents of holy women who led the way in the Old Testament," we must turn now to his second interpretation.

This second interpretation is much better suited to its context, a discussion of charity. Here Gobi makes clear that behind both interpretations lies the concept central to the meaning of Christianity: that the birth of Christ brought a New Law, charity, to supersede the law articulated in the Old Testament. The seminal discussion of this concept occurs in the writings of St. Paul. Paul says, for example, "Christ redeemed us from the curse of the Law" (Galatians 3.13) and "But when the fullness of time came, God sent His Son, born of a woman, born under the Law, that he might redeem those who were under the Law" (Galatians 4.4–5; also Romans 7.4). The highest virtue of the New Law—indeed, the meaning of the New Law itself—is charity: "For the whole Law is fulfilled in one word: Thou shalt love thy neighbor as thyself" (Galatians 5.14; also Romans 13.8–10). Charity thus replaces the provisions of the Old Law, and is extolled as the most sublime of virtues: "So there abide faith, hope and charity, these three; but the greatest of these is charity" (1 Corinthians 13.13). Since Christ replaced the Old Law with the New Law of charity, the ruler in Gobi's version of the Judgment passes over the virtues honored under the Old Law when he goes to award the apple, or Christ, and the humble woman who receives the prize becomes polysemous, representing both the Virgin Mary and the virtue of charity.

Gobi elaborates his second interpretation, however, into an allusive and resonant meditation on the mystery of Christ's coming into the world. He attributes charity's beauty to her robes, not made from wool, "but from the flesh of Christ," thus referring to the essence of the Incarnation and its mystery: the Word was made flesh. Since charity motivated Christ's sacrifice and constituted his central message for man's redemption, "charity" could indeed have been cloaked in flesh when Christ took human form. Gobi was not the first to see Christ's humanity as metaphoric clothing for his divinity. Origen, for example, had much earlier said, "For the Word came into the world by Mary, clad in flesh. . . . So when the Word was shown to men . . . it was not shown them without suitable vesture. There it is covered by the veil of flesh."[102]

In this second interpretation, Gobi abandons the neat equivalencies of his first approach to the Judgment. Here each detail is potentially multivalent. First the humble woman's cloak, or Christ's flesh, becomes assimilated brilliantly to the robe for which lots were cast at the Crucifixion: "thus woven that it could not be divided" (see John 19.23–24). Then the cloak itself begins to take on the characteristics of charity, most strikingly in that it "concealed a multitude of sins" (1 Peter 4.8).

Gobi's second interpretation of the Judgment is a *tour de force*, but in its central concerns it is related to the Judgment's treatment in the other preachers' manuals we have considered. The friars' interpretations are predictably characterized by an emphasis on Christian themes, particularly the central drama of Christianity: sin and redemption. Thus interpretations of the Wedding and Judgment can see in the classical fable the creation, fall, and redemption, or they can focus on the conflicts engendered in every man's soul by the fallen will. The philosophy of history and the moral psychology on which the interpretations are based are Augustinian or at least ultimately traceable to Augustine's influence, and understandably so, given the tendency of popular thought to be conservative.

Rich and diverse as they were, the treatments of the Judgment and the three lives in these fourteenth-century preachers' manuals, by their nature intellectually conservative, were informed by the spirit of Fulgentius. A reevaluation of the three lives themselves, however, was already well underway, and the Fulgentian interpretation of the Judgment was about to be supplanted by one based on an Aristotelian scheme. By the mid-thirteenth century, Aristotle's authority was well established in the universities.[103] The influence of Aristotelianism directly affected attitudes toward the active life, as seen for example in the shift from Augustine's dim view of human society to that of Aquinas, who considered political life natural to man and fundamentally good.[104]

By the thirteenth century, discussions of the three lives themselves were patterned after Aristotle. In the *Tresor*, for example, Brunetto Latini identifies the three modes of life as follows: "The one life is of concupiscence and greed, the other is the life of a citizen, that is of reason and courage and honor, the third is contemplative."[105] He characterizes the active life as a life of good works and correct use of worldly things, but ranks it below the contemplative life (2.123). In the *De Regimine Principum*, Egidio Colonna, a student of Aquinas, condemns the life of pleasure but sees the contemplative and active lives as almost equal in value:

> in the manner of living in the delight of the body, the philosophers put no sovereign goods, because it is the life of a dumb beast, but in the manner of living in contemplation and in knowledge of truth they put a sovereign good of this mortal life which they call the happiness of understanding and knowing; in the manner of associating reasonably with men they put another sovereign good, which they call the happiness of doing the works of virtue.[106]

Some Italian humanists even exalted the active life over the contemplative.[107]

This interest in the Aristotelian scheme of the three lives is reflected in the interpretation which Boccaccio gives the Judgment of Paris in his monumental *De Genealogiis Deorum*, which he began about 1350 and worked at for the rest of his life.[108] Drawing on classical authors, commentators, fathers of the church, the Third Vatican Mythographer, and a mysterious "Theodontius," Boccaccio arranged the classical gods and heroes into a complex genealogical scheme which made Demogorgon the father of the race.[109] His treatment of the Judgment's fable, in book 6, chapter 22, reflects his scholarly aim. He offers an unexceptionably classical version of the story, including the dream of Hecuba (on which he cites Cicero's *De Divinatione*), a reference to Paris's cohabitation with Oenone, and a brief, general allusion to the reputation for justice which caused Jove to make Paris the goddesses' judge. He presents the standard details of Discord's revenge and makes the goddesses show themselves to Paris nude in a wood which he identifies as Mesaulon.[110]

Unlike Bersuire, Boccaccio does not wish to interpret every detail of his story. He calls attention to the presence of "fictions"; wishing to "enucleate" them (*enucleare*), he expounds their deeper significance (1.304). The fictions are those episodes in which the gods of the ancients interact with men; presumably the rest of the story does not need to be "enucleated" because it stands as history.

For the Judgment of Paris, Boccaccio explicitly recommends the opinion of Fulgentius, summarizing the late-classical mythographer thus: "For he says that human life is tripartite. The first part is called theoretical, the second practical, the third 'phylargical.' In common words, we call these lives contemplative, active, and voluptuous" (1.304). He goes on, however, to refer his readers, as Fulgentius of course had not, to the first book of the *Ethics* to learn which life Aristotle regards as best. Boccaccio defines none of the three lives, and a reader consulting the *Ethics* would find that, though Aristotle recommended the contemplative life, he also regarded the active life as suitable to men. Boccaccio has thus superimposed upon Fulgentius the classical scheme of the three lives.[111]

It is not until a little after 1400, however, that the new esteem for the active life brought about by the influence of Aristotle is spelled out in an interpretation of the Judgment. Sometime between 1370 and 1380, an anonymous Frenchman produced an allegorical poem, the *Echecs amoureux*, based on the Judgment of Paris.[112] In this work the narrator is asked to give his opinion of Paris's decision among the goddesses. When he agrees with Paris's choice, he is invited to enter the garden of Pleasure, where he is conquered at chess by a beautiful young maiden. The poem breaks off as Pallas offers alternatives to the young man's pursuit of love. The *Echecs amoureux* itself will be discussed in Chapter 4; of interest here is the fact that a few decades later it inspired a commentary, the first written in French on a French poem.[113] The commentator is particularly interested in explaining the poem's mythological references.[114] Early in his commentary, he allegorizes a series of "portraits" of the gods and goddesses, and he later focuses specifically on the Wedding of Peleus and Thetis and the Judgment. His first and most elaborate interpretation of the Judgment is, as we shall see,

profoundly Aristotelian in its evaluation of the life represented by
Juno.[115] Earlier, however, he wavers between Fulgentius and Aristotle as he explains the allegorical significance of Juno herself in
his "portrait" of the goddess.

First Juno's traditional associations are harmonized with each
other and with a version of the active life which, if it is not precisely Aristotelian, is regarded positively as the life appropriate to
man living in society:

> this active life is ordained for living well and honestly and . . . one
> pursues it to acquire riches and the worldly goods which are neces-
> sary to us and . . . this life is given to riches as the contemplative life
> is devoted to the wise.[116]

The goddess's traditional association with air, based on the ancient
etymology, follows naturally from her connection with wealth
("the air surrounds the earth, which preserves and contains within
itself all the riches and worldly goods") as does her old identification as goddess of birth: "Juno" means "she who helps the new,"
that is, the newborn, because both young and old need riches to
live (f. 125r).[117] Suddenly, however, the commentator abandons this
positive view of the goddess and her wealth as he interprets Juno's
traditional attributes in a passage probably based on the verbal
"portrait" of the goddess in Bersuire's prologue to his *Ovidius
Moralizatus*.

Following the quintessentially medieval Bersuire, the commentator reverts to the old Fulgentian bias against wealth. He begins
with Juno's scepter:

> When the figure then shows us that Juno carries a scepter in her hand
> like a great queen, this signifies that wealth is the principal lady and
> queen of the world and that riches rule and dominate all. And, briefly,
> just as the subjects obey the king, thus all, with one common accord,
> obey wealth.[118]

Far from being the moderate wealth which situates the middle
class between the extremes of want and excess, the wealth which
Juno signifies seduces and enslaves those who devote themselves to
getting and spending. Further negative significance is attached to
the cloud which covers her head: it shows that "riches desire to be

hidden and put aside" or that "those who have them gladly hide themselves and turn their heads away for fear lest someone ask them for something" or that "those who are superabundantly rich are also blind and conceited and they do not know well who is their friend or enemy."[119] Even the rainbow which traditionally surrounds the goddess's head is given negative significance:

> The rainbow which also shines around this goddess which appears to us bright and gleaming signifies the riches of the world which cause rich people to gleam and shine and to seem more wise and virtuous than they often are, just as this rainbow is a marvel appearing in the cloud and a thing which is not in fact what it appears to us.[120]

That the rainbow often appears following a slight shower, but rapidly vanishes, signifies "the adulations, the appeals, and the feigned friendships with which the rich often find themselves surrounded and in the end deceived."[121] The peacocks with which Juno is traditionally associated—licking her feet, as Bersuire has it— show that the rich are surrounded by people "who want to honor and serve them even as far as kissing the foot."[122]

As had Bersuire and the author of the *Ovide moralisé*, the commentator on the *Echecs amoureux* offers suggestions for interpretation, not a definitive reading of his text; like any scholar, he depends on his sources. Thus Juno's value changes according to the sources he consults. The same kind of variation occurs when he turns to the classical story on which the *Echecs amoureux* is based, the Judgment of Paris. For the Wedding of Peleus and Thetis and the Judgment, he offers a wide assortment of interpretations clearly related to those of other mythographers: Fulgentius, Bersuire, even Bernard Silvestris,[123] but the Aristotelian bent of the commentary as a whole pervades his first and most elaborate interpretation of the Judgment.

The commentator begins with an explanation of the three lives themselves. The "moral philosophers," he explains, have determined that three modes of life are possible to man: contemplative, active, and voluptuous. The first, or contemplative,

> is the life in which man, leaving aside worldly things and things which appeal to the senses, applies himself to speculation and to the

knowledge of truth and especially of celestial and divine things; its principal and first end is to love and know God.[124]

The second, or active, "is the life in which man wants to live in society and in community and always conduct himself reasonably among others, following the works of virtue."[125] The third, or voluptuous, "is the life in which man wants to pursue bodily delights and the pleasures of the world more than reason and virtue wish."[126]

Though this is reminiscent of Fulgentius—it even assimilates the classical ideal of contemplation to the Christian search for knowledge of God[127]—it departs from the scheme of the late-classical mythographer in one very important way: the characterization of the active life. For Fulgentius, the active life was almost as reprehensible as the voluptuous: "insatiable for possessions, sly in grasping at them, assiduous in guarding them," and so on.[128] Here, rather, the active life is the virtuous life of man in society, as it was for Aristotle and medieval thinkers influenced by him, such as Brunetto Latini and Egidio Colonna. The Aristotelian influence is made clear by what follows, a passage which seems to echo the *Nicomachean Ethics* 10.8:

> these three manners of living come from a conception the philosophers had because they considered that man was of a nature halfway between dumb beasts and the angels of heaven. And thus that he resembled in some way the beasts, on the one hand, and, on the other hand, the angels. And therefore they said further that insofar as he resembled the beasts thus also the life of pleasure was appropriate for him, and insofar as he was, on the other hand, similar to the angels thus also the contemplative life and the knowledge of truth was appropriate for him, and insofar as he himself was man and, with respect to his proper and true nature, thus also the active life was appropriate for him; it makes man live reasonably in society.[129]

When the commentator turns to his interpretation of the Judgment itself, it is this classically influenced scheme rather than the Fulgentian one that he applies to his analysis of each goddess's significance. This application of the Aristotelian scheme of the three lives to the Judgment may well be his own idea, particularly since the commentary is permeated with Aristotelianism. What he says of Pallas and Venus is not unusual. Pallas is identified as goddess of wisdom and thus assigned to the contemplative life, the life led by "those who use their intelligence and understanding in the study and in the knowledge of the high, secret things of nature and especially of God and of divine things."[130] Not surprisingly, the classical search for truth has been assimilated to the Christian search for God. Venus is identified as goddess of love and delight, and thus assigned to the voluptuous life, the life led by "those who gladly pursue bodily delights and especially by young lovers who seek nothing but idleness and pleasure."[131] The interpretation of Juno is, however, necessarily somewhat different from what we are familiar with, and it is considerably longer than the discussions of Pallas and Venus, as if the commentator were aware that in assigning a nontraditional definition of the active life to this goddess, he had a certain amount of explaining to do, particularly since he keeps Juno's old connection with wealth. In order to justify a positive interpretation of the wealth thus associated with the active life, he depends chiefly on Aristotle's *Politics* 4.9, in which the philosopher explains why a constitution based on the middle class offers the best form of government.

For Aristotle, the middle class represents the virtuous mean. The very rich are disobedient and undisciplined; the very poor lack spirit and are unable to rule. A community composed of rich and poor would be a community of masters and slaves. Since, ideally, a state is a community of equals, one composed primarily of the middle class would be best. Further, the middle class neither envies the goods of others, as do the poor, nor is envied by others, as are the rich. Thus it enjoys greater security than do the other two classes.[132] The commentator uses Aristotle's endorsement of moderate wealth as he attempts to harmonize the wealth of the Fulgentian active life with the political responsibility demanded by the classical active life:

> Juno, who is the goddess of riches, signifies the active life which is appropriate for the rich because riches and worldly goods are indeed necessary in this active life because otherwise one would not be able to live [that life] well enough. One could also say that this active life is appropriate for the rich because in such a life it is necessary to be directed by reason and to live according to virtue because the community could not otherwise endure or last long, and it is not right or

possible for those who live thus to be poor—if one understands the matter correctly—because virtue is the only source of wealth and it is vice that makes man poor and indigent as the wise philosophers say. And therefore Aristotle says that in every reasonable community one should have great care for virtue. Without doubt also virtue makes [one] have enough and having enough makes a person rich because very little suffices nature. And therefore Aristotle says furthermore that moderate wealth is the best of all and in every city the most to be recommended because it easily obeys reason because wealth too great or also too small does not easily obey [reason] because those who are too rich and too powerful do not know how to obey nor do they want to. And those who are too poor do not know how to govern or rule and therefore as he says also the city is more permanent and more peaceful by nature where there are more people of moderate wealth because people of moderate wealth do not thus desire nor seek nor wish the riches of others as the poor do because they have enough wealth nor also do the poor envy them at all nor also desire their moderate wealth as they do excessive wealth. The active life is then especially appropriate and suitable to the rich whose wealth accords with virtue and therefore the philosophers put in this life the second human felicity which lies in the work of prudence because she [is] queen and lady of all the other moral virtues and because she also directs and rules them all as was said before.[133]

In this explanation of why Juno, goddess of wealth, should be patron of the active life, then, the commentator makes strategic use of the Aristotelian notions summarized above. Aside from one lapse into equivocation—"virtue is the only source of wealth"—we are on firm Aristotelian ground, with the moderately wealthy man also the man of virtue and reason, untempted and untroubled by the wealth or envy of others.

Aristotelian too is the commentator's summary statement of the life most to be recommended. Citing Aristotle, he identifies the contemplative life as the best: "it surpasses and exceeds in dignity and perfection every other mode of life because it is a divine life, as Aristotle says, and because the felicity which is placed in this life is also called divine and the best of all."[134] For Aristotle's gods, in whose nature the contemplative man shares, the commentator of course substitutes the Christian God: "because in the knowledge of God and his majesty and in the consideration of his exception-

ally great, infinite good . . . lies the principal end of contemplation."[135] As does Aristotle, he identifies the active life as that which
is "more suitable and advantageous to man,"[136] and he condemns
the voluptuous life as "better the life of a beast than it is the life of
a man."[137]

The interpretation of the Judgment which appears in the commentary on the *Echecs amoureux*, with its new view of the active
life, reflects advanced ideas. It draws on the Greek sources which
had radically affected the study of philosophy in the universities. A
second French interpretation of the Judgment produced around the
same time is, however, profoundly conservative. It seeks in the
Judgment not philosophical themes but religious ones. Looking
back to the era of chivalry as a golden age, it draws from the Judgment interpretations which reflect the view that earthly knighthood images a spiritual service in which the Christian gentleman
is a knight of Jesus Christ.

Christine de Pisan's *Epitre d'Othéa*, written about 1400,[138] has
been described as "a double courtesy book."[139] The work is orga-
nized into one hundred chapters, each consisting of a brief, rhymed
texte, drawn from classical mythology, a *glose*, which provides the
mythological background necessary to understand the *texte* and
applies its lesson to practical knighthood, and an *allegorie*, which
extracts from the *texte* a spiritual application. In structure, the
work is indebted to the medieval *sommes*, or *summae*, of virtues
and vices.[140] Christine has arranged her stories to illustrate virtues,
sins, articles of the Creed, and so on. Whereas the *glose* to each text
provides a moral or tropological interpretation, pertaining to man's
actions, the *allegorie* provides an interpretation pertaining to matters of belief. This allegory can deal with the central mysteries of
the Christian faith—creation, fall, redemption—and also, more
broadly, man's relationship with God.[141] This distinction between
types of interpretation is a legacy of biblical exegesis,[142] and we
have seen it operating in other interpretations of the Judgment.

We should expect in a work produced for a noble audience in the
later Middle Ages some reflection of those chivalric ideals which
had become all the more important as their relevance to real life
declined. That is indeed what we find. Running through the entire
work, beginning with the fiction that Hector, the perfect knight, is

the beneficiary of the advice contained in the *Othéa*, is an appeal to literal and figurative knighthood. The *glose* offers moral instruction applicable to the Christian knight, and by extension, to everyone who fights the good fight. The *allegorie*, on the other hand, deals with matters relevant to the spiritual knight's quest for his ultimate destiny, the "noblesse" which is his as a son of God: [143] either matters of belief in the narrow sense or instructions for conforming the spirit to the image of Christ.

Christine's interpretations of Wedding and Judgment observe this distinction between the practical and the spiritual. Among her one hundred lessons, she includes a chapter each on Discord, the judgment of the goddesses, and Paris's dream. Discord is first, in chapter 60; the *texte* reads, "Flee the goddess of discord; evil are her bonds and her cord. She disturbed the wedding of Peleus. Many people were gathered there then." [144] The *glose* supplies, chiefly from the *Ovide moralisé*, the fable to which this brief verse refers. [145] It then reveals the moral lesson hidden within the fable: the good knight should flee discord, a source of harm and an ugly habit. A spiritual interpretation of the *texte* appears in the *allegorie:*

> As it is said that one ought to flee discord, thus ought the good spirit to flee all impediments of conscience, and Cassiodorus on the Psalter says that contention and riots are to be avoided; above all, says he, flee contention and riot because to contend against peace is madness; to contend against his sovereign is insanity and against his subject is great villainy. Thus St. Paul the apostle says, "Not in strife and jealousy" [Romans 13.13]. [146]

Here discord is seen as a disruption of the soul which would hinder the realization of its ultimate destiny.

Chapter 73 deals with Paris's judgment of the goddesses: "Do not judge as Paris judged because one receives many hard desserts; many have reaped evil by handing down a bad decision." [147] The *glose* narrates, from the *Ovide moralisé* and Machaut's *Dit de la fonteinne amoureuse*, [148] the fable of the Judgment, then draws a moral lesson. Because his thoughts were on love, rather than chivalry or knowledge, Paris gave the golden apple to Venus. Pythagoras says, however, "The judge who does not judge justly deserves all evil" ("Le iuge qui ne iuge iustement dessert tout alm"). Thus the good knight should not emulate Paris. Though Christine follows Fulgentius, criticizing Paris's rejection of the chivalry and wisdom offered by Pallas, but unconcerned by his indifference to Juno's prizes, her view is not the traditional one, interested only in the personal implications of Paris's choice. When she condemns his error as bad judgment, Christine reveals that she shares the perspective of her audience: a noble's mistake was more than personal. She summarizes Paris's error as "handing down a bad decision" ("male sentence octroyer" in the *texte*), alluding to his role as judge. The *allegorie* too is more interested in judgment than in choice, but it deals with a private virtue rather than a public one: "The good spirit should keep from making judgment on others" ("Le bon esperit se doit garder de faire iugement sur aultruy"), for our Lord said, "Do not judge, that you may not be judged. For with what judgment you judge, you shall be judged" (Matthew 7.1–2).

For these two chapters, Christine has used the "classical" version of the Judgment. When the goddesses approach him, Paris is a shepherd, exiled from the royal household following Hecuba's prophetic dream. Christine knew also, probably from the first redaction of the *Histoire ancienne*,[149] the version of the Judgment deriving from Dares, in which the Trojan prince falls asleep while hunting and dreams his adventure with the goddesses. It is this alternative version of the Judgment to which she turns for chapter 68: "Do not base a great undertaking, whether for good or evil, on a vision or a false illusion—remember Paris."[150]

The *glose* explains that Paris's dream caused Troy to be destroyed. The practical lesson is certainly relevant to the nobility: base important undertakings on decisions reached in councils; do not base them on visions. A spiritual interpretation of the story follows in the *allegorie:* not basing a great undertaking on a dream means avoiding presumption and arrogance. Any good one has received is a free gift from God.

Christine had to provide her own interpretations for the dream-Judgment of the Dares tradition, not previously moralized. She also invented, by choice, interpretations for the classical Wedding and Judgment, even though these episodes were already moralized in her major source, the *Ovide moralisé*. Christine preferred to draw her own lessons because of the particular audience, purpose, and structure of the *Othéa*. Christine's readers were nobles whose lives were molded by the ideals of chivalry. She wanted her lessons to shape Christian gentlemen for both their earthly and heavenly destinies. Her structure, too, demanded interpretations of a particular kind, since each fable had to apply to both the flesh and the spirit.

Christine's moral interpretations particularly reflect the culture at which they are aimed, the courtiers who, as Rosemond Tuve puts it, "must wage the moral battles described, under conditions localized in the France of 1400."[151] Christine views society as an ordered hierarchy dependent for the maintenance of its order on the noble class that she addresses. Thus Discord is that contention and debate which disrupt the harmonious functioning of society, and the knight is urged to maintain social harmony. Her interpretation of the Judgment, too, is shaped by her view of the knight's role in the social hierarchy. Paris's chief error is not his wrong *choice*—though Christine cautions against rejecting chivalry and wisdom for love. She emphasizes, rather, that Paris's judgment was unjust. The allegory traditionally drawn from the Judgment—the allegory of the three lives—has an application which is first personal and only secondarily social. The fable makes concrete the motions of the soul faced with an existential question: what kind of person shall I become? A noble's choice of chivalry, riches, or love is ultimately relevant to society, but Christine wished more immediate application for the fable. Nobles were not only society's protectors and rulers but also its judges. To fulfill his role, the noble had to be a just judge. Thus Christine made Paris's failure as a judge his primary error. Swayed by the promise of Helen, he did not award the apple to the goddess who rightfully deserved it. Christine's moral interpretation of Paris's dream, too, is crucial to the noble's role. Troy fell because Paris heeded his vision, leading an army into Greece and stealing Helen. Christine advises her noble audience that rather than following the advice of their dreams, they should follow the advice of their councils.

The spiritual interpretations often follow from the tropological. They deal, however, not with the knight's place in the social hierarchy but with the soul's growth in perfection to resemble the perfect knight, Jesus Christ. Thus the fable is all the more important since it now images the unseen. As Discord disrupted the feast, discord disrupts the soul. The warning is clearer and more powerful as we envision the disruptive goddess's effect on the festivities. When she turns to the spiritual interpretation of Paris's judgment of the goddesses, Christine is guided by her moral application. Wishing to be consistent with her emphasis on Paris's unjust judgment rather than his unwise choice, she turns to the gospel injunction, "Do not judge, that you may not be judged." Finally, in the spiritual interpretation of Paris's dream, the good spirit is urged to acknowledge its place before God, rejecting the vanities of arrogance and presumption.

In this chapter, dealing with explicit allegorizations of the Judgment, we have seen how the meaning drawn from the story could change to reflect the preoccupations of a milieu or an audience. In the twelfth century, William of Conches and Bernard Silvestris saw the Judgment as an allegory for the human involvement in *temporalia*—a lesson to be heeded by the philosopher who sought to transcend the mundane. In the fourteenth century, the authors of numerous preachers' manuals saw in the Judgment and its related episodes useful exempla for moral instruction, as well as allegories of Christianity's most profound mysteries. In the fourteenth century, too, more than one scholar reevaluated Juno, as Aristotelianism encouraged a new respect for the active life. Finally, in the fifteenth century, Christine de Pisan used lessons drawn from the Wedding and Judgment to shape Christian gentlemen, applying the stories to the lives of her noble patrons. Yet in spite of the various interpretations drawn from the story, we have observed that the Fulgentian scheme, which saw the three goddesses as the three lives, was remarkably persistent. In the next chapter we shall see further applications of the Judgment's long allegorical tradition. But where the allegorizations considered in this chapter were explicit, those considered in the next will be implicit. Only a long tradition of explicit allegory, however, from Fulgentius up into the later Middle Ages, could have made possible the applications we shall next encounter.

4

The Choice of Paris

Some allegory resides in the mind of the beholder; other allegory resides in the work itself. This distinction is a crucial one: it is the distinction between allegory that is *imposed* and allegory that is *intended*. When Bernard Silvestris, Pierre Bersuire, Christine de Pisan, and the other writers considered in Chapter 3 used the Judgment as a vehicle for philosophy, the Christian mysteries, or moral lessons, they imposed allegorical interpretations on it.[1] Their impositions were obvious; they *explained* to us what they saw in the story. We did not need to debate whether the stories which they interpreted had been intended as allegories; it was clear that the interpretations were being arbitrarily imposed from outside.[2]

Alongside the tradition of imposed allegory, however, there flourished a complementary tradition of intended allegory. In this tradition, works owed their allegory to the intentions of their authors. During the later Middle Ages, the allegorical poem usurped all other literary forms to become for several centuries the prevailing literary fashion.[3] It was during these same centuries that the Judgment of Paris received its most significant literary treatment. The fable provided the inspiration for three allegorical dream visions produced in France in the third quarter of the fourteenth century: Guillaume de Machaut's *Dit de la fonteinne amoureuse*, Jean Froissart's *Espinette amoureuse*, and the anonymous *Echecs amoureux*.

In each work, the narrator or a major character reenacts Paris's choice among the goddesses. The Judgment's own long development as history and allegory neatly merges with late-medieval literary fashion so that the fable's use in the three works seems both brilliant and inevitable. The tradition that, starting with Dares, had made the Judgment a dream gave the story a natural application to the dream-vision format, while the centuries of allegorical interpretation imposed on the story gave it an allegorical dimension most appropriate to the aims of those who produced intended allegories in the dream-vision genre. The Judgment brings to these three dream visions meanings that it owes to the allegorical tradition. Thus valid interpretation of the three works rests upon a knowledge of the Judgment's allegorical background.

Considering these three uses of the Judgment will make it possible to answer some questions about the role of classical myth in medieval literature, about the sorts of interpretations one can legitimately see in works that incorporate stories with lives of their own, and about the nature of intended allegory in the later Middle Ages. I will argue that these three works are examples of intended allegory, that is, that they are to be read as if their surfaces image unseen truths put there by their authors. Therefore, I would like to begin by defining the way intended allegory works in the medieval dream vision and by surveying the conventions which I will argue mark these works as intended allegory.

The dream visions of the fourteenth century trace their inspiration to a work begun over a century earlier, the *Roman de la Rose.* In devising the form of his poem—a form from which his continuator Jean de Meun felt no need to depart—Guillaume de Lorris exploited a set of conventions whose compatibility had been discovered several decades before by the author of *Li Fablel dou dieu d'amours.*[4] Establishing an important vernacular tradition, that poet had combined the theme of love with the dream-vision format, personified abstractions, and a garden setting to create an allegorical love vision.

The operation of allegory in the medieval dream vision is inextricably linked with the genre's other conventions. The word "allegory" means "to speak other than openly"[5]—thus its Latin name, *inversio*, and its classical definition: to say one thing and mean another.[6] More precisely, though, and particularly in the case of medieval allegory, heir to the philosophical allegory of the ancient world, the relationship between allegory's two levels is that of sensible to intellectual. Since action is crucial to allegory, the figure is often described as a continued or extended metaphor.[7] The interplay among characters on the literal level of the work shows the relationship among the abstract or intellectual concepts with which the work deals. The characters define themselves through their actions.[8]

In a sense, then, the surface of an allegory is a puzzle. The reader must determine the precise significance of each character, that character's part in the whole, and the author's point. Because the form is open-ended, interpretation can be difficult.[9] Earlier medieval allegories may have offered interpretive keys at their conclusions, but the happenstance of Guillaume's *Roman de la Rose* being unfinished perhaps made it fashionable for allegorists to exploit allegory's natural relationship with enigma.[10]

In medieval literature, allegory was quintessentially related to irony, another figure which is open-ended and which says one thing to mean another.[11] Allegory and irony are crucially linked in Jean de Meun's part of the *Roman de la Rose* as the reader perceives in the play of characters the manipulation of ideas by which Jean leads him to draw his own conclusions about the love Amant seeks.

Since allegory's surface exists to communicate abstract ideas, it often uses surreal techniques to set those ideas into motion.[12] For this reason, an allegorical poem frequently employs the convention of a dream or vision so that the author can justify his unrealistic surface. Thus perhaps the most obvious signal that a medieval writer intends his work to be scrutinized for allegory is his use of the dream or vision format.[13] Dreams are enigmatic but filled with meaning, and writers early exploited the dream or vision as a means of putting a character in touch with his deepest impulses or with a world of reality beyond the personal. Classical and medieval dream theory complemented this literary use of the dream form.[14] In his systematization of ancient dream lore, Macrobius reserved for last and best place the *somnium,* which he defined as a dream "that conceals with strange shapes and veils with ambiguity the true meaning of the information being offered, and requires an interpretation for its understanding."[15] He saw in Cicero's Dream of Scipio both a *somnium* and a *narratio fabulosa,* or fiction which presents beneath a veil matters of sacred import.[16] In the Middle Ages, John of Salisbury picked up the Macrobian dream categories and made explicit the connection between Macrobius's *somnium*, or enigmatic dream, and allegorical writing. He defined the *somnium* as a dream which "stretches before the body of truth a curtain, as it were, of allegory."[17]

Guillaume de Lorris's direct model for the format of the *Roman de la Rose*, *Li Fablel dou dieu d'amours*, had already used the dream in combination with a love garden and personified abstractions. The dream had a long tradition as a device for validating the use of allegory in an otherwise realistic context.[18] The format was not new, but the popularity of the *Roman de la Rose* crystallized the genre for its subsequent practitioners. Thus the dream-vision format can signal that a work should be probed for allegory. The format shows us that the author is working in the tradition of that most famous medieval allegory, the *Roman de la Rose*, and there is a kind of natural connection, early recognized by dream theorists, between dreams and allegorical expression.

These dreams do not, however, as a modern reader might suppose, reveal only the idiosyncrasies of the dreamer's psyche—and this for two reasons. First, the medieval author of an allegorical dream vision was not interested in exploring the mind of an individual but rather in using the dream-allegory format as a means of dealing with a world more real than the narrative's surface.[19] Medieval allegory is used to *broaden* beyond the personal the realm with which an author deals, rather than to restrict it to the psyche of one individual character. Second, personal dreams use a private symbol system derived from the dreamer's own experience. Conversely, the medieval dream vision, with its aim of opening rather than restricting, uses what Rosemond Tuve has called "great public images."[20] An image which appears in an allegory with the purpose of representing an abstraction must pull its weight; thus the reader must see through the image to the abstraction which it signals. The surest and most usual way for a writer to make his symbols function is to tap into a tradition in which there is available a vocabulary of images whose possible meanings and interrelationships are already known to the audience. A writer working in the genre of the allegorical dream vision has available a vocabulary of symbols whose meanings are already established on account of their having functioned elsewhere.

Thus, working in a format that sets up in the mind of the reader an expectation of allegory, the writer draws on a vocabulary of symbols, already rich in meaning, which he can exploit and manipulate to serve his own purposes. It is not that the meanings of these symbols are totally circumscribed, but that the symbols delimit areas of meaning which the writer can play off against one another to create an allegorical surface whose accurate interpretation is available to a reader sharing the same cultural and literary tradition. Such motifs serve to place the work in the allegorical tradition, thus signaling to the reader that it is to be read allegorically, and they also usually possess accreted meanings deriving from their use and function in the tradition or traditions to which the writer is heir. We cannot deny to any writer working within a literary tradition—and what writer is not?—the meanings he can generate by manipulating images known to his audience from other contexts.

The characters who populate the late-medieval dream visions—both personifications and figures from classical mythology—are the most obvious examples of images available to an author by virtue of the fact that he is working in the genre of the allegorical vision poem. Personification of abstractions is often seen as the defining characteristic of allegory, or at least its most natural form.[21] Yet in a work such as the *Roman de la Rose*, Venus, a classical goddess, functions on the same plane as Amor, Deduit, Natura, and Genius—personified abstractions. Since a medieval audience would be aware of a god's traditional significance, a god would import into an allegory a nucleus of preexisting meanings from other works, classical and medieval, in which he had appeared.[22]

Besides characters with meanings ready to be deployed in the service of an author's purpose, writers also had available images whose traditional contexts had given them ready-made significance. The primary image known to those working in the genre of the allegorical dream vision was the garden. Though the garden was already long associated with the literature of love and had already been incorporated into the dream vision by the author of the *Fablel*, the combination of garden and dream was so rich in possibility that had the link not existed, Guillaume might well have forged it for himself.

The garden owed its accumulated meanings to three great traditions: Judeo-Christian, classical, and medieval.[23] The most famous garden in the Judeo-Christian tradition is of course the garden of Eden, with its paradoxical associations. It evokes man's perfect bliss in his unfallen state and the promised return to Eden for the regenerated human race, but it also recalls man's fall from grace. Nor can we escape the strong sexual connotations which biblical commentary had seen in the episode of man's fall.[24] Classical tradition too had its gardens; Ernst Robert Curtius has identified the *locus amoenus* or pleasance as a classical *topos*,[25] and the pleasance was frequently associated with love and the goddess of love in Latin literature.[26] Finally, the Provençal love lyric combined themes from Judeo-Christian and classical thought, employing the enclosed garden as a frequent locus for lovers' meetings and thoughts of love.[27]

The accumulated meanings the garden had gathered from these traditions made it ideally suited to Guillaume's purpose in the *Roman de la Rose*, as well as to that of his continuator Jean and all their imitators in the allegorical tradition. Because of the garden's associations with love and passion in the classical and Provençal traditions, the garden was the appropriate setting for a medieval poem purportedly dealing with romantic love. Yet the image was usefully ambiguous because the garden also had profound spiritual implications. It could evoke the state of unfallen man or the restored bliss offered the blessed, a parallel which Jean de Meun exploited when he made Genius contrast the garden of the white sheep with the garden of the Rose. These gardens are superficially identical, and each is devoted to love, yet the meaning of each garden is determined by the nature of the love for which it provides the setting. Thus the image itself is ripe for irony, and Jean, particularly, exploits it to its fullest potential. As the archetypal scene of temptation and fall, too, the garden lends itself to Guillaume's and Jean's purposes, particularly since the fall of man had come to have sexual connotations in the commentary tradition. The setting recalls that most famous story, and a similar pattern of temptation and fall causes us to seek and reflect on the common theme. The image seems to demand allegorical interpretation, both because it offers a rich complex of accreted meaning and because it evokes a pattern—temptation and fall—which is one of allegory's most natural themes.[28] The garden can also indicate that a poem is operating allegorically because it signals that a writer is working in the tradition of the *Roman de la Rose*. But not every poem in which a garden appears is an allegory. The writer must *use* the image in such a way as to exploit the rich body of significance that it owes its literary history. Because details are important to allegory, a detailed and precisely described garden is more likely to have allegorical significance than is one that is dispatched in a few lines.

Another image frequently used by the authors of medieval dream visions is the fountain; like the garden, its meaning is complex because of the traditions that lie behind it. The three gardens considered above almost always included fountains. In the Judeo-Christian tradition, there are the spring of Eden (Genesis 2.6) and the river of paradise with its four streams (Genesis 2.10–14). The classical *locus amoenus* usually includes a spring or brook, whereas in the Provençal love lyric the walled gardens associated with love often have fountains.[29] Because of the ambiguity it had derived from its use in these traditions, the fountain was richly applicable to the purposes of allegory and its related irony, suggesting refreshment for both the spirit and the body. When Guillaume de Lorris created the love garden of the *Roman de la Rose,* he had available immediately from *Li Fablel dou dieu d'amours,* but ultimately from these three traditions, the fountain as an important feature of the enclosed garden.[30] He adapted the fountain to his purpose brilliantly, however, by making it the well of Narcissus. Thus he added depth to the image by bringing in a classical figure whose meaning as an exemplum of self-love would be known to his audience. He also set up an implicit comparison, with ironic reverberations, between this fountain, with its implications of sterility, and the nourishing, fructifying fountains of Christian tradition.

The richest images available to the authors of allegorical dream visions, then, are double in their significance. The garden can serve human love or reflect the divine; the fountain can refresh or titillate. The most powerful personifications and mythological figures have this doubleness too. Amor's name evokes the myriad varieties of love, not just sexual, and Venus's double nature as Venus *scelestis* and Venus *celestis* goes far back in mythographic tradition.[31] If the key images and figures of the genre are ripe with potential for double meaning, but the writer is committed by his form, in its own essence and by its near alliance with irony, to work only on the surface, leaving unstated the interrelationship of ideas that is his work's aim, how then can the reader know whether Venus is good or bad, whether the fountain is nourishing or sinister? It is here that the writer's invention comes into play. He must be allowed his own initiative in the use of details, those details whose role in allegory is crucial because they shape that evaluation of character and action which is essential to allegory's success.[32]

It is thus the writer's *handling* of a multivalent image like the garden that restricts the range of meanings it can have. Of course, there is a constant play back and forth between the part and the whole, as the developing context limits meaning, but each image and each incident contribute to that context. A valid reading of an allegory must allow for the significance of each detail.[33]

Complex as an allegory's surface may be, then, with figures and images pointing to depths of meaning, allegorical plots are usually very simple.[34] Writers of allegory restrict themselves to a few basic narrative patterns, such as quest, marriage, or battle, because the patterns themselves can signal to the reader that a work is an allegory and can give important clues to its meaning. The very familiarity of a pattern makes the reader recall other such patterns and try to apply their significance to the work at hand.[35]

Allegory's themes, too, are simple. The writer of an allegory is fashioning a fable to which he hopes his audience will supply the gloss. To C. S. Lewis, allegory's natural theme is temptation, whereas to Rosemond Tuve, "there is in one sense only one allegorical theme, loss and salvation."[36] This simplicity of theme may be related to the fact that allegory's richest figures and images are multivalent—good Venus and bad Venus, fructifying fountain and sterile fountain—and that it is the writer's manipulation of his enigmatic surface, supplying details which magnify or diminish, that allows his meaning to emerge. With strong, basic oppositions as allegory's native themes, he manipulates his characters and images into opposing camps as he pits ideas against one another.

As Tuve has brilliantly shown, however, allegorical themes fall into two categories: moral allegory and strict allegory. Moral allegory pertains to matters of action, whereas strict allegory pertains to matters of belief, dealing with man's place in the universe. To

Tuve, medieval allegory depends on a "conception of man, as that creature whose property it is to be salvationis capax, who belongs to the kind that may be delivered from the ravishment of death and united to the heavenly original whence it sprang." The only real theme for strict allegory, she argues, is "the mystery of the soul's victory." Jean de Meun, she asserts, "is one of the few extant demonstrations that it is possible to have a secular allegory in the strict mediaeval sense, extending its explorations beyond moral interests to consider beliefs."[37]

Let us return now to the dream visions which are to occupy us in this chapter. The authors of these works have used the profoundly significant story of the Judgment, and its characters with their preexisting identities, to elaborate a surface through which the reader can glimpse the play of ideas—either moral, in the case of the first two works, or philosophical, in the case of the last—which is each work's *raison d'être*.

The earliest of the three works is Guillaume de Machaut's *Dit de la fonteinne amoureuse*, written between 1357 and 1364. The main character of the *Fonteinne amoureuse*, a lovelorn young nobleman, reenacts Paris's choice of love, receiving from Venus's hands the woman whom he desires.[38] To make the parallel clear, Machaut has Venus narrate the story of the Judgment. Machaut's use of the dream-vision form and his careful attention to details point to an allegorical dimension for the Judgment. The Judgment's allegorical significance is not *explained* as it was in the examples considered in Chapter 3; rather, our understanding of the truth Machaut intends us to perceive beneath the surface of the *Fonteinne amoureuse* develops from his manipulation of the poem's surface details.

Taking on the the persona of a poet-clerk much like himself, Machaut tells the story of an adventure with a young nobleman who is suffering from unrequited love. As a guest at the young man's court, his narrator, awake in the early hours of the morning, overhears and transcribes a lengthy *complainte* in which the miserable lover laments that he must soon leave his country, with no hint from his lady that his love is returned. He prays that as Morpheus made known to Alcyone the death of her husband Ceys, the god will make his lady understand that he is half dead of love. The *complainte* ends at dawn, and the narrator sets out to find the unhappy lover whose lament he has overheard. He makes his way to a hall filled with courtiers. Soon, to cries of "Here is my lord!" a handsome noble enters, obviously suffering from the physical effects of love. Approaching him privately, the narrator is cordially received. The nobleman invites him to enter his beautiful private garden and leads him to a fountain decorated with scenes from the story of Troy. This is the "fonteinne amoureuse"; those who drink its water fall hopelessly in love. He himself has drunk so much that he is nearly dead of love. He prays the narrator to write him a poem expressing his love longing, confiding that he must soon go into exile and leave behind the lady whom he so hopelessly loves. The narrator produces his copy of the noble's own *complainte* and explains how he came to transcribe it. Tired from their wakeful night, the two soon fall asleep. They dream that Venus appears, carrying a golden apple. She explains its significance by telling the story of the Judgment and then presents the lovelorn nobleman with his lady, who exchanges her ring for his. The two dreamers awake to find that their vision is gone but that the nobleman now wears his lady's ring. A few days later, the narrator accompanies the nobleman to the coast for his departure.

The *Fonteinne amoureuse* has traditionally been interpreted as a flattering portrait of the Duc de Berry, written to commemorate his marriage to Jeanne d'Armagnac and his journey to England as a hostage under the Treaty of Brétigny. The identification of the lovelorn nobleman as the duke was based on Ernest Hoepffner's solution to the anagram in the poem's prologue (lines 40–41).[39] I have argued elsewhere that Hoepffner's solution to the anagram is not convincing, and thus that the many references to the central character's departure, imprisonment, and exile cannot be considered evidence that the poem is about the adventures of a historical figure.[40] Moreover, I believe that Machaut's narrator is a fictional creation whose evaluation of the story he tells is not Machaut's own.[41] Indeed, rejecting the Duc de Berry as the poem's central character and Machaut himself as the narrator makes possible a far clearer view of the poem. If the *Fonteinne amoureuse* does not deal with Machaut's patron, it need not be a piece of flattery. Instead, Machaut has used the Judgment of Paris to reflect on the implications of a noble's devoting himself to love.

Though Machaut's narrator insists at the outset that his story will contain no villainy, claiming to prefer the unpleasantness of a thunderstorm to *mesdit* or caluminous speech (23–29), the *Fonteinne amoureuse* actually criticizes the nobility. By making his narrator a garrulous clerk who recalls himself from apparent digressions with lines such as, "But I wander from my purpose" (189), Machaut creates an excuse for passages inappropriate to a work which appears to glorify the life of the court. It is implied, for example, that some seek their lord's grace by flattery, adulation, plunder, and theft, rather than honor (177–80), and we are told that there are many whom one ought to serve well and believe badly—serve by doing what they demand but believe that they want to deceive (185–88). The young nobleman's entrance is followed by a passage intensely critical of the nobility. One can be rich in beauty but poor in loyalty, strong as Renouard but recreant and a coward. One who knows not a page of good can believe himself wise. Conversely, one can be rich yet have to beg for the common necessities of existence (1161–68). The criticism is explicit: "I say it for the rich men" (1169)—if they are not loyal, courageous, generous, and wise. They ought to arm themselves willingly because that is their *metier*. They ought to uphold justice and guard the Church, orphans, and widows (1170–83). Yet justice is in flight, the Church is destroyed, and widows and orphans are destitute. Unless God has mercy on the *preudommes* who are thus shirking their rightful duties, they will pay dearly for their error (1184–98).

Charles Muscatine declared Machaut's style incompatible with serious meaning.[42] Indeed, the elegance of his works has always belied their deeper purposes. If the *Fonteinne amoureuse* seems a romantic idyll with its gracious court, its walled pleasance, its ornamental fountain, its beautiful ladies, and its songs of love, Machaut's courtly style is self-conscious—a matter of choice, not an unthinking response to convention. Machaut states explicitly that his poem's surface is an elegant falsehood. He virtually announces his allegorical purpose and his irony by alerting his readers to a second layer of meaning in the *Fonteinne amoureuse*. He plays with double-meaning statements which seem to invite his audience to reexamine its values. After the passage in which he contrasts the

noble class's ideal with its reality, playing on the meanings of words
such as "rich," "poor," and "wise," he concludes, "Now I want to
leave this matter and return to the first because sometimes one
makes things worse by speaking of good and truth" (1201–4). He
thus implies that the poem's courtly surface is neither good nor
true. The surface elegance, though, may be necessary if Machaut is
to present his ideas to a noble audience.

A passage very early in the poem seems to invite his audience to
look beneath the surface of the poem for its truth:

> Now I pray those who read it, who choose the good from the bad, if
> there is any, that they be willing in the reading to leave aside the bad,
> to choose the good. Because when the thing is truly perfect [*bien
> eslite*], one naturally enjoys it more, and ladies and he who reads it
> ought to take greater pleasure in it, and let him by whom it will be
> read be numbered among the elect [*esleüs*]. (13–22)

"Eslite" can mean "perfect," but it can also mean "chosen out";
Machaut plays with the same root in "esleüs." Perhaps the reader
who *chooses out* the deeper meaning from beneath the courtly surface is a *chosen* one who sees a deeper meaning to the work, while a
less perceptive audience considers the courtly portions the "good"
and the criticisms "bad."

Crucial to Machaut's aim in the *Fonteinne amoureuse* is the
poem's structure as a dream vision. The dream-vision form both demands and justifies allegorical interpretation. Here two traditions
we have traced from ancient times come together. For Dares the
dream was a rationalizing device; without demanding belief in the
pagan supernatural, it explained why Paris felt entitled to Menelaus's wife. Generations of medieval historians found the motif
useful as they produced histories of the ancient world for Christian
Europe. Now the dream of the Judgment serves a different but related purpose. It creates an expectation of allegory and thus allows
into the *Fonteinne amoureuse* a world of ideas both more and less
real than that with which the poem's surface deals.

Machaut may have been inspired by one particular source, though,
when he decided to place the Judgment of Paris in the context of a
dream. He took his Judgment mainly from the *Ovide moralisé*,

which uses the classical version of the story rather than that of Dares. When the divine embassy approaches him, Paris is a shepherd who does not know that he is really the son of a king. Machaut elaborated the story in various ways, however, and two details lead to an additional source for the episode.

Paris carries with him a richly ornamented bow and a set of arrows which Hecuba gave him; he is a very good archer, we are told, "if the history [or story] does not lie" (1891–98). The only place I have seen a reference to Paris's skill in archery is the second redaction of the *Histoire ancienne*, discussed in Chapter 2. Clearly influenced by the tradition of Dares and Benoît, the version of the Judgment in this history makes Paris sleep when the goddesses approach but then wake up for the Judgment. Machaut could easily have supplemented the *Ovide moralisé* with a history such as this; he even implies that he used such a source when he says, "if the history does not lie." That Machaut was familiar with a version of this widespread work is suggested too by his acquaintance with the ancient tradition that Paris was beautiful. Venus calls Paris "very beautiful" (1883). The second redaction of the *Histoire ancienne* knew this tradition, but the *Ovide moralisé* did not.

In keeping with his poem's structure as a dream vision, Machaut has included the enclosed garden, whose traditional associations made it richly enigmatic. The garden itself could serve as an isolating device, cutting characters off from the mundane in a landscape whose features could have an allegorical dimension. In the *Fonteinne amoureuse*, the narrator and the nobleman enter the garden before their dream begins, yet the garden has unrealistic elements—the images and details essential to a work of allegory.

Although it is appropriate for the nobleman to lead the narrator into his private garden, the garden of the *Fonteinne amoureuse* has characteristics it would not need if its function in the poem were purely realistic. After a description of its beautiful meadows, closely planted trees, and echoing birdsong, the narrator says that the garden contains all fruits, trees, flowers, plants, and everything of good that can be found (1349–65). In fact, it is more beautiful than even the terrestrial paradise (1367–70). In its perfection, this garden cannot fail to recall the many associations which the garden had by this time accumulated in Western literature, thus creating expectations for the poem's action to fulfill or play against. Like the garden of the *Roman de la Rose*, it evokes the traditional love garden, and so we expect Machaut's poem to deal with romantic love. The garden also recalls its spiritual counterpart, however. Thus we wait to see whether the love it offers will have a spiritual dimension or seem barren because the garden creates an expectation that the poem's action does not fulfill. Further, the association with the garden of Eden suggests that perhaps a choice will occur.

The garden is such an enigmatic image, with associations both spiritual and sensual, that Machaut's purpose in using it could easily be obscure. We must look, however, for those details which magnify or diminish,[43] thus focusing the image morally. The nobleman explains to his guest that the garden was once the trysting place of Cupid, Jupiter, and Venus (1381–89), making the significance of the garden clearer. Jupiter was responsible for the end of the golden age.[44] When he seized control of his father's throne, he established a reign based only on delight, described by Jean de Meun in the *Roman de la Rose* (20071–84 [3.103]). It is most appropriate then that Jupiter should value the garden for the pleasure it gives him, yet the garden thus becomes associated with the licentious activities of the pagan gods and with the end of the golden age. More than one thinker—including Jean de Meun—had seen in the pagan golden age an analogue to the Christian garden of Eden.[45] The mention of Venus and Cupid also helps to place the garden morally. Venus was linked with the end of the classical golden age; an ancient tradition had it that she was born from Saturn's severed genitals when Jupiter castrated his father.[46]

Frequently connected with the garden in both its heavenly and earthly manifestations, the fountain is also a richly ambiguous image. Machaut's *fonteinne amoureuse* enamors those who drink from it—no mortal creature can escape (1408–10). The fountain has made many a lady joyful, but many a lover has died of love on its account (1412–20). In case its fatal powers are not sufficient to place the fountain morally, Machaut provides abundant details to identify the *fonteinne amoureuse* as an inversion of the fructifying fountain his audience would have known from the Judeo-Christian tradition.

The fountain, we are told, was Jupiter's idea (1393). Its base, a great pillar of ivory, is decorated with the story of Narcissus. Therefore, sheep, harts, and "brown beasts" refuse to drink from it (1304–9). The marble portions feature scenes from the story of Troy, including Paris's seduction of Helen. Venus is depicted as the *maquerelle* who brought the lovers together, and she carries the smokeless torch with which she enflamed Helen's passion (1313–24). There are also scenes of battle (1330–40). Water enters the fountain through a golden, twelve-headed serpent (1343–48). Venus is responsible for the carvings on the ivory base and marble basin— she commissioned Pygmalion to do them—and Jupiter gave the gold from which the serpent was made (1394–98).

Through details, then, Machaut makes the meaning of this particular fountain clear, subtly diminishing with a well-chosen word or an ironic juxtaposition. The fountain is decorated with scenes from the story of Troy. This type of *ecphrasis* was a common literary technique with its roots in ancient times.[47] In some cases, scenes used for decorative purposes in literary descriptions have no particular significance, or their significance is purely thematic. In the *Fonteinne amoureuse*, however, the scenes on the fountain work with other details in the poem to focus the allegory. The fountain might seem to depict Paris and Helen on its marble basin because it celebrates the romantic love which they exemplify. Yet Venus is described as Paris's *maquerelle*, a procuress or bawd (1320), and Helen's love for Paris is presented as a fevered and undignified response to Venus's torch (1321–24). Like Jean de Meun, Machaut undercuts a courtly approach to love by showing its basis in lust. Juxtaposed with Paris and Helen's love on the fountain is the unsuccessful love of Troilus for Briseÿda. Further, the tragic effects of Paris's love for Helen are indicated by a scene depicting the battle between Hector and Achilles.

Other details bring with them long-established meanings from earlier contexts. Machaut borrowed from the *Roman de la Rose* the association between Narcissus, the classic paradigm of self-love, and a fountain that provokes love (1430–1520 [1.44–47]). Making the fountain's base depict the story of Narcissus implies that the love offered by the *fonteinne amoureuse* is based—literally—on love of self, as the lover admires in his lady's eyes his new courtly self. It is significant too that sheep and harts refuse to drink from the fountain *because* Narcissus's story is depicted on its base. Both sheep and harts are associated in Christian tradition with fountains which offer the water of salvation. In the second part of the *Roman de la Rose,* Genius describes the garden of the Good Shepherd, in which the good sheep drink from a fountain that quenches their thirst and preserves them from sickness and death, and he contrasts this fountain with the fountain of Narcissus in the garden of Pleasure (20356–94 [3.112–13]). The hart figures in Psalm 41, where the psalmist compares the desire of the virtuous man for God with the desire of the hart for the fountain. Thus, the fact that sheep and harts avoid the *fonteinne amoureuse* suggests that the water which it offers does not satisfy or nourish. It is appropriate too that Pygmalion is the sculptor who decorated the fountain with the stories of Troy and Narcissus. He is associated, as is the fountain, with idolatrous love.

Finally, there is the twelve-headed serpent through which water enters the fountain and whose gold was furnished by Jupiter. The serpent seems misplaced in a garden of love, but its image has great power to indicate a moral slant. One thinks of the Eden story with its own garden, and one thinks of temptation and fall. Interpreting the Judgment, Machaut's main source, the *Ovide moralisé,* calls Satan "the chief [*chiez*] of wrath and discord."[48] Medieval French allows a nice pun: *chiez* can mean either "head" or "chief," so the chief of discord is given visual form as a serpent with twelve heads, and the fountain thus becomes linked with Satan's seduction of Eve in the garden of Eden. It is further appropriate that Jupiter gave the gold from which the serpent was made. He was associated in the *Roman de la Rose* with the end of the classical golden age, which Jean de Meun had made Genius compare to the garden of the Good Shepherd (20166–20236 [3.106–8]). Thus the world over which Jupiter presides is implicitly a fallen one. The ironic implication is that when he deprived the world of its golden age, its unfallen Eden, he transmuted the "gold" into this tempting fountain; its water does not restore blessedness but induces a hopeless love which kills its victims.

Machaut, then, uses the conventions established by the genre of the dream vision to create a landscape with profound moral overtones. It is not the mere presence of the fountain, for example, nor the fact that the adventure takes place in a pleasant landscape—we have seen a similar setting and similar details in Benoît and other writers who handled the Judgment. It is the fact that Machaut has provided details which clearly lead us to *interpret*. His dream is a dream vision, and all the details which surround it are the apparatus of allegory. His garden recalls the Eden of Adam and Eve's temptation and fall, and it evokes the decline of the classical golden age. The setting is charged with meaning, and as his characters act, they define themselves morally against this backdrop.

The nobleman who is the poem's main character is not an allegorical figure, nor is the poet-clerk who functions as narrator. The nobleman is merely a typical nobleman, the narrator a typical clerk. The meaning of the nobleman's actions, though, is clarified first by the allegorical landscape and second by Venus's narration of the Judgment.

The dream, then, is crucial to Machaut's purpose in the *Fonteinne amoureuse*. The dream communicates hidden truth: the narrator says that he considers it "true and good," whoever else might consider it a fable (1567–68). In the dream, Venus tells the nobleman that she has brought him his lady, then turns to the narrator and, in answer to his unspoken question about the writing on her golden apple, tells the story of the Judgment. The Judgment is a fable. When the narrator says he considers the dream true, he means that, though the story might seem opaque, he sees the truth beneath its surface. The Judgment's allegorical dimension is made clear again: "When Venus had finished her speech, in which there was no fable [*parabole*]—because anyone could understand it—she said to *me* without more delay . . . " (1625–28; my italics). The words without fable were Venus's words to the nobleman; what follows—the story of the Judgment—*is* fable, a veiled truth appropriate to an enigmatic dream.

Venus begins her story with the Wedding of Peleus and Thetis, but Machaut makes her glance ahead to the fall of Troy and the suffering of its citizens (1633–60), as if he wants to keep before the eyes of his audience the tragic effects of Paris's love. Venus then continues her narrative with a detailed description of the wedding festivities. All the gods and goddesses were invited except Discord.

Angry, she arrived without invitation and threw before Juno, Pallas, and Venus the golden apple which Venus now carries, crying in a loud voice, "Let it be given to the most beautiful!" (1737). Each goddess claimed the apple, and a furious debate ensued. At last, Mercury took the apple and referred the task of judgment to Jupiter, but Jupiter, fearing the anger of the two goddesses he would have to reject, passed the duty on to Paris of Troy.

Led by Mercury, the three goddesses approached Paris as he tended his animals in solitude. He was very beautiful, says Venus—much too beautiful to watch sheep: "Because he was decked out so fine that he seemed well to be the son of a king" (1885–86). He carried an elaborate bow given him by his mother, Hecuba. Mercury revealed to Paris his true ancestry: he was not the son of shepherds but of Priam and Hecuba. His mother's dream of a flaming torch that would destroy the city almost resulted in his death, but Hecuba arranged for him to be taken away and raised in obscurity. After explaining his background, Mercury entrusted Paris with the Judgment of the goddesses. Each goddess presented her case to the shepherd, and each offered him a gift in exchange for the apple. Pallas would make him the wisest man in the world, and Juno would make him richest, but Venus would give him the most beautiful woman who ever existed. Swayed by the promise of Venus, Paris claimed her as his goddess and awarded her the apple. Her gift was the love of Helen.

Since Machaut took the outline of his Judgment from the *Ovide moralisé*, he must have been aware of the episode's allegorization there. The author of the *Ovide moralisé* used the interpretation which, stemming ultimately from Fulgentius, had come to dominate medieval treatments of the Judgment. In the *Ovide moralisé*, the golden apple is compared to the apple that caused Adam and Eve's fall, and Paris is given a choice among Juno's active life, Pallas's contemplative life, and Venus's voluptuous life. The voluptuous life is "very harmful and damaging" (11.2441–42). He who prefers it to the others is "determined and eager to seek all fleshly delight" (11.2428–29). As Paris chooses Venus, the *Ovide moralisé* says, "For this gift, one should lose . . . all other paradise" (11.2113–14). The significance of Paris's choice is summarized thus:

By Paris, who gave the apple to Venus, one might signify a man who places all his intent on living pleasurably in the world, at ease and in repose, and has no interest in any other matter except to carry out his foolish will, even though sorrow might come of it. (12.829–36)

The moral interpretation of the Judgment is relevant to the *Fonteinne amoureuse* because the plot of the poem reenacts the Judgment.[49] Machaut makes his young nobleman resemble Paris, and thus the interpretation of the Judgment colors our moral evaluation of the poem's main character. In describing how the young prince Paris looked when the divine embassy approached him for judgment, Venus says, "he was decked out so fine that he seemed well to be the son of a king" (1885–86). The nobleman, who is likewise the son of a king, is described in nearly identical words. As he is introduced early in the poem, the narrator says, "he was decked out so fine that he seemed well to be the son of a king" (1157–58). Machaut departs from the *Ovide moralisé* to make Paris an archer who owns a beautiful bow. As the nobleman enters his private park, a chevalier offers him a "very fine bow" (1294). He refuses it, explaining that his garden pleases him enough, but it is clear that he must often use the bow and thus a further parallel with Paris is established. But the most important parallel is the role of Venus in the lives of the two men. As depicted on the fountain, Venus is the go-between who united Paris with his beloved, Helen. Now, in the *Fonteinne amoureuse,* she presents the nobleman, who seems, like Paris, to be the son of a king, with his beloved lady. That Froissart, basing his *Espinette amoureuse* on Machaut's poem, made his narrator explicitly reenact Paris's judgment of the goddesses suggests that he saw Machaut's nobleman reenacting Paris's role.

The poet makes it clear that accepting his lady from Venus represents for the nobleman a choice of lives as crucial as was Paris's choice when he awarded the apple to Venus. Completing her story of the Judgment, Venus quotes Paris's statement of commitment to a life of love (2133–37). But the sleeping nobleman, complains Venus, knows nothing of her power, has no faith in her, and does not call upon her when he endures the torments of love. Nor has he offered her any sacrifices. These oversights, though, have been due to folly or ignorance, and she has determined to have pity on him

by uniting him with his lady (2145–70). By the time the nobleman's lady has assured him of her love and the two dreamers have
awakened, the man has, like Paris, firmly committed himself to
Venus and love (2543–47). He determines further that he will build
a temple to the goddess where henceforth he will offer sacrifice
(2557–60). That he now wears on his finger the ruby that his lady
placed there while taking his diamond for herself (2522–26) suggests that indeed his choice was real: that his dream was not just
the imagined satisfaction of his desire but a firm commitment to
the life represented by Venus.

The poem's plot is then as simple as the plot of any allegory: it
deals with a choice. By the end of the *Fonteinne amoureuse*, the
nobleman has so firmly committed himself to Venus that he has
promised to build a temple to the goddess and worship her henceforth. In order to emphasize the parallel with the Trojan prince's
choice of Venus and to create an atmosphere that invites allegorical
interpretation, Machaut has made Venus relate in a dream the whole
story of the Judgment. The myth's long tradition of allegorization, represented by one of Machaut's sources, the *Ovide moralisé*,
makes it hard to see the Judgment as anything other than a fable
whose deeper significance has moral application.

If we take into account the garden and the fountain, and the fact
that the nobleman's situation parallels that of Paris, it seems obvious that Machaut is criticizing the nobleman's actions. His garden and fountain parody their spiritual counterparts. Rather than
offering repose and nourishment, they create restless longings for
insubstantial goods. With its suggestion of the garden of Eden, the
garden is the locus for a fall, and the nobleman chooses Venus there,
as did Paris, an act which the *Ovide moralisé* had seen as the
choice of damnation. Like Christine de Pisan's *Othéa*, Machaut's
Dit de la fonteinne amoureuse sees a nobleman's responsibilities as
a serious issue, and Machaut uses allegory to indicate where this
particular nobleman falls short.

In the *Espinette amoureuse*, written late in 1369 and strongly influenced by the *Fonteinne amoureuse*, Jean Froissart is even more
explicit than was Machaut in identifying one of his characters with
Paris.[50] Early in the poem, Froissart's narrator reenacts Paris's judgment of the goddesses, and the rest of the *Espinette amoureuse*

shows the implications of his choice. Froissart's narrator is not a noble responsible for the welfare of those he governs, but a young man at the age when young men turn to love. His reenactment of the Judgment confirms the direction that his life will take: he is a lover but his love is destined to be unrequited. Through almost four thousand lines, he attempts to win mercy from a lady who, it becomes more and more obvious, has no interest in him. Though the comical details of the affair suggest that Froissart regards the young man's devotion to love as folly, the allegorical implications of the Judgment are crucial too in evaluating the love which the narrator pursues.[51]

Given an opportunity to revise Paris's judgment, the narrator declares that the Trojan prince's choice of Venus and her gift of Helen was correct. In gratitude, Venus promises that he will soon experience love. Her promise appears to come true when the narrator meets a young lady and is immediately smitten with her. He sees her frequently and tries to reveal his love. Eventually he hears that she may soon be married, and in his despair he succumbs to a fever which lasts over three months. At length recovered, he goes abroad, taking with him his lady's mirror, given him by her *confidante*. One night, asleep with the mirror under his pillow, he dreams that he sees in it the image of his beloved and that she tells him she loves him faithfully. He returns to France, where the young woman eventually agrees to accept his love, though almost immediately afterward she explains that because of scandal-mongers he must avoid her presence. One evening he encounters her as he lurks near her house. He asks her to come near, but she rebuffs him, then approaches and tugs at his forelock, pulling out some hairs. He decides that her act was a lover's gesture, and the *Espinette amoureuse* concludes with songs in praise of love.

Like Machaut's *Dit de la fonteinne amoureuse*, this work has often been considered autobiographical. Its narrator journeys abroad, as Froissart traveled to England, and is entertained as a well-known poet. Further, the *Espinette amoureuse* includes an anagram which the narrator says reveals his name and that of his lady.[52] The journey abroad need not mean, though, that the entire poem is a true story or that Froissart's intention in writing it was to record his own experience. The details of the journey in the *Espinette amoureuse* do not harmonize precisely with what is known of Froissart's life from the *Chronicles*,[53] and the journey may derive from literary influence rather than fact: in Machaut's *Dit de la fonteinne amoureuse*, the lover laments a journey which will separate him from his beloved.[54] Further, were the poem based on Froissart's own experience, the details of the journey would be incompatible with the age of his narrator at the time of the love affair. The adventure which the *Espinette amoureuse* recounts began in its narrator's youth; he played children's games (143–50; also 127–32) and was still under the patronage of Mercury (421–26). At this age, he could hardly have been in real life a well-known poet. Nor is it likely that so young a man would truly have been to Narbonne and traveled through France and to Avignon (794–95) as Froissart makes his narrator claim at one point. In these sections of the poem, Froissart is attributing to his fictional persona details of his own experience. Again there is literary precedent. Machaut's narrators too reflect aspects of their creator when he makes them poet-clerks who are welcomed into noble households.

Nor must we interpret the anagram as evidence that the poem is based on a true story. The narrator tells us (4183–85) that his name and that of his lady appear in four lines between "Nous fumes" (3338) and "Le tamps" (3426). From these eighty-eight lines, the following four, picked out by Fourrier, have been accepted as those to which Froissart refers:

> *Je ha*ntoie la tempre et tart,
> Dont *frois*, dont chau*s*, navrés dou d*art*
> D'Amours, et lors de flours petites,
> Violettes et *margerites*
> Semoie dessus le tapis. . . . (3386–90)[55]

> [I lurked there early and late, whether it was cold or hot, wounded by the dart of love, and I strewed small flowers, violets and daisies, on the carpet. . . .]

Froissart's name is obvious, as is the word *margerite*, and it has been assumed that since Froissart celebrated the name *Marguerite* in other poetry, the *Espinette amoureuse* chronicles an affair with the woman whom he elsewhere praises.[56] The Marguerite whom

Froissart celebrated in his other work need not, however, have been a woman with whom he was in love. Many late-medieval poets wrote poetry celebrating the marguerite, or daisy, and exploited the pun on the name *Marguerite* without necessarily referring to a real-life love affair.[57] What better name for a fictional beloved in the *Espinette amoureuse* than a name for which convention had sanctioned poetry of praise?[58] Further, the anagram teases us: there are *two* names to confuse the reader. "Violettes et margerites" line 3389 reads.[59] Further, the lady's surname has never been satisfactorily identified,[60] and judging from the anagram's form, I doubt that a surname is present. The syllables appear in the order in which they are to be read, and *margerites* appears at the end of the fourth line. A final point calls into question the identification of either flower as a woman's name. When he directs the reader's attention to the anagram, Froissart says that he wanted to arrange it without naming name, surname, or letter (4179–80). How could he thus intend the whole word *margerite* or *violette* as the solution to the puzzle? The anagram, then, does not seem convincing evidence that the *Espinette amoureuse* is autobiographical.

It is important to establish the fictional nature of the *Espinette amoureuse* because viewing the work as autobiography impedes an understanding of Froissart's purpose. The poem is not a celebration of the author's youthful romance, but rather a fiction whose every detail Froissart has wrought in such a way as to reveal his narrator's folly in choosing, like Paris, a life of love and then persisting in his choice despite the overwhelming evidence that his love is not returned.[61]

Froissart's narrator has a certain distance, both chronological and psychological, from the younger self whose story he tells.[62] It is clear that he is older because he says that in his youth he valued a chaplet of violets to give the girls more than he now values a count's gift worth twenty marks of silver (289–93). He often laments, too, from his more mature perspective, the sorrows that love has brought him. Recounting his first meeting with the lady whom he was to love, he states that since then he has paid dearly (834). The poem opens with the reflection that if young people knew the sorrows that love brings, they would not want to attempt it (1–8).

Though the narrator admits he suffered greatly on account of his love, he does not understand the reason for his suffering and continues to praise love as the source of all good. He says, for example, that the recollection of his love provides his life with a sweet nourishment (62–66). A man cannot better use his time, he asserts, than in loving well because love nurtures noble qualities (78–83). Love and his lady have taught him a good way to grow in value; the fault is his if he has not retained all the good they brought him (115–19). If he had any excuse, it is that perhaps he was too young and ignorant (124–26). It does not occur to him that if he has not profited from love it is because love does not bring profit. He believes that love itself is above reproach and that any dissatisfaction he feels is his own fault (127–38, 277–82). Having fallen in love, he regards himself as perfected (798–99). Acknowledging how he has suffered, he says that he has nevertheless enjoyed all that love taught him (835–36). Summarizing his experiences at the end of the poem, he concludes that he would have nothing of value were it not for love (3871–72) and that no matter what happens, he will love no one but his lady (3902–3).

Since the narrator remains committed to his lady and to love throughout the *Espinette amoureuse*, Froissart's criticism of the affair can only be indirect. Thus the Judgment of Paris plays a crucial role in the poem's meaning. The Judgment appears early in the work because the choice that the narrator makes when asked his opinion of Paris's decision determines the adventure which the *Espinette amoureuse* chronicles.

Froissart keeps separate, in a way that Machaut did not, the visionary and nonvisionary portions of his poem, and the setting of the vision is not so rich in significant details as was the case in the *Fonteinne amoureuse*. Nevertheless, the vision is presented in such a way as to show unmistakably that it is a dream vision in the tradition of the *Roman de la Rose* or the *Fonteinne amoureuse* and thus invites allegorical interpretation. In its clear identification as a dream vision and in its introduction of supramundane characters, in fact, the Judgment portion of the poem differs considerably from the later dream in which the narrator seems to see his beloved.[63]

On a lovely May morning, the narrator enters a little garden where birds sing as if in contest. Sitting beneath a hawthorne bush—the *espinette* of the poem's title—he is suddenly "caught up in a

thought" (395). Before him he sees Mercury and the three goddesses. Mercury calls him by name, as if he knows him well, claiming that the narrator has been in his patronage since the age of four.
He introduces the three goddesses and explains that they are arguing over Paris's decision to award the golden apple to Venus. Juno is
angriest: Paris could have won vengeance on the Greeks but chose
rather the worthless Helen, the deaths of his family, and a cruel
war. Mercury asks the narrator's opinion of Paris's choice. The narrator fears that he will be unable to answer well because he is ignorant of sense and ruler of few possessions, but Mercury urges that
he is therefore better able to tell the truth. The narrator concludes
that since Paris knew he was a king's son who would eventually
possess a fortune and since he felt young, strong, and brave, he did
not want to give the apple to Juno or Pallas. Thus his choice of
Venus was correct because he fell in love with Helen and made her
his sovereign lady. Mercury departs, leaving the narrator melancholy. He would gladly have remained with the god the length of a
summer, he says; he profited greatly from Mercury's presence and
considers himself his son (525–30). Juno and Pallas leave also, but
Venus remains behind, promising the narrator a great reward for his
judgment: he will love, obey, and fear a beautiful young lady.

Froissart's use of the Judgment has much in common with Machaut's and was most likely inspired by the *Fonteinne amoureuse*,[64]
but Froissart's treatment of the episode is in certain respects original. Though he gives much less play to the story's narrative possibilities (perhaps assuming that the tale was already familiar to his
audience), he changes the characters of some of the deities involved. Following classical tradition, he associates Pallas with arms
rather than wisdom (493–500),[65] but he transforms Juno's traditional hatred for the Trojans into a promise that, had Paris chosen
her, she would have favored the Trojans in the war (440–44),[66] having apparently forgotten that, had Paris chosen Juno, the war would
never have started. Most striking, though, is his treatment of Mercury, who has an expanded role in the Judgment.

Froissart stresses Mercury's traditional associations with learning and eloquence, associations strengthened by the occasional
portrayal of the god as a scribe, teacher, or even bishop.[67] Mercury
is introduced as a "man of great renown" (400), under whose patron-

age children learn to walk and speak (401–4). He has had the narrator in his tutelage from early childhood.[68] The narrator admires Mercury and enjoys his company (407–8); when the god departs, he feels a sense of loss: "I would willingly have been with him a summer longer" (527–28).

Since Froissart identifies Mercury as a figure of authority, Mercury's gloss on the Judgment is probably significant. Mercury says that Paris was foolish when he gave the apple to Venus; he lost power and dignity for a little vanity. His father, his brothers, and his mother died cruel deaths, and thousands of men went to war. The evil apple was dearly bought by the Trojans, and the love Venus promised was miserably requited because by it Paris brought war to the Trojans (445–66). Mercury clarifies the Judgment's moral implications and makes the narrator's decision in favor of Venus seem the action of a fool. When the narrator has declared himself in sympathy with Paris's choice, Mercury pulls back and states, "I knew it well! All the lovers take that road" (523–24). Mercury sees the narrator's decision as a choice between paths or roads, a theme to be made concrete in the *Echecs amoureux*.

That the decision in favor of Venus was unwise becomes obvious during the narrator's subsequent experience in love. Paris won Helen but caused the fall of Troy; the narrator of the *Espinette amoureuse* cannot even win his lady. Venus promised that he would love (564–66), but she never promised that his love would be returned. The words with which she granted the narrator his reward were, in fact, ambiguous: "Gentle son, is it a fine thing to do this? You can prove [*prouver*] it here" (536–38). *Prouver* can mean "test" as well as "prove." The young man may believe that his adventure will *prove* his choice of Venus correct, but he is actually *testing* the wisdom of that choice. To watch the progress of the relationship is to see that his love is unsatisfying and unprofitable. In his belief that his lady cares for him, he is only deluding himself.[69]

The narrator's overtures toward his lady are ignored, willfully misunderstood, and refused. Early in the affair, he sends her a book in which he has inserted a *balade* declaring his love; when she returns the book, the *balade* is untouched (945–59). He picks her a rose but must beg her to accept it (986–1002). When he finally confesses his love, she asks, "Is it sensible that you should want to love me?" (1121–22). At the suggestion of her *confidante,* he writes a song requesting love. The lady responds that he is asking for a lot (1296) and adds that he can have none of it. Despite these signs of indifference, the narrator is convinced that his lady is gradually coming to love him. He believes he can read her unspoken feelings in her face, interpreting her glances as looks of love (1179–82, 1227–32, 1928–30).

The dream in which his lady seems to grant the narrator her love, thus impelling him to return to France, is a further example of self-delusion. Like an *insomnium* in which the lover "dreams of possessing his sweetheart,"[70] it reflects his own desires and provides a rationalization for his lady's indifference. In the dream, she states that her heart and her love are his (2833, 2905), thus granting him that for which he has longed, and she also explains that she has always loved him secretly (2966–67). Henceforth she will show her love (2968). Her previous behavior was a test of his loyalty (2971–74). Fear of scandal-mongers, too, has caused her to abstain from revealing her love (2771–75). Even the story he cites as precedent for seeing one's distant beloved in a mirror is an example of wishful thinking (2673–2724). Ydoree and Papirus were separated lovers whose magic mirrors allowed each to have the other's image always present. To compare his lady and himself to this pair is to beg the question whose answer can come only from the lady.

The dream persuades the narrator to persist in his unhappy affair even though subsequent developments in the relationship make his persistence obvious folly. The lady's response when he at length greets her and affirms his love is to look at him, laugh, look away, and declare to the *confidante* that he is no worse for his voyage (3314–24). His devotion only amuses her. Testing his obedience, she threads flowers on currant thorns and makes him kiss them, twice pricking himself, then she laughs (3529–31). Perhaps most cruelly, she finally agrees to accept him as her loyal, secret servant, but then almost immediately claims that because gossips are criticizing the affair, she will speak to him no more and he must stay away from her house.

Even her final, startling act of mockery, however, does not deter the narrator from his devotion to his lady. As she passes him one evening, he asks her to come near, but she rebuffs him. Then she approaches and violently tugs his forelock. She quickly returns to her house while he remains behind, sadly contemplating this strange gesture and almost repenting the folly of his devotion. His talent for rationalization soon takes over, however, and he concludes that his lady would never have teased him if she did not love him. In his mind, the incident becomes cause for rejoicing, and he writes a *balade* and a *lay* pledging his continued service. As the poem ends, he is determined to persist in his love.

The *Espinette amoureuse* examines the power and effects of romantic love in the life of an individual. The young man who is the poem's hero is precisely the age at which young men tend toward love, and it is almost, but not quite, inevitable that when asked to comment on Paris's choice he should choose love. In the *Joli buisson de jonece*, Froissart was to make the planets patrons of life's stages. As in the *Espinette amoureuse*, Mercury would be placed in charge of a child's development from age four to fourteen (1625–32), the child then being handed over to Venus for ten years. I knew it well, says Mercury, when the narrator has chosen; every lover chooses that path.

The Judgment functions allegorically here in that the dream-vision form and the conventional landscape bring meaning to the narrator's choice of Venus. The narrator is like Amant in the *Roman de la Rose:* a typical young man about to embark on life. Confronted with Mercury and the three goddesses in a landscape that recalls the garden of the *Roman de la Rose*, he chooses Venus. Because Froissart makes the narrator explicitly reenact the Judgment of Paris in a landscape with allegorical significance, we are justified in seeing the Judgment's traditional allegorical significance in Froissart's use of it here.

Froissart exploits the Judgment's allegorical resonance by pursuing the choice-of-lives theme all through the *Espinette amoureuse*. The narrator's vision of the goddesses and his endorsement of Paris's decision only confirm a choice that he already made long ago. Very early in the poem, he states that his nature inclines toward love (48–51). He later declares, in a context which makes clear what his choice will be, "We have only a little while to live; thus it is good to choose a life. . . ." (73–74). That his choice of love is truly the choice of a *life* is shown when he learns from Venus the full significance of endorsing Paris's choice: He will be her *servans rentieri* [in a sense, her "serf"] for ten years (605–6). Thus his choice of Venus has confirmed his own tendency toward love, the dream both revealing his own nature and giving him an opportunity, which he does not take, to make a wiser choice.

Perhaps, however, Froissart means to imply that, though young men are inevitably drawn to love, a wiser choice is available. Traditional interpretations of the Judgment had stressed that Paris was free to choose among the three lives; it was to his grief that he chose the worst. Because he agrees with Paris's choice, the narrator must give Venus ten years as *servans rentieri*, and then remain *all his life* in her service (607–8). Young men tend toward love from the age of fourteen to twenty-four, as Froissart's scheme in the *Joli buisson de jonece* was to have it (1637–38); by choosing Venus in the reenactment of the Judgment, the narrator condemns himself to serve her for his entire life.

The *Joli buisson de jonece* can shed considerable light on Froissart's use of the Judgment. In this later work, which looks back on the events narrated in the *Espinette amoureuse*, the narrator concludes that Venus lied to him. He continued to love his lady without return for ten years, but by the end of the *Joli buisson de jonece* he has exchanged romantic love for spiritual commitment: he has at last chosen another life.[71]

Froissart's poem is less serious than was Machaut's. Machaut used the Judgment to reflect on the nature of his nobleman's love affair. He stressed the parallel between Paris, the prince who destroyed his father's kingdom, and this "king's son" who, like Paris, accepted his lady from the hands of Venus. The welfare of the realm was at stake in the *Fonteinne amoureuse*, and using the Judgment was only one of the indirect ways by which Machaut criticized the preoccupations of his audience. In the *Espinette amoureuse*, on the other hand, the youth's actions harm no one but himself, and they amuse an audience which cannot help but recognize the great gulf between what he believes about his love and what is true. The parallel with the Judgment serves a further comic purpose as well. Machaut's narrator had many similarities to Paris; Froissart's does not. We thus move from the sublime to the ridiculous as an episode from classical epic finds its parallel in the adventures of an anonymous youth, and the juxtaposition makes for humor. His Helen will not cooperate with his romantic dream. She mocks his failure to take decisive action—Paris raped Helen—with a gesture that evokes the *carpe diem* theme. He has failed to seize time by the forelock.

The *Espinette amoureuse* uses the Judgment to construct an allegory with moral overtones. The portion of the poem devoted to the dream vision is allegorical in that it uses the dream-vision apparatus to invite us to look beneath the work's surface and then presents a situation, the narrator's agreement with Paris's choice, whose pattern recalls the pattern of the Judgment itself. We thus see the poem's narrator as an Everyman whose act has moral implications; his behavior demonstrates a wrong choice, and the humorous results of that choice confirm our impression that he was foolish.

The next work we shall consider, the *Echecs amoureux*, is much more profound. It is an example of that "strict allegory"—to use Tuve's term—which, like the *Roman de la Rose*, deals with man's role on earth, his relationship with the creator, and his final destiny. Written between 1370 and 1380 by an unknown author,[72] the *Echecs amoureux* is, in fact, modeled on the *Roman de la Rose*.[73] The poem treats the adventures of a young man sent out by Nature to learn of the world. The Judgment provides a structure for the poem's encyclopedic content, and the Judgment's traditional allegorizations shape an evaluation of the choice with which the work deals.

On a spring morning the narrator is lying awake in bed.[74] Suddenly rapt in a vision, he sees before him Nature, the ruler and queen of the world. She scolds him for laziness and urges him to study the world's beauty and learn to praise its creator. He should realize the worthiness of his position as a human being by leading a virtuous life. Two paths are available to him. The first path goes from the east to the west; it is the path of reason. The second path goes from the west to the east; it is the path of the senses. Since man is a reasonable being, he should take the first path, keeping his eye on celestial things and despising earthly things. This path leads to heaven. He should follow Reason, who is Nature's friend. The two are in full agreement.

Following Nature's instructions to see the world, the narrator sets out, wandering on his path until he forgets where he started (Galpin, p. 284). His first adventure is an encounter with Mercury, Pallas, Juno, and Venus; Mercury tells him the story of Paris's judgment and asks for his opinion of Paris's choice. When the narrator declares that never has a judge judged better, Mercury departs, commenting, "I knew it well. Everyone takes that road" (Sieper f. 9b). Venus then promises the narrator that, if he keeps her commands and performs her service, she will give him a young woman one hundred times more beautiful than Helen. The narrator places himself body and soul in the service of Venus, who assures him that she and Nature are in full accord. To win the love of the maiden, he is to befriend Venus's sons, Pleasure and the God of Love, in their garden. Venus directs him toward the garden, saying he is already on the way.

Before he reaches the garden, however, the narrator must pass through the wood of Diana. Diana criticizes the path the narrator follows and chastises him for his choice of Venus. She warns him against the garden to which he seeks admittance, suggesting that he remain in her wood. According to Diana, he has misunderstood the words of Nature, who never wished him to enter the garden.[75]

Leaving Diana, he sets out again, finally reaching the garden, which he recognizes as that described in the *Roman de la Rose*. Admitted by Idleness, he happily explores, meeting Pleasure and the God of Love and their company. He sees Sweet Looks, who carries the God of Love's marvelous bows and arrows. He also sees the rosebush, the place where Jealousy imprisoned Fair Welcome, and the fountain of Narcissus. All seems very beautiful. In the fountain, he sees the crystal stones which, as the lover in the *Roman de la Rose* discovered, reflect the contents of the garden. As he gazes into the stones, he sees that the God of Love and his company have retreated to a lovely spot near a corner of the garden. Curious, he joins them and discovers that Pleasure is playing chess with a beautiful young woman. When the game ends, the God of Love commands the narrator to play against the girl. The game, which the young woman easily wins, is revealed as an allegory for the process by which she gains the narrator's love. For the rest of the poem, his goal will be to obtain a rematch so that he may conquer her heart in return.

Though the narrator has lost the game, the God of Love is pleased with his performance and enlists him as his liege man. The narrator pledges himself to the god but is then left alone with new, disturbing thoughts. He is happy when he considers the great merit of the damsel and the fact that eventually he will be able to revenge himself in the game, but sometimes his strong desire to reach his goal causes him great pain. He rejoices that his lady's goodness offers him hope, and that she seems to be the one promised him by Venus, but he despairs when he considers how unworthy he is. In short, he is now afflicted with all the hopes and fears of a lover.

Eventually the God of Love comes to comfort him. The god reminds him of Venus's words, assuring him that the damsel with whom he played is she whom Venus promised. He describes the great power of the goddess to bend lovers to her will. The narrator asks for Love's help in winning the chess game, and the god gives him the commandments of love. He should have faith and imagine the best; he should be loyal, secret, and diligent. If he follows this advice, the god assures him, he will soon gain victory over the damsel. The narrator is reassured and rehearses to himself what he will say when he encounters the young woman.[76]

Now Pallas comes to the narrator and warns him about the life he has chosen. Man should be ruled by reason rather than the delight which Venus offers and which wrongs Nature. Pallas gives the narrator Ovid's rules for the cure of love and identifies the three lives: the voluptuous life of Venus, the active life of Juno, and the contemplative life—her own. This last, which consists in the contemplation of divine mysteries, is the best of the three. She urges the narrator to choose the contemplative life by studying in the schools of Paris; his second-best choice would be the active live. The extant remainder of the poem—sixty-nine folios in the Dresden manuscript—is devoted to a treatise on the active life which discusses everything from the duties of kings to the appropriate location for a wine cellar, breaking off with rules for an art of money-changing.

One of the few analyses of the *Echecs amoureux* is that of Pierre-Yves Badel, who considers the work in his study of the *Roman de la Rose* in the fourteenth century.[77] Badel's main point is that the love which the God of Love represents is natural, reasonable, and good; thus the narrator obeys Nature's directive when he pursues it.

Badel's interpretation of the *Echecs amoureux* depends on his interpretation of the *Roman de la Rose.* He holds that Jean de Meun approves a naturalistic approach to love,[78] and he argues that although the *Echecs amoureux* takes its setting from Guillaume de Lorris, this setting is infused with themes handled by Jean de Meun.[79] Since the poem uses so much of Jean de Meun, the garden of Pleasure is not being condemned, even if it does represent the voluptuous life.[80] Badel must thus insist that the author of the *Echecs amoureux* is renouncing the traditional significance of the Judgment.[81] A careful analysis of the *Echecs amoureux* will show, however, that its author exploits to the fullest the Judgment's traditional interpretation.

Only one manuscript of the *Echecs amoureux* known in modern times included the portion of the poem in which the narrator meets Mercury and the goddesses. Because the manuscript was nearly destroyed in World War II, we cannot know for certain all the details of this episode. Some ideas can be gained, however, from John Lydgate's rehandling of the poem, *Reson and Sensuallyte,* and from the detailed summary Ernst Sieper produced and the passages he transcribed before the manuscript was damaged.[82] Because Sieper does not summarize Mercury's narrative of the Judgment, it is impossible to know precisely what details the author of the *Echecs amoureux* included there. The narrative occupied about two folios (Sieper ff. 8b–9b), however, and so must have been fairly extensive. From what Sieper does include, it can be determined that the author of the *Echecs amoureux* knew a version of the story with the golden apple, and, assuming that Lydgate preserved at least the outlines of the narrative, one can safely say that the *Echecs amoureux* used a classical version of the Judgment that made Paris a shepherd and traced the goddesses' conflict to the Wedding of Peleus and Thetis.[83] In Lydgate, Juno's bribe is goods and riches, Pallas's wisdom and victory, and Venus's the fairest lady in the world, Helen (1995– 2043). Sieper prints a passage which suggests that in the original, Juno promised at least riches and Pallas at least wisdom (f. 9b).

Though we do not know the precise details of the Judgment as Mercury told the story, we know a reasonable amount about the episode in which the Judgment is reenacted by the narrator of the *Echecs amoureux.* Most striking is the great amount of description lavished on the four divinities as they confront the narrator to ask his opinion of Paris's choice.

Pallas, identified as daughter of Jupiter and sister of Phoebus, is associated with both war and wisdom. She is mistress of weapons and chivalry and awards victory to warriors who trust in her. She also strengthens men for virtuous life and gives understanding of divine secrets; she makes mortal men resemble the immortal gods (Sieper ff. 5b–6a). Her form is perfect in its symmetry, and her color has a fresh beauty which is not earthly, though she is as old as or older than Nature. One can scarcely look at her, so bright are her eyes. Her beauty is impossible to describe, and her size is constantly changing. Sometimes it is normal; sometimes it reaches to heaven and beyond (Sieper f. 6a). Her clothing, made with her own hands—she is also goddess of weaving—is woven of imperishable stuff and seems unearthly. Her long and wide garment, suitable for a noblewoman, is iridescent, showing three colors. She has a lance, a helmet impervious to any weapon, and a shield on which is depicted the head of a monster (the gorgon) (Sieper f. 6a–b). To show the beauty of her face, she has removed her helmet, revealing a crown given her in paradise by God the heavenly father. So costly is it that it compares with none but Nature's. Swans fly about her head (Sieper f. 6b).

Juno is identified as mistress of the world. She is both wife and sister of Jupiter, he who has ruled since the overthrow and mutilation of Saturn changed the age of gold to silver. Now the world has declined to a bad alloy, an authorial voice interjects, and law, faith, and justice are ignored. Juno is also the mistress of earthly realms and riches, dispensed for her by the blind goddess Fortune. Juno is exceptionally beautiful; no one who sees her can resist looking again and again (Sieper f. 6b). Her mantle of gold cloth, studded with gems, gleams with a hundred colors. Her crown is golden with precious stones. Around her head is a rainbow, and in her hand she carries a scepter. Peacocks accompany her (Sieper f. 7a).

Born from the foam when Saturn's severed genitals were thrown into the sea, Venus is the powerful goddess of love and fleshly pleasure (Sieper f. 7a–b). All youthful graces are hers. Her close-fitting red mantle reveals her form so that she seems naked. At her waist is a rich belt, on her gleaming head a crown of red roses. In her right hand she carries a brand whose fatal effect is more powerful than Greek fire. In her left hand she carries a golden apple, and doves fly around her head (Sieper f. 7b).

Mercury is the stepson of Juno, who raised him kindly, feeding him her own milk. Because he is the god of eloquence, the gods use him for their messenger, and he is chamberlain, secretary, and intimate notary to Phoebus. On earth, he is god of merchants; he helped men invent money and reckoning. Prophets and philosophers are also under his patronage (Sieper ff. 7b–8a). The god appears youthful, with attractive stature, well-formed members, and a handsome face; his eyes are green, his nose shapely, his teeth fine. He moves quickly, as a messenger should, and all colors appear in his changeable clothing. Like no other staff, even that of Moses, is the staff he carries in his right hand; with it he leads souls from the underworld. His other hand bears a flute whose music is so sweet that it puts to sleep all who hear it; with it he deceived Argus. At his side is his crooked sword, and on his back are wings (Sieper f. 8a–b).

The ultimate inspiration for these descriptive passages is Fulgentius, who had seen in the Judgment an allegory of the three lives and had provided for each goddess a description whose details revealed her nature as an allegorical image.[84] Unlike Fulgentius, however, at least as far as can be determined from Sieper's summary, the author of the *Echecs amoureux* did not explicitly allegorize the attributes with which he provided the three goddesses. In omitting explicit allegorization, the author of the *Echecs amoureux* was thus faithful to the aims of allegorical narrative, since the allegorical surface should be an enigma whose interpretation lies with the reader.

No one source is responsible for the details in these portraits of the goddesses and Mercury.[85] Clearly the author is a man of considerable learning, familiar with the usual attributes of the classical divinities. In the case of Mercury, for example, he must have combined material from more than one source. The curved sword is as old as or older than Ovid's *Metamorphoses*, and included frequently in discussions of the god,[86] as is his powerful rod, the caduceus. Frequently, too, the god is given a flute, but usually it is the rod and not the flute that has the power to induce sleep.[87] The sleep-inducing flute comes ultimately from the story of Mercury, Argus, and Io; it appears, for example, in Ovid's *Metamorphoses*, whence it is picked up by Bersuire, who provides it with an allegorical interpretation.[88] The whole story is later used in the garden episode of the *Echecs amoureux* to illustrate the destructive effects of jealousy in love (4651–4703). Much else in the *Echecs amoureux*'s description of Mercury is not in Bersuire, however, but can be traced piecemeal to other handbooks.

The author ranged farthest afield in describing the goddess of wisdom and war. For many details, he went not to a mythographer's treatment of Pallas but to the description of Lady Philosophy in Boethius's *Consolation*.[89] Like Pallas in the *Echecs amoureux*, Lady Philosophy has eyes of great brightness[90] and a color so fresh that it belies her great age. Her size is changeable, sometimes normal, sometimes reaching to heaven and beyond, and her imperishable clothing has been made with her own hands, a detail which harmonizes nicely with Pallas's traditional patronage of weaving.

By using the conventional spring-morning setting and making the poem unfold within a vision, the poet makes it clear that he intends to produce a work in the tradition of the *Roman de la Rose* and that he wants to be read allegorically. Thus, as is characteristic of allegory, his plot is simple. It deals with a choice and easily lends itself to an allegorical theme. The title by which Lydgate's rehandling of the work came to be known, *Reson and Sensuallyte*, states perfectly the conflict between abstractions bodied forth in the *Echecs amoureux*. Here, as elsewhere, the three alternatives of the Judgment are reduced to two.

The conflict between abstractions is made concrete with landscape and characters, each detail of the surface contributing to the work's meaning. A central image in the poem and one with a long tradition in allegorical expression and interpretation is the traveler's choice of road or path.[91] The motif recalls the contrast between the broad way to destruction and the narrow way to everlasting life in Matthew 7.13–14, as well as the popular apologue of Hercules at the crossroads.[92] In the *Echecs amoureux*, the choice between paths has been superimposed on the choice represented by the Judgment to emphasize the allegorical thrust of the poem. Nature describes to the narrator the paths that are available to him: the path of reason, which runs from the east to the west, and the path of the senses, which runs from the west to the east. This image of paths whose opposite directions signify the conflict between competing impulses is very old,[93] but the immediate source here was probably Alain de Lille's *De Planctu Naturae*. There Nature's diadem travels from the east to the west.[94] As the narrator's movements in the poem are traced, the significance of the path as an allegorical image becomes clear.

The poem's landscapes too have allegorical significance. In keeping with the theme of conflict between sensuality and reason, the author offers two landscapes whose contrast is obvious: the garden of Pleasure and the wood of Diana. Little needs to be said about the garden, since it is identified explicitly with the garden of the *Roman de la Rose* (Kraft 43–90) and thus represents the life of sensuality. Opposed to the garden is the wood of Diana, which of course represents reason and virtue. That the joys of Diana's landscape are lasting is suggested by the fact that its leaves remain green through heat and cold and its fruit is not subject to decay (Sieper f. 12a). In a passage reminiscent of Jean de Meun's contrast between the garden of the Good Shepherd and the garden of Pleasure, Diana compares her wood with the garden. She explains that the fruits of her trees have the power to prolong human life, while the pleasures of the garden are dangerous and deceptive (Sieper ff. 14b–17a).

The narrator's movements through the poem's landscapes reveal his moral state. He has already forgotten where he started—forgotten his relationship to Nature as a reasonable man—when he meets Mercury and the goddesses. As soon as he has confirmed Paris's choice of Venus, Mercury declares, "I knew it well. Everyone takes that road" (Sieper f. 9b),[95] thus making it clear that in choosing Venus the narrator has chosen a particular path. It is then logical that when, convinced of the joys to be had in love, he asks Venus how to reach the garden, she should tell him that he is already on the way (Sieper f. 11b). The fact that his path leads through the wood of Diana, though, offers him another possible direction for his life. The wood is long and narrow, easy to walk through (Sieper f. 12a). It must cross at right angles the path that he follows; thus choosing to enter it would require choosing a route that forks off to the side. Diana knows that it would be hopeless to put the narrator on a path other than the one which leads to the garden, but says that she will explain herself so that he later might recall her words (Sieper ff. 12b–13a).

The poem's characters function as allegorical images too. Not only do the three goddesses of the Judgment bring to the work their identifications with the three lives, but the *Echecs amoureux* also includes personifications whose names signal their roles in that play of ideas which is the work's *raison d'être*. Thus by her appearance, words, and actions, Nature reveals the author's view of nature and its operation; the God of Love and Pleasure, too, stand for realities beyond themselves. The characters divide neatly into two camps, of course, each aligning himself or herself with one side in the conflict with which the poem deals. On the side of reason are Nature, Diana, Pallas, and Juno; on the side of sensuality are Venus, Pleasure, the God of Love, and all the inhabitants of the garden.

Nature's role in the scheme of the poem is admittedly complex. She urges the narrator to go out and see the beauty of God's creation, following the path of reason and avoiding the path of sensuality. This advice seems to rule out the garden of Pleasure as a suitable destination. Indeed, Diana tells the narrator as much. Confronting Venus and the God of Love with his qualms about the garden, however, the narrator is assured that both they and Pleasure and Idleness are under the guidance of Nature and cooperate with her in the task of replenishing the species. This news is puzzling; one begins to imagine with the narrator that perhaps the love offered by the garden is natural, reasonable, and praiseworthy. Pallas comes along, though, to castigate him for choosing a life of love and to condemn the voluptuous life, just as we should expect.

An important key to the significance of Nature in the *Echecs amoureux* is the *De Planctu Naturae*, long recognized as a chief source for the figure of Nature in the poem.[96] In the *De Planctu Naturae*, as in the *Echecs amoureux*, Nature is the subvicar of God whose duty is to achieve permanence in an impermanent world. She constantly replenishes the species as their members are claimed by death (col. 445). She and all the creation she rules are good, except for man, whose fallen nature is shown by the rent in Nature's tunic just at the place where the human race is represented (col. 437). Man has been endowed by Nature with reason (col. 443), but reason and passion war within him, and he has chosen passion (cols. 443, 448).

The portrayal of Nature in the *Echecs amoureux* has also been influenced by the *Roman de la Rose*.[97] Jean de Meun's Nature, as is well known, can be traced back to Alain's. Like her counterpart in the *De Planctu Naturae*, her task is to keep pace with the work of death by constantly replenishing the species. To this end she labors at her forge night and day. Jean's Nature, however, differs in an important way from Alain's, for Jean's Nature is fallen. As George D. Economou puts it, Nature in the *Roman de la Rose* "operates as procreatrix outside the Christian context within which Alain's Natura acts."[98] Jean, he says, "limit[s] her moral sphere to a demand for fruitful procreation."[99] Perhaps when Jean created his version of Nature and her priest Genius, then made Genius pronounce an anathema against those who refuse Nature the tribute they owe her, he was parodying the *De Planctu Naturae*. It is far more likely that, with his figures of Nature and Genius, Jean was asserting a truth about sexuality in a fallen world than that he was advocating a naturalistic approach to sex.[100] The Nature who appears to the narrator at the opening of the *Echecs amoureux*, describes the paths that are available to him, and advises him to follow reason is, however, the Nature of Alain's *De Planctu*, not Jean's *Roman*. It is Alain's Nature who laments man's sensuality and his abandonment of his reasonable nature. The Nature whom the God of Love serves is that of the *Roman de la Rose*, blind to man's higher self.[101]

The *De Planctu Naturae* and the *Roman de la Rose* can also elucidate the meanings of Venus, Pleasure, and the God of Love, clarifying their relationships with one another and with Nature. In the *De Planctu Naturae*, Alain uses a fable detailing the relationship among Nature, Venus, and Venus's two sons in order to explain man's fallen sexuality.[102]

So that men would willingly follow Nature's plan and reproduce themselves, Nature appointed Venus as her deputy. Venus was to be assisted by her husband, Hymen, and her son, Cupid (col. 454). Yet even this "good" Cupid, legitimate offspring of Venus and the god of wedded love, was not blameless. Nature criticizes the love that Cupid represents, calling it madness and explaining, "It is not strange if in this portrayal of Cupid I intersperse slight signs of blame, although he is allied to me by the connection of own blood-relationship."[103] Venus, however, is even worse. Nature taught her rules to ensure that her aim was the production of offspring in marriage (cols. 456–57), but Venus became bored and at length committed adultery with Antigamus. From their union was born Jocus, or Mirth (cols. 459–60). Thus natural and reasonable love, sanctioned by marriage, fell, to be replaced by a love which primarily seeks delight.

In the *Echecs amoureux*, therefore, when Venus assures the narrator that Nature rules her and that she aids Nature in her work of replenishing the species (Sieper f. 10a–b), she is in a sense correct, but she hides a part of the truth—that she has rebelled against Nature's rules. The God of Love and Pleasure are Cupid and Jocus, the sons of Venus. The God of Love likewise assures the narrator that the love he represents is agreeable to Venus and profitable to Nature (Kraft 2047–58), and he too is correct. It is true that the love he urges profits Nature, though when he tells the narrator that if he places all his intent in this love, he will be welcomed by Nature (Kraft 2059–68), he has in mind rather the fallen Nature of the *Roman de la Rose*. That the God of Love views Nature as a force which is bent, as in the *Roman de la Rose*, on perpetuating the species by any means, and which does not work within the law of God, is shown by a speech which hilariously reveals the natural—but not reasonable—character of the love he offers. At the bidding of Venus, his mother, he asserts, he often sends Nature some of his followers, who so happily fall to work with forge and hammer that they nearly "unbrain" (*s'en eschervelent*) themselves (Kraft 2095–97). The God of Love even insists that Pleasure and Idleness serve Nature (Kraft 2291–2362). Yet Pleasure is Jocus, illegitimate offspring of Venus and Antigamus, rejected by Nature in the *De Planctu Naturae*, and it is hard to imagine that the Nature of the *Echecs amoureux* would welcome the service of Idleness, since she earlier urged the narrator not to be idle.

The figures of Diana and Pallas, too, are important to the analysis of sexuality which the author of the *Echecs amoureux* has carried over from the *De Planctu Naturae* and the *Roman de la Rose*. Badel sees Diana as a representative of the monastic life.[104] He must assume then that the author of the *Echecs amoureux* makes her warn the narrator against the garden not because it is really bad but only because *she*, as a virgin, considers any kind of sexual love bad. It is true that she is presented as the epitome of chastity. Her pure white clothes cover her whole body, and her simple headdress seems to identify her as a member of an order. With her ivory bow and arrows, she hunts wild beasts in order to keep Idleness away. In her wood are trees which are always green and fruit which does not spoil (Sieper f. 12a–b). Diana's wood and her way of life conflict profoundly with the way of life represented by the garden of Pleasure, and she warns the narrator about its dangers. Diana makes it very clear, however, that she renounced love only when love fell.

Once, says Diana, her wood was full of gods and men, but all has changed on account of Venus, who, because of what Jupiter did to Saturn, has drawn everyone to her side (Sieper f. 13a–b). She is alluding to the fable of Venus's birth from Saturn's severed genitals, thrown into the sea by his son Jupiter, marking the end of the golden age. At least as old as Ovid is a link between the end of the golden age and the end of sexual innocence.[105] Now chastity, justice, faith, and truth have fled, she says, and no one lives a virtuous life, but all strive after pleasure (Sieper f. 13b). Thus Diana identifies the love offered by the garden as a fallen love in opposition to Nature's aim for the narrator.

That Diana does not condemn all love, but only love which is an outgrowth of man's fallen sexuality, is shown, however, by an important passage in her speech. Devising a fable of her own, she sees in the court of King Arthur an unfallen age, an age of gold, in which love was natural and reasonable. Love did not spoil the knights but enhanced their daring (Sieper f. 13b). I cannot agree with Badel's argument that Diana's speech represents praise of courtly love in general and that thus, in condemning the garden, Diana cannot be condemning courtly love.[106] The thrust of Diana's speech is not to identify the love of Arthur's era as a praiseworthy courtly love. Rather, she shows that she does not object to all love but only to the fallen love represented by the garden.

Pallas too is ranged with Nature and Diana on the side of reason. Like the character Reason in the *Roman de la Rose*, she comes to the narrator after he has been exposed to the pleasures of the love garden, and she attempts to dissuade him from the life he has chosen. Her function in the poem is determined by traditional interpretations of Pallas as the representative of wisdom and virtue. Details of her description enhance her identity as reason's most authoritative voice. In creating his version of Pallas, the author of the *Echecs amoureux*, as we have seen, drew on the figure of Lady Philosophy in the *Consolation of Philosophy*. The parallel is easy and natural, and it certainly heightens Pallas's role as a figure of wisdom and authority—a figure who surely ought to be heeded.

The harmony between Pallas and Nature is stressed again and again. Only Nature's crown, for example, can compare to that of Pallas (Sieper f. 6b), and Pallas's goals for man are the same as those of Nature. Nature shows that a bent toward contemplation is natural to man. Her mantle depicts man with his head raised to the heavens while beasts look to the earth, a powerful image—as old as or older than Ovid's *Metamorphoses* (1.84–86 [Loeb 1.9])—for man's share in divinity. Man's reason separates him from the beasts, Nature tells the narrator, thus making it possible for him to know spiritual things (Sieper f. 4b). She wishes him to go through the world and contemplate its beauty, learning to praise the creator who made it all—certainly an injunction to the contemplative life.

Pallas's aims for the narrator are similar. She strengthens men for a virtuous life, imparts understanding of divine secrets, and makes them, though mortal, like the immortal gods (Sieper ff. 5b–6a). She argues that the narrator should leave the life he has chosen and follow reason, the foremost property of man, which raises him above the beasts and makes him godlike (Sieper f. 46b). Man wrongs Nature, she argues, when he goes against reason (Sieper f. 47a). It is Pallas's task in the *Echecs amoureux*, then, to lay out the alternatives to the life of love that the narrator has chosen, explicitly evoking the connection between his choice among the three goddesses and the three lives, contemplative, active, and voluptuous, which generations of interpreters had made commonplace in allegorizations of the Judgment.

The contemplative life as she presents it is precisely what Nature had seen as the narrator's goal. The definition of this life has been strongly influenced by Aristotelianism, in that it is seen not as service of God but as study of God's creation. Pallas advises the narrator to go to the university at Paris if this is the life he decides to pursue.

The significance of Pallas, though, has been distorted by Badel.

According to him, she represents the contemplative life, possibly the clergy, and she, with Diana, opposes not what he sees as morally neutral love in harmony with Nature (the love represented by the garden of Pleasure and sought by the narrator) but passionate love, which she regards as the "voluptuous life." Badel believes that the theme of the *Echecs amoureux* denies any conflict among the three lives represented by the Judgment of Paris. In his view, the poem presents the three lives not in opposition to one another, but as a hierarchy in which each has merit.[107]

But in order to preserve the argument that the love offered by the garden is natural and reasonable, one must somehow get around the fact that Pallas condemns it as being opposed by Nature and Reason. Badel does this by arguing that Pallas condemns some other type of love than that offered by the garden. In order to support this argument, he implies that Pallas is a misguided prude. Yet it is obvious that Pallas is condemning precisely the love urged by Venus and the God of Love and offered in the garden of Pleasure.

Pallas clearly tells the narrator that by serving love, he wrongs Reason and Nature (Sieper f. 46a). She does not say, "Were you to serve amour-passion, you would wrong Reason and Nature." She says rather that the love in which he is enmeshed as a result of his sojourn in the garden wrongs Reason and Nature. Pallas persistently links Reason with Nature and sees love opposed to both (Sieper f. 47a).

The choice of Paris is thus not presented as a hierarchy of three goods. The poem represents a conflict or debate in which Paris's choice among three is assimilated to the scheme of the *Roman de la Rose*, that is, to a struggle between the voices of reason and the life represented by the garden.

But what of the active life? Juno's connotation is at first slightly negative. The author chooses to mention her husband Jupiter's role in ending the age of gold, and he evokes the uncertain nature of Juno's gifts by recalling that they are dispensed by Fortune (Sieper f. 6b). Later, however, as Pallas offers the narrator alternatives to the life he has chosen, the active life is presented as worthy and suitable for man. Criticizing the life represented by the garden of Pleasure, Pallas says, "Briefly, in this life, there is neither much of use nor of true happiness."[108] The other two lives contrast with this one: "The other two are not such, but are profitable and fine."[109]

Juno represents the political life, the life of man in society, not the scramble for possessions which Fulgentius found nearly as reprehensible as the life represented by Venus:

> The second life belongs to Juno, who for her part holds sovereign rule over all worldly wealth. This life is very reasonable. It is the honest and praiseworthy life that one ought to lead in cities and in noble communities which are ruled by reason because Juno wants one always to devote oneself attentively to living virtuously.[110]

Note that Juno's life is explicitly linked with reason, thus confirming her place on the side of Pallas and Nature. The distinction between the two good lives, active and contemplative, is seen, following Aristotle, as governed by the distinction between prudence, the highest moral virtue, and wisdom (Venice 188r–189v).

Though Pallas is given the task of describing—even advocating—the active life as well as her own, the author of the *Echecs amoureux* does not regard all *three* lives as good in varying degrees. Rather, he is strongly influenced by the Aristotelian view, in which the active life has its own value. Pallas's discussion of the active and contemplative lives is clearly based on the Aristotelian scheme. Perfect happiness lies in the pursuit of wisdom, since the highest good is the good of the soul. One also needs sufficient power and wealth, though, and therein lies the happiness afforded by the active life, whose highest virtue is prudence. It is because he has used the Aristotelian scheme of the three lives that the anonymous author of the *Echecs amoureux* does not find it necessary to oppose the active and contemplative lives to one another, not because he views all three lives as equally good.

Like the *Roman de la Rose*, then, the *Echecs amoureux* plays off against one another characters with clear allegorical identities, each seeking to win the narrator to his or her point of view. As has been the case before, the three possibilities of the Judgment have been simplified to that most basic temptation, the choice between good and evil. Superimposed on the fable of the Judgment, in fact, is the theme of opposing paths. Nature makes this theme explicit early in the poem, and it is implicit in the landscape against which the allegory works itself out. As the narrator wanders in the landscape, he chooses the path that will be his destiny, the path to the garden, and he rejects the chance to sojourn in the wood of Diana. His choice of paths reiterates with a different allegorical image the choice that he made when given the opportunity to reconsider Paris's choice.

Venus's identity in the fable of the Judgment is crucial to her role in the *Echecs amoureux*. She is the voluptuous life, and when the narrator affirms Paris's decision in her favor, he signifies his choice of the voluptuous life. All the world takes that road, says Mercury disgustedly, evoking his role as moral commentator in the *Espinette amoureuse*. Ranged on Venus's side in the drama are Pleasure and the God of Love, who have figured in other allegorical treatments of sexuality and who thus have well-established meanings.

The Judgment and its allegorical interpretations provide the *Echecs amoureux* with both structure and meaning. The plot is simple: a choice of lives or paths. As in the *Roman de la Rose*, though, ideas are put into motion by characters whose allegorical significances are transparent. When the work's meaning and thus its *raison d'être* depend on the significance of each figure, it hardly seems fair to ask, with Badel, that the author abandon the usual and customary significances of the figures he has chosen to use. Venus is as sinister as she has ever been, and the narrator's choice is clearly as foolish a choice as it was for Paris.

The *Echecs amoureux* is the fullest allegory we have considered. Like the *Roman de la Rose*, the entire work operates on an allegorical level, with abstractions constantly in play. In the *Fonteinne amoureuse*, an individual character made an individual choice, but his choice gained significance from its parallel with the Judgment of Paris and from the setting in which it occurred. In the *Espinette amoureuse*, the narrator seemed akin to the lover in the *Roman de la Rose*, an Everyman who chose the voluptuous life in a setting with an allegorical dimension. His subsequent experiences particularized him, though, as he then followed out the implications of his choice against a naturalistic background. The parallel with the Judgment of Paris enriched our understanding of his action's significance and made us understand why his love could not succeed. In the *Echecs amoureux*, however, the allegory is deeper and broader—truly cosmic allegory.

To borrow a claim that Tuve made for Jean de Meun, the *Echecs amoureux* "talks about going to heaven."[111] It deals with man as a creature who is, as Tuve puts it, *salvationis capax.*[112] The threefold choice offered Paris provides a structure for the work's encyclopedic content: a survey of the choices available to all mankind, not merely to the poem's narrator. We are rational animals that lust for God, summoned to higher things while voices whisper to us from below, and the *Echecs amoureux* is about our human condition. The unknown author's grand vision of human possibility is rendered the more poignant by his profound debt to Aristotle, whose view of man's potential was scarcely less sublime than that of Christ.

The accomplishment of the poet who composed the *Echecs amoureux* was made possible partly by the conventions of the genre in which he worked, a distinctive literary phenomenon which did not last beyond the fourteenth century. The magnitude of his accomplishment is made clearer when we compare the original work with the translation which John Lydgate produced in about 1408. Lydgate turned the first 4,873 lines of the *Echecs amoureux* into 7,042 lines of English, breaking off while describing the chess figures in the garden of Pleasure.[113] The untitled translation has come to be known as *Reson and Sensuallyte*, a phrase which indicates the work's theme more precisely than does the name by which the original, likewise untitled by its author, has come to be known.[114] If we examine what Lydgate did to the *Echecs amoureux*, though, we can see that the dream visions of the fifteenth century indeed represent a falling off from the great period of the allegorical poem.

Because the only manuscript in which the opening part of the *Echecs amoureux* appears is seriously damaged, it is impossible to know in what respects, if any, Lydgate's unexceptionably classical Judgment departs from its model. Certain variations from the French source, though, appear in details surrounding the narrative of the Judgment, variations which give *Reson and Sensuallyte* a character different from the work which it translates.[115] Above all, Lydgate seems to have wanted to emphasize the work's edifying nature and to make it even more edifying.[116]

Just before the narrator is to hear the story of the Judgment and offer his opinion of Paris's choice, Lydgate reminds his audience that *Reson and Sensuallyte* is the story of a dream, and he seems to request not only intellectual but also spiritual attention. "And thogh I slept," says the narrator after he has described the appearance of the divine embassy, "myn hert awook" (1834). The line, a direct translation from the *Song of Songs'* "Ego dormio et cor meum vigilat" (5.2), implies that a mind freed by sleep from mundane affairs is receptive to higher things. Lydgate the author-translator is aware that the details of an enigmatic dream can yield profound truths.

In his treatment of Mercury and the three goddesses, the author of the *Echecs amoureux* had added, from various sources, considerable descriptive material, supplying the four divinities with traditional attributes in order to provide a surface whose details would invite allegorical interpretation. Lydgate went one step farther. He followed extremely closely the descriptions of Mercury and the goddesses in his source—minor variations are not worth mentioning—but then he went on to provide explicit allegorical interpretations. This desire to explain allegorical images rather than letting them speak for themselves suggests a loss of faith in the power of allegorical expression, and seems to coincide with the end of that great era of allegorical narrative which began with the *Roman de la Rose*. In *explaining* the attributes, Lydgate removed the enigma.

Thus the description of Pallas includes generally the same material found in the *Echecs amoureux*—she is daughter of Jupiter, sister of Phoebus, and the rest—but added to this material are explicit moralizations. An example is the detail, ultimately from Boethius, that though the goddess is very old, her color is fresh and young. Lydgate first reproduces the description:

> And hir colour and hir hiwe
> Was euere y-lyche fresh and nywe,
> And yet this lady, wys and sage,
> Was ryght olde and of gret age. (1103–6)

Then, in case it is not obvious to the reader why the goddess of wisdom and the contemplative life would appropriately be both old and young, along comes the explanation, ultimately from Fulgentius:

> For wisdam neuer may apalle,
> Nor of Nature neuer sterve,
> For which she called ys Mynerve,
> That ys to seyne in special
> A thing that ys ay inmortal. (1110–14)[117]

The rich suggestiveness of the surface, with its beautiful enigmatic woman, has been simplified and reduced to one explanation for which the allegorical image then just seems to *stand* in a mechanical way.

One more example of this reductive explanation in the description of Pallas will suffice. The author of the *Echecs amoureux*, it will be recalled, had unaccountably associated the goddess of wisdom with swans rather than the traditional owl.[118] It is Lydgate, though, who provides the explanation for the attribute: as swans sing before death, so should men, being glad to leave the world (1247–77). That the passage is indeed an addition to the original is clearly indicated by the marginal gloss, one of many provided by an unknown hand—very possibly Lydgate's own—who was familiar with the source and thus could indicate the departures made in the translation.[119] As the explanation of the swan's significance begins, the marginal gloss advises, "These are the words of the translator" (1245).

For Mercury, too, Lydgate's text provides some explicit allegorizations. As had the *Echecs amoureux*, Lydgate reports that though Mercury was begotten by Jupiter on the daughter of Atlas, the god was kindly raised by Juno, who felt no resentment toward her foster child. Lydgate, however, provides for this detail an interpretation which draws on Mercury's traditional links with learning and commerce:

> [Juno] bisyly dide hir cure
> To yive him mylke to hys norture:
> The whiche thinges doth signifye
> That wisdam and philosophie

Yfostred ben with rychesse,
And also eke I dar expresse,
Marchaundyse nor eloquence
Ne shold[e] ha noon excellence,
But Iuno, goddesse of rychesse,
Ne dyde her hool[e] besynesse
To yive hem mylke to her fosterynge. (1629–39)

It is appropriate that Mercury be explicitly linked with wisdom and philosophy here, since, as in the *Echecs amoureux*, his comment on the narrator's choice of Venus seems to evaluate the young man's decision: "Al this worlde gooth the same trace / And stondeth in [the] selve case" (2107–8). As the story of the Judgment was passed on through the centuries, Mercury's growing association with learning gave him an expanded role as a kind of commentator on Paris's choice, a role he also plays in the *Espinette amoureuse*.

For Juno and Venus, it is the marginal glosses alone which interpret details of the goddesses' descriptions, whereas in the treatments of Pallas and Mercury, they summarized interpretive material which had already been worked into the translation. The close relationship thus revealed between the glosses and the text—in some cases the glosses take over a task that elsewhere is handled by text and gloss working together—is a powerful argument that the glosses are Lydgate's own.

Opposite the description of Juno, for example, appears a gloss which, drawing on her old cosmic identification with air, explains *why* Juno is goddess of riches and then explicitly identifies her with the active life (there was no corresponding gloss explicitly identifying Pallas with the contemplative life): "Juno is called goddess of riches because the lower air encircles the earth in which all treasures and all riches are contained, which signifies the active life which is dependent on riches" (1354). A gloss likewise provides an explanation, foreign to the treatment of Juno in the *Echecs amoureux* itself, for the goddess's great beauty: she is beautiful "because riches attract the hearts of men and especially of the greedy" (1365). Thus an idea present in the original French text—that anyone who once looked at Juno would be compelled always to look again, undeterred even by Cerberus—takes on a deeper significance; the goddess's power of attraction is really the power of wealth to attract those who seek it:

> But euere ylyche desirous,
> Al thogh that cruel Cerberus
> Sholde haue rent hem and y-gnawe,
> And her throte asonder drawe.
> For the nerer that they went,
> Ay the more her hert[e] brent,
> And the more gan presse and siwe,
> Without[e] power to remywe. (1381–88)

For Venus, too, allegorizations are handled by glosses rather than incorporated into the text. Thus we get the explicit identification of Venus with the voluptuous life: "Venus is carnal concupiscence or the planet which inclines [men] to concupiscence and she signifies the voluptuous life which is devoted to fleshly matters" (1434), and later, opposite the description of her "firy bronde" (1578), "The poets imagined this on account of the heat of desire."

Since his translation of the *Echecs amoureux* leaves off in the midst of describing the chessboard, Lydgate does not get to the section of the poem in which Pallas remonstrates with the narrator and explains that two other lives are available besides that which he has chosen. Thus it is impossible to know what Lydgate's approach to these lives would have been. His description of Juno early in the poem, however, suggests that he had in mind the original Fulgentian scheme of the three lives rather than the Fulgentius *cum* Aristotle of the text he translated. Working through the poem from the beginning, as Lydgate was, he may not have been entirely familiar with the version of the three lives that was to be revealed later in the text on which he labored. He has also obviously supplemented his treatment of early parts of the poem with references to handbooks, where he would have found a Fulgentian approach to the Judgment. In the *Echecs amoureux* itself, Juno was ranged on the side of Pallas, and the active life that she represents was explicitly described as reasonable, but Lydgate seems to have seen instead a negative Juno like that of Fulgentius.

Lydgate makes more explicit the passage in his source which described Jupiter's putting an end to the golden age by his overthrow

of his father, Saturn—included in the description of Juno because
she is introduced as Jupiter's wife. We cannot make too much of
this point, because we are dependent on Sieper's summary for a
knowledge of what details were present in the original, yet it appears that Lydgate may have taken further than his source the idea
that successive states of decay have brought the world to the age of
false alloy. Lydgate seems to have added the lines

> Swich falsnesse regneth now this day,
> Thorgh coveytise, that feyth ys gon;
> For now vnnethe ther ys noon
> That loueth but for lucre of gode. (1332–35)

As we saw above, Lydgate treats Juno's connection with riches
much more negatively than did his source. Juno's beauty is explained by saying that she is beautiful because riches attract the
hearts of men and especially the greedy. In the marginal gloss that
links Juno to the active life, the active life is defined as the life dependent on riches. Thus the link between Jupiter, her husband, and
the world's eventual decline to a state in which covetousness holds
sway is eminently appropriate.

Not only do the marginal glosses point up the moral significance
of the goddesses; they also explicitly gloss the Judgment. Opposite
the lines in which Lydgate's narrator relates how he confirmed
Paris's choice of Venus (2071–83), two long Latin glosses explain
that when a youth reaches the age of discretion—note the parallel
with the *Espinette amoureuse*—a threefold choice of lives is offered and that, because youths pursue passion, they choose the voluptuous life.

The *Echecs amoureux* needed neither explicit interpretations
nor marginal glosses in order for its meaning to be clear, and neither, I would argue, did Lydgate's translation. The explicit interpretations and the glosses "close up" the work's potential as a true
allegory whose rich enigma draws the reader into engagement with
the text. Yet Lydgate for some reason—the temper of the times perhaps—found it necessary to gloss his own poem.

The dream visions of the later fourteenth century were the high
point of the Judgment's development. The historical tradition had
helped to link the dream with the episode, and by Machaut's time,

the dream vision was just reaching its peak. It is true that dream visions of the fifteenth century and beyond kept the form without the substance, but the dream visions of the later fourteenth century were still faithful to the tradition of the *Roman de la Rose*. They were powerful works whose allegory and irony examined serious moral questions and the ultimate issues of human purpose and destiny.

5

The Meaning of the Judgment

The fourteenth-century dream visions considered in Chapter 4 were the most important works to isolate the Judgment from its place in history or remove it from the allegorizing context of a preachers' manual or mythographical compendium. Their use of the fable was distinctive in that each made a character reenact Paris's choice among the goddesses. These three dream visions were not, however, the only works to use the Judgment as a separate episode. From the Latin Middle Ages to the fifteenth century and beyond, the Judgment appeared in works of all kinds. Each application reflects, as did the allegorizations considered in Chapter 3, a writer's period, milieu, and purpose, yet the applications we shall consider here are neither imposed nor intended allegory. The moral significance of the Judgment may be the reason that a writer has chosen to use it, but he uses the story as an example or as an illustration, neither drawing from it an explicit moral or spiritual meaning nor depending on his audience to read the fable as an allegory.

By the eleventh century the Trojan War was an important theme for medieval Latin poets.[1] Length and complexity made the classical epic an intimidating model, however, and so shorter works developed individual episodes from the saga. The Judgment of Paris was first used in medieval literature by the Latin poets of the eleventh century. For Godfrey of Reims, the story provided inspiration for two graceful compliments.[2] His *Satyra de Quadam Puella Virgine* argues that if the lady whom the poem flatters accompanied the three goddesses to the Judgment, it is she who would win the prize;[3] his letter to Enguerrand asserts that, confronted, as was Paris, with the nude Venus, Enguerrand would never have been swayed by her charms.[4] A third verse letter, the *Godefridus ad Lingonensem Episcopum*, makes more extensive use of Trojan themes. A wonderful chlamys worn by Calliope features a scene, "De Paride," which figures Paris's theft of Helen, thus calling to mind the Judgment. Godfrey reminds Venus: "You told him [Paris] when you were nude: / 'Do you see this glory? I will give you [a woman] not inferior.'"[5]

Baudri of Bourgueil used the Judgment of Paris in his imitation of *Heroides* 17.[6] Helen informs Paris that she knows his background well:

> You, the arbitrator, were ordered to pronounce judgment among the goddesses that thus litigious minds might be calmed. Jupiter wisely removed himself from the judgment, and, all the same, he would have been well enough able to decide the quarrel which Discord, angry because she was excluded from the table of the goddesses, initiated among them with the apple that she threw; but, wise, he wanted to offend neither of the goddesses; at last he ordered them to submit to the decrees of Paris; moreover you put an end [to the argument] by means of judgment, thus I understood the thing, thus I know too; indeed I also know what were the gifts promised you, what Venus and Juno promised, and what Minerva, or which or whose promise you preferred.[7]

Godfrey and Baudri aimed to imitate the classics; they did so with considerable success. The Judgment did not yet appear in a narrative context because no medieval writer had attempted an epic on the classical model. The art of letter writing, on the other hand, was congenial to the eleventh-century humanist.[8] Copying Ovid, Baudri narrated the Judgment, as had his model, because it was the pretext for Paris's affair with Helen. Godfrey practiced the *ars dictaminis*, and the Judgment furnished the material of a compliment or an exercise in *descriptio*.

By the twelfth century, however, not only had Latin imitations of the classical epic been produced, but the genre had given way to the vernacular romance. At home on medieval soil, the heroes of the ancients had become medieval knights whose interests and aims were those of the audiences for which the romances were written. The romances were a kind of history too, and the Judgment appeared in the *Eneas* and the *Roman de Troie* because it was the historically crucial explanation of how the conflict between the Greeks and Trojans began. The twelfth century also saw the Judgment put to literary uses in which it was separated from the story of Troy. So popular were romances based on classical themes, like the *Eneas* and the *Roman de Troie*, that they soon spawned imitations whose subject matter was drawn from a wide variety of nonclassical sources.[9] Written between 1155 and 1173, *Floire et Blancheflor* is one of the so-called "Graeco-Byzantine" romances, whose inspiration has been traced to Greek influence.[10] Certainly its plot is reminiscent of what has come to be called the Greek romance.

As the story begins, a pagan queen and her serving maid, the captured daughter of a French knight, have both borne children. The children, a boy and a girl, are raised together and soon fall in love. Attempting to separate them, the pagan king sends his son Floire away; he sells Blancheflor in exchange for a beautiful cup decorated with scenes of Troy, carried off from the city by Aeneas but later stolen by thieves. The Judgment of Paris is depicted on the cup's cover:

> Up above on the cover was incised how Venus, Pallas, and Juno thus came to hear the Judgment of Paris when they quarreled over a golden apple which they found; on it was inscribed [that] the most beautiful of them should have it. They delivered this apple to Paris and enjoined him to give it to the most beautiful; he would certainly not go unrewarded. Each made him a solemn promise, should the judgment be to her: Juno abundance of riches, Pallas strength and knowledge; Venus promised him that he should have the woman that he requested. The picture showed very well the love of Paris and his effort, how he prepared his ships and sailed the sea for her. (454–75)

Floire et Blancheflor's editor, Margaret Pelen, traces this episode to the *Eneas*.[11] There is no doubt that the *Eneas* contributed to the popularity of the Judgment and thus partly accounts for its inclusion here. The cup is even linked with Aeneas in the account of its origin. The direct source for the Judgment in *Floire et Blancheflor* is, however, probably not the *Eneas* but a version of the *Excidium Troiae* or the *Compendium Historiae Troianae-Romanae*.[12] The Judgment in *Floire et Blancheflor* goes on to refer to Paris's preparing his boats to claim Helen, as do the *Excidium Troiae* and the *Compendium Historiae Troianae-Romanae*, whereas the version in the *Eneas* leaves off just after the Judgment.

The author of *Floire et Blancheflor* has used the classical version of the Judgment, in which Paris's encounter with the goddesses is not a dream but a real event. Yet he has downplayed the story's supernaturalism. He never refers to the rival beauties as goddesses, and he omits all reference to the Wedding of Peleus and Thetis by making Juno, Pallas, and Venus merely *find* the golden apple. Because the episode is not integral to his plot, he need not be too concerned about its plausibility. A fable need not be true to be decorative. Its decorative function here recalls Godfrey of Reims's use of the story as one of the episodes illustrated on the elaborate chlamys of Calliope, an example of medieval *descriptio*.

The Judgment is appropriate to its context because Paris's own story delicately parallels that of Floire, the hero of the romance.[13] As he seeks the return of his beloved, he contemplates the image of Paris and Helen on the cup: "Love said to him: 'You may win out; here Paris is leading his beloved away.' 'Ah, God! Will I see the day that I thus lead Blancheflor away?'" (1517–20).

Paris's drama is over, but on the cup he inhabits a timeless world. Just as the heroes of classical literature, made eternal by their authors' art, provided models for the centuries to emulate, so the story preserved on the cup inspires the hero of this twelfth-century romance. Godfrey of Reims had praised a friend by insisting that he would not have repeated Paris's judgment. In the romance tradition, however, Paris is worthy of emulation. Benoît condemns none of his characters for loving, though in the *Roman de Troie* love undoes better men than Paris.

A second Graeco-Byzantine romance, *Athis et Prophilias*, written towards the end of the twelfth century by one "Alexander," also uses the Judgment of Paris.[14] In this complex story, Athis the Athenian relinquishes his fiancée to his friend Prophilias the Roman and then falls in love with the latter's sister, Gäite. She, however, is betrothed to King Bilas, who arrives to claim his bride, camping outside Rome in an elaborate tent. He spirits the young woman away, but Prophilias and the Romans win her back, and Bilas's tent is used by the newlyweds as they celebrate their union. On the walls of the tent are depicted scenes from the Trojan saga: the dream of Hecuba, the Judgment of Paris, the fall of Troy, and the wanderings of Aeneas. The story of the Judgment is told in detail.

Juno hands Paris the apple Discord has made and, reminding him of his noble ancestry, asks him to choose which of the three goddesses is the noblest and most lovely. Pallas and Venus likewise urge him to be fair. Paris tells them to return in three days for his decision. In the interval, they come to him separately and offer gifts: Juno will make him the richest man in the world, Pallas will make him the wisest and most knightly, and Venus will give him the most beautiful woman. As the romance puts it, "She had the apple, and he the woman."[15]

The influence of the tradition represented by the *Excidium Troiae* and the *Compendium Historiae Troianae-Romanae* is immediately obvious, though this influence has not to my knowledge been previously noticed. The distinctive tradition is seen in such details as the goddesses' going unaccompanied to the Judgment and Paris's delaying his decision for three days. It is also seen in the scope of the scenes included on the tent, which include the dream of Hecuba and the wanderings of Aeneas. Like *Floire et Blancheflor*, then, *Athis et Prophilias* uses a classical version of the Judgment, and its author is even less concerned than was the author of *Floire et Blancheflor* to blunt the supernaturalism of his story. He refers to the goddesses as goddesses, and he includes the apple's origin at the hands of Discord. Here too, though, the story serves a decorative purpose, providing the romance's author with an opportunity to exercise his skill at *descriptio*. Since the scene is decorative rather than essential to the story, it need not be realistic. Halfway through his description of the Judgment, the author injects a disclaimer: "So says the tale of the ancients" (5714). Recalling the disclaimers of historians such as Vincent of Beauvais, "concerning which thing the following fable was invented," or Jacopo da Bergamo, "as the poets tell," he thus notifies his audience that the Judgment comes to him as fable, not as historical fact.

The Trojan material, however, functions artistically within the scheme of the romance. Because the Trojan scenes are the only extended classical references in the entire narrative, the author must have chosen them because he had some purpose in mind. The stories depicted on Bilas's tent provide a fixed and timeless precedent for the mortal struggles of the romance's characters. Episodes which parallel the conflict of Paris and Menelaus over Helen occur all through *Athis et Prophilias*. The story opens with a reference to the founding of Rome after the fall of Troy. It was Vergil, of course, who made Aeneas translate the Trojan heritage from Troy to Rome, and in this story, Rome carries on the tradition of Troy. Prophilias the Roman, like Paris the Trojan, falls in love with a Greek woman, the promised wife of his friend Athis. Here the conflict is resolved amicably, as friendship prevails over love, but later war ensues when the outraged Bilas arrives like a latter-day Menelaus to camp outside the walls of Rome and claim Gäite, the woman to whom he has been betrothed. In another episode, Thelamon, duke of Corinth and Ephesus, gathers an army to aid Bilas in revenging himself on the Romans for stealing his intended wife. At the height of the conflict, participants assure one another that their struggle is in no way inferior to the Trojan War. Eventually, however, Bilas falls in love with Savine, the sister of Athis, and the romance ends in rejoicing.

Love conquers all in this story; it is a positive force and a worthy motive for action. Thus, though the romance's author laments the sufferings caused by Paris's choice of Venus,[16] there is little, if any, sense that Paris or his actions are being condemned. In the love-triangle of Bilas, Gäite, and Athis, it is Bilas, like the *jaloux* of the courtly love lyric, who is the villain. The heroic ideals which kept the Greeks at the walls of Troy for ten years have given way to the ideals of romance. *Athis et Prophilias* ends, not in the fall of a noble city, but in Bilas's reconciliation with his former enemies.

In these anecdotal uses of the Judgment, the story certainly does not always bring with it the moral force it had in the allegorical tradition stemming from Fulgentius. When Godfrey says that Enguerrand would not have judged as Paris did, of course we are to understand that Paris's choice was wrong, but Godfrey is equally capable of flattering a woman by telling her that she could carry off the prize of beauty from the three goddesses. Among uses of the Judgment discussed in this chapter, several have been examples of *descriptio.* The story ornaments a garment, a cup, a tent, and the poet enjoys evoking a scene whose appeal is visual as well as literary. This application of ancient—and later medieval—material was of course extremely common and owes much to classical and medieval art.[17] One could scarcely attribute the same motive to every writer who ever enriched the surface of a work with *descriptio;* only context can determine what, if any, purpose led him to one story rather than another. I have tried to show that in the Graeco-Byzantine romances, the Judgment was chosen not for the meaning it had acquired in the allegorical tradition but rather because certain graceful parallels between the ancient fable and the plots of those romances added an extra dimension.

By the fourteenth century, however, the story was much more likely to carry considerable moral force—and this for three reasons. Writers like Andreas Capellanus, Guillaume de Lorris, and Jean de Meun had begun to question the basis of the love which the romances celebrated; further treatments of Paris's choice in works of explicit allegory had built up a longer tradition of condemnation for the lust that attracted him to Venus and thus led him to Helen; and, particularly relevant to the next work which we shall consider, Guido de Columnis had put the heavy hand of the moralist to the Trojan story and in his treatment of the Judgment had done all he could to suggest that Paris submitted to demonic forces when he judged the goddesses.

In the mid-fourteenth century, the Italian humanist Convenevole da Prato, once Petrarch's teacher, drew on the Judgment of Paris for a poem included in his *Panegyricus* for King Robert of Naples, a man of learning and a generous patron of the arts.[18] Produced during the last decade of the king's reign and most probably between 1334 and 1343, the work exists in three sumptuous manuscripts.[19] The poem based on the Judgment gains part of its effect from being presented on a lavishly illustrated page which shows Paris awarding the apple to Venus as the other two goddesses look on. The words of the poem function almost like the dialogue of a drama or pageant, two uses to which the Judgment was later to be put.

Seated in the center, Juno is giving her opinion of Paris's choice:

"This royal son has been deceived and ensnared. Tricked by beauty, now, as a judge, he has been eaten up by poisons. His judgment has been turned by promises and immersed in filth. In degenerating from his honorable ancestors, see which of us three the king chooses—her, because he wants such a one for himself. Without fault, Robert, the crowd seeks a better judgment: wealth and possessions. It beseeches me with prayers and adores my divinity with vows." Thus does her wild envy submit rather badly [an authorial voice intrudes]. Subject to a single judgment, Juno says indignantly, "That woman is pleasing to the vain, the lustful, and the profane. Venus is beloved to the lustful because she is a full pit, and she is the food of pleasure, and also, however, of anxiety."[20]

From the left side, Pallas responds:

"Surely, Juno, these things are known to Robert. That Medea [i.e., witch] speaks to the king, she who bewitches—Venus and her worse offspring. Afterwards, she will obtain interest on this usury [i.e., Paris's enjoyment of Helen], believe me. In time to come, they [the Greeks] will investigate the perjuries of Laomedon. Having nearly avenged yourself, be silent now until the reins of Trojan customs are broken or forced by siege. See, spouse of Jove, and now laugh. She herself will be punished, she who made the chain from love. It is not fitting for you, a queen, to have wild will in your mouth, but [instead] to wish holy goodness."[21]

She then comments, perhaps to herself, perhaps to the audience,

"This Paris spurns me because he does not see the light well, and he praises Venus who always deceives him badly. This man, like a fool, because he is ignorant of true piety, gave away the rights I am owed because he foolishly turned over the fruit to the vain, senseless female who destroys Troy."[22]

Venus, sitting on the right side and receiving from Paris the prize for her beauty, an apple with leaves and stem still attached, says, "Oh, sweet Paris, son of Priam, most welcome and fulfilled at our altars, pay no attention to these hypocrites." Under her breath, though, she comments, "It will not happen that I will be grateful to you, truthful with a true gift."[23]

Paris, ignoring the authorial exhortation to "cleverly hear the warnings and commands of Pallas," says, "Accept this lovely fruit, you, the lovelier goddess, for I judge that you are the dwelling place of beauty, my living hope."[24] The drama is summed up thus: "When beauty promises loveliness, judgment forsakes the brilliance of light or ancestral good."[25]

By showing the foolish choice that Paris made, Convenevole puts in relief Robert's noble character, as Godfrey of Reims had earlier flattered Enguerrand. After Juno has railed against Paris's foolish lust and the depravity of Venus's followers, Pallas reminds her, "Surely, Juno, these things are known to Robert." In order to stress the parallel between the two men, Paris is referred to as a king rather than as a prince. "See which of us three the king chooses," says Juno, referring to Paris. "That Medea speaks to the king," says Pallas.

Yet Robert has made his choice too, and not the choice that traditional interpretation of the Judgment sanctioned. He is a king, not a monk; moreover, he is a king noted for his political successes. How to reconcile with the position and power of the man to whom this work is dedicated the time-honored interpretation of the Judgment which made Juno almost as bad as Venus? Writing when he wrote and for whom he wrote, Convenevole could scarcely affect to despise money and power; his immersion in his milieu is suggested by images in the poem drawn from the burgeoning economic life of fourteenth-century Italy: "fenus / Ex hac usura capiet," he says of the debt Venus will collect for Paris's pleasure; "she will obtain interest from this usury." Convenevole makes the Judgment flatter his patron, however, by shaping to his own purpose the familiar material with which he started.

The drama is taking place at the moment of Paris's decision in favor of Venus, but the goddesses already anticipate the effects of his choice. Pallas contemplates the ten-year siege and the destruction of the city when she tells Juno that since revenge is near, she should be silent until Troy falls. Paris himself, she assures the angry goddess, will pay for his enjoyment of Helen as Venus claims interest on his pleasure, and Venus, too, will be punished, presumably by the downfall of the Trojans, whom she favors. Pallas is also aware of *how* Paris's choice of Venus will lead to the war, as her reference to the perjuries of Laomedon shows. Laomedon's culpability for the first destruction of Troy had, in late-classical and medieval tradition, become indissolubly linked with the Trojan War and Troy's second fall.

In creating an identity for each goddess, Convenevole seems most indebted to Fulgentius. Pallas is associated with wisdom rather than war. Commenting on Paris's foolish choice, she observes that he chooses Venus because he does not see the light (*lumina*), and at the end of the poem, Pallas's gift is described as "the brilliance of light" (*lucis splendorem*). Convenevole is obviously thinking that the life Pallas would offer seeks spiritual illumination as its goal.

Convenevole's Venus could easily be a descendant of Fulgentius's. Not only is she condemned as a source of the pleasure which would distract from more worthy pursuits, but there is a strong antisexual, almost misogynist, bias to the portrayal of the goddess. Recalling the approach to the Judgment taken by Convenevole's countryman, Guido de Columnis, about a century earlier, Venus is presented as a witch or sorceress. Pallas describes her as a "Medea"—who was famed in medieval tradition as a witch—and says that she "bewitches" (*fascinat*). Images of poison and decay are associated with her appeal: Paris "has been eaten by poisons" (*uiris*); his judgment has been "immersed in filth"; Venus is a "full pit" (*puteus*). She is, further, portrayed as deceitful, her seeming fairness a trap for the unwary. Juno says that Paris has been "tricked by beauty," Pallas that he will pay for his pleasure in Helen. Venus herself admits under her breath that her gift will prove false. She is the food of pleasure and anxiety, says Juno, recalling the love contraries of courtly tradition, while Pallas refers to the chain of love, suggesting the moralist's warning against love's power.

It is in his treatment of Juno, however, that Convenevole makes the adjustments which allow the Judgment to flatter rather than condemn. The premise of the exchange between her and Pallas, which in fact takes up most of the poem, is Juno's particular anger at Paris's choice, even though both goddesses were slighted. Here Convenevole has drawn, of course, on the *Aeneid* 1.26–27: "deep in her heart lie stored the judgment of Paris and her slighted beauty's wrong." Pallas speaks not of herself but of Juno. Her speech is devoted in large part to describing the revenge that Juno will obtain as a result of Paris's rash act. It is Juno who addresses Robert directly.

Influenced by Fulgentian tradition, Convenevole has made Juno offer wealth rather than royal power. The "better judgment" that she opposes to Paris's choice of Venus is "wealth and possessions" (*censum . . . nactaque*). At the end of the poem, the gift of Juno that Paris is said to have rejected is "ancestral good" (*bonum patrium*). Despite the fact that the gifts themselves suggest Fulgentian tradition, however, Juno and what she represents are not condemned as in Fulgentius. With no irony intended by Convenevole, she pronounces the crowd that worships her in pursuit of wealth and possessions as "without fault." Clearly, Convenevole had in mind Aristotle's positive estimation of the active life when he created this portrait of the goddess, despite the fact that he made her offer riches rather than sovereign power. The "ancestral good" which she has at her disposal could be taken as a call to the life of the nobility, whose inherited wealth brought with it the responsibility of service. As an Italian humanist writing to honor a king noted for his patronage of the arts but also for his political *savoir faire*, Convenevole has taken just the approach to the Judgment that one would expect. Though he has succeeded in making respectable Juno and what she represents, his treatment of the Judgment is nevertheless extremely conventional—and closely related to the allegorical tradition. He certainly expected his audience to be familiar with the Judgment's traditional moral interpretation. The choice of Venus is shown to be completely wrong, and the bent toward love which might make a man choose Venus and the gift she offers is presented as blind lust, worthy of the most severe condemnation.

About half a century later, Christine de Pisan took the Judgment as the inspiration for a *balade*,[26] an application which contrasts with her treatment of the theme in the *Othéa*, discussed in Chapter 3. In the *Othéa*, we had an example of imposed allegory; explicit moral and spiritual meanings were drawn from the story. Here the treatment is purely allusive. Christine expects her audience to know the fable of the Judgment and to bring to her poem an understanding of what Paris's choice meant in moral terms, but the *balade* is certainly not an allegory, nor did Christine write it with the intention of giving moral instruction.

> If I could know Pallas, I would never lack joy and all good because I would be on the path of comfort, bearing the load with which Fortune has overwhelmed me. But I am weak to endure such great

weight if she does not come to share part, to aid me through her powerful effort. Would God she might!—because I have no comfort from Juno.

Pallas, Juno, and Venus once wanted to argue their case before Paris; each said that in her opinion she was more beautiful and her great power more perfect in everything than that of the others; they wanted to entrust themselves to Paris, who judged that Venus ought to be held more beautiful and powerful. He said, "Lady, I want you because I have no comfort from Juno."

For the apple of gold, then, Venus came to help him gain Helen; on account of it he was afterwards dead and undone. I have nothing to do with her [Venus], but my heart would be revived with joy if the worthy Pallas, by whom misdeeds are forsaken and all goods retained, deigned to keep me for her servant: no more would I have to desire to come to great good, because I have no comfort from Juno.

These three powerful goddesses make the world endure, their discord notwithstanding, but may God make me remember Pallas, because I have no comfort from Juno.[27]

The *balade* would be meaningless to one unacquainted with the Judgment and its long interpretive tradition stemming from Fulgentius. One must know that Pallas is wisdom, Venus lust, and Juno wealth. As wisdom, Pallas represents those intangible goods over which Fortune holds no sway. Thus she can be called upon to sustain the narrator. Consistent with the Fulgentian condemnation of Venus, Paris's choice of that goddess is directly connected with his death; taking disaster as a typical effect of devotion to Venus, the narrator rejects her. Juno's association with wealth, however, is what gives the poem its wit: the *balade* is obviously a complaint to the poet's purse.

In the mid-fifteenth century, René of Anjou used Paris's judgment of the goddesses to illustrate the inveterate lover's fatal attraction to love and beauty. In the *Livre du cuer d'amours espris*, written in 1457, René's narrator describes a dream in which his heart is removed from his body by Love to go in search of Mercy.[28] Accompanied by Desire, the heart travels through a landscape which abounds in personifications inspired by the *Roman de la Rose*. Its many adventures represent allegorically the travails which a lover must suffer at his lady's hands. At the "hospital of love," the heart tours the cemetery of famous lovers, studying the *blasons* which describe their fame and whose placement—high or low—reflects the nature of their love.[29] One of the lovers is Paris, whose shield, azure with three golden toads rampant, and a little lower than the previous shield, that of Hercules, is accompanied by the following legend:

> Paris is my rightful name—handsome and gracious, the perfectly noble shepherd, sweet and tuneful, and son of King Priam, powerful and good: he who had from the goddesses the worthy gift. Presenting the apple to me, in truth, instead of to all those [others] who hoped to serve love, they said that none of them approach me in beauty. I was worthy of the woman and most valiant in arms. But the appetite for love was so delightful to me that I had to come, pensive and languorous, to put my *blason* here—I cannot excuse myself—because of Helen the beautiful, whom I loved so much. (127–28)

After further adventures, the heart repairs to the hospital of love to live out the rest of its days.

René has followed the tradition which makes Paris the beautiful shepherd of Troy—more beautiful than all the other servants of love, the goddesses tell him. He is presented as a lover who, unable by nature to resist the gift offered by Venus, loved Helen too well and thus met his end. René is clearly aware of the Judgment's allegorical significance. As Paris describes his fate, there is a note of melancholy, a sense that he knows he chose the worst choice offered him. "I was worthy of the woman and most valiant in arms," he says, referring to the old opposition between the *hēdonē* of Venus and the *aretē* of Pallas. "But the appetite for love was so delightful to me that I had to come . . . here." Paris's bent for love was the undoing of a man who could have chosen the better gift and won knightly fame—thus has he deserved three golden toads rampant as his device. The fact that his *blason* is lower than others suggests that in the panorama of loves which the work offers, his is not the noblest.

The heart, too, gains only grief from its pursuit of Mercy in the *Livre du cuer d'amours espris*. Heir to centuries of literary *complaintes*, René knows that love is more often bitter than sweet. He wishes to delineate the psyche of a lover and show the pass to which one can be brought by love, and his dream vision gives nar-

rative form to the impulse of countless lyrics. René's aim is psychological more than moral or eschatological; Paris and the other
famous lovers in whose company he is buried offer not a warning
that love can bring grief, but rather a testimony to love's great
power.

Probably dating from some time in the fifteenth century, four
stanzas of English rhyme royal present the Judgment of Paris as
a "disgising" or masque in which Paris is approached by Pallas,
Venus, and Minerva, each of whom speaks to him and offers him
gifts.[30] "Sone of pryam jentil paris of troye," says Pallas, "Wake of
thi slep" (1–2). She asks him to award the apple to the fairest of the
three, promising as her gifts

> honour conquest nobley loos and pris
> victorye corage force and hardynesse
> good Aventure and famous manlynesse. (10–12)

Venus counters, offering

> glad aspecte with fauour and fayrnesse
> and love of ladyes also while that ye leve
> famous stature and princely semlynesse
> Acordyng to your natyf gentilnesse. (16–19)

Last to speak is Minerva (the anonymous poet has mistakenly seen
Pallas and Minerva as two separate goddesses and has substituted
one of them for Juno), who tells Paris,

> Thou art a prince borne be discent
> And for to Rule thi Roial dygnyte
> j shall the yeve first entendement
> Discrecion prudence in Riht of jugement. (23–26)

As in the *Seege of Troye*, Paris is sleeping when he is approached by
the divine embassy but is then awakened by the goddesses. Thus,
the Judgment is not a dream. Venus's gifts also recall the *Seege of
Troye*: here she offers to make him fair and give him the love of
ladies; there Venus offered to make women love him, and "Jubiter"
offered to make him the fairest man. The poet has made two separate goddesses of the goddess of war and wisdom. His Pallas offers
gifts traditionally associated with the Greek Athena—victory and

valor—while his Minerva offers gifts from the later tradition: prudence, discretion, and understanding. There is also some suggestion here of the sovereignty traditionally associated with Juno, since these gifts are described as suitable to a royal prince.

The poem comes to no formal conclusion; it sets forth the contrasting characters of the rival goddesses without revealing Paris's decision or making any moral evaluation of the choices he is offered. I would argue, though, that by this stage in the Judgment's history, when the episode was presented with no interpretation, the audience was called upon to supply the most familiar one and to gloss the fable with the allegory of the three lives. Specific details would not be important. We have seen much variation in the evaluation of Juno and the life she represents, but we have seen no positive evaluation of Venus in the allegorical tradition. From about the mid-fourteenth century, there was scarcely a positive interpretation of Paris's decision unless the exemplum was explicitly turned to a nontraditional purpose.

In the later Middle Ages, then, an unglossed use of the Judgment depended for its meaning on the audience's awareness of the tradition which condemned Paris's choice of Venus as the action of a fool ruled by lust. The interpretation of the Judgment which made Paris's choice among the goddesses' gifts a choice among lives of contemplation, action, and pleasure was by far the most common. Some writers, however, used the Judgment for purposes which departed from its accepted meaning. Thus the Judgment was occasionally pressed into service in surprising contexts. When the Judgment was put to use in a way that did not draw on its traditional significance, however, the new application had to be explained. Such explanation was not needed when a writer drew on the meaning which centuries of allegorical interpretation had made familiar.

John Gower saw in Benoît's version of Paris's Judgment and his subsequent rape of Helen an illustration of the evils of sacrilege. Completed in 1390, Gower's *Confessio Amantis* uses the fiction of a lover's confession to organize a handbook of lovers' deadly sins. Each sin is subdivided, and the subdivisions are illustrated with exempla, for which Gower often had recourse to Guido's or Benoît's narratives of the Trojan saga.[31]

Sacrilege, which Gower makes a subdivision of avarice (5.6961ff.), is said to be committed when lovers talk with their ladies at mass, take rings or gloves from their ladies' hands, or dress themselves lavishly in order to show off before their ladies in church (7032–90). Sacrilege is a branch of avarice because in such flirtations the lover may win things with which he is unwilling to part: "For wel mai be he stelth away / That he nevere after yelde may" (7091–92). Though Gower's lover-narrator doubts that he has the ability to steal his lady's affection, he agrees that she is a great distraction to him at mass and that he would certainly commit such sacrilege if he could. To help him amend his will, Genius offers a tale illustrating the wrongs of sacrilege. There follows, from Benoît,[32] a long Trojan narrative which begins with the first destruction of the city, includes Paris's judgment of the goddesses (7410–33), culminates in his theft of Helen from the temple at which he had first made her acquaintance earlier that day, and concludes with a brief reference to the fall of Troy—all owing to Paris's sacrilege.

Only the late-classical version of the story would have served Gower's purpose here. The anonymous rehandler who gave the "Dares" version of the saga its final form took from Dracontius the episode in which Paris stole Helen from the temple on Cytherea at which she observed religious rites. Gower is using the material as a cautionary tale. Paris's actions are linked ultimately to the fall of his city, and his choice of Venus is wrong because it led him to the sacrilege in which Gower sees his greatest fault. This is a clever and original application of Paris's story. It is interesting too in that usually the classical version of the Judgment and theft, rather than that of Dares, is brought forth for moral application. In those cases, however, the story is usually completely detached from its context. Here, on the other hand, Gower has inserted almost a miniature history—necessary, though, in order to show the context and the effects of Paris's sin.

An even more original application of the Judgment appears in Christine de Pisan's *Le Livre du chemin de long estude*, completed in 1403.[33] As the work opens, its narrator is seeking in books for comfort following the death of her beloved. After reading *The Consolation of Philosophy*, she falls asleep and has a vision in which, led by a lady who identifies herself as Almethea, she follows "the road of long study." Visiting St. Sophia in Constantinople, the ruins of Troy, and the like, they make their way to heaven, where they meet the four queens who rule the world, Wealth, Nobility, Chivalry, and Wisdom, currently engaged in a debate. As Reason presides, the four queens try to determine which of the four qualities they represent is most crucial to good government. The discussion has reached an impasse when a "worthy and wise doctor," Reflection, suggests that, like the goddesses who quarreled over the prize of beauty, the four queens could benefit from the opinion of an arbitrator.

In order to illustrate that an arbitrator can help settle such arguments, Reflection recalls the Wedding of Peleus and Thetis and the Judgment of Paris. Attended by all the gods, the wedding was held "in the places where the destinies have their seats." Pallas, Juno, and Venus sat together at a table. Suddenly Discord arrived uninvited and threw before them a golden apple inscribed, "Let it be given to the most beautiful!" As each claimed the apple, great debate arose. Seeking judgment, they came before Jupiter, and each persisted in demanding the prize. Finally, so that Jupiter should not incur the losers' ill will, the goddesses agreed to take their quarrel to "the excellent shepherd of Troy." Mercury led them to Paris, who awarded the apple to Venus (6149–92).

Christine could well have taken this material from the *Ovide moralisé.*[34] The origin of the goddesses' quarrel at the Wedding of Peleus and Thetis is crucial to her purpose, and so she uses the classical version of the story: Paris is a shepherd, and the adventure is not a dream. Since the episode functions as an exemplum rather than as part of a history, she does not need to establish its historical validity by rationalizing Paris's meeting with the goddesses.

The relevance of the Judgment to its context is clear. Christine ignores and clearly expects her readers to ignore any negative connotations associated with the incident. Once the problem of connotations is out of the way, though, useful parallels abound. Christine's four queens argue before Reason as the three goddesses argue before Jupiter. The debate in the *Chemin de long estude* takes place in heaven. Christine's version of the Judgment, in a passage which recalls the Clementine *Homilies* (see Chapter 1), situates the Wedding of Peleus and Thetis "in the places where the destinies have their seats"—that is, in the heavens, among the stars. Christine's four queens are personified abstractions; the three goddesses are very nearly so. Wisdom and Chivalry suggest Pallas's traditional areas of patronage, while Wealth and Nobility call to mind those of Juno. Each of the four queens represents a sphere with a certain claim to princely power, and each goddess represents a sphere of human activity. Jupiter, sometimes interpreted as Divine Reason, easily parallels the personified Reason before whom the queens argue.

Christine makes the story serve her distinctive purpose. Most of the episode is taken up with her description of the argument before Jupiter; only a few lines at the beginning explain its origin, and a few at the end treat Paris's judgment of the goddesses. Christine ignores the bribes Paris was offered, making the story more self-contained. We are not reminded that Venus offered Paris Helen, and thus we are not led to reflect on the Judgment's place in history. Christine concludes merely by saying that Venus got the apple over which she had taken such pains. Recalling the Judgment's crucial relationship to the destruction of Troy might lead us to reject the goddesses' quarrel as an appropriate parallel for the debate among Christine's four queens. She thus succeeds in making the story serve her purpose without creating any unintentional irony. As a court poet, Christine excels at applying her learning to the interests and needs of her audience. The character of a king was a serious issue in the Middle Ages, and Christine here considers what qualities in a man make for good government. The moral she takes is not, however, the obvious lesson of Paris's choice. Her use of the Judgment reminds us that the context in which a classical story appears is more important than any meaning it may have acquired from earlier applications.

In Gower's *Confessio Amantis*, we saw an interpretation of the Judgment in which Paris's greatest error was not his choice of Venus but rather this theft of Helen from the temple; in Christine de Pisan's *Chemin de long estude*, we saw Paris's resolution of the goddesses' quarrel held up as a model of effective arbitration. The most surprising applications of the Judgment, however, remain to be examined: those in which Paris is seen as an example for lovers. Despite the long tradition which saw in his choice of Venus and subsequent pursuit of Helen the actions of a fool, Paris could nevertheless be invoked occasionally as the very model of a lover, a young man whose judgment of the goddesses reflected every lover's natural bent toward love and beauty.

Though in the *Dit de la fonteinne amoureuse*, Guillaume de Machaut exploited the Judgment's allegorical dimension, in the *Confort d'ami*, which immediately preceded the *Fonteinne amoureuse*, he used the Judgment only for an obvious parallel between the situation of Paris and that of his patron, ignoring any possible moral implications raised by the comparison. Completed in 1357, the *Confort d'ami* was written for Charles the Bad, king of Navarre, while he was imprisoned by John the Good, king of France.[35] It has four main sections. The first uses exempla from the Bible to show Charles that God aids those who trust in Him; the second gives him advice about conducting himself in prison—he should observe *mesure, patience,* and the like; the third comforts him, by means of classical exempla, in his separation from his lady; and the fourth offers him a virtual handbook's worth of advice to princes.

The Judgment of Paris appears in the third section of the work, where it is pressed into service to urge Charles that hope will help him withstand separation from his lady. "When Paris went to seek Helen . . . he went in hope to have her love and her acquaintance" (2645–47), the episode begins, and a short version of the Judgment follows (2652–63). The version of the story is similar to that which Machaut used in the *Fonteinne amoureuse*: Paris is a shepherd, the adventure is not a dream, and the goddesses' traditional associations with wisdom, love, and wealth are recalled.[36] This classical version of the Judgment, with its implication that Paris's adventure was real, seems to have been acceptable to authors who used the story as an exemplum because exampla were seen as fables with useful applications, not as stories whose historical truth was crucial to their validity.

Though Machaut mentions that Paris's choice of Venus led to the destruction of Troy, there is no justification for reading the exemplum as a moral lesson which ironically contradicts the stated aim of the passage: to urge that hope aids a lover and to present Paris as a model to be emulated. The structure of the work is too different from that of the *Fonteinne amoureuse* for us to try to see a moral application for the Judgment here. The *Fonteinne amoureuse* is a work whose use of dream-vision conventions compels an allegorical reading and an awareness of the irony associated with allegory. The fact that no explicit moral is drawn from the Judgment forces us to look for what is implicit. The *Confort d'ami* is a poem of advice and consolation in which exempla reinforce points already made explicitly. Further, Machaut includes an image which seems to sum up love's place in human life. Romantic love is to divine love as an embroidered picture is to the living creature it portrays (2771–72). Love is thus used well, he implies, by those who see it as an image of divine love, not an end in itself. By the fourteenth century, the rituals of courtly love were so conventionalized that one could scarcely speak of love without invoking the personifications with which the *Roman de la Rose* had rendered accessible the lover's psyche. Though the *Roman de la Rose* satirically lays bare the lust at the root of the dreamer's love and mocks him because he believes that courtliness can disguise the true basis of his attraction to the Rose, later medieval literature treats of many loves, not just the madness of youth. Even literature which deals with responsible love, however, employs the language of courtliness, and only careful reading can show whether a work endorses the love with which it deals or undermines it by means of irony and satire.

In the *Confort d'ami*, then, Paris figures as an exemplary lover. His determination in sailing to Greece to win from her husband the woman he had been promised by Venus shows that every lover must nerve himself with hope if he wishes to succeed in his quest. Thus the Judgment itself comes along not as a moral lesson but merely as a necessary clarification: Paris claimed Helen because he once judged the goddesses and won for his pains a beautiful woman.

Paris appears as an exemplary lover, too, in William Nevill's *The Castell of Pleasure*, a dream vision ultimately inspired by the *Roman de la Rose*.[37] Written a little before 1518,[38] it is scarcely a work of the Middle Ages, yet its inspiration is certainly medieval, and it represents an interesting application of the Judgment.

As the poem begins, its narrator announces that his book's purpose is to provide pleasure for gentlefolk who enjoy youth with amorous "dyleccyon": "Layenge a parte / all wylfull vayne desyre // To conforte them that brenne in louynge fyre" (27–28). The printer, who figures as a character in the work, objects that nowadays everyone just wants money and frivolous pleasures instead of books. The narrator then tells the story of a dream he had after reading Ovid's *Metamorphoses,* and the remainder of the poem chronicles his dream adventures. He and Morpheus journey to a beautiful castle whose gates, echoing the introductory dialogue between the narrator and the printer, offer a choice between the way of worldly wealth and the love of beauty. Pointing out the parallel between this choice and the fable of Hercules at the crossroads, he chooses the way of love. Entering the castle through the gate of love, he has a series of adventures which represent allegorically the psychological effects of love. The Judgment of Paris figures in a debate between Disdain and Pity over the fate of Desire, who has gone in quest of Beauty. Disdain mentions Paris to support her argument that Beauty should reject Desire, arguing that though Paris had pledged himself to Oenone, he broke his troth once he judged the goddesses. Pity argues, however, that he then committed himself totally to Helen:

> . . . accordynge to his wordes he made grete labour
> Hertely requyrynge my lady hym to redresse
> Promysynge her the utterest of his lytle power. (671–73)

Disdain replies that he pursued Helen only because of her riches or "grete parentage" (674–75). Pity agrees that though some men may pursue women only for material benefits, personal gain is not Desire's motivation. Though several additional exempla are introduced, the debate ends inconclusively. Just then, however, Credence appears to announce that Beauty will marry Desire if Desire wishes. The narrator awakes when the noise of the wedding celebration makes Morpheus vanish. Sad that his vision has fled, the narrator meditates on the transitory quality of human existence. He determines to follow virtue and try always to love.

Nevill sees love in a totally positive light. With no sense of irony, Desire's winning of Beauty is celebrated, and amorous "dyleccyon" is seen as a worthy pursuit for youth. Even the parallel with Hercules at the crossroads is intended positively; the implication is that the narrator chose correctly when he rejected the pursuit of wealth in favor of love.

The pull between wealth and love is a theme that runs through the entire work, and again we see the more complex choice among three abstractions reduced to the simpler choice between two. Wealth is the villain here, but rather than being opposed to contemplation, it is opposed to love—which in earlier interpretations of the Judgment was more commonly wealth's partner in ignominy. The gates of the castle offer the choice between wealth and love, and the narrator emulates Hercules in choosing the correct alternative, which here turns out to be love. Love and money are seen as the only possible explanations for Paris's pursuit of Helen, and love is upheld by the sympathetic Pity as the worthy motive, while the cynical Disdain sees money as the more likely one. In a curious way, in fact, love and contemplation have been conflated and set off against the third alternative, the active life: Nevill's introduction contrasts pursuing wealth with making a book about love. As a fit topic for study, love has become a valid object of the contemplation which the allegory of the three lives had for almost two millennia held out as most worthy for man.

The sixteenth century brought a striking shift in applications for the Judgment. The theme was popular in poetry, drama, masque, and pageant; most commonly it served, as it had long before served Godfrey of Reims, as a device for the flattery of ladies. More than one noblewoman, and even Queen Elizabeth herself, was claimed worthiest to win the prize for beauty.[39] Many a medieval woman might have longed to hear herself praised as the face that launched a thousand ships or the goddess that delivered Helen into her lover's hands, but in the thirteenth, fourteenth, and even fifteenth centuries, all but a few references to the Judgment came too heavily laden with allegorical freight to allow the comparison to pass as a compliment. The Renaissance had other uses for the Judgment, but that is another book.

Epilogue: The Judgment and the Meaning of History

At the close of a detailed treatment of the Judgment written in the early sixteenth century by Jean Lemaire de Belges, Paris questions the nature of the experience he has just had. Was it a dream, an ecstasy, a fantasy, or an illusion? Or was it real? In medieval treatments of the Judgment, the episode was either fact or fable. If its context required that it be fact, it was rationalized, usually by having Paris's encounter with the goddesses occur in a dream, an expedient deriving from the *De Excidio Troiae Historia* of "Dares the Phrygian." When the Judgment did not appear in a historical context, the classical version of the story was used. The classical version was a tale told by poets; it was not true, but it pointed to truths. It was an allegory which taught moral lessons or revealed the secrets of the cosmos. In the Renaissance, however, this neat division no longer held sway.

In Lemaire's *Les Illustrations de Gaule et Singularitez de Troye,* which he began in 1500, the context required that the Judgment be historical, but Lemaire was drawn to the classical version of the story because it offered him scope to display his rhetoric and erudition. Having told the story in its classical form, however, he then invoked Dares's expedient. Perhaps Paris's experience was merely illusory.[1] Yet Lemaire included as well the allegorizations which traditionally validated the nonhistorical Judgment. Contradicting all that the word "history" implies, he treated the Judgment as a poetic fiction whose *raison d'être* was not its historical truth but rather its utility in conveying truths of moral and spiritual significance. *Les Illustrations* is thus an appropriate coda to this study. Lemaire draws together the three traditions we have followed from antiquity, yet he is a man of the Renaissance. His three goddesses are not precisely what they were for Fulgentius and those who followed him. His approach to the allegorization of the Judgment, moreover, shows that the old Fulgentian tradition was losing ground.

Lemaire purports to write history. By the time book 3 of the *Illustrations* appeared in 1513, he was the historiographer for Louis XII of France.[2] As a history, he intended the work to go beyond the scheme of Fredegarius, the main source for those who traced the Trojan origin of the Franks.[3] Lemaire would show that not only did fleeing Trojans come to the shores of France after the fall of Troy, but that Troy and Gaul could trace their origins to founders who shared common descent from Noah. His inspiration for this new link between Troy and the nations of Europe was the recently published *Antiquitatum Variarum Volumina XVII* by Giovanni Nanni of Viterbo (Rome, 1498), supposedly a history of the world based on previously unknown texts.[4]

Drawing on Nanni, Lemaire begins his history with Noah's adventures after the flood. By chapter 19, Noah's descendant Hercules has founded the Duchy of Burgundy in Gaul, his son Tuscus has founded Tuscany in Italy, and his remote descendant Dardanus has founded Troy. As Rhemus, the thirty-second king of Gaul, is founding Reims, Laomedon is killed in the first destruction of Troy, and Priam comes to the throne. This synchronization of world history yields, however, in chapter 20, to what has been aptly characterized as "the romance of Paris."[5] Leaving behind Nanni for other sources, Lemaire devotes the remaining twenty-four chapters of book 1 and most of book 2 to the adventures of the Trojan prince.

Lemaire elaborates his sources into a narrative of great interest and charm.[6] While he doubtless relied on handbooks for an overview of his story and for certain erudite details, the spirit and atmosphere of his Judgment show the unmistakable influence of two classical treatments of the theme: that of Ovid, in the *Heroides*, and that of Apuleius, in *The Golden Ass*.[7] From the former comes the psychological depth of his characterizations;[8] from the latter comes the scene's pageantry and splendor.

Lemaire's Judgment begins with the Wedding of Peleus and Thetis. Starting with a basic outline of the story, Lemaire displays his erudition while at the same time creating an episode steeped in magic and the supernatural. He makes the apple with which Discord provokes the goddesses' quarrel come from the garden of the Hesperides, an unusual detail that he may have known from the pseudo-Clementines.[9] Having established his command of classical lore, he goes on to create for the episode the atmosphere of a fairy tale. It is not enough that Discord should write around the apple in the time-honored fashion, "Let the gleaming golden apple be given to the most beautiful" (1.30 [p. 222]); she also, like an evil queen in a children's story, poisons it. Having thrown the apple, she plunges down into hell, her home. Thus Lemaire merges classical with Christian supernaturalism and, in order to create a distinctive and dramatic version of the wedding episode, introduces motifs that evoke popular story.

As the goddesses prepare to depart from Mount Olympus for the meeting with their judge, Lemaire provides each with an equipage incorporating the traditional details of her cult. His desire to create an effect of pageantry is probably to be traced to his acquaintance with the Judgment scene in *The Golden Ass*, but his raw material is most likely drawn from Boccaccio's *De Genealogiis Deorum*— the detailed descriptions with which Boccaccio had accommodated each goddess to his genealogical plan. Juno's chariot, prepared by her messenger, Iris, is pulled by peacocks harnessed with gold collars. Lemaire knows from Boccaccio that Iris is the daughter of Thaumas[10] and that the peacocks' painted tails are the eyes of Argus.[11] Venus's chariot, prepared by the three Graces, is pulled by six swans and twelve doves—Boccaccio had said that her chariot was drawn by swans.[12] Pallas is borne to the scene of judgment by wings fastened to her shoulders and feet—Boccaccio had mentioned her "winged sandals."[13] Thus Lemaire weaves together details to surround the ancient gods with splendor.

Leaving behind his glorious Olympians, Lemaire shows his versatility by sketching with equal skill the simplicity of Paris's rustic state. The identification of Paris's valley as Mesaulon leads us to his major source for this section, Boccaccio's judgment scene. From Boccaccio's dry summary—"[The goddesses], as they say, showed themselves nude to that Paris, under the thick shade of the grove which is called Mesaulon" (6.22 [1.303])—he fashions a charming pastoral. Paris leans against a great hollow crag carpeted with grass and moss. He is surrounded by his dogs and his pasturing flocks. His food is a bit of bread with dates and fresh mulberries that he has gathered (1.30 [pp. 227–29]).

It is here that Mercury and the goddesses find him and request his aid as judge. Lemaire's Judgment is a *tour de force* of spectacle and erudition in which he makes of the classical story a splendid pageant. Again drawing on Boccaccio's discussions of the individual goddesses in the *De Genealogiis Deorum*, Lemaire combines materials sanctioned by classical tradition with details from his own imagination in order to create for each goddess a portrait laden with significance. Not only does each detail bear silent witness to hidden truths, but Lemaire has provided, probably from Boccaccio too, explicit interpretations of the goddesses' iconography to an extent that makes his Judgment an important link in the allegorical tradition discussed in Chapter 3.

Juno's clothing is intended to reflect her traditional association with wealth and sovereignty, as well as her cosmic identification with the air. Her dress is purple, the color of royalty, and garnished with great pearls, while her azure cloak is ornamented with figures alluding to her connection with the atmosphere: birds, clouds, rain, and hail. Her belt, woven of gold thread, is covered with studs and bosses of enameled gold and gems. Her scepter is made of aloe wood from the terrestrial paradise (1.31 [pp. 231–32]). Many of her attributes have deeper significance: peacocks are placed in her service, for example, because nobles always seek exquisite adornments to win the attention of the people and also because peacocks are royal, proud, haughty birds and very loud.

Though he identifies her as the goddess of wealth and opulence, Lemaire's Juno is associated much more with sovereignty than with wealth per se. The life she represents is not the reprehensible scramble for possessions that it was for Fulgentius, but rather a life of inner and outer nobility—a life rather like the lives of the noble patrons for whom Lemaire wrote. He has been unable to free himself entirely from the legacy of Fulgentius; a trace of *contemptus mundi* is evident when, thinking of the connection between riches and fortune, he says that the great speed of Juno's chariot indicates fortune's instability (1.31 [p. 232]). Yet the interpretation of Juno's iconography is for the most part neutral, if not positive.

If he has retained as part of his portrait of Juno her traditional association with wealth, Lemaire has skillfully assimilated it to his evaluation of the goddess as representative of the noble life—a life for which the resurgence of Aristotelianism had created a positive climate. Stressing her association with sovereignty, Lemaire sees her wealth as a concomitant of nobility.

Juno naturally advocates the life she represents, yet she does not merely defend riches; she defends a mode of existence in which riches are seen as the appropriate prerogative of the ruling class. Since Lemaire was more familiar with medieval monarchy than with Athenian democracy, he sees the active life not as the life of a Greek citizen but as the life of a medieval king. The riches and opulence with which Juno is identified are seen as inspiring a certain *noblesse oblige:* be courageous, Juno exhorts Paris. Put aside pastoral rusticity and aspire to royal stature. I am called Juno, *quasi iuuans omnes,* that is to say, "aid of all," or Lucina, because I give light entrance to all noble hearts and distribute worldly riches to the worthy. Paris is encouraged to reclaim the nobility that Juno knows is his: high marriages, royal crowns, terrestrial monarchies—you are capable of these things as much for the antiquity of your origin as the magnificence of your person. She criticizes those who live in leisure and solitary dreams of philosophy, passing their days uselessly. They cannot obtain her treasure, she warns, because they do not enjoy action. Men of royal vocation should not think about literature, moral virtues, and the like (1.31 [pp. 233–35]).

Though it is clear that Lemaire was acquainted with the Fulgentian tradition, the portrait of the active life that Juno presents varies from Fulgentius's scheme in important ways. Lemaire barely criticizes the wealth with which Juno is associated, but he stresses her link with royal power. The life she offers Paris would surely have been seen by the members of Lemaire's audience as worthy and good, a life like their own. Despite its lack of concern for the moral virtues, this life is ranked with the contemplative as lasting in value. Juno's parting words to Paris reveal the allegorical significance of his choice: "Are you not ashamed to prefer the voluptuous and unprofitable life to the active and contemplative lives? Are you not ashamed to put aside the lasting for the transitory?" (1.33 [p. 258]). Significantly, she allies herself with Pallas, acknowledging the worth of Pallas's gifts and ranking them with her own against the worthless gauds of Venus. Thus we see reflected the classical scheme in which the active and contemplative lives are worthy choices separated by a wide gulf from the worthless and self-indulgent life of pleasure.

Pallas's appearance reflects her connection with wisdom and war. Her threefold garments, changeable in color, are her own creation: Lemaire knew from Boccaccio that Pallas was credited with the invention of woolworking and cloth.[14] Figured on her robes are the seven liberal arts, the seven virtues, and images of warfare and human prudence. The triple nature of her garments and the changeable quality of the colors show that sapience is hidden from the ignorant. The goddess is armed because she founded the science of warfare and because prudence is always well equipped with defense against those who wish her ill. Pallas wears the crested helmet and the aegis with which she is often depicted in art, and she carries her crystalline shield and her lance. Each attribute reveals something of her nature; the owl which surmounts her helmet signifies, for example, that a prudent man sees as clearly by night as by day. Lemaire betrays his application of Pallas's significance to the lives of his noble patrons when he explains that her attendants, Fear, Terror, Diligence, and Wisdom—inspired by Apuleius's Fear and Terror—all belong to wise princes (1.31 [pp. 236–37]).

When Pallas speaks, moreover, it becomes clear that what she offers Paris is not the contemplative life with which she was associated by Fulgentius, nor even the warrior's life of earlier tradition, but rather the life of a soldier-prince. She can speak only of war, not of rule, however, lest she encroach upon the territory of Juno. Urging Paris to turn away from Juno and Venus, she offers him a plethora of virtues without which, she says, her brother Mars would never be able to conduct his battles. It is no accident that these rewards—eloquence and knowledge of history are only two from a long list—sound more like the attributes of an ideal prince than the ornaments of the contemplative life (1.31 [pp. 238–39]). When Pallas at last turns to that contemplation with which she is traditionally associated, she offers it not as an end in itself, but as a means of relaxing from the demands of public life and developing administrative abilities (1.31 [p. 239]). These results are hardly what Aristotle had in mind when he saw in the happiness gained from speculation man's highest aim.

Catering to the interests of his noble audience, then, Lemaire exalts the arts of government, going even further than Aristotle in praising the active life. Not only is it nearly as good as the highest life offered man; it is really almost better. The twofold role of nobility as defender and ruler is reflected in the complementary portraits of Pallas and Juno.

If the portraits of Pallas and Juno depart from Fulgentian tradition, Lemaire's picture of Venus is even more surprising. He emphasizes her beneficent aspects. Venus's appearance reflects her link with love and fertility, as well as her identification with the planet that bears her name. Her *undercote* is the color of grass in the spring, evoking her old association with the season of growth.[15] Her *houppelande,* whose design recalls her identity as the evening star,[16] is yellow and gold, alternating with blue and embossed with silver stars (1.32 [p. 241]). Depicted on the borders of her garments are animals of both sexes and small nude children.[17] So finely woven is her clothing that when the wind presses it against her body, her form is revealed. Lemaire may have recalled that in *The Golden Ass,* Venus's thin silk smock, her only garment there, was sometimes lifted by the wind, other times pressed to her body, revealing the outline of her limbs.[18] A black velvet ribbon around her forehead displays a star-shaped carbuncle representing the planet Venus at night. A chaplet of myrtle adorns her elaborately dressed blond hair, and she carries a bouquet of red and white roses (1.32 [pp. 241–42]).[19] She wears her characteristic belt, or *cestos,* whose significance Boccaccio had already altered from Homeric tradition, where it represented Aphrodite's power to awaken sexual desire.[20] For Lemaire, as for Boccaccio, it restrains the "unduly wayward lasciviousness of Venus."[21]

In creating his distinctive portrait of Venus, Lemaire drew on traditions that acknowledged the complex nature of the goddess, who had long been considered under two aspects, one beneficent and the other destructive.[22] The *locus classicus* for this distinction in the ancient world is Plato's *Symposium:* "Does anyone doubt that she is double? Surely there is the elder, of no mother born, but daughter of Heaven, whence we name her Heavenly; while the younger was the child of Zeus and Dione, and her we call Popular."[23] Lucretius, whom Lemaire claimed to have read, includes both Venuses in the *De Rerum Natura*,[24] and the distinction between the two Venuses passed into medieval thought as a commonplace useful in discussions of love and sexuality. It was handed on by such writers as Remigius of Auxerre,[25] John Scotus Erigena,[26] Alain de Lille,[27] Bernard Silvestris,[28] and the Third Vatican Mythographer, who cited Remigius's simple formulation: "According to that same Remigius, however, there are two Venuses: one chaste and modest, who is said to be present at honest loves, the other voluptuous, goddess of passion."[29]

This formulation made its way into Boccaccio's *De Genealogiis Deorum*, from which Lemaire drew much else that he applied to his portraits of the goddesses. Boccaccio devoted separate chapters to the two Venuses, whom he identifies as *Venus magna*, daughter of Caelum and Dies (3.22), and *Venus secunda*, born from the severed genitals of Caelum or Saturn (3.23)—Boccaccio scrupulously acknowledges variations in the story from source to source. (A third Venus, inventor of prostitution, is given Jove and Dione as parents [11.4].) As Earl Schreiber points out, however, Boccaccio had a certain amount of difficulty keeping each Venus in her own moral sphere.[30] *Venus magna*, for example, shares with *Venus secunda* certain attributes, such as doves, whose meanings are inevitably associated with lasciviousness. If Boccaccio tended, though, to give his good Venus some negative associations, the opposite is true of Lemaire.

Although he makes her the daughter of Jupiter and Dione, and mentions her link with prostitution (1.32 [p. 244]), Lemaire's Venus is nevertheless beneficent. He has emphasized the goddess's positive aspects and subtly altered the negative interpretations of her iconography. Thus we have trouble accepting Paris's choice as the moral outrage it was considered in traditional allegorizations of the Judgment. In Lemaire's portrait of Venus, her garments evoke her crucial role in the cycles of nature, and her belt, the *cestos*, represents the limits placed on passion by shame and the laws of society.

Turning to his explicit interpretations of Venus, we see that

Lemaire has also changed some traditional explanations of her iconography. He includes, for example, her roses—she carries a bouquet and then later wears a rose garland around her loins—but he omits the allegory which connects the prick of roses with desire or the pangs of conscience, as in Fulgentius or Boccaccio.[31] Furthermore, Venus's roses are usually red, a color traditionally taken to represent the redness of shame.[32] Lemaire has given her both red and white roses, as if to temper the lustful associations of red with the purity implied by white.[33]

When Venus speaks to Paris, she stresses her power over gods and men, but she also emphasizes her role in maintaining the stability of the universe. The entire mechanism ("la machine totalle") of the world, she says, would dissolve and fall into ruin if it were deprived of her loving harmony (1.32 [p. 245]). No medieval writer we considered applied to Venus's role in the Judgment her association with the concord of elements in the composition of the universe. The idea is, however, extremely old.

Empedocles had seen the universe as governed by φιλία and νξῖκος, love and hate. While love held the elements together, hate strove to separate them.[34] Heraclitus applied this scheme to the union of Ares and Aphrodite in *Odyssey* 8, thus seeing the myth as a cosmic allegory, an idea which was passed along by Plutarch in his *Moralia*.[35] Zeno borrowed the theme from Homeric exegesis and made Aphrodite represent the power which holds the elements in composition.[36] We saw in Chapter 1 that a positive view of Venus as σύγχρασις, or that mixture which creates harmony out of the warring elements, was picked up in Stoic interpretations of the Judgment.[37] For the Middle Ages, the most striking statement of this theme appeared in the *Consolation of Philosophy:* the often-quoted meter 8 from book 2. Boethius replaced the goddess's name with that which she personified—love—but his statement of love's crucial role in the cosmos was certainly indebted to the classical and late-classical tradition sketched above.[38] The same notion is expressed in Bernard Silvestris's characterization of the good Venus as "the music of the world."[39] It seems clear that Lemaire is dealing with this idea when he makes Venus responsible for uniting the diverse elements which make up the world. In doing so, however, he departs from Boccaccio, who says nothing about this aspect of the goddess. It is possible that Lemaire was familiar with the Boethian passage itself, since Boethius too had linked chaste marriages with Venus's role as universal concord (book 2, meter 8, 22–25) and since Boethius's "soluere machinam" (21) parallels Lemaire's "la machine totalle . . . se dissolueroit" (1.32 [p. 245]).[40]

It is understandable that no widespread medieval tradition had seen in the Venus of the Judgment the love which binds the elements and moves the sun and other stars. Even the tradition of good Venus and bad Venus rarely makes universal concord a facet of the good Venus. For both manifestations of the goddess, the stress is usually on fertility and sex. That Lemaire is truly making a departure from the prevailing view of Venus is further seen in his handling of the *cestos.*

For Boccaccio, the *cestos* had been given Venus not by Nature or by poets but by the authority of laws. Its purpose was to control wandering lasciviousness (3.22 [1.144]). Boccaccio's Nature is the Nature of the *Roman de la Rose;* she could scarcely have furnished Venus with useful restraint because she herself functions outside the moral order. Thus law rather than Nature furnished the belt. Lemaire makes a crucial change in Boccaccio's wording. About the *cestos* he says, "Dame Nature herself forged it once and gave it to her, so that the unduly wayward lasciviousness of Venus should be checked and restrained by proper shame, and also by the authority of conjugal laws" (1.32 [p. 242]). Clearly very different from that envisioned by Boccaccio, Lemaire's Nature is like that of the *De Rerum Natura* of Lucretius, an author whom he lists as a source,[41] or like Nature in the *De Planctu Naturae* and the *Anticlaudian* of Alain de Lille, or, near his own time, the *Echecs amoureux.* She represents a natural moral law directing man's potentially destructive sexual impulses into channels sanctioned by society.[42] That Lemaire was familiar with the complex of ideas we find in Alain is suggested by the fact that he makes Genius a priest of Venus in another work, his *La Concorde des deux langages.*[43]

After Lemaire has exhausted the narrative possibilities of his drama—Paris's choice, Venus's triumph, Juno's anger, and so on— he moves on to the next order of business: expounding the story's deeper significance. With respect to the Wedding, he first explains what the story means "according to the historical sense," citing as his source Dictys of Crete, who had indeed euhemerized the tale. That those who assembled for the wedding were called gods, demigods, and heroes simply means, says Lemaire, that the relatives of the bride and groom were royalty, nobility, and ladies adored on earth as if they were goddesses (1.35 [p. 271]). He next provides a physical explanation from Fulgentius: the ancient philosophers thought each god and goddess had power over a part of the human body and thus they made each god present at the nativity of Achilles to make a perfect man (1.35 [pp. 271–72]).

For his interpretation of the Judgment, too, he follows Fulgentius, though he adds some new material as well. The poets meant it to be understood, he says, that Paris had the planet Venus in his horoscope; she ruled at the hour of his birth and inclined him to amorous and venerian things. For the golden apple, which is not in Fulgentius's Judgment but only in his treatment of the Wedding, Lemaire provides an original interpretation. Following the classical tradition which makes Paris beautiful—Fulgentius had specifically said that he was not[44]—Lemaire makes the golden apple represent Paris's "noble" head, which was round and "of golden splendor like the apple." That he gives the apple or his head to Venus, says Lemaire, means that he gives his understanding to the voluptuous life. The strongest condemnation of Paris's choice comes when, in connection with his Fulgentian interpretation of the Judgment, Lemaire cites Firmicus Maternus on the type of character to be expected of one with Paris's horoscope: such a conjunction of planets produces "weddings full of strife, and marriage without peace . . . from which can follow wondrous tumult of deadly war. . . . And all this brought about by venerian cupidity" (1.35 [p. 273]).

Finally, Lemaire offers an extended interpretation of the Wedding and Judgment from the late-classical *Recognitions* of St. Clement. He is the first we have seen to resurrect this source. After explaining that the dishes at the banquet of the gods represent the study of philosophy, which is available to any man who wishes to taste of it, he makes Paris signify the man of crude understanding who rejects chastity and virtue to follow sensuality, bringing ruin not only to himself but to all his house (1.35 [pp. 274–75]).

Lemaire's interpretations of the Judgment represent no distinctive departure from medieval tradition. Venus is identified with destructive sexual passion, and Paris's choice of her is seen as his undoing. Yet two things about the interpretations are disturbing. One is the very fact of their existence: though the exegetical tradition had shown that the historical truths of the Bible could yield up spiritual truths without losing their historical validity, those who allegorized the fables of the ancients had always done so on the premise that the stories themselves were not true. When he allegorizes the events of his history, Lemaire undercuts the notion that he is writing history. The second disturbing thing is that the content of the interpretations clashes with Lemaire's earlier portrait of Venus: Paris's choice of Venus is wrong, yet the goddess herself is portrayed in a positive light. Both contradictions can be explained by the same phenomenon; the key is the late date of *Les Illustrations.*

The medieval traditions of interpretation, particularly moral interpretation, were becoming less important by 1500.[45] Lemaire is original, but he applies his originality to his narrative of the Judgment rather than its interpretation. Dozens of commentators had seen in the Judgment a choice of lives, and Lemaire uncritically took the interpretations that were at hand. He hastens over them; the one from the pseudo-Clementine *Recognitions,* particularly, is offered nearly word for word. The Judgment itself seems to have lost its vitality as an exemplum condemning the life of pleasure: Lemaire was drawn to it for its aesthetic possibilities instead. Thus Venus herself still fascinates. When he deals with the goddess of love and her attributes, Lemaire rethinks tradition, and in rethinking, he revives it. The Middle Ages knew a good Venus and a bad Venus, but as long as the Judgment still held sway as an allegory, the Venus associated with it had to be the destructive goddess. Lemaire's positive Venus can function only in a treatment of the Judgment which no longer takes seriously the Fulgentian moralizations.

We have followed the Judgment from its earliest appearances in the ancient world up to the beginning of the Renaissance. By far the most important tradition has been the allegorical, which, primarily through the influence of Fulgentius, made the Judgment evoke for centuries the choice among three modes of life. Had the Judgment's strong allegorical associations not been sufficient, however, to make it ideally suited to the dream-vision genre, its long tradition as a historical episode had equipped it to function in the dream-vision form. Ever since the *De Excidio Troiae Historia* of "Dares the Phrygian," Paris's encounter with the goddesses had been merely a dream he dreamed after a tiring hunt. Surely the three dream visions which use the story—Machaut's *Dit de la fonteinne amoureuse*, Froissart's *Espinette amoureuse*, and the anonymous *Echecs amoureux*—represent the Judgment's most striking literary applications. Yet the story's power to teach while delighting is demonstrated too by its use in a context such as Convenevole da Prato's flattery of Robert of Naples, implying that he would have resisted Venus's charms. In *Les Illustrations de Gaule et Singularitez de Troye*, however, the Judgment's significance is no longer primarily moral. By the year 1500, elements of the goddesses' old Fulgentian associations still linger beneath the surface of the fable, but we can no longer hear or see them very well.

Appendix: The Judgment of Paris in Medieval Art

The Judgment of Paris was a popular artistic theme in its own right during the classical period.[1] During the Middle Ages, however, its treatment in art was confined largely to illustrations in manuscripts of works dealing with the matter of Troy. It began to appear as a subject for miniatures only after the beginning of the fourteenth century; at least, extant representations of the theme date exclusively from that relatively late period. Many of the works which include the Judgment—histories, for example—lent themselves to presentation in lavishly produced and illustrated volumes. Though its appearance in medieval art is thus limited almost entirely to the illustration of the Trojan legend, the depiction of the theme in art represents a substantial tradition in the Middle Ages. The illustrations are based exclusively on the textual tradition; thus there is a sharp break with classical representations of the Judgment. By the same token, though, the art reflects precisely the literary traditions we have traced.

A review of several outstanding examples of the Judgment in art will reveal that the artistic traditions faithfully reflect the clearly differentiated literary traditions that we have considered. It will become clear also that the artistic traditions, though derived from the literary traditions, go on to flourish independently. Thus a work whose text reflects the classical version of the Judgment might well be illustrated with a picture that shows the rational version. Or a miniature whose details derive from the distinctive classical version of the Judgment passed on in the *Excidium Troiae* and the *Compendium Historiae Troianae-Romanae* might illustrate a text which knows only the details of the standard classical version.

The most common type of Judgment encountered in medieval art is that derived from the tradition of Dares. In this tradition, it will be recalled, Paris only dreams of his adventure with the goddesses. The popularity of this version in art is probably due to the fact that, through the *Historia Destructionis Troiae* of Guido de Columnis, the dream-Judgment became the most respected and widespread version. Many subsequent histories of Troy were based on the *Historia Destructionis Troiae*, and miniatures which illustrated the Judgment in these works tended to follow the artistic traditions established in illustrated manuscripts of Guido's history.

Figure 1 shows an early depiction of the Judgment from a manuscript of the *Historia Destructionis Troiae* produced in Northern Italy during the 1300s. This particular miniature has been studied in some detail by Hugo Buchthal, who regards it as one of the oldest extant medieval depictions of the theme.[2] Buchthal believes that the exemplar of the scene was based directly on Guido's text rather than on an existing miniature of the Judgment. Guido, it will be recalled, copied Benoît de Sainte-Maure's *Roman de Troie*, but he changed some of the details of the Judgment. This miniature clearly depicts Guido's Judgment, not that of Benoît. As in Guido's text, the horse is tied to a tree, and Paris has his bow and quiver. The spring, mentioned by Benoît but not by Guido, is missing. Buchthal also thinks that the model is responsible for the oriental-style clothing and the Byzantine elements, possibly borrowed from a cycle accompanying a Byzantine version of the Troy story. He suggests that these elements may be "an attempt to authenticate [the narrative] by evoking its Eastern Mediterranean background and setting."[3]

More than one scene has been fused in this miniature. Artists who depicted the Judgment of Paris as handled by Guido had problems to overcome. How is it possible to depict the action of a dream? Does the dreamer see himself? If so, does he see himself asleep or awake? And if the goddesses disrobe, at what point in the action should the scene be frozen? The first problem is solved here

Figure 1. The Judgment of Paris, from the *Historia Destructionis Troiae* of Guido de Columnis, fourteenth century (Codex Bodmer 78, Biblioteca Bodmer, Geneva, f. 17 v). Reprinted by permission.

by using the continuous method. First Paris is shown asleep, and then he is shown, as if the dream scene were viewed from without, taking part in the Judgment of which he dreams. In fact, he seems just on the point of awarding the prize to the goddess he has chosen; thus the artist must depict the goddesses nude, since Paris presumably has had his opportunity to look them over before arriving at his decision.

Figure 2 demonstrates the continuity of the artistic tradition represented by Figure 1. It is a miniature from a manuscript of Raoul Le Fèvre's *Recueil des histoires de troyes* produced in 1495.[4] The portion of the *Recueil* dealing with the Trojan War was a French translation of Guido's *Historia*. This miniature presents a much more elegant version of the Judgment, which reflects the *Recueil's* status as a ducal commission. Paris is asleep, as if prepared to dream. We recognize the familiar bow and arrows which Guido

Figure 2. The Judgment of Paris, from the *Recueil des histoires de troyes* of
Raoul Le Fèvre, 1495 (B.n. fr. 22552, Paris, f. 214 v). Phot. Bibl. Nat., Paris.

Figure 3. The Judgment of Paris, from the *Epitre d'Othéa* of Christine de Pisan, late fifteenth century (Ms. Bodley 421, Bodleian Library, Oxford, f. 51 v). Reprinted by permission.

Figure 4. The Judgment of Paris, from the *Excidium Troiae,* fourteenth century (Ms. Ricc. 881, Biblioteca Riccardiana, Florence, f. 55 r). Reprinted by permission.

Figure 5. Paris and the Rival Bulls, from the *Fulgentius Metaforalis* of John Ridwall, fifteenth century (Ms. Pal. Lat. 1066, Vatican Library, Rome, f. 229 r). Reprinted by permission.

Figure 6. The Judgment of Paris, from the *Dit de la fonteinne amoureuse* of Guillaume de Machaut, fourteenth century (B.n. fr. 22545, Paris, f. 129 v). Phot. Bibl. Nat., Paris.

Figure 7. The Three Lives, from the *Ovide moralisé*, early fourteenth century (Bibl. municipale o.4 [1044], Rouen, f. 286 r). Reprinted by permission.

Figure 8. The Goddesses as the Three Lives, from a commentary on the *Echecs amoureux*, around 1500 (B.n. fr. 143, Paris, f. 198 v). Phot. Bibl. Nat., Paris.

Figure 9. The Goddesses as the Three Lives, from the *Fulgentius Metaforalis* of John Ridwall, fifteenth century (Ms. Pal. Lat. 1066, Vatican Library, Rome, f. 230 v). Reprinted by permission.

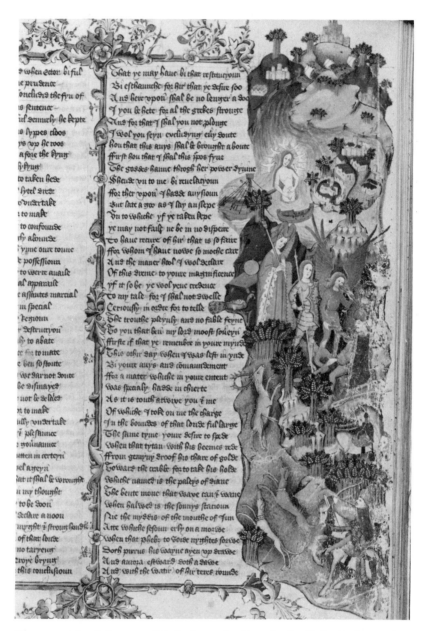

Figure 10. The Judgment of Paris, from the *Troy Book* of John Lydgate, after 1460 (Rylands English Ms. 1, John Rylands University Library of Manchester, f. 42 r). With the permission of the John Rylands University Library of Manchester.

gave him. He is dressed not in the Byzantine-inspired garb of Figure 1, but in a splendid suit of armor appropriate to his status as the son of a king: the tradition Guido used had no episode in which Paris was rejected by his parents to be raised in obscurity. Mercury has been added to the scene, reflecting Guido's text but not the older illustration of the *Historia* shown in Figure 1. The god is lavishly dressed in a long, ermine-lined gown. Though the miniature seems to show the embassy's initial approach to the judge, the goddesses are already nude.

The most interesting variation here is the sumptuous fountain. This fountain was not in Guido's text, though Benoît's Judgment included a spring. The version of Guido's Judgment incorporated into the *Recueil* placed the episode in early May, probably because by the later Middle Ages the dream-vision tradition had made May the appropriate time for a visionary experience. The same tradition can explain the fountain in this scene. The spring at which Benoît imagined the Judgment occurring must have been a natural spring, yet here we have an elaborate fountain which recalls the fountain of the *Roman de la Rose* and its progeny in both literature and art. By the date that this manuscript was produced, too, Lydgate's *Troy Book* and the second redaction of the *Histoire ancienne* had added fountains to the setting of the Judgment.

So widespread was the pictorial tradition deriving from Guido's *Historia* that it acquired a life of its own, being pressed into service to illustrate even the classical version of the Judgment. Over forty manuscripts of Christine de Pisan's *Epitre d'Othéa* survive, many designed so that each of the one hundred chapters is illustrated with its own miniature.[5] The *Othéa* was Christine's most popular book, deriving its popularity in part from its lavish illustrations, which Christine apparently conceived as an integral part of the work.[6] In many manuscripts, the miniatures seem based specifically on Christine's text; some manuscripts were even designed under her direction.[7] But consider the depiction of the Judgment which illustrates chapter 73 in Oxford Bodl. 421 (Figure 3), produced in the last third of the fifteenth century, possibly in northern France:[8] it clearly represents the artistic tradition deriving from Guido's Judgment. The sketch seems hastily done, as well, suggesting that the manuscript in which it appears was not carefully designed but that the miniatures were based upon models that were readily available. On the other hand, certain amusing details suggest that the artist may have known enough of the text he illustrated to depart from his model and comment on Paris's story.

Chapter 73 of the *Othéa* deals with the Judgment itself rather than Paris's dream; it is based on the *Ovide moralisé* and Guillaume de Machaut's *Dit de la fonteinne amoureuse,* which derive from classical tradition. (Chapter 68 deals with Paris's dream, but the cycle in Oxford Bodl. 421 includes no picture for chapter 68.) Though the text of chapter 73 relies on classical tradition, in this particular miniature Paris sleeps with closed eyes and head on hand, as in Dares. The woodsy setting is that of Dares, Benoît, and Guido. The most telling links with Guido are the tethered horse and the nudity of the goddesses. Note that for all the difference in the miniature's style, the horse is similar to the horse in Figure 1, whereas the elaborate fountain recalls the fountain in Figure 2. But there are unexpected elements: Paris's helmet seems to have an entire bird for its crest, and, another novelty, the elaborate fountain's major ornament is a small urinating figure. One is tempted to see in the bird on Paris's helmet and in the prominent penis of the figure on the fountain interpolations by a witty but not very skilled artist who knew enough of the story he illustrated to comment visually on Paris's reputation as a lover.[9]

Much less common in medieval art are depictions of the version of the Judgment which I have labeled the classical version. The most obvious reason for the infrequency of this version in the pictorial tradition is that the dream version of the Judgment was really the most widespread in literature. There are, however, a few miniatures which depend on the tradition in which the Judgment is not a dream. These miniatures even reveal specific links with the tradition of the *Excidium Troiae* and the *Compendium Historiae Troianae-Romanae,* which transmitted to the Middle Ages a distinctive version of the classical tradition.

We found our earliest extant miniature of Guido's version of the Judgment in a manuscript of Guido's *Historia.* Likewise, our earliest depiction of the Judgment as handled by the *Excidium Troiae* and the *Compendium Historiae Troianae-Romanae* is in a fourteenth-century manuscript of the *Excidium,* Ms. 881 in the Biblioteca

Riccardiana (Figure 4).[10] The artist has fused more than one scene in the miniature. The cluster of figures on the left, with identical hair, faces, clothing, and feet, must be successive views of Paris; the artist is suggesting the passage of time during which the goddesses come secretly to Paris with their bribes. The separate approach of each goddess is indicated by the three arches, which, however, accommodate only two goddesses, Juno and Minerva. Each goddess gestures as if pleading to be chosen most beautiful. Venus has escaped from her arch, which nevertheless echoes her gesture in its upper curve, and she appears in the scene intended to represent the day fixed by Paris for the goddesses to return for judgment. The artist has depicted the climactic moment in which Venus throws aside her garments as she offers Paris a beautiful wife. He has conflated that moment with Paris's awarding Venus the prize, the golden apple. In his capacity as judge, Paris now appears seated in regal splendor within his own arch, having donned a robe which gives him a magisterial air.

A second miniature which clearly shows the influence of this distinctive version of the story is found in a fifteenth-century manuscript of John Ridwall's *Fulgentius Metaforalis* from the Vatican Library (Figure 5).[11] The *Fulgentius Metaforalis*, itself a work of the fourteenth century, does not include the Judgment of Paris, but some manuscripts of the work incorporate a version of the story.[12] The miniature conflates three scenes. Paris, distinguishable by his grand clothing and his crown, observes the struggle between his own bull and its rival, as goats graze in the foreground. On the right, two companion shepherds seem to witness and comment on the action, as if Paris had already judged the bulls: in the *Excidium Troiae* and the *Compendium Historiae Troianae-Romanae*, Paris's judgment in favor of the rival bull earns him a reputation for justice. Simultaneously, on the left, the three goddesses approach for *their* judgment, having been sent to Paris by Jupiter because his reputation for justice has already spread. That they, unlike the shepherds on the right, are not intended to be immediately *in* the scene is suggested by the little ridge of landscape that at the far left separates them from the black bull. As in the *Excidium Troiae* and the *Compendium Historiae Troianae-Romanae*, the goddesses approach Paris themselves without the intervention of Mercury.

A relationship with the tradition of the *Excidium Troiae* and the *Compendium Historiae Troianae-Romanae* is also found, surprisingly, in a miniature from a fourteenth-century manuscript containing Guillaume de Machaut's *Dit de la fonteinne amoureuse* (Figure 6).[13] Machaut had used the classical version of the story, which he knew from the *Ovide moralisé*. But the miniature includes details which allude specifically to the distinctive version of the story found in the *Excidium Troiae* and the *Compendium Historiae Troianae-Romanae*. On the left are the three goddesses, virtually indistinguishable from one another. Mercury has nothing of the divine herald about him, but with his fashionable sleeves and long, slit cloak, furred on the inside, resembles an elegant nobleman. That the divine embassy approaches against a dimensionless, patterned background suggests their otherworldly origin, whereas Paris's setting is more naturalistic, a rocky hillside surmounted by a clump of trees. The artist has been faithful to the classical version of the story that Machaut used, dressing Paris in a humble cowled tunic whose looseness and intermediate length show its rusticity, in contrast with the extremes of fullness, tightness, length, and shortness in the dandyish Mercury's garb. Paris's garment seems to be fastened at the waist by a rope, whose frayed ends the artist has placed in Paris's hand, perhaps in order to emphasize his humble costume. True to Machaut's text, Paris carries a bow in his hand, though its awkward position suggests that perhaps the artist fashioned it out of something else in a model, such as the club which the shepherd Paris more commonly carries (e.g., Morgan 396, f. 113v). In Machaut's text, Paris watches only sheep, and so the two bulls, much larger and more detailed than the sheep, are puzzling, until we remember the tradition represented by the *Excidium Troiae* and the *Compendium Historiae Troianae-Romanae* in which Paris rewards with a crown the rival bull which conquers his own.

The allegorized Judgment has its artistic tradition too. A depiction of the three lives accompanies the *Ovide moralisé* in Rouen Bibl. municipale o.4 (1044), produced early in the fourteenth century (Figure 7).[14] In this miniature, which appears in a manuscript that Carla Lord has characterized as the "ancestor of all surviving illustrated *Ovide moralisé* manuscripts,"[15] it is difficult to know whether we are being shown the three goddesses or personifications of the three lives. Clearly the depiction of the lives, if they are the lives and not the goddesses, has been influenced by the fact that they are represented allegorically by the goddesses.

In the center of the miniature, the life of pleasure is depicted as a woman with an elaborate coiffure and a sumptuous gown; she holds a small mirror into which she gazes as she combs her hair. It would be hard to imagine a more appropriate representation of the voluptuous life. Because the flesh knows many pleasures and succumbs to many sins, definitions of the life represented by Venus usually try to leave room for all possibilities. The medieval moralist, however, most often focuses on lust when he decries the life given over to the senses. Venus's own traditional identification with passion fosters this narrowing of definition, as does Paris's particular sin in choosing Helen, so that the voluptuous life is implicitly the life of *luxuria* or lust. Further, both *luxuria* and Venus could be depicted holding mirrors,[16] so that the familiar iconography of a beautiful woman combing her hair and gazing into a mirror serves as a characterizing device for both Venus and the life she represents.

The active life is represented by the figure on the left holding a distaff and spindle. The image seems almost to recommend the active life as a wholesome contrast to the self-absorption of the voluptuous. Yet the figure's elaborate coiffure and clothing suggest a woman who is concerned with worldly affairs; they suggest, in fact, the traditional view of Juno as goddess of wealth and sovereignty.

The image of the contemplative life, a cloaked religious reading a large book, evokes Fulgentius more than it does the *Ovide moralisé*. It was Fulgentius who had seen in the bishops, priests, and monks of his era the philosophers of old and their search for truth. He thus implied that the love of learning was an activity not incompatible with contemplation. The contemplative life as described in the *Ovide moralisé* is a life in which the love of learning has been completely overshadowed by the desire for God. It is a life available to any Christian, not just a religious, and the author of the *Ovide moralisé*, whose aim is prescriptive rather than descriptive, urges it upon all who will hear him. That the figure here is feminine might suggest that the artist has expanded the meaning of the contemplative life, as did the author of the *Ovide moralisé*. But it might also suggest that he saw in the figure both the contemplative life *and* Pallas, and thus made the figure feminine because he glimpsed the contemplative life through the image of the goddess.[17]

A miniature from a manuscript of the commentary on the *Echecs amoureux* produced around the year 1500, B.n. fr. 143, gives us another version of the goddesses as personifications of the lives they represent (Figure 8).[18] In the foreground are the narrator and Pleasure. The narrator is depicted as an older man in a heavy cloak, Pleasure as an elegant young man leading a dog. The artist has conflated the fictional first-person narrator, a young man, with the mature author who actually produced the work. Above and to the left is the wood of Diana; contrasting with it is the walled garden of Pleasure. Nature stands at its gate holding a key because it is she who at the poem's opening tells the narrator that he should explore the world. In the miniature, the garden signifies the world; thus the artist has put all three goddesses inside it.

Though each goddess is clearly labeled with her own name, the figures in the miniature do not represent only the goddesses as they function on the literal level of the *Echecs amoureux*. Each has attributes which show as well her allegorical significance. Venus is nude, as she is for Fulgentius and other mythographers, not because she is nude in the *Echecs amoureux*, but because her nudity is significant allegorically. The mirror into which she gazes suggests her association with *luxuria*, recalling the depiction of the voluptuous life in Figure 7, while the tree beneath which she stands may be intended for the rosebush of the *Roman de la Rose*—or the tree of Eden, with Venus as Eve. Her position in the lower half of the picture suggests Fulgentius's ranking of the life of pleasure as lowest of the three available to man.

Juno's elaborate outfit suggests her association with wealth and sovereignty; the little structure near which she stands looks more than anything else like the townhouse of a bourgeois who owes his worldly prosperity to his pursuit of the active life. Juno's position midway between Venus and Pallas of course suggests the ranking of the life she represents—more Aristotelian than Fulgentian here.

Pallas is depicted at the top of the picture because she represents the highest life available to man. Her simple dress and loose, garlanded hair suggest her enduring youth. The structure behind her with its impressive crest is perhaps the university to which the author of the *Echecs amoureux* suggested that those who wish to pursue the life of contemplation should repair.

The first illustration of the allegorized Judgment that we considered depicted the lives themselves, not the goddeses, though the iconography of the lives was influenced by the fact that they were represented allegorically by the goddesses. In the miniature accompanying the commentary on the *Echecs amoureux*, it was the goddesses themselves who were depicted, yet their accoutrements alluded to the three lives as well. Figure 9 is a miniature from the fifteenth-century manuscript of the *Fulgentius Metaforalis* mentioned above. It illustrates Fulgentius's allegorized Judgment, even though the text of the *Fulgentius Metaforalis* does not include the Judgment. In this miniature, we have a depiction of the goddesses as the three lives that goes even further toward allegorical representation. The figures themselves are surreal, saddled with an improbable confusion of attributes, yet through these improbable details we glimpse the unseen.

Above and to the right, the artist has depicted Fulgentius's initial description of the three lives: contemplative, active, and voluptuous. The heavily bearded figure in severe dark robes represents the contemplative life. The more fastidiously barbered gentleman in furred hat and furred cloak represents the active life. The elegantly dressed youth represents the voluptuous life. They seem to be discussing the relative merits of the three goddesses.

Each goddess is portrayed with the attributes that reveal her allegorical significance. Below on the right is Venus. As Fulgentius had specified, she is naked, floating in the sea, and surrounded by the three Graces, who depart from Fulgentius's scheme in being clothed. The artist has given her a chaplet of the roses with which Fulgentius had linked her, and he has also scattered roses over her nude body and stuck them onto the points of her crown. The crown and scepter are not in Fulgentius but are perhaps intended to suggest her triumph in the beauty contest or her role as queen of love.

Below on the left is Juno. That she and Venus share the lower panel of the picture echoes Fulgentius's negative evaluation of the two. Her connection with sovereignty is suggested by the castle beneath her. Fulgentius had linked her with riches and given her a scepter because of the association between riches and dominion. Thus the artist has placed a scepter in her left hand while with her right she handles coins on a counting table. He has also included her veiled head, her peacock, and her rainbow.

Above is Minerva, with Jove in the background, the juxtaposition intended to suggest her birth from his head. Her preeminent position suggests her place in Fulgentius's scheme. The artist has included her plumed helmet and her breastplate with the gorgon's head, as well as her long spear. He has also included her owl, and he has attempted to convey its allegorical significance: "wisdom has its flashes of lightning even in the dark."[19] The plant in her left hand may be intended for an olive, often associated with the goddess of wisdom, though not mentioned by Fulgentius. The cruciform structure on which she is placed is doubtless intended to suggest Fulgentius's identification of the contemplative life with "the life led . . . by bishops, priests, and monks."[20]

The final depiction of the allegorized Judgment we shall consider appears in a manuscript of Lydgate's *Troy Book* produced sometime after 1460, and now in the John Rylands Library at the University of Manchester (Figure 10).[21] This miniature conflates the allegorized Judgment with the dream-Judgment of the Dares tradition, as had Lydgate in the text of the *Troy Book*.

Reading the picture from the lower right, we see Paris hunting in company with his dogs and wounding the stag that he pursues. We then see his riderless horse tethered to the branch of a tree. Above the horse, Paris reclines with closed eyes against a rock as Mercury taps him with his caduceus, the sleep-inducing rod, and plays his flute, also known to induce sleep. Mercury is accompanied by his cock, which is perched above Paris's head, recalling in a curious but inexplicable way the bird on Paris's helmet in Figure 3. Behind Mercury is Pallas, in armor and bearing a shield and a spear; her owl sits in a tree above Paris. Next is Juno, wearing queenly garments, carrying a scepter, and followed by a peacock. Above, in a river that descends from the top of the scene, is Venus, nude and surrounded by doves. At the left of the picture, behind Juno, is a table with a large golden apple on it.

The artist has managed to depict in the same scene the hunt which led Paris to the site of his dream, and then the dream itself.

The origin of the goddesses' quarrel at the Wedding of Peleus and Thetis is suggested by the table with the apple on it, and the allegorical significance of each goddess is represented by her clothing and attributes. Like Lydgate's text, the miniature fuses the episode's historical elements with its allegorical significance.

The Greeks based their art on religious themes, but the myths were their religion, and depictions of the Judgment were widespread in the ancient world. Most medieval art drew its themes from Christianity. Thus medieval depictions of the Judgment lived only between the covers of books, where their purpose was purely illustrative. The Judgment flourished in literature, we have seen, but the artists who depicted the theme worked only in the service of texts.

The following abbreviations are used in the Notes.

ALGRM	*Ausführliches Lexikon der griechischen und römischen Mythologie*
CCSL	*Corpus Christianorum Series Latina*
CSEL	*Corpus Scriptorum Ecclesiasticorum Latinorum*
MGH	*Monumenta Germaniae Historica*
PL	*Patrologiae Cursus Completus, Series Latina*
RECA	*Real-Encyclopädie der classischen Altertumswissenschaft*

Notes

Chapter 1. The Judgment of Paris in the Ancient World

1. The story's early literary sources are discussed in Friedrich Creuzer, *Griechischer Thongefässe der Grossherzoglich Badischen Sammlung in Karlsruhe* (Heidelberg: C. F. Winter, 1839), 7–11; F. G. Welcker, *Alte Denkmäler*, 5 (Göttingen: Dieterichschen Buchhandlung, 1864), 366–432; Gustav [?] Türk, "Paris," *ALGRM*, ed. W. H. Roscher, 3, 1 (Leipzig: Teubner, 1897–1902), cols. 1586–92, 1607–31; Ernst Wüst, "Paris," *RECA*, ed. August Pauly and Georg Wissowa, 18, 4 (Waldsee: Alfred Druckenmüller, 1949), cols. 1492–1501; Ludwig Weniger, "Das Urteil des Paris," *Sokrates*, 73 (1919): 1–18; Ludwig Preller, *Die griechische Heldensage*, vol. 2 of *Griechische Mythologie*, ed. Carl Robert, 4th ed. (Berlin: Weidmann, 1923), 1071–77; T. C. W. Stinton, *Euripides and the Judgement of Paris*, Journal of Hellenic Studies Supplementary Paper no. 11 (London: Society for the Promotion of Hellenic Studies, 1965). For a brief survey of the theme from ancient times to the nineteenth century, see Marc Rosenberg, *Von Paris von Troja bis zum König von Mercia: Die Geschichte einer Schönheitskonkurrenz* (Darmstadt: L. C. Wittich'schen Hofbuchdruckerei, 1930). For a more detailed survey, see Charles Vellay, *Les Légendes du cycle troyen*, 2 vols. (Monaco: Imprimerie Nationale, 1957), 1.67–74, 79–81. On possible preliterary origins of the story, see Türk, "Paris," col. 1588; Stinton, *Euripides*, 5–10; Karl Reinhardt, "Das Parisurteil," in *Tradition und Geist* (Göttingen: Vandenhoeck and Ruprecht, 1960), 16; H. J. Rose, *A Handbook of Greek Mythology*, 6th ed. (London: Methuen, 1958), 106–7.

2. Trans. Richmond Lattimore (Chicago: University of Chicago Press, 1961), 24.28–30 (p. 476).

3. For the Judgment's appearance in the *Cypria*, see Welcker, *Alte Denkmäler*, 367; Türk, "Paris," cols. 1586–87; Wüst, "Paris," cols. 1495–98; Weniger, "Urteil des Paris," 1; Stinton, *Euripides*, 1–8; A. Severyns, "Pomme de discorde et Jugement des déesses," *Phoibos*, 5 (1950–51): 154–57; for the relationship between these two summaries and the *Cypria*, see [Eduard] Schwartz, "Die apollodorische Bibliothek," *RECA*, ed. August Pauly and Georg Wissowa, 1, 2 (Stuttgart: Alfred Druckenmüller, 1894), cols. 2875–86.

4. *Hesiod, the Homeric Hymns, and Homerica*, trans. Hugh G. Evelyn-White, Loeb Classical Library (Cambridge: Harvard University Press, 1936), 489–91.

5. James George Frazer, trans., *The Library,* by Apollodorus, 2 vols., Loeb Classical Library (Cambridge: Harvard University Press, 1921), 2.173.

6. *The Fragments of Sophocles,* ed. A. C. Pearson (Cambridge: Cambridge University Press, 1917), 29–31.

7. Charles Burton Gulick, trans., Loeb Classical Library, 7 vols. (Cambridge: Harvard University Press, 1927–41), 15.687c (Loeb 7.181). For the date, see 1.viii. The Judgment of Paris in Sophocles is discussed by Reinhardt, "Parisurteil" 17; Stinton, *Euripides,* 8–9; Wüst, "Paris," cols. 1497, 1499; it is Pearson's fragment 361, *Fragments of Sophocles,* 30–31.

8. Pearson, *Fragments of Sophocles,* 30. I am indebted to Bruce Heiden for this translation.

9. Wüst, "Paris," col. 1497; Preller-Robert, *Griechische Heldensage,* 1074–75.

10. Hermann Luckenbach, *Das Verhältnis der griechischen Vasenbilder zu den Gedichten des epischen Kyklos* (Leipzig: Teubner, 1880), 569–70.

11. Discussed in Stinton, *Euripides,* 13–39; Türk, "Paris," col. 1587. I used the translation of Arthur S. Way, Loeb Classical Library, 4 vols. (Cambridge: Harvard University Press, 1912).

12. Wüst, "Paris," col. 1497.

13. *Andromache,* 289; *Helen,* 35.

14. *Andromache,* 275, 280–81; *Helen,* 29; *Iphigeneia at Aulis,* 575–77, 1291.

15. *Andromache,* 274–77; *Iphigeneia at Aulis,* 1300–1307.

16. *Andromache,* 279–90; *Helen,* 23–26; *Iphigeneia at Aulis,* 1308–9.

17. For discussion of the work and its date, see R. C. Jebb, *The Attic Orators from Antiphon to Isaeos,* 2 vols. (1875; rpt. New York: Russell and Russell, 1962), 2.100–106. See also Türk, "Paris," col. 1588; Wüst, "Paris," col. 1498; Stinton, *Euripides,* 19.

18. Isocrates, 3, trans. Larue Van Hook, Loeb Classical Library (Cambridge: Harvard University Press, 1945), 83–85.

19. On "overdetermination" in the Judgment, see Stinton, *Euripides,* 10.

20. H. J. Rose, ed., *Hygini Fabuli* (1934; rpt. Leyden: A. W. Sythoff, 1963), 68. The translation in the text is mine. The *Fabulae* have also been translated by Mary Grant, *The Myths of Hyginus,* University of Kansas Publications: Humanistic Studies, no. 34 (Lawrence: University of Kansas Press, 1960).

21. Rose, *Handbook,* 128, n. 17, calls Eris's spoiling the banquet with the apple a "good folktale theme."

22. Luckenbach, *Verhältnis der griechischen Vasenbilder,* 592; L. von Sybel, "Eris," *ALGRM,* ed. W. H. Roscher, 1, 2 (Leipzig: Teubner, 1884–86), col. 1338.

23. W. H. Roscher, "Athene," *ALGRM,* ed. W. H. Roscher, 1, 1 (Leipzig: Teubner, 1884–86), col. 682.

24. Propertius alludes to a version of the Judgment in which the goddesses disrobe before Paris (Elegy 2.2). On the nudity of the goddesses in Alexandrian treatments of the Judgment, see Türk, "Paris," col. 1591; Weniger, "Urteil des Paris," 9; Wüst, "Paris," col. 1497; Preller-Robert, *Griechische Heldensage,* 1075.

25. Trans. Grant Showerman, Loeb Classical Library (Cambridge: Harvard University Press, 1947), 201–3.

26. Trans. William Adlington, rev. Stephen Gaselee, Loeb Classical Library (Cambridge: Harvard University Press, 1915), 526–33.

27. Lucian, 7, trans. M. D. Macleod, Loeb Classical Library (Cambridge: Harvard University Press, 1961), 203–5.

28. Lucian, 3, trans. A. M. Harmon, Loeb Classical Library (Cambridge: Harvard University Press, 1921), 385–409.

29. An exception is the Judgment's inclusion in *The Rape of Helen* by the sixth-century Greek writer Colluthus, trans. A. W. Mair, Loeb Classical Library (Cambridge: Harvard University Press, 1963).

30. *Servianorum in Vergilii Carmina Commentariorum*, ed. Edward K. Rand et al., 2 vols. (Lancaster, Pa.: Lancaster Press, 1946), 2.29–30. The commentary is discussed in [Paul] Wessner, "Servius," *RECA*, ed. August Pauly and Georg Wissowa, 2nd series, 2 (Munich: Alfred Druckenmüller, 1923), cols. 1836–44. A more detailed narrative of the Judgment appears in the tenth-century manuscript of Servius and is printed by Georg Thilo and Hermann Hagen, *Servii Grammatici qui feruntur in Vergilii Carmina Commentarii*, 1 (1881; rpt. Hildesheim: G. Olms, 1961), 22–23. On it see Edmond Faral, *Recherches sur les sources latines des contes et romans courtois du moyen âge* (Paris: Edouard Champion, 1913), 172–73, n. 5.

31. *Interpretationes*, in G. Fabricius's 1561 edition of Vergil, ed. Heinrich Georges, 2 vols. (Leipzig: Teubner, 1905–6), 1.14.

32. Euripides, *Tragoediae et Fragmenta*, ed. August Matthiae, 4 (Leipzig: Weigel, 1817), 148–50. I am indebted to Bruce Heiden for the following translation:

"Hera, Athena, and Aphrodite, as well as other deities, were invited to the wedding of Peleus and Thetis. Since the wedding was without Discord, Discord became angry and prepared a golden apple, on which she wrote, 'The apple for the fair.' She mounted the roof and threw it near the three goddesses. They read the apple and became angry at one another, each claiming that she herself was more beautiful than the others. Therefore they went to Zeus and asked him to award the apple to the fairest. But he avoided a decision because it did not seem to have been devised for the good, and it was not seemly—for if he had awarded it to Hera, he would have been thought to have given it to her because she was his wife, if to Athena, because she was his daughter, if to Aphrodite, he would seem to have honored his sister. Fearing this, therefore, and hoping to avoid blame, he made Alexander the son of Priam the judge of the goddesses. He was then a cowherd beside Mount Ida, and Zeus thought that he would decide impartially and without favoritism. Therefore the goddesses went to him with Hermes, whom Zeus had sent along, and they bid him award the apple to the most beautiful. They also promised to give greater gifts to him if he decided the contest for this one and not for that. Hera promised a kingdom if she were not deprived of the apple, since kingdoms were her province. Athena promised conquest in war, and to be worsted by no enemy; for she is a warlike goddess. Aphrodite offered Helen, and through her she charmed the man, and won, and took the apple as the reward of what she had promised."

33. E. Bagby Atwood, "The Rawlinson *Excidium Troiae*: A Study of Source Problems in Mediaeval Literature," *Speculum*, 9 (1934): 379–404, and "The *Excidium Troiae* and Medieval Troy Literature," *Modern Philology*, 35 (1937): 115–28; W. A. Oldfather, "Notes on the *Excidium Troiae*," *Speculum*, 11

(1936): 272–77; E. Bagby Atwood and V. K. Whitaker, eds., *Excidium Troiae* (Cambridge: Mediaeval Academy of America, 1944), xi–lxxxv.

34. Atwood and Whitaker, *Excidium Troiae*, xv, xxxi; Atwood, "The *Excidium Troiae*," 116.

35. Atwood and Whitaker, *Excidium Troiae*, xvi.

36. Ibid., *Excidium Troiae*, xi.

37. Atwood, "The *Excidium Troiae*," 116.

38. Atwood and Whitaker, *Excidium Troiae*, 3–5.

39. *Compendium Historiae Troianae-Romanae*, ed. Henry Simonsfeld, *Neues Archiv der Gesellschaft für ältere deutsche Geschichtskunde*, 11 (1886): 239–51. For Wedding and Judgment see 242–43.

40. As told, for example, in Hyginus's Fable 79 (Rose, *Hygini Fabuli*, 59–60).

41. [Carl Olaf] Thulin, "Iuno," *RECA*, ed. August Pauly and Georg Wissowa, 10 (Stuttgart: J. B. Metzler, 1917), cols. 1115–16.

42. [Ferdinand] Haug, "Hera," *RECA*, ed. August Pauly and Georg Wissowa, 8 (Stuttgart: J. B. Metzler, 1913), cols. 396–97.

43. The theme is discussed by Wüst, "Paris," cols. 1489–92. For bibliography on the relationship between the birth of Paris and the Judgment, see Stinton, *Euripides*, 22, n. 1; H. D. Jocelyn, ed., *The Tragedies of Ennius* (Cambridge: Cambridge University Press, 1967), 202, n. 1.

44. Stinton, *Euripides*, 55.

45. Fragment 82. See *The Odes of Pindar*, trans. John Sandys, Loeb Classical Library (Cambridge, Mass.: Harvard University Press, 1968), 545–47.

46. Wüst, "Paris," col. 1489; Stinton, *Euripides*, 22, 53, appendix 1, 64–71; Jocelyn, *Tragedies*, 202.

47. Dream: *The Daughters of Troy*, 922; exposure: *Iphigeneia at Aulis*, 1284–91; shepherds: *Iphigeneia at Aulis*, 575–77, 1291.

48. Wüst, "Paris," cols. 1489–92.

49. Rose, *Hygini Fabuli*, 67. A similar story is told in the *Library* of Apollodorus, 3.12.5 (Loeb 2.47).

50. A number of works have studied the origins and development of allegory in the ancient world. See, for example, Paul Decharme, *La Critique des traditions religieuses chez les Grecs* (Paris: Alphonse Picard et Fils, 1904); Gilbert Murray, *Five Stages of Greek Religion* (New York: Columbia University Press, 1925), ch. 4; Franz Cumont, *Recherches sur le symbolisme funéraire des Romaines*, Bibliothèque Archèologique et Historique, 35 (1942; rpt. New York: Arno Press, 1975), 1–32; Jean Pépin, *Mythe et allégorie: Les origines grecques et les contestations judéo-chrétiennes* (Paris: Editions Montaigne, 1958); Paule Demats, *Fabula: Trois études de mythographie antique et médiévale*, Publications Romanes et Françaises, 122 (Geneva: Librairie Droz, 1973), 5–60.

51. Stinton, *Euripides*, 8.

52. 12.510c (Loeb 5.295).

53. Decharme, *Critique*, 290.

54. Stinton, *Euripides*, 26–27.

55. Pépin, *Mythe et allégorie*, 156–59.

56. Ibid., 125; Decharme, *Critique*, 260–61.

57. On their approach, see Decharme, *Critique*, 259–353, especially ch. 10; Pépin, *Mythe et allégorie*, 125–31. The Stoics are discussed in Murray, *Five Stages*, chs. 3–4.

58. [Hans] von Arnim, "Chrysippos," *RECA*, ed. August Pauly and Georg Wissowa, 3 (Stuttgart: Alfred Druckenmüller, 1899), col. 2502; discussed in Pépin, *Mythe et allégorie*, 129–31; Decharme, *Critique*, 312–13.

59. *Stoicorum Veterum Fragmenta*, ed. Hans von Arnim, 3 (1903; rpt. Stuttgart: Teubner, 1979), sect. 25, fr. 4 (p. 197).

60. Discussed in Decharme, *Critique*, 348; Jean Daniélou, "Die Hochzeit von Thetis und Peleus im hellenistischen Allegorismus," *Antaios*, 3 (1961): 247–48.

61. *In Homeri Iliadem*, ed. Gottfried Hermann (Leipzig: Weigel, 1812), 42–43. A similar, but briefer, formulation appears in Tzetzes' *Antehomerica*, ed. Friedrich Jacobs (Leipzig: Weidmann, 1793), 12–13. I am grateful to Anthony B. Breen for translating this material for me. The *Antehomerica* passage is discussed in Daniélou, "Hochzeit," 247–48.

62. Decharme, *Critique*, 322–24.

63. *Symposium*, trans. W. R. M. Lamb, Loeb Classical Library (Cambridge: Harvard University Press, 1932), 180 (p. 109).

64. [Karl] Tümpel, "Aphrodite," *RECA*, ed. August Pauly and Georg Wissowa, 1 (Stuttgart: Alfred Druckenmüller, 1894), col. 2771; Daniélou, "Hochzeit," 248; Félix Buffière, *Les Mythes d'Homère et la pensée grecque* (Paris: Société d'Edition Les Belles Lettres, 1956), 146, 159, 169.

65. Murray, *Five Stages*, ch. 5.

66. On the dates of the *Recognitions*, of the *Homilies*, and of their common source, see Hans Waitz, *Die Pseudoklementinen, Homilien und Rekognitionen: Eine quellenkritische Untersuchung*, Texte und Untersuchungen zur Geschichte der altchristlichen Literatur, NF 10,4 (Leipzig: J. C. Hinrichs, 1904), 30, 255; *Die Pseudoklementinen, 1 (Homilien)*, ed. Bernhard Rehm and Johannes Irmscher, 2nd ed., rev. Franz Paschke (Berlin: Akademie-Verlag, 1969), vii–viii; Daniélou, "Hochzeit," 244.

67. On the presence of this passage in the common source, see Waitz, *Pseudoklementinen*, 30–32; on its possible source, ibid., 252–54; Pépin, *Mythe et allégorie*, 396; M. R. James, "A Manual of Mythology in the Clementines," *Journal of Theological Studies*, 33 (1932): 262–65.

68. *Die Pseudoklementinen, 2 (Rekognitionen in Rufins Übersetzung)*, ed. Bernhard Rehm (Berlin: Akademie-Verlag, 1965), 10.41 (pp. 352–53). The translation in my text is based on that of Thomas Smith in *Ante-Nicene Fathers*, ed. Alexander Roberts and James Donaldson, rev. ed., 8 (New York: C. Scribner's Sons, 1925), 203. The passage is discussed in Pépin, *Mythe et allégorie*, 400–403.

69. For interpretations of the passage, see Pépin, *Mythe et allégorie*, 402–3; Daniélou, "Hochzeit," 245–46, 255.

70. Daniélou, "Hochzeit," 246.

71. On this tradition, see Jean Seznec, *The Survival of the Pagan Gods: The Mythological Tradition and Its Place in Renaissance Humanism and Art*, trans. Barbara F. Sessions, Bollingen Series, 38 (1953; rpt. Princeton: Princeton University Press, 1972), ch. 2, esp. 37–40.

72. Seznec, *Survival of the Pagan Gods*, 40–42.

73. [Samson] Eitrem, "Hermes," *RECA*, ed. August Pauly and Georg Wissowa, 8 (Stuttgart: J. B. Metzler, 1913), cols. 781–82.

74. Rehm and Irmscher, *Pseudoklementinen*, 1, ς. 14–15 (pp. 111–12);

trans. Peter Peterson, in Roberts and Donaldson, *Ante-Nicene Fathers*, 8.265.

75. Cf. Daniélou, "Hochzeit," 248–54.

76. This identification is without precedent, according to Daniélou, "Hochzeit," 249–50.

77. See Severyns, "Pomme de discorde," 161, n. 49a, on the link between the apple in the Wedding and Judgment and the apples from the garden of the Hesperides.

78. Daniélou, "Hochzeit," 251.

79. Sallust, *Concerning the Gods and the Universe*, trans. Arthur Darby Nock (Cambridge: Cambridge University Press, 1926). On the work, see Murray, *Five Stages*, 217–30.

80. Intimate of Julian: Nock, *Concerning the Gods*, ci; Murray *Five Stages*, 217; statement of beliefs: Murray, *Five Stages*, 217–19.

81. Seznec, *Survival of the Pagan Gods*, 85; Nock, *Concerning the Gods*, xcvii–c; Murray, *Five Stages*, 219.

82. Nock, *Concerning the Gods*, ch. 4 (p. 7). Sallust's interpretation is summarized in Creuzer, *Griechische Thongefässe*, 11, and Türk, "Paris," col. 1592.

83. Analyzed by Nock, *Concerning the Gods*, xlix.

84. Daniélou, "Hochzeit," 246–47.

85. Daniélou, "Hochzeit," 247, argues that here they complete rather than oppose one another.

86. *Procli Diadochi in Platonis Rem Publicam Commentarii*, ed. Wilhelm Kroll, 2 (Leipzig: Teubner, 1901), 263. I am indebted to Bruce Heiden for this translation.

87. Discussed in Demats, *Fabula*, 36–37, 55–60. Leslie George Whitbread, trans., *Fulgentius the Mythographer* (Columbus: Ohio State University Press, 1971), 3; page references in my text are to Whitbread's translation.

88. Demats, *Fabula*, 57–58; Hans Liebeschütz, *Fulgentius Metaforalis: Ein Beitrag zur Geschichte der antiken Mythologie im Mittelalter* (Leipzig: Teubner, 1926), 3–5.

89. Fulgentius, *Opera*, ed. Rudolf Helm (1898; rpt. Stuttgart: Teubner, 1970), 2.1 (pp. 36–37).

90. Ibid., 2.1 (pp. 37–38).

91. Ibid., 2.1 (pp. 38–39).

92. Whitbread's note on the passage gives possible explanations for the etymologies: *Fulgentius the Mythographer*, 67.

93. Fulgentius, *Opera*, 2.1 (pp. 39–40).

94. For the three lives in the ancient world, see Fritz Schalk, "Il tema della *vita activa* e della *vita contemplativa* nell'umanesimo italiano," *Umanesimo e scienza politica: Atti del Congresso Internazionale di Studi Umanistici*, ed. Enrico Castelli (Milan: Marzorati, 1951), 559–66; Edgar Wind, *Pagan Mysteries in the Renaissance*, rev. ed. (New York: W. W. Norton, 1968), 81–82.

95. Trans. Paul Shorey, Loeb Classical Library, 2 vols. (Cambridge: Harvard University Press, 1969–70), 9.7 (Loeb 2.371–73).

96. *Politics*, trans. Harris Rackham, Loeb Classical Library (Cambridge: Harvard University Press, 1959), 7.13.6–9 (pp. 605–9).

97. *Nicomachean Ethics*, trans. Harris Rackham, Loeb Classical Library (Cambridge: Harvard University Press, 1947), 1.5 (pp. 13–15).

98. The three lives are also defined in the *Eudemian Ethics*, trans. Harris Rackham, Loeb Classical Library (Cambridge: Harvard University Press, 1935), 1.4 (p. 209).

99. *Politics*, 7.13.7 (p. 607).

100. *Nicomachean Ethics*, 10.7 (p. 619).

101. *Nicomachean Ethics*, 6.12 (pp. 365–67).

102. Wind, *Pagan Mysteries*, 81, says Fulgentius borrowed the three lives specifically from Plutarch.

103. Roscher, "Athene," col. 682.

104. Whitbread has noted a relationship between Hyginus and Fulgentius and posited a common source: *Fulgentius the Mythographer*, 22.

105. *Nicomachean Ethics*, 1.5 (p. 15).

106. On the rationalizing-historical approach, see Seznec, *Survival of the Pagan Gods*, 11–36; Pépin, *Mythe et allégorie*, 49–50, 146–67 and passim; Decharme, *Critique*, 371–411.

107. Demats, *Fabula*, 12–14; cf. Pépin, who regards all interpretation of myth as allegory: *Mythe et allégorie*, 149, and Seznec, who applies the term "allegory" to *moral* interpretation alone: *Survival of the Pagan Gods*, 85, n. 3.

108. Decharme, *Critique*, 68–69.

109. Ibid., 113–40.

110. Ibid., 268–69; Pépin, *Mythe et allégorie*, 148–49.

111. Decharme, *Critique*, 371–72, 393–94.

112. Seznec, *Survival of the Pagan Gods*, 11–12; Pépin, *Mythe et allégorie*, 148–49; Decharme, *Critique*, 371–72; John Daniel Cooke, "Euhemerism: A Mediaeval Interpretation of Classical Paganism," *Speculum*, 2 (1927): 397.

113. Decharme, *Critique*, 375.

114. Ibid., 381–82.

115. On the later history of euhemerism, see Seznec, *Survival of the Pagan Gods*, 15–36.

116. Quoted by Weniger, "Urteil des Paris," 14, n. 2. Bruce Heiden has translated the passage for me. Discussed in Weniger, "Urteil des Paris," 14; Preller-Robert, *Griechische Heldensage*, 1075; Türk, "Paris," col. 1591.

117. On him and the tradition, see Demats, *Fabula*, 10; Buffière, *Mythes d'Homère*, 228–48; Decharme, *Critique*, 403–11; Pépin, *Mythe et allégorie*, 149–50.

118. "Sciendum Alexandrum, qui alio nomine Paris dicebatur, non Deas judicasse, sed, cum sapientia excelleret, laudationem in eas scripsisse. Hinc fabulae datus locus, eum inter Palladem, Junonem, et Venerem sententiam dixisse." *Opuscula Mythologica Physica et Ethica Graece et Latine* (Amsterdam: Henricum Wetstenium, 1688), ch. 10 (p. 89).

119. Discussed in Preller-Robert, *Griechische Heldensage*, 1076; Türk, "Paris," cols. 1591–92.

120. Dio Chrysostom, 1, trans. J. W. Cohoon, Loeb Classical Library (Cambridge: Harvard University Press, 1932), 453–57.

121. Dio Chrysostom, 2, trans. J. W. Cohoon, Loeb Classical Library (Cambridge: Harvard University Press, 1939), 247–69. Page references in the text refer to this edition.

122. This work is lost, but an abridgment has been preserved in the *Library* of Photius, trans. René Henry, 6 vols. (Paris: Société d'Edition Les Belles Lettres, 1959–71), 190 (3.69).

123. See H. W. Stoll, "Melos," *ALGRM*, ed. W. H. Roscher, 2, 2 (Leipzig: Teubner, 1894–97), col. 2648.

124. *Interpretatio Chronicae Eusebii Pamphili, PL*, ed. J.-P. Migne, 27 (Paris: J.-P. Migne, 1846), cols. 33–702.

125. "Alexander Helenam rapuit. Trojanum bellum decennale surrexit: causa mali, quod trium mulierum de pulchritudine certantium praemium fuit, una earum Helenam Pastori judici pollicente" (col. 262).

126. On them, see Nathaniel Edward Griffin, *Dares and Dictys: An Introduction to the Study of Medieval Versions of the Story of Troy* (Baltimore: J. H. Furst, 1907), 6–13, and "Un-Homeric Elements in the Medieval Story of Troy," *Journal of English and Germanic Philology*, 7 (1907–8): 38–48.

127. Griffin, "Un-Homeric Elements," 37.

128. Griffin, *Dares and Dictys*, 15, n. 2. Dares may have been preferred for other reasons as well; cf. Eugène Collilieux, *Etude sur Dictys de Crête et Darès de Phrygie* (Grenoble: Drevet, 1886), 20–21.

129. Griffin, *Dares and Dictys*, 17; "Un-Homeric Elements," 37–38.

130. Griffin, "Un-Homeric Elements," 35. On Dares: Otmar Schissel von Fleschenberg, *Dares-Studien* (Halle a. S.: Max Niemeyer, 1908), 128–33 and passim; on Dictys: Griffin, *Dares and Dictys*, 23–33.

131. Griffin, *Dares and Dictys*, 14–15, n. 1; 80–81, n. 2; 108; and "Un-Homeric Elements," 36, n. 1; 51. Schissel von Fleschenberg, *Dares-Studien*, 128.

132. On their relation to sophist and rationalizing tendencies, see Griffin, "Un-Homeric Elements," 52.

133. Collilieux, *Etude sur Dictys et Darès*, 17; Carl Wagener, "Beitrag zu Dares Phrygius," *Philologus*, 38 (1889): 120–24; Schissel von Fleschenberg, *Dares-Studien*, ch. 12, 134–57.

134. *De Raptu Helenae*, ed. Fridericus Vollmer, *MGH Auctorum Antiquissimorum*, 14 (Berlin: Weidmann, 1905), lines 31–40 (p. 157).

135. Dares Phrygius, *De Excidio Troiae Historia*, ed. Ferdinand Meister (Leipzig: Teubner, 1873), ch. 7 (p. 9); R. M. Frazer, Jr., trans., *The Trojan War: The Chronicles of Dictys of Crete and Dares the Phrygian* (Bloomington: Indiana University Press, 1966), 138–39.

136. According to Schissel von Fleschenberg, *Dares-Studien*, 136–37, the source was probably a Latin mythographic compendium.

137. Lattimore, *Iliad*, 5.638–42, 5.648–50, 21.441–57 (pp. 145, 430); see Preller-Robert, *Griechische Heldensage*, 234.

138. Schwartz, "Die apollodorische Bibliothek," cols. 2881, 2884.

139. Trans. C. H. Oldfather, Loeb Classical Library (Cambridge: Harvard University Press, 1967), 4.32, 4.42 (pp. 445–47, 475–77). See Demats, *Fabula*, 83, n. 75.

140. Rand, *Servianorum Commentariorum*, 265–66.

Chapter 2. The Judgment as History

1. A. E. Parsons, "The Trojan Legend in England," *Modern Language Review*, 24 (1929): 253, 255–57, and see Maria Klippel, *Die Darstellung der fränkischen Trojanersage in Geschichtesschreibung und Dichtung vom Mittelalter bis zur Renaissance in Frankreich* (Marburg: Beyer und Hausknecht, 1936); Karl Heisig, "Zur fränkischen Trojanersage," *Zeitschrift für Romanische Philologie*, 90 (1974): 441–48; George Gordon, "The Trojans in Britain," *Essays and Studies by Members of the English Association*, OS 9 (1924): 9–30.

2. For Godfrey of Reims's and Baudri of Bourgueil's use of the Judgment, see Chapter 5.

3. André Boutemy, "Le Poème *Pergama Flere Volo* et ses imitateurs du XIIe siècle," *Latomus*, 5 (1946): 240–41.

4. Boutemy, ed., "Le Poème *Pergama*," 244; on its influence see also Jürgen Stohlmann, ed., *Anonymi Historia Troyana Daretis Frigii* (Wuppertal: Henn, 1968), 150–51, 155; Edmond Faral, "Le Manuscrit 511 du 'Hunterian Museum' de Glasgow: Notes sur le mouvement poétique et l'histoire des études littéraires en France et en Angleterre entre les années 1150 et 1225," *Studi Medievali*, NS 9 (1936): 43–51.

5.   Flamma Paris patrie, forme quo iudice die
         Troia caput Frigie flosque iaces Asie!
         Iunonem ledit, Veneri dum pastor obedit;
         Cum iudex sedit, tot tibi dampna dedit! (9–12)
The text is based on the edition of *Viribus, Arte, Minis* in Johann Huemer, *Mittellateinische Analekten* (Vienna: n.p., 1882), 16–20. Professor Jürgen Stohlmann, who is preparing a new edition of the poem, has kindly supplied me with his corrections for the passage. Petrus himself is discussed in Boutemy, "Le Poème *Pergama*," 234–44; Faral, "Le Manuscrit 511," 46–47.

6.   Conveniunt ad eum Iuno, Minerva, Venus.
         Iudicium querunt, pulcherrima que sit in ipsis,
         Promittunt eciam munera, queque suum:
         Iuno decus, Pallas vires, Citherea puellam;
         Sed Veneri tribuit vincere victus ea. (38–42)
The text is based on the edition of André Boutemy, "La Version parisienne du poème de Simon Chèvre d'Or sur la Guerre de Troie," *Scriptorium*, 1 (1946–47): 269–86. I am grateful to Professor Jürgen Stohlmann, who is preparing an edition of the work, for providing me with corrections from the manuscripts. Simon is discussed in Stohlmann, *Anonymi Historia*, 150–51; F. J. E. Raby, *A History of Secular Latin Poetry in the Middle Ages*, 2nd ed., 2 vols. (Oxford: Clarendon, 1957), 2.70–71; André Boutemy, "La Geste d'Enée par Simon Chèvre d'Or," *Le Moyen Age*, 52 (1946): 243–44. The *Ylias* exists in at least three versions. The oldest and shortest deals in 150 lines with the adventures of Paris and the siege of Troy (in *PL* 171.1447–51, where it is attached to Petrus Sanctonensis and attributed to Hildebert). To this Simon then added a second section treating the adventures of Aeneas. (Boutemy, "La Geste d'Enée," edits this second part; he says [244] that the first part of this version is much like version one). The third version, from which I quote above, doubled the poem's volume. For discussion of the three versions and their relationship, see Boutemy, "La Version parisienne," 267, and "La Geste d'Enée," 243.

7. For the concept, see Erwin Panofsky and Fritz Saxl, "Classical Mythology in Mediaeval Art," *Metropolitan Museum Studies*, 4 (1932–33): 268; Erwin Panofsky, "Renaissance and Renascences," *Kenyon Review*, 6 (1944): 216–17, 219–20; Erwin Panofsky, *Studies in Iconology* (1939; rpt. New York: Harper and Row, 1972), 26–31.

8. Jean Frappier, "La Peinture de la vie et des héros antiques dans la littérature française du XIIe et du XIIIe siècle," in *Histoire, mythes et symboles: Etudes de littérature française* (Geneva: Droz, 1976), 21–54, especially 21–32; Edmond Faral, *Recherches sur les sources latines des contes et romans courtois du moyen âge* (Paris: Edouard Champion, 1913), 391–419.

9. Faral, *Recherches*, 410; Raymond J. Cormier, *One Heart, One Mind: The Rebirth of Virgil's Hero in Medieval French Romance*, Romance Monographs, 3 (University, Miss.: Romance Monographs, Inc., 1973), 21 and n. 16.

10. Albert Pauphilet, "Eneas et Enée," *Romania*, 55 (1929): 213; for the work's relationship with its source, see also 196 and passim: cf. F. M. Warren, "On the Latin Sources of *Thèbes* and *Enéas*," *PMLA*, 16 (1901): 382–85, who thinks that the source was a Latin prose romance based on the *Aeneid*. The *Eneas* has been studied in detail by Cormier, *One Heart*, and is discussed generally in Frappier, "La Peinture," 42–43, and Faral, *Recherches*, 410–15.

11. Trans. H. Rushton Fairclough, rev. ed., 2 vols., Loeb Classical Library (Cambridge: Harvard University Press, 1960), 1.26–27 (Loeb 1.243).

12. Ed. J.-J. Salverda de Grave, 1 (Paris: Edouard Champion, 1925), lines 101–82. The *Eneas* has been translated by John A. Yunck (New York: Columbia University Press, 1974).

13. E. Bagby Atwood and Virgil K. Whitaker, eds., *Excidium Troiae* (Cambridge: Mediaeval Academy of America, 1944), xxxviii. Before the publication of the *Excidium Troiae*, other sources were proposed in Salverda de Grave, *Eneas*, xxix (Ovid) and Edmond Faral, "Le Récit du jugement de Paris dans l'*Enéas* et ses sources," *Romania*, 41 (1912): 101 (Donatus and Hyginus). (This same material is reprinted in Faral's *Recherches*, 74–75.)

14. Atwood and Whitaker, *Excidium Troiae*, 4.

15. Its wide circulation is shown by its influence. See Atwood and Whitaker, *Excidium Troiae*, xxiii–xxiv, xxxiv–li. W. A. Oldfather, "Notes on the *Excidium Troie*," *Speculum*, 11 (1936): 273, n. 1, suggests that the redaction of the *Excidium Troiae* edited by Atwood and Whitaker was produced in France.

16. Léopold Constans, ed., *Le Roman de Troie*, by Benoît de Sainte-Maure, 6 vols. (1904–12; rpt. New York: Johnson Reprint Corporation, 1968), 6.190; cf. Edmond Faral's review of Constans's edition, *Romania*, 42 (1913): 100, and my discussion below in this chapter and in n. 24 concerning the relationship between the *Roman de Troie* and the *Eneas*.

17. Benoît himself acknowledges his use of Dares, lines 93–110 (Constans, *Le Roman de Troie*, 1.6–7); he also uses Dictys after 24425. On his use of Dares, see R. M. Lumiansky, "Structural Unity in Benoit's 'Roman de Troie,'" *Romania*, 79 (1958): 410; Faral's review of Constans's edition, 100–101; cf. Warren, "Latin Sources," 377, and Constans, *Le Roman de Troie*, 6.344 and passim.

18. On his adaptation of his sources, see Lumiansky, "Structural Unity," 410–24; Frappier, "La Peinture," 43–46; Ernst Meybrinck, *Die Auffassung der*

Antike bei Jacques Milet, Guido de Columna und Benoît de Ste-More (Marburg: M. G. Elwert, 1886), 4–17; Marc Rosenberg, *Von Paris von Troja bis zum König von Mercia: Die Geschichte einer Schönheitskonkurrenz* (Darmstadt: L. C. Wittich'schen Hofbuchdruckerei, 1930), 29–31.

19. Meybrinck, *Auffassung der Antike*, 4.

20. A verse translation of the Bible made in the mid-thirteenth century by the Walloon Jehan Malkaraume inserts Benoît's entire *Roman de Troie* in the Book of Exodus. Jehan claims the romance as his by replacing Benoît's name with his own in the *Roman's* prologue. Drawing on the historical synchronizations of Eusebius, Jerome, and others in deciding where to insert the *Roman de Troie* in sacred history, he locates Laomedon's rude reception of the Argonauts in the time of Moses. See Jean Bonnard, *Les Traductions de la Bible en vers français au moyen âge* (Paris: Imprimerie Nationale, 1884), 55–64.

21. Constans, *Le Roman de Troie*, 3855–3928.

22. Ibid., 6.236, n. 3.

23. Frappier, "La Peinture," 23–25, stresses the medieval respect for such sources as history.

24. Faral's review of Constans's edition, 101–2, establishes the dependence of the *Roman de Troie* on the *Eneas*; see also Faral, *Recherches*, 74–75, 172–74, 187. For other evidence that the *Eneas* preceded the *Roman de Troie*, see Ernest Langlois, "Chronologie des romans de Thèbes, d'Eneas et de Troie," *Bibliothèque de l'Ecole des Chartes*, 66 (1905): 113–20. Cf. Constans, *Le Roman de Troie*, 6.236–37; Meybrinck, *Auffassung der Antike*, 47.

25. Paul Zumthor, *Histoire littéraire de la France médiévale* (Paris: Presses Universitaires de France, 1954), 254–55.

26. Zumthor (ibid., 254) dates it between 1225 and 1250; on it see also William Allan Neilson, *The Origins and Sources of the Court of Love*, [Harvard] Studies and Notes in Philology and Literature, 6 (Boston: Ginn, 1899), 41; Howard Rollin Patch, *The Other World According to Descriptions in Medieval Literature* (1950; rpt. New York: Octagon Books, 1970), 199; Ernest Langlois, *Origines et sources du Roman de la Rose* (Paris: Ernest Thorin, 1891), 15–18.

27. "Celtic Dynastic Themes and the Breton Lays," *Etudes Celtiques*, 9 (1961): 453. Examples of the theme from early Irish literature appear in Standish H. O'Grady, ed. and trans. *Silva Gadelica*, 2 vols. (London: Williams and Nogate, 1892), 2.222; "The Adventures of Lomnochtan of Sliabh Riffe," *Gaelic Journal*, 9 (1898): 294; Arthur C. L. Brown, *The Origin of the Grail Legend* (Cambridge: Harvard University Press, 1943), 213–14.

28. Bromwich, "Celtic Dynastic Themes," 460; see also Tom Peete Cross, "The Celtic Elements in the Lays of Lanval and Graelent," *Modern Philology*, 2 (1915): 589.

29. Bromwich, "Celtic Dynastic Themes," 444; the hunt in Arthurian literature is also discussed in Lucy Allen Paton, *Studies in the Fairy Mythology of Arthurian Romance*, 2nd ed. (New York: Burt Franklin, 1960), 14–18 and passim.

30. Zumthor, *Histoire littéraire*, 213, dates it to the end of the twelfth century.

31. Cross, "Celtic Elements," 599–608; passage quoted at 608. For a similar theme with a hunt included, see Myles Dillon, *The Cycles of the Kings* (London: Oxford University Press, 1946), 39–40.

32. A. J. Bliss, ed., *Sir Orfeo*, 2nd ed. (Oxford: Oxford University Press, 1966), liv.

33. "Classical Threads in 'Orfeo,'" *Modern Language Review*, 56 (1961): 162–63.

34. "Story-Patterns in Some Breton Lays," *Medium Aevum*, 22 (1953), 62.

35. Ibid., 79–81; Bliss cites examples of the motif in other narrative *lais: Sir Orfeo*, xxxv–xxxvi.

36. Discussed in Cross, "Celtic Elements," 592, n. 2.

37. The theme of fairy gifts is common in Celtic lore; see Cross, "Celtic Elements," 630, as well as Cross's *Motif-Index of Early Irish Literature*, Indiana University Publications Folklore Series, 7 (Bloomington: Indiana University Press, 1952), F 340, and John Arnott MacCulloch, *The Mythology of All Races*, 3 (1918; rpt. New York: Cooper Square, 1964), 90. It is frequently in dreams that fairies make their promises of gifts to mortals: Cross, *Motif-Index*, D 1731.2.1. For magic sleep, see Tom Peete Cross, "The Celtic Origin of the Lay of Yonec," *Review Celtique*, 31 (1910): 434–35; 446–47; 452, n. 2. Three is the usual number of wishes granted by fairies: Stith Thompson, *Motif-Index of Folk Literature*, 6 vols. (Bloomington: Indiana University Press, 1955–58), s.v. "wishes." Celtic lore even provides an analogue for the apple that the goddesses carry; see Paton, *Studies*, 39, n. 2; Alfred Nutt, "The Happy Otherworld," in *The Voyage of Bran*, ed. Kuno Meyer (London: David Nutt, 1895), 142–43.

38. Lumiansky sees Benoît's interest in love as a key to the poem's unity: "Structural Unity," 411 and passim.

39. On the role of anachronism in the survival of the classics, see Panofsky, "Renaissance," 217, 219–22.

40. Robert Kilburn Root, "Chaucer's Dares," *Modern Philology*, 15 (1917): 1–22.

41. Geoffrey B. Riddehough, "A Forgotten Poet: Joseph of Exeter," *Journal of English and Germanic Philology*, 46 (1947): 254; the work is also discussed in Walter Bradbury Sedgwick, "The *Bellum Troianum* of Joseph of Exeter," *Speculum*, 5 (1930): 49–76; Raby, *Secular Latin Poetry* 2.132–37; citations are to *Frigii Daretis Yliados Libri VI*, in Joseph Iscanus, *Werke und Briefe*, ed. Ludwig Gompf, Mittellateinische Studien und Texte, ed. Karl Langosch, 4 (Leiden: Brill, 1970); the work has been translated by Gildas Roberts, *The Iliad of Dares Phrygius* (Cape Town: A. A. Balkema, 1970).

42. Sedgwick, "The *Bellum Troianum*," 60, says Joseph omits Paris's actual decision.

43. Jürgen Stohlmann, "Albert von Stade," *Die deutsche Literatur des Mittelalters: Verfasserlexikon*, ed. Karl Langosch, 2nd ed. (Berlin: de Gruyter, 1978), 1, col. 145; on Albert's life, see cols. 143–44. I used the edition of Theodor Merzdorf (Leipzig: Teubner, 1875).

44. Stohlmann, "Albert von Stade," cols. 149–50; Stohlmann, *Anonymi Historia*, 188.

45. "Albert von Stade," col. 151.

46. Brian Woledge, "La Légende de Troie et les débuts de la prose française," in *Mélanges de linguistique et de littérature romanes offerts à Mario Roques*, 2 (Bade: Editions Art et Science, 1953), 313–24.

47. Identified by Kathleen Chesney, it is unedited and exists in three manu-

scripts: Ms. Douce 196, B. n. nouv. acq. fr. 9603, and Grenoble Ms. 861; see "A Neglected Prose Version of the *Roman de Troie*," *Medium Aevum*, 11 (1942): 46–49.

48. *Le Roman de Troie en prose*, ed. Léopold Constans and Edmond Faral, Les Classiques Français du Moyen Age (Paris: Champion, 1922). The work is discussed in Constans's edition of Benoît's *Roman de Troie*, 6.264–318, and Paul Meyer, "Les Premières Compilations françaises d'histoire ancienne," *Romania*, 14 (1885): 65–67; for the date, see ibid., 66.

49. (Cologny-Genève: Fondation Martin Bodmer, 1979).

50. Ibid., 8. It also exists in fragmentary form in British Library Lansdowne 229 and Oxford Queens College CVI. See Vielliard, *Roman de Troie en prose*, 8, and, on the latter, Woledge, "Légende de Troie," 320.

51. The prose *roman* in Rouen 1049 has not to my knowledge been studied. For the relationship between Benoît and the prose *roman* edited by Constans and Faral, see Meyer, "Premières Compilations," 65; for the Judgment scene, see Constans and Faral, *Roman de Troie*, 35–36. For the relationship between Benoît and the Bodmer prose *roman*, see Vielliard, *Roman de Troie en prose*, 10–23; I have compared the Judgment in the two works, and they are close in essential details. On the relationship of the Southern version to Benoît, see Chesney, "A Neglected Prose Version," 49–52; I have studied the Judgment as it appears in Ms. Douce 196, folios 15v–16r, and have found it to be very close to Benoît in essential details.

52. Woledge, "Légende de Troie," 319; Chesney, "A Neglected Prose Version," 53; Giuliana Carlesso, "La versione sud del 'Roman de Troie en prose' e il volgarizzamento di Binducci dello Scelto," *Atti dell'Istituto Veneto di scienze, lettere ed arti*, 124 (1966): 525; cf. Constans's introduction to his edition of Benoît's *Roman de Troie*, 6.330–31.

53. Chesney, "A Neglected Prose Version," 52.

54. Ed. Nathaniel Edward Griffin (Cambridge: Mediaeval Academy of America, 1936), 61–63. The work has been translated, with some inaccuracies, by Mary Elizabeth Meek (Bloomington: Indiana University Press, 1974). See Ruth Morse's review in *Medium Aevum*, 44 (1975): 66–67. In his notes on p. 61, Griffin prints for "Minori" (India) the alternative reading "Maiori," which is closer to the wording of the Southern version of the prose *roman*, at least as it appears in Ms. Douce 196.

55. For general comparisons with Benoît, see Hugo Buchthal, *Historia Troiana: Studies in the History of Mediaeval Secular Illustration* (London: Warburg Institute, 1971), 38, and Meybrinck, *Auffassung der Antike*, 48.

56. See generally on Friday as a day of ill luck: Alexander H. Krappe, *The Science of Folklore* (1929; rpt. New York: W. W. Norton, 1964), 220; particularly for Guido, who was a Sicilian: Giuseppe Pitrè, *Usi e costumi credenze e pregiudizi del popolo siciliano*, 4 (Florence: G. Barbèra, [1952]), 269–85.

57. Francis X. Newman, "*Somnium*: Medieval Theories of Dreaming and the Form of Vision Poetry" (Ph.D. diss., Princeton University, 1962), 50–55.

58. *PL*, ed. J.-P. Migne, 75 (Paris: J.-P. Migne, 1849), 827–28; discussed in Newman, "*Somnium*," 91–95.

59. For Isidore, see *Sententiarum Libri Tres*, 3.6, *PL*, ed. J.-P. Migne, 83 (Paris: J.-P. Migne, 1850), 669; see Newman, "*Somnium*," 95, n. 87.

60. *Policratici sive De Nugis Curialium et Vestigiis Philosophorum Libri*

VIII, ed. Clement C. J. Webb, 2 vols. (Oxford: Clarendon, 1909), 2.15 (1.92–93).

61. Hans Liebeschütz, *Fulgentius Metaforalis: Ein Beitrag zur Geschichte der antiken Mythologie im Mittelalter* (Leipzig: Teubner, 1926); Friedrich von Bezold, *Das Fortleben der antiken Götter im mittelalterlichen Humanismus* (Bonn: Kurt Schroeder, 1922).

62. Ed. Thomas Duffus Hardy, 2 vols. (1840; rpt. Vaduz: Kraus Reprint, 1964), 1.354–57; discussed in von Bezold, *Fortleben der antiken Götter*, 63–64.

63. Von Bezold, *Fortleben der antiken Götter*, 72.

64. John B. Friedman, *Orpheus in the Middle Ages* (Cambridge: Harvard University Press, 1970), 188; see also Henry Charles Lea, *Materials Toward a History of Witchcraft*, ed. Arthur C. Howland, 3 vols. (1939; rpt. New York: Thomas Yoseloff, 1957), 1.81–82.

65. *De Nugis Curialium*, ed. and trans. M. R. James, rev. C. N. L. Brooke and R. A. B. Mynors (Oxford: Clarendon, 1983), 4.11 (pp. 350–65); discussed in von Bezold, *Fortleben der antiken Götter*, 72–74.

66. Lynn Thorndike, *A History of Magic and Experimental Science*, 8 vols. (New York: Columbia University Press, 1934–58), 4.277, 328; on the general significance of St. John's Day, see Krappe, *Science of Folklore*, 271.

67. For the historical development of the idea up to the time of Guido, see Jeffrey Burton Russell, *Witchcraft in the Middle Ages* (Ithaca: Cornell University Press, 1972), esp. chs. 4, 5, and 6. Russell presents convincing evidence that Lea and others were wrong in placing the rise of witchcraft as late as the mid-thirteenth century; see 31, 133; cf. too Thorndike, *History of Magic*, 2.973. In their introduction to a collection of original sources, *Witchcraft in Europe, 1100–1700: A Documentary History* (Philadelphia: University of Pennsylvania Press, 1972), Alan C. Kors and Edward Peters date the codification of witch lore from about 1100 (5).

68. Russell, *Witchcraft*, 18, 53–54 and passim; Kors and Peters, *Witchcraft in Europe*, 8; and see the story from William of Malmesbury's *Gesta Regum Anglorum* printed in Kors and Peters (ibid., 32–35) and also in Hardy's edition, 1.351–54.

69. Von Bezold, *Fortleben der antiken Götter*, 29–32.

70. Ibid., 31.

71. Ibid.

72. E.g., Russell, *Witchcraft*, 15.

73. Webb, *Policraticus*, 2.15 (1.92); trans. Joseph B. Pike, *Frivolities of Courtiers and Footprints of Philosophers* (Minneapolis: University of Minnesota Press, 1938), 80.

74. Webb, *Policraticus*, 2.15 (1.92–93); Pike, *Frivolities*, 80.

75. On its relationship to Guido's *Historia*, see Meybrinck, *Auffassung der Antike*, 4; Gustav Häpke, *Kritische Beiträge zu Jacques Milets dramatischer Istoire de la Destruction de Troye la grant* (Marburg: M. G. Elwert, 1899), 5; for the date and biographical information on Milet, ibid., 1–2.

76. Meybrinck, *Auffassung der Antike*, 6–7.

77. Häpke, *Kritische Beiträge*, 3–4.

78.   Ce fust ou temps que toute fleur
       Verdoye pour commencement
       Et que le rossignol apprent
       Les amoureux a eulx deduire

Et que par chanter doulcement
Il les veult a amour induire.

(Paris: J. Driart, 1498), n.p. There is no critical edition of the work; Stengel's 1883 edition is only a reproduction of the 1484 *editio princeps;* see Häpke, *Kritische Beiträge,* 6. Häpke has collected from the oldest manuscripts variant readings up to line 14279; see 63–125.

79. George Doutrepont, *La Littérature française à la cour des ducs de Bourgogne* (1909; rpt. Slatkine Reprints, 1970), 171; he lists them on pp. 171–76; Alphonse Bayot, *La Légende de Troie à la cour de Bourgogne,* Société d'Emulation de Bruges, Mélanges, 1 (Bruges: L. de Plancke, 1908), 34; he lists them on pp. 38–44.

80. Doutrepont, *La Littérature française,* 147–49; Bayot, *La Légende de Troie,* 35–37.

81. Doutrepont, *La Littérature française,* 159–60, 168.

82. Ibid., 147–49, 152.

83. See Doutrepont, 172, who discusses them on pp. 172–73; and Bayot, *La Légende de Troie,* 18, who discusses them on pp. 18–23. See also H. Oskar Sommer, ed., *The Recuyell of the Historyes of Troye,* by Raoul Le Fèvre, trans. William Caxton, 2 vols. (London: David Nutt, 1894), 1.xxxiv–xxxvi.

84. Sommer, *Recuyell,* 1.lxxi; for the date, see Doutrepont, *La Littérature française,* 174; Bayot, *La Légende de Troie,* 33.

85. Doutrepont, *La Littérature française,* 173–74; Bayot, *La Légende de Troie,* 25–26.

86. Bayot, *La Légende de Troie,* 32; Sommer, *Recuyell,* 1.lviii–lx.

87. Bayot, *La Légende de Troie,* 23, 27–28, 33; Doutrepont, *La Littérature française,* 173–74, agrees with Bayot's analysis.

88. (Bruges: Colard Mansion, 1476[?]), n.p. This edition is discussed in Bayot, *La Légende de Troie,* 15. According to Bayot, this version is similar to that from which Caxton made his translation.

89. See especially Gordon, "Trojans in Britain," 9–30.

90. *Historia Brittonum cum Additamentis Nennii,* ed. Theodor Mommsen, *MGH,* 13 (Berlin: Weidmann, 1898), 150–53.

91. Gordon, "Trojans in Britain," 12–18; Parsons, "Trojan Legend," 253–57.

92. Gordon, "Trojans in Britain," 20.

93. The relationship between Guido's *Historia* and these three works has been studied by C. David Benson, *The History of Troy in Middle English Literature: Guido delle Colonne's Historia Destructionis Troiae in Medieval England* (Totowa, N.J.: Rowman and Littlefield, 1980).

94. Other English versions of Guido are the "Barbour" Fragments and Bodleian Library Rawlinson Ms. Misc. D. 82. See Mary Elizabeth Barnicle, ed., *The Seege or Batayle of Troye,* Early English Text Society, OS 172 (London: Oxford University Press, 1927), 229.

95. Barnicle, *Seege,* xxx.

96. Ibid., xxxiii–xxxv.

97. Ibid., lvii–lviii, and here Barnicle also surveys previous scholarship on the source; Elmer B. Atwood, "The Youth of Paris in the *Seege of Troy,*" *Texas University Studies in English,* 21 (1941): 7, and "The Judgment of Paris in the *Seege of Troye,*" *PMLA,* 57 (1942): 343.

98. Barnicle, *Seege,* lix–lx; Atwood, "Youth," 7; Atwood, "Judgment," 343.

99. Atwood, "Youth," 8–9 and passim; Atwood, "Judgment," 343–44 and passim.

100. See especially Atwood, "Youth," passim. Barnicle, who wrote before the discovery of the *Excidium Troiae*, noted these elements. She rejected the hypothesis of the "enlarged *Roman de Troiae*" and said they came separately from different sources (lix–lxviii). Possibly the presence of this material is also why Constans said the poem had the same Latin source as Simon Aurea Capra: *Le Roman de Troie*, 6.343, n. 4.

101. Atwood, "Judgment," 344–53.

102. I use Barnicle's edition of the *Seege* and follow the version in manuscript L (Lincoln's Inn 150), which she considers the most accurate and complete of the three in which the first version of the work is preserved. The Judgment appears on pp. 38–48. Barnicle prints in app. A a second version, quite different from the first, preserved in Harley 525. It will be discussed below.

103. Barnicle, *Seege*, lxix–lxx.

104. On mist which sets a hero apart from his companions as a theme in Celtic tales, see Bromwich, "Celtic Dynastic Themes," 447, 453. For an example of the theme, see Marie Louise Sjoestedt, ed., "Le Siège de Druim Damhghaire," *Revue Celtique*, 43 (1926): 23.

105. Russell, *Witchcraft*, 13, 18, 101; see also George Lyman Kittredge, *Witchcraft in Old and New England* (Cambridge: Harvard University Press, 1929), 119.

106. Printed by Andrew G. Little in *Studies in English Franciscan History* (New York: Longmans, Green, 1917), app. 3, 230; trans. G. R. Owst, "*Sortilegium* in English Homiletic Literature of the XIVth Century," *Studies Presented to Sir Hilary Jenkinson*, ed. J. Conway Davies (London: Oxford University Press, 1957), 278.

107. Russell, *Witchcraft*, 111.

108. Barnicle, *Seege*, xlvi–xlvii.

109. Ibid., 175 (lines 399–400).

110. Ed. George A. Panton and David Donaldson, 2 vols., Early English Text Society, 39 and 56 (London: N. Trubner, 1869, 1874). Date: Walter Clyde Curry, "The Judgment of Paris," *Modern Language Notes*, 31(1916): 114; dialect: James Root Hulbert, "The 'West Midland' of the Romances," *Modern Philology*, 19 (1921–22): 1–16; cf. Panton and Donaldson, 2.xv–xvi.

111. The editors discuss the work's relationship with Guido: 2.viii–ix.

112. Ed. J. Ernst Wülfing, 2 vols., Early English Text Society, OS 121–22 (London: EETS, 1902–3). Wülfing dates the poem to 1400: vol. 1, Temporary Preface, n.p. Dorothy Kempe says it may date from before 1343: "A Middle English Tale of Troy," *Englische Studien*, 29 (1901): 5; see pp. 6–12 on the relationship between the *Laud Troy Book* and Guido's *Historia*.

113. Henry Bergen, ed., *The Troy Book*, by John Lydgate, 4 vols., Early English Text Society, ES 97, 103, 106, 126 (London: EETS, 1906–35). For the date, see 1.ix; also Walter F. Schirmer, *John Lydgate: A Study in the Culture of the Fifteenth Century*, trans. Anne E. Keep (London: Methuen, 1961), 42–43, 50. On its relationship with Guido, see Bergen, *Troy Book*, 1.ix; Schirmer, *John Lydgate*, 43; Alain Renoir, *The Poetry of John Lydgate* (Cambridge: Harvard University Press, 1967), 64–67.

114. Bergen, *Troy Book*, Prologue, 360–75; subsequent citations give book and line references to this edition.

115. On his erudition, see Schirmer, *John Lydgate*, 44.

116. E. Bagby Atwood, "Some Minor Sources of Lydgate's *Troy Book*," *Studies in Philology*, 35 (1938): 26–27.

117. Bayot, *La Légende de Troie*, 14–15.

118. Sommer, *Recuyell*, 1.lxxxii–lxxxiii.

119. Ibid., 1.lxxxiii–lxxxv. Citations are to Sommer's edition.

120. Meyer, "Les Premières Compilations," 1.

121. For date and patron see, ibid., 57; Guy Raynaud de Lage, "Les 'Romans antiques' dans l'histoire ancienne jusqu'à César," *Moyen Age*, 63 (1957): 268; for authorship, see ibid., 268. The author was possibly Wauchier de Denain, Paul Meyer suggests in "Wauchier de Denain," *Romania*, 32 (1903): 585. For oral presentation, see Meyer, "Les Premières Compilations," 57.

122. Listed in Meyer, "Les Premières Compilations," 49–51. See also Woledge's appendix to "Légende de Troie," 321–22, and D. J. A. Ross, "The History of Macedon in the *Histoire ancienne jusqu'à César*," *Classica et Mediaevalia*, 24 (1963): 181, n. 2.

123. D. J. A. Ross, "Some Notes on the Old French Alexander Romance in Prose," *French Studies*, 6 (1952): 138.

124. Raynaud de Lage, "Les 'Romans antiques,'" 267.

125. Ibid., 279; Buchthal, *Historia Troiana*, 4–5. On the importance of prose as a medium of factual communication, see Woledge, "Lègende de Troie," 318–20. Buchthal, *Historia Troiana*, 4–5, says Dares "was evidently taken to be a more reliable historian than the imaginative poet Benoît."

126. I consulted the following manuscripts of the first version of the *Histoire ancienne*, all from the British Library: Add. 15268, Add. 19669, Add. 12029, Eg. 912, Roy. 16.G.VII. They are among those listed by Woledge, "Lègende de Troie," 321–22. The accounts of the Judgment of Paris in these manuscripts are identical but for minor scribal variations. I quote from Roy. 16.G.VII, which seems to have suffered the least scribal mishandling of the group. For a notice of the manuscript, see David Casley, *Catalogue of the Manuscripts of the King's Library* (London, 1734), 291. Contractions have been silently expanded.

"Aprez parla paris et dist a son pere que il feist apparillier le nauie si yroit en grece se il vouloit et il auoit si es diex sa fiance que se il y aloit que il vaincroit si sez annemis que il en aroit los et repaireroit arriere a toute victoire. Or entendez sire pour quoy ie di ceste chose. na mie encore long temps que ie estoie alez chacier en la forest. et la sapparut a moy en dormant mercurius qui grans diex est et sires si me fu auis que il amena o lui .iii. deesses. Junone et uenerem et minerua. adonc me rouua mercurius et dist que ie feisse iugement et deisse la quelle de ses trois estoit la plus belle et bien sachiez que assez me promistrent sens et prouesce Juno et minerue et venus de grece pource que ie la deisse la plus belle me promist la plus belle feme du monde et ie la belle dame couuoitay et dis deuant toutes les autres que venus estoit la plus belle" (f. 711).

127. Every manuscript of this redaction of the *Histoire ancienne* which I examined had the same wording for this line. Wisdom and strength are, however, traditionally Minerva's promises, but we must go back to Hyginus to find them combined in a source that would have been available in 1223. Curiously, the

two goddesses' traditional promises are reversed in a late twelfth- or early thirteenth-century school exercise, where Juno offers *vim*, strength, and Pallas
omen, solemnity or magnificence. See Faral, "Le Manuscrit 511," item 6, "Quis
Partus Trojae," lines 41–42 (pp. 21–22). At least one version of the Judgment
with the promises confused may have circulated in a compendium or handbook—the sort of reference that a student or historian would consult.

128. I have located two other historical compilations which include the
Judgment of Paris, both from the British Library: Roy. 19.E.VI and Roy. 18.E.V.
The Trojan material in each follows the tradition of Dares, beginning with the
story of the Golden Fleece. The Judgment is a dream which Paris recounts in
Priam's council. With respect to the Judgment, though, the two differ from each
other and from the more common tradition represented by Roy. 16.G.VII. In
Roy. 19.E.VI, Mercury brings only Juno and Venus to Paris, and each promises
him the most beautiful woman in Greece; in Roy. 18.E.V., the goddesses approach Paris without Mercury, and Juno hands him the golden apple, telling
him to award it to the most beautiful of them. There are no promises. We can
see from the variations in these two versions further evidence that writers
tended to vary the details of the Judgment as an infinitely malleable episode
within an established narrative structure that they followed quite faithfully—
usually that of Dares or Benoît.

129. Buchthal, *Historia Troiana*, 5.

130. Meyer, "Les Premières Compilations," 63, 75.

131. Ibid., 63–65. According to Ross, "The History of Macedon," 181, n. 2,
eight manuscripts of this redaction are extant; Woledge, "Légende de Troie,"
323, lists ten; Léopold Constans, "Une Traduction française des Héroïdes
d'Ovide au XIII siècle," *Romania*, 43 (1914), 178, lists some which contain in-
terpolated *Heroides*, also characteristic of the second redaction.

132. Paraphrased from my translation. I consulted, all from the British Library, Roy. 20.D.I., Add. 25884, Stowe 54. Add. 25884 (despite Woledge, "Légende de Troie," 321) follows the *second* redaction, at least in the episode of the
Judgment. I print below the episode from Add. 25884, amending from the other
two manuscripts when necessary and expanding contractions. For a brief notice
of B.L. Add. 25884, see *Catalogue of Additions to the Manuscripts in the British Museum in the Years MDCCCLIV–MDCCCLXXV*, 2 (London: Longmans,
1877), 230.

"Le tiers ot nom paris qui fut moult beau et de noble faiture et maniere et
estoit le plus beau et le plus plaisant aux dames qui oncques feust en son temps
mais il nestoit pas le plus cheualereux mais a merueilles estoit bon archier et
bon veneur et par raison bon cheualier mais non mie si bon comme furent ses
freres. . . . Une nuit estoit la roine ecuba couchee auec son mary le roy priant.
Celle nuit habita le roy a la royne puis sendormy celle dame et en ce somme
songa vn songe que de son songe lui aparoit que de son ventre issoit vne torche
ardant et lui sembloit que celle torche ardoit toute la cite de troie et en songant
ce songe fremissoit et se remuoit et paroit quelle souffrist grant paine quant
vint au matin le roy lui demanda que celle auoit la nuit eu et la dame lui dist
quelle auoit vn songe songie moult merueilleux et lui dist que il lui auoit paru
en son songe que vne torche lui issoit du ventre qui toute la cite de troie ardoit.
Quant le roy lentendi si pansa bien en son cuer que ce signifioit et li arupi-
cenieismes li distrent que la dame auoit conceu vn enfant par qui toute la cite

de troie seroit arse et destruite. Quant li rois uit ce si commanda a sa feme quelle occeist lenfant quelle auoit ou corps car grant peril pourroit par lui venir. quant la dame ot enfante Si lui print pitie de son enfant si ne le voult pas tuer mais lenuoia par vn sien secret messaigier en vne ville a vn sien secret vavasseur qui le nourry bien et doulcement et lappelerent par son droit nom alixandre et quant il fut grant et parcreus si print a femme la deesse cenona qui lui donna de nobles dons et de gracieux. . . . Un jour auint que icellui alixandre estoit alez veoir ses bestes et son aumaille a vn manoir que son seigneur tenoit Si trouua es prez soubz vne roche prez dune clere fontaine vn torel bel et fort et gras mais il ne sauoit dont il estoit ne de quelle part il estoit venus car il estoit estranges et se combatoit icellui torel a vn des siens toreaux. longuement dura la bataille et paris les regarda sans aidier ne sans nuire a lun ne a lautre tout coiement et quant vint a la fin son toreau fut vaincu si fist vne couronne de flours et couronna le torel estrange en signe de victoire. Ceste chose fut sceue communement par tout le pais et en fut moult loez et fut dit quil estoit loial et droicturiez et vrais justicier.

Vn jour auint que la deesse juno et la desse palas dame de sapience et dame venus sassemblerent ensemble pour joye et feste demener mais quant setota la deesse vist que les autres deesses ne lauoient pas apellee a la feste si en fut forment yree contre elles. Si se apensa de semer entrelles semance de discorde. Si fist vne pome de fin or ou il auoit escript ceste pome soit donnee a la plus belle. Et quant les dames orent festoie si entrerent en vn vergier par grant deduit sur vne belle fontaine et puis sassistrent illec pour dire lun a lautre ce quil leur delictoit et plaisoit adont passa par lair la deesse feconda et laissa cheoir la pome entrelles. quant celles dames virent la pome si lurent les lettres et si dist chascune quelle la deuoit auoir. Et auec ce dit chascune la raison pourquoy elle la deuoit auoir et moult estriuerent les dames entre elles et moult grant fut la discorde si que ala fin lune des dames Si dist que mieux vauldroit quelles queissent vn bon proudomme loial qui en sceust droictement jugier et quelles se en y meissent du tout sur lui. A ceste chose sacorderent toutes. Si se mistrent a la voie pour aler hors de la forest si alerent tant que par auenture sembatirent et vindient a vne fontaine soubz vn oliuier la ou paris se dormoit. Lors dist lune a lautre veez cy paris le fils au roy priant nul plus loial de lui ne pourroit estre trouuez et bien y paru au torel estrange que il couronna le quel auoit vaincu le sien. de grant loiaulte lui vint Que il fist ce a vn estrange aussi comme il eust voulu que len eust fait au sien. Se vous voulez accordons nous et si nous enmettons sur ce quil nous en dira. A ce furent toutes accordees si senvindrent a paris et si le sueillerent quant paris les vist Si leur fist grant joie et grant honneur et que vous iroie je racontant la choison lui conterent toute comment il leur estoit auenu. Si lui donnerent la pomme en sa main et lui distrent quil la donnast a la plus belle selon son jugement et se mistrent dutout sur lui. . . . Ma dame juno la premiere lui pria et le semond que il la lui donnast et quelle lui feroit aide toutes les fois que mestiez lui en seroit et lui mettroit en son secours toutes les fortes et bonnes vertus du ciel. . . . Ma dame pallas lui redist et raconta que se il la lui donnoit quelle lui aideroit et donroit sens et sauoir Car elle estoit deesse de sapience et jamais ne seroit quelle ne lui feist aide toutes les fois que il en auroit mestier en aucune maniere. . . . Ma dame Venus cointe noble et plaisant soutiue et deceuant li fist de son pouoir preut et si lui fist entendre et par raison lui monstra et lui dist paris se tu es loial homs tu me doie la pome donner par raison car la pome doit estre donnee a la plus belle et tu vois tout apartement que je suis la plus belle se tu fais droit je laurai et se je lay je te donray telle grace que toutes les femmes te ameront se tu veulx que tu auras la plus belle du monde a amie a briefment parlez tant lui dist et promist que il lui donna la pomme deuant les autres par droit jugement si en furent moult courrouciees mais quiconques eust de ce courrux ma dame Venus en ot la joie et lonneur." (ff. 116v–117v).

133. Meyer, "Les Premières Compilations," 65; Constans, "Une Traduction," 193; Woledge, "Légende de Troie," 322–23.

134. Chesney, "A Neglected Prose Version," 64, has commented on its more complete Judgment, referring specifically to the version in Douce 353.

135. For background on Mannyng, see Beryl Smalley, *English Friars and Antiquity in the Early Fourteenth Century* (New York: Barnes and Noble, 1960), 21–23.

136. Ibid., 22.

137. Gordon, "Trojans in Britain," 11–21.

138. Robert Manning of Brunne, *The Story of England*, ed. Frederick J. Furnivall (1887; rpt., n.p.: Kraus Reprint, 1965). Subsequent references are to line numbers in this edition.

139. Elmer Bagby Atwood, "Robert Mannyng's Version of the Troy Story," *Texas University Studies in English*, 18 (1938): 5.

140. Ibid., 9.

141. Ibid., 10, points out that a ball rather than an apple appears as well in the *Istorietta Trojana*.

142. Cf. Atwood, "Robert Mannyng's Version," 10–11.

143. Kittredge, *Witchcraft*, 29–30; Russell, *Witchcraft*, 13–15, 23, 53–54, 117–18. An example of a medieval English tale in which a witch flies is Ralph of Coggeshall's narrative of the witch of Reims (1176–80), printed by Kors and Peters, *Witchcraft in Europe*, 44–47.

144. Kors and Peters, *Witchcraft in Europe*, 10–11; Russell, *Witchcraft*, 133, 168; Thorndike, *History of Magic*, 3.9, 21–35.

145. Kittredge, *Witchcraft*, 50–55 and passim; on Mortimer, 53.

146.   3 yf þou euer þurgh folye
    Dydyst ouȝt do nygrómauncy.
    Or to þe deuyl dedyst sacryfyse
    Þurgh wychcraftys asyse,

    . . . .

    Þou hast synned & do a-mys,

    . . . .

    Wycchëcraft men clepyn hyt al:
    Beleue nouȝt yn þe pyys cheteryng. . . . (lines 339–55)
Robert of Brunne's "Handlyng Synne," ed. Frederick J. Furnivall, 2 vols., Early English Text Society, OS 119, 123 (1901, 1903; rpt. Millwood, N.Y.: Kraus Reprint Co., 1978), 1.13. Discussed in Kittredge, *Witchcraft*, 51; I use Kittredge's version of the passage in my text. On the substitution, Kittredge, *Witchcraft* 51; Furnivall, *"Handlyng Synne,"* lines 501–62 (pp. 19–20).

147. Europe: Kors and Peters, *Witchcraft in Europe*, 7–8; England: Kittredge, *Witchcraft*, 24–25.

148. Russell, *Witchcraft*, 124, 165.

149. Smalley, *English Friars*, 47–48; on Vincent see also B. L. Ullman, "A Project for a New Edition of Vincent of Beauvais," *Speculum*, 8 (1933): 312–26.

150. On the influence of Eusebius, see Jean Seznec, *The Survival of the Pagan Gods: The Mythological Tradition and its Place in Renaissance Humanism and Art*, trans. Barbara F. Sessions, Bollingen Series, 38 (1953; rpt. Princeton: Princeton University Press, 1972), 14.

151. "Causa autem belli fuit ut scribit eusebius quod trium mulierum de pulcritudine certantium premium fuit vna earum helenam pastorali iudice pollicente." Vincent of Beauvais, *Speculum Historiale* [Strassburg: Johann Mentelin, 1473], bk. 3, ch. 60.

152. Churchill Babington, ed., *Polychronicon Ranulphi Higden Monachi Cestrensis*, 9 vols. (London: Longmans, Green, 1865–86), 1.ix. Babington also prints Trevisa's English translation of the work.

153. Ibid., 1.ix, xiii.

154. Completed April 18, 1387: ibid., 1.lv, n. 2.

155. Babington, ibid., 2.xxxvi, gives Dares as one of Higden's sources for the Argonautic expedition and the Trojan War.

156. "[H]e see in his slepe Mercury to haue brou3t to hym Venus and Minerua to iugge of the beawte of theyme. Then Minerua promisede to hym sapience, if that he wolde preferre here beaute; and Venus promisede to hym oon of the feireste women of þe worlde to his wife." Babington, *Polychronicon*, 2.409.

157. Seznec, *Survival of the Pagan Gods*, 21, discusses the work briefly. I used the edition of Bernardinus de Benaliis (Venice, 1486). The Trojan material appears in book 3.

158. "[I]n maximam iustitie famam euasit: et adeo magnam (vt poete tradunt) vt litigantibus de formositate: pallade: iunone et venere propter aureum pomum a discordia eis in conuiuio periectum: in quo scriptum erat: Detur digniori: quod cum in litigium maximum incidissent: a Ioue per sententia misse sunt: verum cum ob voluptatem veneri id deberi iudicasset: quae eidem pulchriorem orbis mulierem spoponderat a multis iniustus iudicatus est" (f. 611; contractions have been silently expanded).

Chapter 3. The Judgment as Allegory

1. *Epistularum*, part 1, ed. Isidorus Hilberg (*Opera*, sect. 1, part 1) *CSEL* 54 (Vienna: F. Tempsky, 1910), letter 22, (p. 190).

2. On the allegorical interpretation of classical myth in the Middle Ages, see Hans Liebeschütz, *Fulgentius Metaforalis: Ein Beitrag zur Geschichte der antiken Mythologie im Mittelalter* (Leipzig: Teubner, 1926); Alma Frey-Sallmann, *Aus dem Nachleben antiker Göttergestalten: Die antiken Gotheiten in der Bildbeschreibung des Mittelalters und der italienischen Frührenaissance* (Leipzig: Dieterich'sche Verlagsbuchhandlung, 1931); Erwin Panofsky and Fritz Saxl, "Classical Mythology in Mediaeval Art," *Metropolitan Museum*

Studies, 4 (1932–33): 228–80; Lester K. Born, "Ovid and Allegory," *Speculum,* 9 (1934): 362–79; Erwin Panofsky, *Studies in Iconology* (1939; rpt. New York: Harper and Row, 1972); Erwin Panofsky, "Renaissance and Renascences," *Kenyon Review,* 6 (1944): 201–36; Edwin A. Quain, S.J., "The Medieval Accessus ad Auctores," *Traditio,* 3 (1945): 125–64; Jean Seznec, *The Survival of the Pagan Gods: The Mythological Tradition and Its Place in Renaissance Humanism and Art,* trans. Barbara F. Sessions, Bollingen Series, 38 (1953; rpt. Princeton: Princeton University Press, 1972); Paule Demats, *Fabula: Trois études de mythographie antique et médiévale,* Publications Romanes et Françaises, 122 (Geneva: Librairie Droz, 1973).

3. For its roots in ancient thought, see Jean Pépin, *Mythe et allégorie: Les Origines grecques et les contestations judéo-chrétiennes* (Paris: Editions Montaigne, 1958); Born, "Ovid," 366.

4. Pépin, *Mythe et allégorie,* 125–31.

5. E.g., ibid., 276–307 and passim.

6. On the early Christian interpretation of the classics, see Quain, "Medieval Accessus," 222–25; Liebeschütz, *Fulgentius Metaforalis,* 1–3; Born, "Ovid," 366–68.

7. Born, "Ovid," 367–68.

8. Exodus 3.22, 11.2, 12.35.

9. Aurelius Augustinus, *De Doctrina Christiana* (*Opera,* part 4, 1) CSEL 32 (Turnhout: Brepols, 1962), 2.40.60 (p. 74); quoted and discussed in D. W. Robertson, Jr., *A Preface to Chaucer: Studies in Medieval Perspectives* (Princeton: Princeton University Press, 1962), 340–41, where he also cites medieval uses of the theme.

10. *Epistularum,* letter 70 (p. 702); quoted in Robertson, *Preface to Chaucer,* 340; cited in Demats, *Fabula,* 39–40. The idea is ultimately Origen's; see Henri de Lubac, *Exégèse médiévale: Les quatre sens de l'écriture,* 1 (Paris: Aubier, 1959), 290–304.

11. *Scriptores Rerum Mythicarum,* ed. Georg Heinrich Bode (Celle: Schulze, 1834), fables 205 and 206 (pp. 142–44). On the identity of the Second Vatican Mythographer, see Max Manitius, *Geschichte der lateinischen Literatur des Mittelalters,* 2 (Munich: Beck, 1923), 656–60, and Pierre Courcelle, *La Consolation de philosophie dans la tradition littéraire: Antécédents et postérité de Boèce* (Paris: Etudes Augustiniennes, 1967), 247; cf. K. O. Elliot and J. P. Elder, "A Critical Edition of the *Vatican Mythographers,*" *Transactions of the American Philological Association,* 78 (1947): 202. On the style and format of the Second Vatican Mythographer, see Elliott and Elder, 199–200; on his sources, 200–202. For a general survey of scholarship, see Richard M. Krill, "The Vatican Mythographers: Their Place in Ancient Mythography," *Manuscripta,* 23 (1979): 175–76.

12. Bode, *Scriptores,* 11.20–23 (pp. 240–41). On the identity of the Third Vatican Mythographer, see Eleanor Rathbone, "Master Alberic of London, 'Mythographus Tertius Vaticanus,'" *Mediaeval and Renaissance Studies,* 1 (1941): 37; Elliott and Elder, "*Vatican Mythographers,*" 205. On his date, Rathbone, "Master Alberic," 37; on his learning and sources, Elliott and Elder, "*Vatican Mythographers,*" 203–5; Henning Sjöström, "Magister Albericus Lundoniensis: Mythographus Tertius Vaticanus," *Classica et Mediaevalia,* 29

(1968): 250–51; on his intellectual milieu, ibid., 249–64. For bibliography and survey of scholarship, see Krill, "Vatican Mythographers," 176–77.

13. (Strassburg: Adolf Rusch, 1477[?]), bk. 6, ch. 34. On Vincent and the *Speculum Maius*, see B. L. Ullman, "A Project for a New Edition of Vincent of Beauvais," *Speculum*, 8 (1933): 312–26.

14. B. M. Royal 12.E.xxi, f. 46r–v. See J. A. Herbert, *Catalogue of Romances in the Department of Manuscripts in the British Museum*, 3 (London: British Museum, 1910), 160; Frederic C. Tubach, *Index Exemplorum: A Handbook of Medieval Religious Tales* (Helsinki: Akademia Scientiarum Fennica, 1969), no. 3604.

15. Ed. Robert A. van Kluyve (Durham, N.C.: Duke University Press, 1968), 12.1 (pp. 169–71). On the date of the work, see van Kluyve's introduction, x; on its debt to the Third Vatican Mythographer, xiv–xv.

16. On the use of classical myth in this milieu, see M. D. Chenu, "*Involucrum*: Le Mythe selon les théologiens médiévaux," *Archives d'Histoire Doctrinale et Littéraire du Moyen Age*, 30 (1955): 75–79.

17. On William, see Brian Stock, *Myth and Science in the Twelfth Century: A Study of Bernard Silvester* (Princeton: Princeton University Press, 1972), 239–40; Edouard Jeauneau, *Glosae super Platonem*, by Guillaume de Conches, Textes Philosophiques du Moyen Age, 13 (Paris: J. Vrin, 1965), 9–10; on his thought and career, ibid., 10–14; Stock, *Myth and Science*, 249–62; Winthrop Wetherbee, *Platonism and Poetry in the Twelfth Century* (Princeton: Princeton University Press, 1972), 29–48 and passim; on the date of his commentary on the *Consolation of Philosophy*, Jeauneau, *Glosae*, 14; cf. Courcelle, *Consolation de philosophie*, 303.

18. Wetherbee, *Platonism*, 93; see pp. 92–98 for Wetherbee's full discussion of the commentary.

19. Ed. Edouard Jeauneau, "L'Usage de la notion d'*integumentum* à travers les gloses de Guillaume de Conches," *Archives d'Histoire Doctrinale et Littéraire du Moyen Age*, 32 (1957): 51–52.

20. For its relationship with the Fulgentian interpretation, see Jeauneau, "L'Usage," 47, 52.

21. Wetherbee, *Platonism*, 96; Jeauneau, "L'Usage," 46. William's interpretation of Orpheus is discussed in John Block Friedman, *Orpheus in the Middle Ages* (Cambridge: Harvard University Press, 1970), 105–9.

22. Jeauneau, "L'Usage," 45.

23. William's interpretation of the Judgment is repeated verbatim in the *Liber Cosmographiae* of John de Foxton, Trinity College, Cambridge, Ms. R.15.21, ff. 49v–50r. I am indebted to John Friedman for this reference. An interpretation of the Judgment appears too in an unpublished Florentine commentary on Martianus Capella which may derive ultimately from William's lectures. See Jane Chance, "The Medieval Sources of Cristoforo Landino's Allegorization of the Judgment of Paris," *Studies in Philology*, 81 (1984): 156–59, and Peter Dronke, *Fabula: Explorations into the Uses of Myth in Medieval Platonism*, Mittellateinische Studien und Texte, 9 (Leiden and Cologne: E. J. Brill, 1974), app. B, 167–83.

24. The passage is printed in Richard A. Dwyer, *Boethian Fictions: Narratives in the Medieval French Versions of the Consolatio Philosophiae*, Medi-

aeval Academy of America Publication no. 83 (Cambridge: Mediaeval Academy of America, 1976), app. 1, 103–8. I use the longer version, though the work was evidently later rehandled by someone who wanted to shorten it; see 62. On the date, see ibid., 14; on sources, 59, 63.

25. Ibid., 63–65.

26. Ibid., 14.

27. On his life, see Stock, *Myth and Science*, 13–14; Winthrop Wetherbee, trans., *The Cosmographia of Bernardus Silvestris* (New York: Columbia University Press, 1973), 20. For the attribution of the commentary on the *Aeneid* to him, see Stock, *Myth and Science*, xii and 36, n. 42; Wetherbee, *Cosmographia*, 20, 135–36, n. 88.

28. *The Commentary on the First Six Books of the Aeneid of Vergil Commonly Attributed to Bernardus Silvestris*, ed. Julian Ward Jones and Elizabeth Frances Jones (Lincoln: University of Nebraska Press, 1977), Preface, lines 10–11 (p. 3). Translations are my own. The work has also been translated by Earl G. Schreiber and Thomas E. Maresca, *Commentary on the First Six Books of Virgils's Aeneid by Bernardus Silvestris* (Lincoln: University of Nebraska Press, 1979). For a general discussion of the work, see Wetherbee, *Platonism*, 105–11; Marc-René Jung, *Etudes sur le poème allégorique en France au moyen âge* (Berne: Editions Francke, 1971), 61–62.

29. Wetherbee, *Platonism*, 106.

30. Ibid., 107.

31. Trans. H. Rushton Fairclough, rev. ed., 2 vols., Loeb Classical Library (Cambridge: Harvard University Press, 1960), 6.63–65 (Loeb 1.511).

32. Jones and Jones, *Commentary*, 46.

33. Ibid., 99. I have been unable to determine what Greek word Bernard had in mind.

34. Wetherbee, *Platonism*, 110, says he took material from Fulgentius, William, and others.

35. On preaching in the Middle Ages, see G. R. Owst, *Literature and Pulpit in Medieval England*, 2nd ed., rev. (1961; rpt. Oxford: Basil Blackwell, 1966) and *Preaching in Medieval England* (1926; rpt. New York: Russell and Russell, 1965); Beryl Smalley, *English Friars and Antiquity in the Early Fourteenth Century* (New York: Barnes and Noble, 1960); J.-Th. Welter, *L'Exemplum dans la littérature religieuse et didactique du moyen âge* (1927; rpt. Geneva: Slatkine Reprints, 1973).

36. Panofsky and Saxl, "Classical Mythology," 256; Demats, *Fabula*, 111 and passim.

37. On medieval interest in Ovid, see. e.g., Edward Kennard Rand, *Ovid and His Influence* (1925; rpt. New York: Cooper Square Publishers, 1963); Fausto Ghisalberti, ed., "Arnolfo d'Orléans, un cultore di Ovidio nel secolo XII," *Memorie del Reale Istituto Lombardo di Scienze e Lettere*, 24 (1932): 157–232; Fausto Ghisalberti, ed., *Giovanni di Garlandia: Integumenta Ovidii, poemetto inedito del secolo XIII* (Messina: Ct. Principato, 1933); Fausto Ghisalberti, ed., "Giovanni del Virgilio, espositore delle 'Metamorphosi,'" *Il Giornale Dantesco*, 34 (1933): 43–107.

38. "'Ovide moralisé': Poème du commmencement du quatorzième siècle," ed. Cornelis de Boer, *Verhandelingen der Koninklijke Akademie van Wetenschappen te Amsterdam, Afdeeling Letterkunde*, NS 15, 21, 30, 37, 43

(Amsterdam, 1915–38). References in my text are to book and line numbers. On date and author, see Joseph Engels, *Etudes sur l'Ovide moralisé* (Groningen: J. B. Wolters, 1945), 46–50.

39. Smalley, *English Friars*, 258.

40. On Ovid as Christian: Demats, *Fabula*, 113–36; Born, "Ovid," 364. For the counterargument: Demats, *Fabula*, 109, 112–13.

41. Demats, *Fabula*, 175.

42. Engels, *Etudes*, 70–71; Demats, *Fabula*, 61–63.

43. Engels, *Etudes*, 66–69; Christian interpretation: 49.

44. Demats, *Fabula*, 68.

45. Ibid., 91.

46. Ibid., 81–82.

47. Ibid., 93–94; on a possible source in the *Fasti* for details of the Wedding, see 80, n. 66. For the Judgment in Fulgentius see Chapter 1, for the Wedding see *Opera*, ed. Rudolf Helm (1898; rpt. Stuttgart: Teubner, 1970), 3.7 (p. 70).

48. On various examples of the tradition, Demats, *Fabula*, 93–94; cf. de Boer, "Ovid moralisé," 24.

49. Engels, *Etudes*, 73.

50. Welter, *Exemplum*, 69, 74–79, 133–34.

51. Aurelius Augustinus, *De Civitate Dei*, *Opera*, part 14, 1–2, *CCSL* 47–48 (Turnhout: Brepols, 1955), 12.15 (part 14, 2, p. 369).

52. 12.14 (part 14, 2, p. 369). On the importance of this theme in Augustine, see Frederick Copleston, *A History of Philosophy*, 2 (Westminster, Md.: Newman Press, 1950), 85–86.

53. Copleston, *History*, 243.

54. For the Augustinian tradition see, e.g., Anselm's *Cur Deus Homo*; on it, see Emile Bréhier, *The Middle Ages and the Renaissance*, trans. Wade Baskin, vol. 3 of *The History of Philosophy* (Chicago: University of Chicago Press, 1965), 40. On *Sentences*: Bréhier, *Middle Ages*, 48–49. On *Summa*: ibid., 114–15.

55. Fulgentius, *Opera*, 3.7 (p. 70); trans. Leslie George Whitbread, *Fulgentius the Mythographer* (Columbus: Ohio State University Press, 1971), 91.

56. *The Works of Geoffrey Chaucer*, ed. F. N. Robinson, 2nd ed. (Boston: Houghton Mifflin, 1961), General Prologue, 282, 275 (p. 19).

57. Fulgentius, *Opera*, 2.1 (p. 36).

58. Bréhier, *Middle Ages*, 123; Copleston, *History*, 216–17 and passim.

59. *De Libero Arbitrio*, *Opera*, part 2, 2, *CCSL* 29 (Turnhout: Brepols, 1970), 2.19.52 (p. 272). Quoted and discussed in Copleston, *History*, 82; the translation in my text is Copleston's.

60. Copleston, *History*, 82.

61. *De Civitate Dei*, 12.24 (*Opera*, part 14, 2, p. 381).

62. Fulgentius, *Opera*, 2.1 (p. 37).

63. Cornelis de Boer, ed., *Ovide moralisé en prose*, Verhandelingen der Koninklijke Nederlandse Akademie van Wetenschappen, Afdeeling Letterkunde, NS 61, no. 2 (Amsterdam, 1954), 3. Citations are to this edition.

64. On Bersuire's life, see Engels, *Etudes*, 23–24. On the work's use by preachers, see Engels, "L'Edition critique de l'*Ovidius Moralizatus* de Bersuire," *Vivarium*, 9 (1971): 22–23; Fausto Ghisalberti, "L' 'Ovidius moralizatus' di Pierre Bersuire," *Studi Romanzi*, 23 (1933): 32.

65. Engels, "L'Edition critique," 21, and *Etudes*, 24–25; Ghisalberti, "L' 'Ovidius,'" 29–30, 66–68; Smalley, *English Friars*, 262–63; Joseph Engels, ed., *Reductorium Morale, Liber XV: Ovidius Moralizatus, cap. i, De Formis Figurisque Deorum*, by Petrus Berchorius (Utrecht: Instituut voor Laat Latijn der Rijksuniversiteit, 1966) (Werkmateriaal—3), iii–iv. For the earlier (Avignon) version of the *Ovidius Moralizatus*, I consulted for ch. 1, "De Formis Figurisque Deorum," the 1509 Paris edition ascribed to Thomas Waleys, and for chs. 2–15 a transcription of the 1509 edition prepared under the editorship of Joseph Engels by the Instituut voor Laat Latijn der Rijksuniversiteit (Utrecht, 1962), cited henceforth as Werkmateriaal—2. For the later (Paris) version, I consulted for ch. 1 Engels's edition cited above (Werkmateriaal—3) and for chs. 2–15 a print of B.n. 16787 in the New York Public Library. B.n. 16787 is discussed as a good example of the Paris version by Engels, Werkmateriaal—3, xx, and Ghisalberti, "L' 'Ovidius,'" 66.

66. On the content of the *Reductorium*, see Engels, *Etudes*, 44.

67. Ghisalberti, "L' 'Ovidius,'" 27.

68. Ibid., 29; Engels, *Etudes*, 25.

69. "Duae vero sequentes historiae seu fabulae non habentur in textu" (Werkmateriaal—2, 187).

70. On the placement, see Engels, Werkmateriaal—3, xi.

71. Ovid, *Metamorphoses*, trans. Frank Justus Miller, 2 vols., Loeb Classical Library (Cambridge: Harvard University Press, 1951–58), 12.4 (Loeb 2.181).

72. Werkmateriaal—3, 1, lines 1–21; see Ghisalberti, "L' 'Ovidius,'" 28, and on his method, 39–42.

73. Werkmateriaal—2, 187–88 (bk. 15, fable 8).

74. "Vel si vis dic quod Peleus et Thetis est Adam et Eva, qui scilicet filium se mayorem scilicet Achillem id est Xristum, de sua progenie produxerunt et sic Xristus [Xristum?] Adam" (Werkmateriaal—3, 53, lines 34–36; I have expanded contractions not expanded by the editors).

75. As does, later, Venus showing herself to Paris nude; see below in this chapter.

76. Werkmateriaal—2, 162–63 (bk. 12, fable 1).

77. "Per istas tres deas sic pacifice conuiuentes intelligo bonos et iustos pacifice conuersantes. Per deam discordiae intelligo inuidos qui quando non vocantur indignantur et seminare discordiam inter ipsos delectantur. Tales consueuerunt inter alios pomum discordiae proiicere. Et verbum detractorium dicere" (Werkmateriaal—2, 163 [bk. 12, fable 2]).

78. "[Vel dic quod pomum discordie significat] bona temporalia: quae pro certo: qui habent vix possunt pacifici esse: quia quilibet vult ipsa habere. Ista sunt quae discordiam seminant et quae suis successoribus lites parant et finaliter bella et destructiones parant. Dea et domina discordiae est auaritia: qua nihil potest melius inter homines dissensionem facere" (Werkmateriaal—2, 164 [bk. 12, fable 2]; I have supplied the missing line from B.n. 16787).

79. Werkmateriaal—2, 163–64 (bk. 12, fable 2).

80. Werkmateriaal—2, 164 (bk. 12, fable 2).

81. For Augustine on the will, see, e.g., *De Civitate Dei*, 14.6–7; *Enchiridion, Opera*, part 13, 2, *CCSL* 46 (Turnhout: Brepols, 1969), 9.30–32 (pp. 65–67).

82. See Augustine, *Contra Duas Epistolas Pelagianorum*, 1.13.27 (*PL*, ed.

J.-P. Migne, 44 [Paris: J.-P. Migne, 1845], 563); Etienne Gilson, *The Christian Philosophy of Saint Augustine*, trans. L. E. M. Lynch (New York: Random House, 1960), 151, 162, 169–70.

83. "Haec igitur tria, memoria, intellegentia, uoluntas." *De Trinitate, Opera*, part 16, 1, *CCSL* 50 (Turnhout: Brepols, 1968), 10.11.18 (p. 330); Gilson, *Christian Philosophy*, 219, 354–55, n. 14.

84. *Spicilegium Bonaventurianum IV* (Grottaferrata: Collegii S. Bonaventurae ad Claras Aquas, 1971), 1.3.2–3; Gilson, *Christian Philosophy*, 219.

85. Placed above *ratio* by Augustine; Gilson, *Christian Philosophy*, 79, 269–70, n. 1.

86. On the handbook, see John B. Friedman, "John de Foxton's Continuation of Ridwall's *Fulgentius Metaforalis*," *Studies in Iconography*, 7–8 (1981–82): 67–69; Smalley, *English Friars*, 109–12. On the assignment of virtues to the gods, see Friedman, "John de Foxton," 68–69; Seznec, *Survival of the Pagan Gods*, 94. In the Paris version of ch. 1, *De Formis Figurisque Deorum*, an allegorization of the chief gods and goddesses, Bersuire associates Juno with memory and refers obliquely to the *Fulgentius Metaforalis* as his source ("ille super Fulgencium") (Werkmateriaal—3, 34, lines 3–5). The corresponding passage is absent, however, in the earlier version, suggesting that his association of Juno with memory there was not due to a connection already made in the mythographic tradition.

87. "[D]ic quod in homine qui dicitur minor indus tres dee id est tres anime potentie primo fueresse[n]t concordes et quia spiritualitas rationi obediebat nulla erat discordia inter partes. Homo cum deo concors erat et inter se talis erat concordia quod nequaquam caro spiritum repugnabat. Denique dea vel deus discordie id est dyabolus vel cum superbia vel concupiscentia pomum vetitum sibi pericat [from *iacio* or *iacto?*] ideo pacem et concordiam enervauit et regum anime dissipauit" (B.n. 16787, f. 58r; contractions have been silently expanded).

88. *De Civitate Dei* 13.13 (*Opera*, part 14, 2, p. 395); the translation in my text is from Robert P. Miller, ed., *Chaucer: Sources and Backgrounds* (New York: Oxford University Press, 1977), 23. See also *De Doctrina Christiana*, 1.24.25, and *De Genesi ad Litteram* 10.12; discussed in Gilson, *Christian Philosophy*, 151.

89. *De Libero Arbitrio*, 1.8.18 (*Opera*, part 2, 2, p. 223); also see *De Civitate Dei*, 14.16.

90. *De Civitate Dei* 22.24 (*Opera*, part 14, 2, p. 847).

91. On concupiscence in Augustine, see Gilson, *Christian Philosophy*, 151, 162, 169–70.

92. Herbert, *Catalogue*, 166–79; Tubach, *Index*, no. 3604; Siegfried Wenzel, *Verses in Sermons: Fasciculus Morum and Its Middle English Poems*, Mediaeval Academy of America, Publication no. 87 (Cambridge, Mass.: Mediaeval Academy of America, 1978), 116–19 and passim (see index); Welter, *Exemplum*, 368–69.

93. "[A]d fontem sedebant tres regine mutuo querentes que pulcrior earum. Venit ergo quarta a longe pomum proiciens aureum in quo sic sculpebatur: 'pulcrior vestrum me habebit.' tunc vnanimiter deum appollinem adiuerunt vt quererent que earum pulcrior esset. Prima erat dea veneris que pro se pulcritudinem corporis allegebat. Secunda dea uesta que honesta morali se

pulcriorem ostendebat. Tercia [illegible] dea cursus que vitam activam designabat. Tunc appollinus dixit venerem pomum debere habere, quia pulcritudo corporalis in tantum excedit alia [sic]. quod multi ob amorem eius mortem vultro incurrebant. Set duobus adhuc non ascensientibus omnes ad deum iouem ascenderunt qui dixit pallas idest dea uesta pomum debere habere et non venus, quia venus de deliciis predicat et gloriatur, nec sinia [?], que in diviciis dominatur, set pallas que in divinis sollicitatur.

"Pomum est vita eterna, tres regine sunt tria genera hominum tripliciter sic viuentes. Pomum proiciens est deus regnum suum omnibus equaliter offerens. Deus appollinis est volupta voluntas volupte [?] et fatue sentencians. Deus iovis est racio racione procedens inflexibilis et verissimus, qui bene deus deorum dicitur quia inpossibile est sibi mentiri" (f. 161r–v).

Siegfried Wenzel has kindly supplied me with this transcription of the passage.

94. On Gobi and the Scala Coeli, see Karl Goedeke, "Liber de Septem Sapientibus," Orient und Okzident, 3 (1865): 397–98; Alfons Hilka, "Historia Septem Sapientum: Die Fassung der Scala celi des Johannes Gobii iunior nach den Handschriften kritisch herausgegeben," Beiträge zur Sprach- und Völkerkunde: Festschrift für Alfred Hillebrandt (Halle: Buchhandlung des Waisenhauses, 1913), 54–55; Thomas Kaeppeli, Scriptores Ordinis Praedicatorum Medii Aevi, 2 (Rome: Sabina, 1975), 442–44; Welter, Exemplum, 76, 290, 319–25.

95. "Refert Helinandus quod quidam uolens inducere bellum in ciuitate troyana. fecit fieri unum pomum aureum. in cuius circumferentia erat scriptum. pulcriori detur. Cum autem omnes nobiliores mulieres fuissent congregate in quodam festo periectum est pomum in medio et perlecta scriptura quelibet dicebat quod suum erat extollens suam pulcritudinem. Cum autem imperator requisitus de iusticia fuisset et intueretur earum pulcritudinem. unam pauperem a ceteris distantem uidit exellentioris forme licet ipsa uon [sic] iungeret se inter pulcras et huic datum est pomum in confusionem aliarum. Pomum est filius dei. proucieus [pronuntians?] spiritus. santis mulieris uirtutes uel sciencie que precesserunt in veteri testamento pauper est uirgo benedicta uel humilitas." ([Louvain, 1485], p. C 3r; contractions have been silently expanded.)

There is no modern edition of the Scala Caeli; older editions of the work are listed in Kaeppeli, Scriptores, 444.

96. "Legitur in hystoria troyana quod cum quidam nobilis multitudinem dominarum ad solenne festum inuitasset. quidam clericus quoddam pomum aureum in cuius circumferencia circum scriptum proiecit in medio. et tenor illius scripture talis erat pulcriori detur Cunque [sic] pomum istud aureum in medio festiuitatis et leticie fuisset repertum et esst lecta scriptura. orta est questio inter mulieres. eo quod quelibet earum proferebat suam pulcritudinem esse excellentiorem et postulabat pomum Cumque fuisset peruentum ad iudicium regis et ille iudicasset habenti faciem pulcriorem et honestiora uestimenta daretur reperta est una preelecta et in habitu honestissima. cui pomum est datum. Hoc enim festum est curia celestis. iste nobilis est spiritus sanctus. domicelle autem uirtutes. pomum filius dei. sed pulcrior est charitas induta raubis preciosissimus non ex pilis ouium uel auimalium [sic] sed ex uisceribus

Christi sic contexta ut non posset diuidi. sic colorata ut omnis bonitas dei representaretur in ea. sic honorata ut ueneretur in curia dei et operiret multitudinem peccatorum. et ideo merito super omnes uirtutes hoc fecit ad Christi incarnationem et ad nostram salutem." (P. C 6r; contractions have been silently expanded.)

97. Frey-Sallmann, *Nachleben antiker Göttergestalten*, 37; 147, n. 4; table 3, no. 4; Seznec, *Survival of the Pagan Gods*, 158.

98. (Strassburg: Johann Mentelin, 1473), bk. 3, ch. 60.

99. Matthew 1.18; see also Matthew 1.20, Luke 1.35.

100. Owst, *Literature and Pulpit*, 17–21, 77–78.

101. Ibid., 17.

102. *Origines in Leviticum*, in *Origines Werke*, 6, ed. W. A. Baehrens, Griechischen Christlichen Schriftsteller der ersten drei Jahrhunderte (Leipzig: J. C. Hinrichs, 1920), 1.1. (p. 280). Quoted in Beryl Smalley, *The Study of the Bible in the Middle Ages* (1952; rpt. Notre Dame: University of Notre Dame Press, 1964), 1; the translation in my text is from Smalley.

103. Bréhier, *Middle Ages*, 116–19 and passim; Copleston, *History*, 207–8, 210–11.

104. F. C. Copleston, *Aquinas* (Baltimore: Penguin Books, 1955), 236–38.

105. Ed. Francis J. Carmody (Berkeley: University of California Press, 1948), 2.4 (p. 177).

106. There is no modern edition of Egidio's Latin text. I quote from the thirteenth-century French translation, *Li Livres du gouvernement des rois:* "en la maniere de vivre en delit de cors les philosophes ne mistrent nus souverains biens, por ce que est vie de beste mue, mes en la maniere de vivre en contemplation et en conoissance de verité il mistrent un souverain bien de ceste mortel vie, qu'il apelent beneüreté d'entendre et de savoir; en la maniere de converser ovec la gent resonnablement il mistrent un autre souverain bien, que il apelent beneüreté de fere les oevres de vertu." Ed. Samuel Paul Molenaer (1899; rpt. New York: AMS Press, 1966), 10.

107. Fritz Schalk, "Il tema della vita activa e della vita contemplativa nell' umanesimo italiano," *Umanesimo e scienza politica: Atti del Congresso Internazionale di Studi Umanistici*, ed. Enrico Castelli (Milan: Marzorati, 1951), 562–65.

108. On the work, see Smalley, *English Friars*, 290–92; Cornelia C. Coulter, "The Genealogy of the Gods," in *Vassar Mediaeval Studies*, ed. Christabel Forsyth Fiske (New Haven: Yale University Press, 1923), 317–41. For the date, see Coulter, "Genealogy," 318; Vittore Branca, *Boccaccio: The Man and His Works*, trans. Richard Monges (New York: New York University Press, 1976), 109.

109. On his sources, Coulter, "Genealogy," 329–33; on the work's organization, 336–37.

110. *Genealogie Deorum Gentilium Libri*, ed. Vincenzo Romano, 2 vols. (*Opere*, 10–11) (Bari: Gius. Laterza & Figli, 1951), 6.22 (1.303).

111. His contemporary and friend Petrarch was less avant-garde. In a brief allusion to the Judgment in the Prohemium of *De Viris Illustribus* (1338), he condemned both Juno's and Venus's lives: "The path is double and precipitous both ways, greed and pleasure. . . . Thus not only Venus but also Juno is pre-

ferred in value by the decision of their judge; only Pallas is neglected." Francesco Petrarca, *Prose*, ed. Guido Martellotti, Letteratura Italiana Storia e Testi, 7 (Milan: Riccardo Ricciardi, 1955), 218.

112. Pierre-Yves Badel, *Le Roman de la Rose au XIVe siècle: Etude de la réception de l'oeuvre*, Publications Romanes et Françaises, 153 (Geneva: Librairie Droz, 1980), 264.

113. Marc-René Jung, "Poetria: Zur Dichtungstheorie des ausgehenden Mittelalters in Frankreich," *Vox Romanica*, 30 (1971): 60; on the date, Badel, *Roman de la Rose*, 290–92; on its relationship with the *Echecs amoureux*, Badel, *Roman de la Rose*, 290–92; Ernst Sieper, *Les Echecs amoureux: Eine altfranzösische Nachahmung des Rosenromans und ihre englische Übertragung* (Weimar: Verlag von Emil Felber, 1898), 98–111. The author of the commentary has recently been identified as Evrart de Conty. See Françoise Guichard-Tesson, "La *Glose des Echecs amoureux:* Un savoir à tendance laïque: comment l'interpréter?" *Fifteenth Century Studies*, 10 (1984): 229.

114. Badel, *Roman de la Rose*, 295–96; on the commentator's aim see also Sieper, *Echecs amoureux*, 111.

115. Badel, *Roman de la Rose*, 313–15, has also noted the Aristotelian influence. If the commentary is by Evrart, the work's Aristotelianism could be explained by its author's association with a milieu interested in the translation of Aristotle's work. See Guichard-Tesson, "*Glose*," 229.

116. "ceste actiue vie est ordonnee pour bien viure et honnestement et . . . y entend on a acquerre richesses et les biens temporelz qui nous sont necessaires et . . . ceste vie est aux richesses donnee aussi que la vie contemplatiue est deue aux sages" (f. 126r–v). Citations of the French text are from a microfilm of B.n. fr. 143. Contractions have been silently expanded. For a description of B.n. fr. 143, see *Catalogue des manuscrits français, Anciens fonds*, 1 (Paris: Firmin Didot, 1868), 10, and Reginald Hyatte, "The Manuscripts of the Prose Commentary (Fifteenth Century) on *Les échecs amoureux*," *Manuscripta*, 26 (1982): 25–26. An edition of the commentary is being prepared by Bruno Roy. The translations are my own. The commentary has also been translated by Joan Morton Jones, "*The Chess of Love* (Old French Text with Translation and Commentary)" (Ph.D. diss., University of Nebraska, 1968).

117. On Juno's traditional association with the air, see Paul Decharme, *La Critique des traditions religieuses chez les Grecs* (Paris: Alphonse Picard et Fils, 1904), 322. F. 125v: "lair auironne la terre qui toutes les richesses et les biens temporelz en soy garde et contient." On Juno as goddess of birth, see [Carl Olaf] Thulin, "Iuno," *RECA*, ed. August Pauly and Georg Wissowa, 9 (Stuttgart: J. B. Metzler, 1917), cols. 1115–16. Clearly the latter etymology is related to that used by Fulgentius: "Iuno enim quasi a iuuando dicta est" (*Opera*, 2.1 [p. 38]), or "For Juno has been named, as it were, from *iuuando*" (*iuvo*, "to help"). (Cf. Whitbread's translation: "Juno is named for getting ahead" [*Fulgentius*, 65]). The extra detail here is derived from splitting Juno's name thus: *iu < iuvo / no < novus.*

118. "Quant la figure donc nous monstre que Juno porte en sa main vng ceptre comme vne grant royne ce signifie que richesse est principal dame et royne du monde et que sur tous les riches regnent et seigneurissent. Et briefment tout ainsi que les subgectz obeissent au roy tout ainsi obeissent tuit communement a richesse" (f. 126v). The essentials of the description are very close

to Bersuire (Werkmateriaal—3, 32–33 [f. 7rb, 53–56 to f. 7va, 1–2]). The interpretations (except for the rainbow, mentioned below) are close to those given on
33–34 (f. 7va, 30–42).

119. "les richesses veulent estre muciees et repuses. . . . ceulx qui les ont se
mucent voulentiers et tournent daultre part la teste de paour que on ne leur
demande riens. . . . ceulx qui sont surhabondamment riches sont aussi aueugles
et oultrecuydez et ne se cognoissent pas bien ne qui leur est amy ne qui en-
nemy" (f. 126 v).

120. "Larc du ciel qui reluyt aussi entour ceste deesse lequel se monstre a
nous cler et resplendissant signifie les richesses du monde qui font les riches
resplendir et reluyre et apparoir sages et vertueulx plus quilz ne sont souuent
aussi que cest arc est vne merueille en la nue apparant et vne chose qui nest pas
de fait telle quelle se monstre a nous" (f. 127r).

121. "[L]es adulacions les aplamemens et les amystiez faintes dont les
riches se treuuent souuent auironnez et en fin deceuz" (f. 127v).

122. ". . . qui les veulent honnourer et seruir iusques au pie baisier" (f.
127v). For the reference in Bersuire, see Werkmateriaal—3, 32–33 (f. 7va, 1–2).

123. E.g., a cosmological interpretation of the Wedding of Peleus and Thetis
(f. 164r–v); Paris as an example of bad judges (f. 163r–v); the quarreling goddesses as examples of the envious (f. 163v); Paris as sense (f. 162v); and the
Judgment as a confirmation of man's free will (f. 162r). Badel lists the commentator's sources but omits Bersuire: Roman de la Rose, 313–14; see also Sieper,
Echecs amoureux, 111.

124. ". . . est la vie ou lomme an lessant les choses temporelles et sensibles
se applicque a speculacion et a la cognoissance de verite et par especial des ce-
lestiaulx choses et diuines dont la fin principal et premiere est dieu aymer et
entendre" (f. 158v).

125. ". . . est la vie ou lome veult viure en compaignie et en communite et
raisonnablement soy tousiours maintenir entre les aultres en ensuyuant les
oeuures de vertu" (f. 158v).

126. ". . . est la vie ou lomme veult ensuyr les delitz corporelz et les plai-
sances du monde plus que raison et vertu ne desirent" (f. 158v).

127. Thinkers nearer in time to the commentator on the Echecs amoureux,
too, had assimilated the Aristotelian ideal of contemplation to the Christian
quest for the knowledge of God. In Aquinas, for example, Aristotle's ultimate
human aim, happiness, becomes an intuitive knowledge of God. See Copleston,
Aquinas, 204.

128. Whitbread, Fulgentius, 64.

129. "[C]es troys manieres de viure vindrent dune consideracion que les philozophes [sic] eurent car ilz considererent que li homs estoit aussi come dune
nature moyenne entre les bestes mues et les anges du ciel Et par ainsi quil res-
sembloit en aucune maniere aux bestes dune part et dautre part aux anges Et
pour ce disoient oultre ilz que selon ce quil sembloit aux bestes selon ce aussi
luy estoit deue la vie delicatiue et selon ce quil estoit daultre part aux anges
ressemblable selon ce aussi luy estoit deue la vie contemplatiue et la cognoissance de verite et selon ce quil estoit en soy homme et quant a sa propre nature
et vraye selon ce luy estoit aussi deue la vie actiue qui lomme fait en compaignie viure et raisonnablement" (f. 158v).

Compare Chapter 1 above.

130. ". . . ceulx qui employent leur sens et leur entendement en la consideracion et en la cognoissance des haultes choses secretes de nature et especialment de dieu et des choses diuines" (f. 159r).

131. ". . . ceulx qui aux delitz charnelz entendent voulentiers et par especial a ieunes amoureux qui ne quierent que oyseuse et delectacion" (f. 159v).

132. Trans. Harris Rackham, Loeb Classical Library (Cambridge: Harvard University Press, 1959), 4.9 (pp. 327–31).

133. "Juno qui est la deesse des richesces signifie la vie actiue qui est deue aux riches pour ce que les richesces et les biens temporelz sont bien neccessaires en ceste vie actiue car aultrement on ny pourroit pas bien suffisamment viure. On pourroit aussi dire que ceste vie actiue est aux riches deue pour ce quil sy conuient ordonner par raison et selon vertu viure car la communite ne se pourroit aultrement soustenir ne durer longuement et ceulx qui ainsi viuent nont mestier de estre poures ne ilz ne le peuent estre aussi au bien entendre car vertus seulement fait lomme riche et vice le fait poure et indigent sicome dient les sages philozophes Et pour ce dit aristote que en toute raisonnable communite on doit auoir grant cure de vertu. Sans faille aussi vertus fait auoir suffisance et suffisance fait la personne riche car pou de chose a nature suffist. Et pour ce dit oultre encores aristote que moyenne richesce est la meilleur de toutes et en toute cite la plus recommandable pour ce quelle obeist de legier a raison car richesce trop grande ne trop petite aussi ny obeissent pas legierement car ceulx qui sont trop riches et trop puissans ne se sceuent soubzmectre ne ne veulent Et ceulx qui sont trop poures ne se sceuent gouuerner ne seigneurir et pour ce est plus durable la cite sicome il dit aussi et plus par nature paisible ou il a plus de peuple moyen car le peuple moyen ne desire pas ainsi ne ne quiert ne souhaicte la richesce des aultres come les poures font pour ce quilz ont richesce suffisant ne les poures aussi nont point sur eulz denuie ne ilz ne desirent aussi point leur richesce moyenne come ilz font la richesce excessiue. La vie actiue est donc especialment deue et conuenable aux riches de richesce accordant a vertu et pour ce en ceste vie mettent les philozophes la seconde felicite humaine qui gist en loeuure de prudence pour ce quelle royne et dame de toutes les aultres vertus moraulx et quelles les adresce et reigle aussi toutes come il fut dit deuant" (f. 159r–v).

134. "quelle surmonte et excede toute aultre maniere de viure en dignite et en perfection pour ce que cest vie diuine come aristote dit et pour la felicite qui est en ceste vie mise elle est aussi diuine appellee et la meilleur de toutes" (f. 160v); see Nicomachean Ethics, 10.7–8.

135. "car en la cognoissance de dieu et de sa mageste et en la consideracion de sa tresgrand infinite bonte . . . gist la fin principal de contemplacion" (f. 159v).

136. "plus a lomme . . . conuenable et propice" (f. 161v); see Nicomachean Ethics, 10.8.

137. "miellx vie de beste que ce nest vie domme" (f. 160v); see Nicomachean Ethics, 1.5.

138. Gianni Mombello, "Per un' edizione critica dell' 'Epistre Othea' di Christine de Pizan," Studi Francesi, 24 (1964): 413–14; on the background of the work see Enid McLeod, The Order of the Rose: The Life and Ideas of Christine de Pizan (Totowa, N.J.: Rowman and Littlefield, 1976), 51–52.

139. Rosemond Tuve, Allegorical Imagery: Some Mediaeval Books and

Their Posterity (Princeton: Princeton University Press, 1966), 44.

140. Ibid., 38–39, 286; for earlier critical reaction to the *Othéa's* structure, see Mary Ann Ignatius, "Christine de Pizan's *Epistre Othea:* An Experiment in Literary Form," *Medievalia et Humanistica,* 9 (1979): 129–31.

141. Tuve, *Allegorical Imagery,* 17–18, also passim, esp. 13, 15, 40–42.

142. Ibid., 45.

143. Ibid., 44.

144.   Fuys la deesse de discorde
       Maulx sont ses liens et sa corde
       Les nopces peleus troubla
       Dont puis mainte gent assembla. (N.p.)

There is no modern edition of the *Othéa.* I used the edition of Philippe le Noir (*Les Cent Hystoires de Troye* [Paris, 1522]). For information on the editions of the *Othéa,* see Josette A. Wisman, "Manuscrits et éditions des oeuvres de Christine de Pisan," *Manuscripta,* 21 (1977), 148. I also consulted Stephen Scrope's English translation, *The Epistle of Othéa,* ed. Curt F. Bühler, Early English Text Society, OS 264 (London: Oxford University Press, 1970).

145. On Christine's sources, see P.-G.-C. Campbell, *L'Epître d'Othéa: Etude sur les sources de Christine de Pisan* (Paris: Edouard Champion, 1924).

146. "Comme il est dit que discorde doit fuir Ainsi doit le bon esperit fuir tous empeschemens de conscience et que contens et riotes soyent a escheuer dit cassiodore sur le psaultier souuerainement dit il fuy contens et riotes car contendre contre paix est enragerie contendre contre son souuerain cest forcennerie et contre son subiect cest grant villenie. Pource dit sainct pol lapostre. Non in contentione et emulatione" (n.p.; contractions have been silently expanded).

147.   Comme Paris ne iuge pas
       Car on recoipt maint dur repas
       Par male sentence octroyer
       Maintz en ont eu mauluais loyer. (N.p.)

148. Campbell, *L'Epître d'Othéa,* 96–100.

149. See ibid., 87–94, on Christine's acquaintance with the *Histoire ancienne.*

150.   Ne fondes sur auision
       Ne dessus folle illusion
       Grant emprinse soit droit ou tort
       Et de Paris ayes recort. (N.p.)

151. Tuve, *Allegorical Imagery,* 45.

Chapter 4. The Choice of Paris

1. On imposed allegory, see Rosemond Tuve, *Allegorical Imagery: Some Mediaeval Books and Their Posterity* (Princeton: Princeton University Press, 1966), ch. 4, 219–333; Jean Pépin, *Mythe et allégorie: Les origines grecques et les contestations judéo-chrétiennes* (Paris: Editions Montaigne, 1958), 78.

2. Of course, different interpreters had different notions about whether the meanings they found in the fables of the ancients were intended by their authors. See, for example, Paule Demats, *Fabula: Trois études de mythogra-*

phie antique et médiévale, (Geneva: Librairie Droz, 1973), 113–36, on the medieval tradition that Ovid was a Christian.

3. On the popularity and spread of this form, see William Allan Neilson, *The Origins and Sources of the Court of Love,* [Harvard] Studies and Notes in Philology and Literature, Vol. VI (Boston: Ginn and Company, 1899), 60–109; Howard Rollin Patch, *The Other World According to Descriptions in Medieval Literature* (1950; rpt. New York: Octagon Books, 1970), 195–229; Marc-René Jung, *Etudes sur le poème allégorique en France au moyen âge,* Romanica Helvetica, Vol. 82 (Berne: Editions Francke, 1971), 327–28; Paul Zumthor, *Essai de poétique médiévale* (Paris: Editions du Seuil, 1972), 132–33.

4. Ed. Achille Jubinal (Paris: Techener, 1834); discussed by Patch, *Other World,* 198–99; Neilson, *Origins,* 41–42; Ernest Langlois, *Origines et sources du Roman de la Rose* (Paris: Ernest Thorin, 1891), 15–17.

5. Angus Fletcher, *Allegory: The Theory of a Symbolic Mode* (Ithaca: Cornell University Press, 1964), 2, n. 1.

6. Pépin, *Mythe et allégorie,* 88–89.

7. Tuve, *Allegorical Imagery,* 233; Zumthor, *Poétique médiévale,* 126, 131, 376–77; cf. Fletcher, *Allegory,* 84.

8. Heinrich Lausberg, *Handbuch der literarischen Rhetorik,* 2 vols. (Munich: Max Hueber, 1960), ¶ 421, 829, 895, 897.

9. Tuve, *Allegorical Imagery,* 220, 259.

10. Hans Robert Jauss, "Allégorie, 'remythisation' et nouveau mythe: Réflexions sur la captivité chrétienne de la mythologie au moyen âge," *Mélanges d'histoire littéraire, de linguistique et de philologie romanes offerts à Charles Rostaing,* 1 (Liège, 1974), 474–75; on allegory and enigma, see Fletcher, *Allegory,* 6; Pépin, *Mythe et allégorie,* 89–90.

11. Tuve, *Allegorical Imagery,* 220, 259–60.

12. Fletcher, *Allegory,* 104–7.

13. Ibid., 348–49.

14. For a general discussion of classical and medieval dream theory, see Francis X. Newman, "*Somnium:* Medieval Theories of Dreaming and the Form of Vision Poetry" (Ph.D. diss., Princeton University, 1962), chs. 1–3.

15. Ambrosius Theodosius Macrobius, *Commentarii in Somnium Scipionis,* ed. Iacobus Willis (Leipzig: Teubner, 1963), 1.3.10 (p. 10); trans. William Harris Stahl, *Commentary on the Dream of Scipio* (New York: Columbia University Press, 1952), 90; Newman discusses Macrobius in "*Somnium,*" 70–77.

16. Macrobius, *Commentarii,* 1.2–3 (pp. 3–12); Stahl, *Commentary,* 85, 90–91. Pépin discusses the passage in *Mythe et allégorie,* 211–12.

17. *Policratici sive De Nugis Curialium et Vestigiis Philosophorum Libri VIII,* ed. Clement C. J. Webb, 2 vols. (Oxford: Clarendon, 1909), 2.15.432a (1.94); trans. Joseph B. Pike, *Frivolities of Courtiers and Footprints of Philosophers* (Minneapolis: University of Minnesota Press, 1938), 81. Newman discusses John of Salisbury's theories of dream interpretation in "*Somnium,*" 135–42.

18. On the history of the tradition, see Langlois, *Origines,* 55–59; on the allegorical nature of the dream vision, see Newman, "*Somnium,*" 300.

19. Jung, *Etudes,* 327–28.

20. Tuve, *Allegorical Imagery,* 22.

21. Ibid., 26; Jung, *Etudes,* 20–23; Zumthor, *Poétique médiévale,* 126–27;

Fletcher, *Allegory*, 26; Stephen A. Barney, *Allegories of History, Allegories of Love* (Hamden, Conn.: Archon Books, 1979), 20–26.

22. Though they offer caveats against importing a figure's traditional associations wholesale into any work in which that figure appears, the following acknowledge that awareness of a figure's previous significance can be a useful aid to interpretation: Richard Hamilton Green, "Classical Fable and English Poetry in the Fourteenth Century," in *Critical Approaches to Medieval Literature*, ed. Dorothy Bethurum (New York: Columbia University Press, 1960), 110–33; Theodore Silverstein, "Allegory and Literary Form," *PMLA*, 82 (1967): 28–32; Paul Beichner, "The Allegorical Interpretation of Medieval Literature," *PMLA*, 82 (1967): 33–38; see also Tuve, *Allegorical Imagery*, 26; Jauss, "Allégorie," 477–81.

23. On the complexity of the image, see Tuve, *Allegorical Imagery*, 266–67; Jauss, "Allégorie," 484.

24. E.g., Augustine, *De Civitate Dei, Opera*, part 14, 2, *CCSL* 48 (Turnhout: Brepols, 1955), 13.13, 13.15, 14.17 (pp. 395, 396, 439–40); Peter Comestor, *Historia Scholastica, PL*, ed. J.-P. Migne, 198 (Paris: J.-P. Migne, 1853), 1072–73.

25. Ernst Robert Curtius, *European Literature and the Latin Middle Ages*, trans. Willard R. Trask, Bollingen Series, 36 (Princeton: Princeton University Press, 1973), ch. 10, "The Ideal Landscape," 183–202, esp. sect. 6, "The Pleasance," 195–200.

26. See A. Bartlett Giamatti, *The Earthly Paradise and the Renaissance Epic* (Princeton: Princeton University Press, 1966), sect. 3, 33–47.

27. Neilson, *Origins*, 26–27; Giamatti, *Earthly Paradise*, 59–60.

28. On typical patterns as a signal of allegory, see Barney, *Allegories of History*, 32–33.

29. Classical tradition: Curtius, *European Literature*, 195–200; on the spring or brook in Claudian: Giamatti, *Earthly Paradise*, 52–53. Provençal love lyric, e.g., ibid., 59–60.

30. On the influence of *Li Fablel*, see Langlois, *Origines*, 26–35 and passim; Patch, *Other World*, 198–99; Neilson, *Origins*, 41–42.

31. Earl G. Schreiber, "Venus in the Medieval Mythographic Tradition," *Journal of English and Germanic Philology*, 74 (1975): 519–35.

32. Tuve, *Allegorical Imagery*, 243, 281, and passim.

33. Ibid., 234–36, 240–41; Fletcher, *Allegory*, 85–87.

34. Tuve, *Allegorical Imagery*, 22, 287, 308–9; Zumthor, *Poétique médiévale*, 132; Fletcher, *Allegory*, 151; Barney, *Allegories of History*, 16–17, 32–33.

35. Barney, *Allegories of History*, 20.

36. C. S. Lewis, *The Allegory of Love: A Study in Medieval Tradition* (1936; rpt. London: Oxford University Press, 1959), 58–61; cited in Fletcher, *Allegory*, 36, n. 20. Tuve, *Allegorical Imagery*, 28, n. 10.

37. Tuve, *Allegorical Imagery*, 17, 308, 245.

38. Ed. Ernest Hoepffner, *Oeuvres de Guillaume de Machaut*, 3 (Paris: Edouard Champion, 1921). Hoepffner dates the poem 1360–61, xxix. His more specific date is based on his identification of the poem's main character as the Duc de Berry, an identification which I do not accept. Citations of the *Fonteinne amoureuse* refer to Hoepffner's edition.

39. Ernest Hoepffner, "Anagramme und Rätselgedichte bei Guillaume de

Machaut," *Zeitschrift für romanische Philologie*, 30 (1906): 407; Hoepffner, *Oeuvres*, 3, xxv–xxviii.

40. Margaret J. Ehrhart, "Machaut's *Dit de la fonteinne amoureuse*, the Choice of Paris, and the Duties of Rulers," *Philological Quarterly*, 59 (1980): 121–23.

41. Ibid., 123–24; the fictionality of Machaut's narrators has also been discussed by James Wimsatt, *Chaucer and the French Love Poets*, University of North Carolina Studies in Comparative Literature, 43 (Chapel Hill: University of North Carolina Press, 1968), 97–102; William Calin, *A Poet at the Fountain: Essays on the Narrative Verse of Guillaume de Machaut*, Studies in Romance Languages, 9 (Lexington: University Press of Kentucky, 1974), 36–38, 151, and passim; and, most recently, Kevin Brownlee, *Poetic Identity in Guillaume de Machaut* (Madison: University of Wisconsin Press, 1984). See 188–90 for his discussion of the narrator in the *Fonteinne amoureuse*.

42. *Chaucer and the French Tradition: A Study in Style and Meaning* (Berkeley: University of California Press, 1957), 99.

43. Tuve's terms, see *Allegorical Imagery*, 281.

44. As, for example, in the *Roman de la Rose* of Guillaume de Lorris and Jean de Meun, ed. Félix Lecoy, 3 vols. (Paris: Honoré Champion, 1966–70), 20166–72 (3.106).

45. For a reading of the *Fonteinne amoureuse* which overlooks the negative connotations of the garden, see Marc M. Pelen, "Machaut's Court of Love Narratives and Chaucer's *Book of the Duchess*," *Chaucer Review*, 11 (1976): 136–39.

46. See, for example, Fulgentius's *Mythologies*, in *Opera*, ed. Rudolf Helm (1898; rpt. Stuttgart: Teubner, 1970), 2.1 (pp. 39–40). For other examples of the theme in the mythographic tradition, see Schreiber, "Venus," 529–30.

47. See, e.g., Alma Frey-Sallmann, *Aus dem Nachleben antiker Göttergestalten: Die antiken Gottheiten in der Bildbeschreibung des Mittelalters und der italienischen Frührenaissance* (Leipzig: Dieterich'sche Verlagsbuchhandlung, 1931).

48. "'Ovide moralisé': Poème du commencement du quatorzième siècle," ed. Cornelis de Boer, *Verhandelingen der Koninklijke Akademie van Wetenschappen te Amsterdam, Afdeeling Letterkunde*, NS 15, 21, 30, 37, 43 (Amsterdam, 1915–38), 11.2413, 520–21. De Boer showed Machaut's debt to the *Ovide moralisé* in "Guillaume de Machaut et l'*Ovide moralisé*," *Romania*, 43 (1914): 335–52.

49. Cf. Brownlee, *Poetic Identity*, who argues that "Machaut has systematically and . . . purposefully 'demoralized' his source." (202)

50. Ed. Anthime Fourrier, Bibliothèque Française et Romane, Textes et Documents, 2 (Paris: Librairie C. Klincksieck, 1963). For the date, see Fourrier's introduction, 32; for the relationship with the *Fonteinne amoureuse*, see 34–37.

51. Zumthor, *Poétique médiévale*, 378, sees the allegory in the *Espinette amoureuse* as only episodic, and based on mythological allusions.

52. F. S. Shears, *Froissart: Chronicler and Poet* (London: George Routledge and Sons, 1930), 11–12, seems to regard the voyage as autobiographical, though he elsewhere speaks as if he sees in the poem a certain authorial distance from the *persona* of the narrator.

53. B. J. Whiting, "Froissart as Poet," *Mediaeval Studies*, 8 (1946): 197–98.

54. Whiting, "Froissart as Poet," 196, suggests that the journey could be borrowed from Machaut.

55. See note to 4179–88 in Fourrier's edition, 184.

56. Fourrier, *Espinette amoureuse*, 184.

57. See, e.g., James I. Wimsatt, *The Marguerite Poetry of Guillaume de Machaut*, University of North Carolina Studies in the Romance Languages and Literatures, 87 (Chapel Hill: University of North Carolina Press, 1970), esp. 60–65.

58. Cf. Shears, *Froissart*, 12, and Whiting, "Froissart as Poet," 206, who says, "Marguerite was a common name and it may well have been Froissart's fortune to have lady and cult fall together."

59. The fact that two names appear in the anagram has also been noted by William W. Kibler, "Self-Delusion in Froissart's *Espinette Amoureuse*," *Romania*, 97 (1976): 80–81.

60. Fourrier, *Espinette amoureuse*, 184; Kibler, "Self-Delusion," 80.

61. Kibler makes much the same point: "Self-Delusion," 81–83.

62. Though Shears seems to regard the work as autobiographical, he too sees a certain distance between the author and the persona of his narrator: *Froissart*, 205.

63. To the narrator, his judgment of the goddesses was a vision rather than a dream. He considers dreams undependable as predictions of the future but observes that his experience of the Judgment was proved true by his subsequent adventures (679–87).

64. Fourrier, *Espinette amoureuse*, 34.

65. E.g., *Heroides* 16 and 17. Fourrier too notes an Ovidian influence, particularly from the *Metamorphoses*, for much of Froissart's mythological material: *Espinette amoureuse*, 35–36.

66. Elsewhere Froissart makes it clear, however, that Juno's gift would have been wealth (487–90); for Juno's hatred of the Trojans, see *Aeneid* 1.25–28.

67. On Mercury as scribe, teacher, or bishop, see Jean Seznec, *The Survival of the Pagan Gods: The Mythological Tradition and Its Place in Renaissance Humanism and Art*, trans. Barbara F. Sessions, Bollingen Series, 38 (1953; rpt. Princeton: Princeton University Press, 1972), 158–61 and figs. 21, 62; Frey-Sallmann, *Nachleben antiker Göttergestalten*, 37; 147, n. 4; table 3, fig. 4; table 6, fig. 9. The associations with eloquence, learning, and wisdom are commonplace; see, e.g., Rabanus Maurus, *De Universo, PL*, ed. J.-P. Migne, 111 (Paris: J.-P. Migne, 1852), 429–30; Isidore of Seville, *Etymologiae*, ed. W. M. Lindsay (Oxford: Clarendon, 1911), 8.11.45–50; the Third Vatican Mythographer, *Scriptores Rerum Mythicarum*, ed. Georg Heinrich Bode (Celle: Schulze, 1834), 9.1 (p. 213, lines 25–40); Pierre Bersuire, "De Formis Figurisque Deorum," *Reductorium morale, Liber XV: Ovidius moralizatus, cap. i*, ed. Joseph Engels (Utrecht: Instituut voor Laat Latijn der Rijksuniversiteit, 1966), 26, lines 12–16; *De Deorum Imaginibus Libellus*, ed. Hans Liebeschütz, in *Fulgentius Metaforalis: Ein Beitrag zur Geschichte der antiken Mythologie im Mittelalter* (Leipzig: Teubner, 1926), 119. See also Patrick J. Gallacher, *Love, the Word, and Mercury: A Reading of John Gower's Confessio Amantis* (Albuquerque: University of New Mexico Press, 1975), 114–15, n. 182.

68. In the *Joli buisson de jonece*, Froissart was to assign a god to each stage

of human life. Mercury was the patron of children from age four to fourteen (ed. Anthime Fourrier [Geneva: Droz, 1975], 1625–32). See p. 175, Fourrier's notes to lines 402–4, 422–23.

69. Kibler too has noted the element of *self*-delusion in the poem.

70. Macrobius, *Commentarii*, 1.3; Stahl, *Commentary*, 88.

71. For a view of the relationship between the *Espinette amoureuse* and the *Joli buisson de jonece* which complements my own, see Michelle A. Freeman, "Froissart's *Le Joli Buisson de Jonece:* A Farewell to Poetry?" in *Machaut's World: Science and Art in the Fourteenth Century*, ed. Madeleine Pelner Cosman and Bruce Chandler, Annals of the New York Academy of Sciences, 314 (New York: New York Academy of Sciences, 1978), 235–47.

72. Christine Kraft, ed., *Die Liebesgarten-Allegory der "Echecs Amoureux": Kritische Ausgabe und Kommentar*, Französische Sprache und Literatur, 48 (Frankfurt am Main: Peter Lang, 1977), 31–32.

73. Ernst Sieper, *Les Echecs amoureux: Eine altfranzösische Nachahmung des Rosenromans und ihre englische Übertragung*, Literarhistorische Forschungen, 9 (Weimar: Emil Felber, 1898), 127–204 and passim; Pierre-Yves Badel, *Le Roman de la Rose au XIVe siècle: Etude de la réception de l'oeuvre*, Publications Romanes et Françaises, 153 (Geneva: Librairie Droz, 1980), 263 and passim.

74. No full edition of the work exists. There are two manuscripts: Dresden, Sächsische Landesbibliothek Oc 66 (D), and Venice, Biblioteca Nazionale Marciana Fr. App. 23 (= 267) (V) (1). The Dresden manuscript was severely damaged in World War II, and I could not obtain permission to study it. Ff. 1–54 were summarized by Sieper in *Echecs amoureux* (cited above, n. 73), and a brief summary of the entire manuscript was made early in this century by Stanley L. Galpin, "*Les Eschez Amoureux:* A Complete Synopsis with Unpublished Extracts," *Romanic Review*, 11 (1920): 283–307. See Badel, *Roman de la Rose*, 263–64, n. 1, for references to summaries that cover later sections of the Dresden manuscript. Sieper's study has been reviewed by Heinrich Spies in *Englische Studien*, 27 (1900): 437–45, and is supplemented by his own "Zu den Echecs amoureux," *Englische Studien*, 28 (1900): 310–12. The Venice manuscript is incomplete. The love-garden portion of the manuscript has been edited by Christine Kraft in the work cited above. For portions of the Venice manuscript not covered by Kraft's edition, I have consulted a microfilm copy obtained with the kind assistance of the Marquis Lelio Pellegrini-Quarantotti. For a discussion of the Venice manuscript, see Domenico Ciàmpoli, *I codici francesi della R. Biblioteca Nazionale di S. Marco in Venezia* (Venice: Leo S. Olschki, 1897), 132–44. For this first section of my summary, I follow mainly Sieper.

75. Kraft's edition picks up here.

76. Kraft's edition ends here. For the remainder of my summary, I follow Galpin and the Venice manuscript.

77. See n. 73.

78. Badel, *Roman de la Rose*, 29–30 and passim.

79. Ibid., 282.

80. Ibid., 284.

81. Ibid., 282.

82. See n. 73. Parenthetical references are to Sieper's folio citations in his study of the *Echecs amoureux*. *Reson and Sensuallyte* has been edited by

Sieper, Early English Text Society, ES 84, 89 (London, 1901–3).

83. Cf. Sieper, *Les Echecs*, 148, who says that the Judgment in the *Echecs amoureux* is close to that of Guido de Columnis. This seems impossible unless Lydgate substituted an entirely different version of the episode in his rehandling. It is more likely that Sieper was confused about the version of the Judgment Guido had used. Some evidence that Lydgate's Judgment is close to that in his source is given by the marginal glosses in *Reson and Sensuallyte*. See below in this chapter.

84. Sieper too sees Fulgentius as the author's ultimate inspiration for his descriptions of the goddesses: *Les Echecs*, 140–41.

85. Sieper too makes the point that there are influences from many different sources: *Les Echecs*, 141–47. I would not, however, put as much emphasis as he does on the *De Deorum Imaginibus Libellus* as a source.

86. Ovid, *Metamorphoses*, trans. Frank Justus Miller, 2 vols., Loeb Classical Library (Cambridge: Harvard University Press, 1951), 1.717 (Loeb 1.53); Fulgentius, *Opera*, 1.18 (p. 30); Petrarch, *Africa*, ed. Nicola Festa (Florence: G. C. Sansoni, 1926), 3.178; Bersuire, "De Formis Figurisque Deorum," Werkmateriaal—3, 25, lines 52–53; *De Deorum Imaginibus Libellus*, 119. On the relationships among the last three works, see Seznec, *Survival of the Pagan Gods*, 170–76.

87. E.g., Bersuire, "De Formis Figurisque Deorum," Werkmateriaal—3, 25, lines 51–52; *De Deorum Imaginibus Libellus*, 119.

88. *Metamorphoses*, 1.682–84 (Loeb 1.51). As Ovid tells the story, both the flute and the wand induce sleep (1.715–16 [Loeb 1.53]). *Reductorium Morale, Liber XV, cap. ii–xv, Ovidius Moralizatus*, ed. Joseph Engels (Utrecht: Instituut voor Laat Latijn, 1962), 43 (fable 12).

89. *The Consolation of Philosophy*, ed. Ludwig Bieler, *CCSL* 94 (Turnhout: Brepols, 1957), 1, prose 1 (p. 2); Sieper recognized the parallel, *Les Echecs*, 142.

90. This detail, though, is typical for Pallas too. See Bersuire, "De Formis Figurisque Deorum," Werkmateriaal—3, 30, line 23; Giovanni Boccaccio, *Genealogie Deorum Gentilium Libri*, ed. Vincenzo Romano, 2 vols. (*Opere*, 10–11) (Bari: Gius. Laterza & Figli, 1951), 4.48 (1.282); *De Deorum Imaginibus Libellus*, 120. Sieper noted the presence of the theme in the *Libellus* also; he also points to the description of Reason in the *Roman de la Rose* as a possible source: *Les Echecs*, 142.

91. On the history of the image and possible sources, see Sieper, *Les Echecs*, 135–37; also see Demats, *Fabula*, 143–45. On the theme in general, see Wolfgang Harms, *Homo Viator in Bivio: Studien zur Bildlichkeit des Weges* (Munich: Wilhelm Fink Verlag, 1970).

92. In the *Deipnosophists*, Athenaeus had explicitly compared the Judgment to the fable of Hercules at the crossroads; see above, Chapter 1. See also Harms, index s.v. "Herakles am Scheidewege," especially 40–49.

93. Sieper, *Les Echecs*, 135.

94. *PL*, ed. J.-P. Migne, 210 (Paris: J.-P. Migne, 1855), col. 433; Sieper, *Les Echecs*, 135, refers also to the lines "Et sicut contra ratam firmamenti volutionem, motu contradictorio exercitus militat planetarum, sic in homine sensualitatis rationisque continua reperitur hostilitas" (col. 443).

95. See Badel, *Roman de la Rose*, 268, on the parallels with the *Roman de la Rose* and the *Espinette amoureuse*.

96. Sieper, *Les Echecs*, 128–30.

97. Ibid., 131–33; Badel, *Roman de la Rose*, 265–66.

98. *The Goddess Natura in Medieval Literature* (Cambridge: Harvard University Press, 1972), 111.

99. Ibid., 123.

100. Some disputants in the modern controversy over the *Rose* are Tuve; D. W. Robertson, Jr., *A Preface to Chaucer: Studies in Medieval Perspectives* (Princeton: Princeton University Press, 1962); John V. Fleming, *The Roman de la Rose: A Study in Allegory and Iconography* (Princeton: Princeton University Press, 1969). On the other side: Badel; Alan M. F. Gunn, *The Mirror of Love: A Reinterpretation of "The Romance of the Rose"* (Lubbock: Texas Tech Press, 1952).

101. Cf. Badel, *Roman de la Rose*, 285.

102. See Richard Hamilton Green, "Alan of Lille's *De Planctu Naturae*," *Speculum*, 31 (1956): 670–72, on Alain's use of this fable in the *De Planctu Naturae*.

103. Col. 456. *The Complaint of Nature*, trans. D. M. Moffat (New York: H. Holt, 1908), 49.

104. Badel, *Roman de la Rose*, 286.

105. See John M. Fyler, "Irony and the Age of Gold in the *Book of the Duchess*," *Speculum*, 52 (1977): 314, 318–19.

106. Badel, *Roman de la Rose*, 286.

107. Ibid., 286, 287.

108.   Briefment en la vie presente
         Na tant soit poy de vtilite
         Ne de vraye felicite. (Venice f. 172r)

109. "Les aultres .ii. ne sont pas teles / Mais sont pourfitables et beles" (Venice f. 172r).

110.   La seconde vie apartient
         A Juno qui a sa part tient
         La seignourie souueraine
         De toute richesse mondaine
         Cheste vie est mult raisonnable
         Chest la vie honneste et loable
         Qu'un doit maintenir es cites
         Et es nobles communites
         Qui sont rieuglees [?] par raison
         Car Juno voelt toute saison
         Qu'un entende songueusement
         A vivre vertueusement. (Venice f. 171v)

111. Tuve, *Allegorical Imagery*, 245.

112. Ibid., 17.

113. On the date, see Sieper's introduction to his edition of *Reson and Sensuallyte* (cited above, n. 82), 2.8. References to the work are to this edition. See also Walter F. Schirmer, *John Lydgate: A Study in the Culture of the XVth Century*, trans. Anne E. Keep (London: Methuen, 1961), 39. On the work's relationship with the *Echecs amoureux*, see Sieper, *Les Echecs*, 213–39.

114. On the lack of a title, see Sieper, *Les Echecs*, 112–13.

115. As Sieper reports, the Judgment of Paris episode in the *Echecs amoureux*, lines 891–2300, became lines 897–2700 in *Reson and Sensuallyte* (*Les Echecs*, 213).

116. Schirmer, *John Lydgate*, 39–40.

117. Fulgentius has, "Minerua denique et Athene Grece dicitur quasi atha-nate parthene, id est inmortalis uirgo, quia sapientia nec mori poterit nec cor-rumpi" (*Opera*, 2.1 [p. 38]).

118. Sieper has suggested the *De Planctu Naturae* (435–36) as the source for the swan of Pallas in the *Echecs amoureux* (*Les Echecs*, 143).

119. Sieper, *Reson and Sensuallyte*, 2.4.

Chapter 5. The Meaning of the Judgment

1. F. J. E. Raby, *A History of Secular Latin Poetry in the Middle Ages*, 2nd ed., 2 vols. (Oxford: Clarendon, 1957), 1.325–26.

2. On Godfrey, see ibid., 1.312–16; André Boutemy, "Autour de Godefroid de Reims," *Latomus*, 6 (1947): 238–54; John R. Williams, "Godfrey of Rheims, a Humanist of the Eleventh Century," *Speculum*, 22 (1947): 29–45.

3. Ed. W. Wattenbach, "Lateinische Gedichte aus Frankreich im elften Jahr-hundert," *Sitzungsberichte der Königlich Preussischen Akademie der Wissen-schaften zu Berlin*, 7 (1891): 109 (lines 89–96); discussed in Williams, "God-frey of Rheims," 35–36.

4. Ed. André Boutemy, "Trois oeuvres inédites de Godefroid de Reims," *Revue du Moyen Age Latin*, 3 (1947): 343 (lines 149–50); on the identity of Enguerrand, see Boutemy, "Autour de Godefroid de Reims," 240–46.

5. Boutemy, "Trois oeuvres," 360 (lines 328–29); on it, see ibid., 364, and "Autour de Godefroid de Reims," 239–40, 246–51; Williams, "Godfrey of Rheims," 36–37.

6. On Baudri, see Raby, *Secular Latin Poetry*, 1.337–48, and *A History of Christian-Latin Poetry from the Beginnings to the Close of the Middle Ages*, 2nd ed. (Oxford: Clarendon, 1953), 277–85. On Baudri and the *Heroides* tradi-tion, see Ernstpeter Ruhe, *De Amasio ad Amasiam: Zur Gattungsgeschichte des mittelalterlichen Liebesbriefes*, Beiträge zur romanischen Philologie des Mittelalters, 10 (Munich: Wilhelm Fink, 1975), 44–49.

7. *Baldricus Burgulianus Carmina*, ed. Karlheinz Hilbert, Editiones Heidelbergenses XIX (Heidelberg: Carl Winter, 1979), 30, lines 6–18.

8. See Ruhe, *De Amasio*, 22–60, and Peter Dronke, *Medieval Latin and the Rise of European Love Lyric*, 2 vols., 2nd ed. (Oxford: Clarendon, 1968), 1.196–220.

9. Urban Tigner Holmes, Jr., *A History of Old French Literature from the Origins to 1300* (New York: Russell and Russell, 1962), 146.

10. For the date, see Margaret M. Pelan, ed., *Floire et Blancheflor*, 2nd ed., Publications de la Faculté des Lettres de l'Université de Strasbourg, Textes d'Etude 7 (Paris, 1956), xii. A second, later, version of the poem does not in-clude the Judgment of Paris. On Greek influence, see Holmes, *History*, 146. All citations of *Floire et Blancheflor* are to Pelan's edition.

11. *Floire et Blancheflor*, xvi.

12. E. Bagby Atwood and Virgil K. Whitaker, eds. *Excidium Troiae* (Cam-bridge, Mass.: The Mediaeval Academy of America, 1944), xliv.

13. The parallel has also been noted by Pelan, xvi.

14. Holmes, *History*, 146; Paul Zumthor, *Histoire littéraire de la France médiévale* (Paris: Presses Universitaires de France, 1954), 214.

15. *Li Romanz d'Athis et Prophilias* (*L'Estoire d'Athenes*), ed. Alfons

Hilka, 2 vols., Gesellschaft für romanische Literatur, Bd. 29, 40 (Dresden, 1912–16), 5719. The Judgment occupies lines 5661–5721 (1.196–98).

16. 5715–21; e.g., "She had the apple, and he the death" (5271).

17. See, e.g., Alma Frey-Sallmann, *Aus dem Nachleben antiker Göttergestalten: Die antiken Gottheiten in der Bildbeschreibung des Mittelalters und der italienischen Frührenaissance* (Leipzig: Dieterich'sche Verlagsbuchhandlung, 1931).

18. On Robert's patronage, see Paolo D'Ancona, *La Miniature italienne du Xe au XVIe siècle*, trans. M. P. Poirier (Paris and Brussels: Librairie Nationale d'Art et d'Histoire, 1925), 45; on the popularity of Trojan themes during this period, Bernhard Degenhart and Annegrit Schmitt, "Frühe angiovinische Buchkunst in Neapel: Die Illustrierung französischer Unterhaltungsprosa in neopolitanischen Scriptorien zwischen 1290 und 1320," in *Wolfgang Braunfels zum 65. Geburtstag*, ed. Friedrich Piel and Jhorg Traeger (Tübingen: Wasmuth, 1977), 71, 74–76.

19. On the date, see Bernhard Degenhart and Annegrit Schmitt, *Corpus der italienischen Zeichnungen 1300–1450*, part 1 (Berlin: Gebr. Mann Verlag, 1968), 58, n. 2, and "Marino Sanudo und Paolino Veneto: Zwei Literaten des 14. Jahrhunderts in ihrer Wirkung auf Buchillustrierung und Kartographie in Venedig, Avignon und Neapel," *Römisches Jahrbuch für Kunstgeschichte*, 14 (1973): 98, n. 131 b; on the manuscripts, Degenhart and Schmitt, *Corpus*, 55; D'Ancona, *Miniature*, 45.

20.   Regius hic natus deceptus et illaqueatus
       Forma delusus nunc iudex uiris abusus
       Arbitrio uerso promissis sordeque merso
       Degenerando probis maioribus aspice nobis
       Ex tribus o qualem rex eligit hanc quia talem
       Se uult experte rerum modo multa Roberte
       Turba petit censum meliorem nactaque sensum
       Me precis implorat uotis me numen adorat
       Sic etiam peius subdit liuor ferus eius
       Judicio Iuno fert indignata sub uno
       Ista placet uanis lasciuis atque profanis
       Est dilecta Venus libiti puteus quia plenus
       Estque voluptatis cibus et tamen anxietatis.

I have used British Library Royal 6.E.IX, f. 22r. Spelling has been regularized. I am grateful to Joseph Salemi for translating this material for me.

21.   [P]ro certo Iuno sunt nota Roberto
       Regi fatur ea quae fascinat ista Medea
       Deteriorque Venus proles sua postea fenus
       Ex hac usura capiet mihi crede futura
       Laomedontis erunt perjuria quae fore querunt
       Ulta sibi pene taceas modo donec habene
       Morum sint fractae Teucrorum siue coactae
       Obsidione uide coniux Iouis et modo ride
       Ipsa dabit penam quae fecit amore catenam
       Non te reginam decet hanc habere ferinam
       Ore uoluntatem set velle piam bonitatem

22.   Me Paris hic spernit quia lumina non bene cernit
       Et Venerem laudat quae semper eum male fraudat.

        Iste prout stultus ueri nescit quia cultus
        Debita iura dedit quod stulta mente resedit
        Pomum vesanae quae perdet Pergama vanae.

23. Dulcis nate Paris Priamo gratissimus aris
        Effectusque meis ne cures his phariseis.
        Non fore gratus ero tibi uerax munere uero.

24. "Palladis audite monitus et iussa perite." "Pulcrius hoc pomum tu pulcrior accipe diua / Formae namque domum te censeo spes mea uiua."

25. "Deserit arbitrium spetie spondente decorem / Lucis splendorem siue bonum patrium."

26. Individual dates for Christine's *balades* are not known, but most of them date from early in her career. See Enid McLeod, *The Order of the Rose: The Life and Ideas of Christine de Pizan* (Totowa, N.J.: Rowman and Littlefield, 1976), 39–41. The poem's concern with money, too, could suggest that it dates from the early days of her widowhood.

27. *Oeuvres poétiques*, ed. Maurice Roy, 1, Société des Anciens Textes Français, 81 (Paris: Firmin Didot, 1886), 214–15.

28. Ed. Susan Wharton (Paris: Union Générale d'Editions, 1980); for the date, see 15. The work is discussed by Douglas Kelly, *Medieval Imagination: Rhetoric and the Poetry of Courtly Love* (Madison: University of Wisconsin Press, 1978), 187–90, 212–18.

29. Kelly, *Medieval Imagination*, 188.

30. Ed. J. A. van Dorsten, "The Leyden 'Lydgate Manuscript,'" *Scriptorium*, 14 (1960): 315–25; for the date, see 318.

31. *The English Works of John Gower*, ed. G. C. Macaulay, 2 vols., Early English Text Society, ES 81–82 (1900–1901; rpt. London: Oxford University Press, 1969). For the date, see 1.xxi; for Gower's sources for his Trojan material, see, e.g., notes, 1.468, 471.

32. See note to line 7195 (2.509).

33. Ed. Robert Püschel (Berlin: R. Damkohler, 1881). The work is discussed by McLeod, *Order of the Rose*, 91–95; for the date, see 95.

34. Cornelis de Boer, ed., "'Ovide moralisé': Poème du commencement du quatorzième siècle," *Verhandelingen der Koninklijke Akademie van Wetenschappen te Amsterdam, Afdeeling Letterkunde*, NS 15 (Amsterdam, 1915), 38–39, n. 1, said that Christine took the passage from Machaut's *Fonteinne amoureuse*, but I do not see in Christine's version Machaut's golden table, which for de Boer proved the relationship. P.-G.-C. Campbell, *L'Epître d'Othéa: Etude sur les sources de Christine de Pisan* (Paris: Edouard Champion, 1924), has also noticed this point, 100–101. Alfred Dressler, *Der Einfluss des altfranzösischen Eneas-Romanes auf die altfranzösische Litteratur* (Borna-Leipzig: Robert Noske, 1907), 50, has also considered her sources for the passage, suggesting, on the basis of the golden apple, Hyginus. Lines 6151–53 suggest the Pseudo-Clementines, however, where she could also have found the golden apple.

35. Ernest Hoepffner, ed., *Oeuvres de Guillaume de Machaut*, 3 (Paris: Edouard Champion, 1921), i. Citations in my text are to this edition. Charles's name indeed appears in the anagram; see ibid., xvii.

36. Hoepffner traces the mythological materials to the *Ovide moralisé*: ibid., viii.

37. Roberta D. Cornelius, ed., Early English Text Society, OS 179 (London:

Oxford University Press, 1930), Preface, 15. All citations of the *Castell of Pleasure* are to this edition.

38. Nevill was born in 1497; the earliest known copy of the work was produced before 1518. See Cornelius, *Castell of Pleasure*, Preface, 9, 58–59.

39. See John D. Reeves, "The Judgment of Paris as a Device of Tudor Flattery," *Notes and Queries*, 199 (1954): 7–11.

Epilogue. The Judgment and the Meaning of History

1. *Les Illustrations de Gaule et Singularitez de Troye*, vols. 1 and 2 of *Oeuvres de Jean Lemaire de Belges*, ed. August Jean Stecher, 4 vols. (Louvain: Lefever, 1882–91), 1.35 (p. 276). On the date, see Georges Doutrepont, *Jean Lemaire de Belges et la Renaissance* (Brussels: Maurice Lamertin, 1934), xi; Paul Spaak, *Jean Lemaire de Belges: Sa vie, son oeuvre, et ses meilleures pages* (Paris: Champion, 1926), 18, 110–11.

2. Doutrepont, *Jean Lemaire de Belges*, xi.

3. *Chronicarum quae Dicuntur Fredegarii Scholastici Libri IV cum Continuationibus*, ed. Bruno Krusch, *MGH*, Scriptores Rerum Merovingicarum, 2 (Hannover: Hahn, 1888).

4. Doutrepont, *Jean Lemaire de Belges*, 5–6.

5. Ibid., 2, 51.

6. Major sources for Lemaire's Judgment, exclusive of allegorical interpretation, could easily be those proposed by Doutrepont (ibid., 306–8): *Heroides* 16 and 17; the commentary on the *Heroides* of Volsc and Ubertino; Apuleius's *The Golden Ass*, bk. 10, with commentary by Beroaldo; Hyginus; Servius; and Boccaccio's *De Genealogiis Deorum*. Some sources Doutrepont mentions are not relevant to our study because he is also considering sources for the Paris-Oenone episode and some material on the youth of Paris. On Lemaire's use of his acknowledged sources, see ibid., 26–40 passim, and annexes, 403–16.

7. He cites Ovid's *Heroides* in his list of sources at the end of bk. 1 (p. 344), and he cites Apuleius's Judgment in 1.35 (p. 272). The sources that he claims are not always the sources that he uses, but in these cases, he is accurate. On his use of these sources, see Doutrepont, *Jean Lemaire de Belges*, 41–42, 306–7, 408.

8. On his use of Ovid, see ibid., 305–6.

9. He claims the *Recognitions* as a source, though this detail is only in the *Homilies*.

10. Lemaire, *Illustrations*, 1.30 (p. 226). Giovanni Boccaccio, *Genealogie Deorum Gentilium Libri*, ed. Vincenzo Romano, 2 vols. (*Opere*, 10–11) (Bari: Gius. Laterza & Figli, 1951), 9.1 (2.439).

11. Lemaire, *Illustrations*, 1.30 (p. 226); Boccaccio, *Genealogie*, 9.1 (2.436–37).

12. Lemaire, *Illustrations*, 1.30 (p. 226); Boccaccio, *Genealogie*, 3.22 (1.142).

13. Lemaire, *Illustrations*, 1.30 (p. 226); Boccaccio, *Genealogie*, 4.64 (1.219).

14. Lemaire, *Illustrations*, 1.31 (p. 236); Boccaccio, *Genealogie*, 2.3 (1.72).

15. See, e.g., Boccaccio, *Genealogie*, 3.22 (1.145).

16. As in ibid., 3.22 (1.148).

17. See ibid., 3.22 (1.144) for her traditional association with the union of animals.

18. Apuleius, *The Golden Ass*, trans. William Adlington, rev. Stephen Gaselee, Loeb Classical Library (Cambridge: Harvard University Press, 1915), 529.

19. Boccaccio gives her myrtle and roses, 3.22 (1.142, 147), but only red roses (see 3.23 [1.152]).

20. *Iliad*, trans. Richmond Lattimore (Chicago: University of Chicago Press, 1951), 14.215–17 (pp. 299–300).

21. Lemaire, *Illustrations*, 1.32 (p. 242); Boccaccio: "santissima atque veneranda legum autoritate illi fuisset appositum, ut aliquali coertione vaga nimis lascivia frenaretur" (3.22 [1.144]).

22. W. H. Roscher, "Aphrodite," *ALGRM*, ed. W. H. Roscher, 1, 1 (Leipzig: Teubner, 1884–86), col. 399; Earl G. Schreiber, "Venus in the Mythographic Tradition," *Journal of English and Germanic Philology*, 74 (1975): 522.

23. Trans. W. R. M. Lamb, Loeb Classical Library (Cambridge: Harvard University Press, 1932), 180 (p. 109).

24. Lemaire, *Illustrations*, bk. 1 (p. 346); Lucretius, *De Rerum Natura*, trans. W. H. D. Rouse, Loeb Classical Library (Cambridge: Harvard University Press, 1937), 3–5, 323–31.

25. *Commentum in Martianum Capellam*, ed. Cora E. Lutz, 1 (Leiden: Brill, 1962), 2.62.11 (p. 180). See D. W. Robertson, Jr., *A Preface to Chaucer: Studies in Medieval Perspectives* (Princeton: Princeton University Press, 1962), 125–26; Doris Ruhe, *Le Dieu d'amours avec son paradis: Untersuchungen zur Mythenbildung um Amor im Spätantike und Mittelalter*, Beiträge zur romanischen Philologie der Mittelalters, 6 (Munich: Wilhelm Fink, 1974), 50–51.

26. Actually three Venuses; see Richard Hamilton Green, "Alan of Lille's *De Planctu Naturae*," *Speculum*, 31 (1956): 667–68; *Annotationes in Marcianum*, ed. Cora E. Lutz (Cambridge, Mass.: Mediaeval Academy of America, 1939), 8.8 (p. 13).

27. "Venus in Venerem pugnans," *De Planctu Naturae*, PL, ed. J.-P. Migne, 210 (Paris, J.-P. Migne, 1855), col. 431. For Alain's use of this figure and its history, see Green, "Alan of Lille's *De Planctu Naturae*," 667–68.

28. *The Commentary on the First Six Books of the Aeneid of Vergil Commonly Attributed to Bernardus Silvestris*, ed. Julian Ward Jones and Elizabeth Frances Jones (Lincoln: University of Nebraska Press, 1977), 9; on it Green, "Alan of Lille's *De Planctu Naturae*," 668.

29. *Scriptores Rerum Mythicarum*, ed. Georg Heinrich Bode (Celle: Schulze, 1834), 11.18 (p. 239).

30. Schreiber, "Venus," 522, 528.

31. Lemaire, *Illustrations*, 1.32 (p. 242) and 1.33 (p. 255); Fulgentius, *Opera*, ed. Rudolf Helm (1898; rpt. Stuttgart: Teubner, 1970), 2.1 (p. 40); Boccaccio, *Genealogie*, 3.23 (1.152).

32. E.g. Fulgentius, *Opera*, 2.1 (p. 40); Boccaccio, *Genealogie*, 3.23 (1.152). On the rose in connection with Venus, see Robertson, *Preface to Chaucer*, 95–96, n. 82.

33. In the commentary on the *Echecs amoureux*, each of the two Venuses has her own rose, red or white. See Chapter 4. The *De Deorum Imaginibus Libellus* gives Venus both red and white roses (ed. Hans Liebeschütz, in *Fulgen-*

tius Metaforalis: Ein Beitrag zur Geschichte der antiken Mythologie im Mittelalter [Leipzig: Teubner, 1926], 118].

34. Félix Buffière, *Les Mythes d'Homère et la pensée grecque* (Paris: Société d'Edition Les Belles Lettres, 1956), 159.

35. On Heraclitus, ibid., 169; on Plutarch, Edgar Wind, *Pagan Mysteries in the Renaissance*, rev. ed. (New York: W. W. Norton, 1968), 86–87.

36. Buffière, *Mythes d'Homère*, 148.

37. On the tradition in classical and late-classical thought, Wind, *Pagan Mysteries*, 87–88, 119.

38. ed. Ludwig Bieler, *CCSL*, 94. Turnhout: Brepols, 1957), 2, meter 8, 1–30.

39. "Legitimam Venerem legimus esse mundanam musicam" (9).

40. Lemaire does not cite Boethius, but he could have known the *Consolation of Philosophy*, which was extremely popular. Colard Mansion had printed a French translation at Bruges in 1477, and this edition had been reprinted by Antoine Verard at Paris in 1494. See Richard A. Dwyer, *Boethian Fictions: Narratives in the Medieval French Versions of the Consolatio Philosophiae*, Mediaeval Academy of America Publication no. 83 (Cambridge, Mass.: Mediaeval Academy of America, 1976), 130.

41. See Lucretius, *De Rerum Natura*, 7 and passim.

42. On the contrasting views of Nature in Alain de Lille and the *Roman de la Rose*, see Ernst Robert Curtius, *European Literature and the Latin Middle Ages*, trans. Willard R. Trask, Bollingen Series, 36 (1953; rpt. Princeton: Princeton University Press, 1973), 117–22, 124–27; George D. Economou, *The Goddess Natura in Medieval Literature* (Cambridge: Harvard University Press, 1972), 106–24; on Nature in Alain de Lille, Green, "Alan of Lille's *De Planctu Naturae*," 663–67.

43. *Oeuvres*, 3.98–135.

44. "Sed bene pastor, quia *non* ut sagitta certus et iaculo bonus et *uultu decorus* et ingenio sagacissimus" (Fulgentius, *Opera*, 2.1 [p. 37]; my italics).

45. In an interesting discussion of Lemaire, Ann Moss points out that a positive view of Venus characterized the Italian neo-Platonist approach to the Judgment: *Poetry and Fable: Studies in Mythological Narrative in Sixteenth-Century France* (Cambridge: Cambridge University Press, 1984), 36.

Appendix. The Judgment of Paris in Medieval Art

1. The most comprehensive catalogue of the theme's occurrence in ancient art is Christoph Clairmont, *Das Parisurteil in der antiken Kunst* (Zurich: n.p., 1951), but see the review of Roland Hampe, *Gnomon*, 26 (1954): 545–51. See also, more recently, Irmgard Raab, *Zu den Darstellungen des Parisurteils in der griechischen Kunst*, Archäologische Studien, no. 1 (Frankfurt: Peter Lang, 1972), 161–97, and bibliography, 11.

2. Hugo Buchthal, *Historia Troiana: Studies in the History of Medieval Secular Illustration* (London: Warburg Institute, 1971). I follow 37–39 in my discussion of the miniature's relation to Guido's text and to a possible model. For the date and provenance, see 20.

3. Ibid., 39.

4. For a description of the manuscript, see Henri Omont, *Catalogue général des manuscrits français*, 4: *Anciens petits fonds français*, 1 (Paris: Ernest Leroux, 1898), 522. I know of two additional miniatures, one in a manuscript, the other in an early printed book, which use the artistic version of the Judgment deriving from Guido to illustrate a text based on Guido: both illustrate Jacques Milet's *Lystoire de la destruction de Troye:* Paris B.n. nouv. acq. fr. 24920, f. 8r; *Lystoire de la destruction de Troye la grant* (Paris: J. Driart, 1498), n.p.

5. For descriptions of the manuscripts, see Gianni Mombello, *La tradizione manoscritta dell' "Epistre Othea" di Christine de Pizan* (Turin: Accademia delle Scienze, 1967).

6. Mary Ann Ignatius, "Christine de Pizan's *Epistre Othea:* An Experiment in Literary Form," *Medievalia et Humanistica*, 9 (1979): 131–39; Millard Meiss, *French Painting in the Time of Jean de Berry: The Limbourgs and Their Contemporaries*, 2 vols. (New York: George Braziller, 1974), 1.23.

7. Mombello, *Tradizione manoscritta*, 14–15; e.g., see the Judgment in London Harley 4431, f. 125 v, illustrating Ch. 68, the dream of Paris. Another miniature of the Judgment which seems to have been devised *ad hoc* to reflect the text of the *Othéa* is Brussels Bibl. Roy. 9392, f. 80v (reproduced on the jacket of this volume).

8. Fritz Saxl and Hans Meier, *Catalogue of Astrological and Mythological Illuminated Manuscripts of the Latin Middle Ages*, 3, fasc. 1: *Manuscripts in English Libraries* (London: Warburg Institute, 1953), 295; on the manuscript see also Mombello, *Tradizione manoscritta*, 225–32.

9. Another miniature which illustrates ch. 73 of the *Othéa* with a picture deriving from the tradition of Guido is Erlangen Universitätsbibliothek 2361, f. 93v.

10. On it, see E. Bagby Atwood and V. K. Whitaker, eds., *Excidium Troiae* (Cambridge, Mass.: Mediaeval Academy of America, 1944), lxxviii–lxxix.

11. On it, see Fritz Saxl, *Verzeichnis astrologischer und mythologischer illustrierter Handschriften des lateinischen Mittelalters in römischen Bibliotheken*, 1 (Heidelberg: Carl Winter, 1915), 8–10.

12. Hans Liebeschütz, *Fulgentius Metaforalis: Ein Beitrag zur Geschichte der antiken Mythologie im Mittelalter* (Leipzig: Teubner, 1926), 56–57.

13. For the manuscript description, see Omont, *Catalogue général*, 520–21.

14. On the manuscript, see Carla Lord, "Three Manuscripts of the *Ovide moralisé*," *Art Bulletin*, 57 (1975): 162–63. For the date, see 163.

15. Ibid., 162.

16. John B. Friedman, "L'iconographie de Vénus et de son miroir à la fin du Moyen âge," in *L'Erotism au Moyen Age: Etudes présentées au Troisième colloque de l'Institut d'études médiévales*, ed. Bruno Roy (Montreal: Aurore, 1977), 51–82.

17. A similar depiction of the three lives appears in a manuscript of the *Ovide moralisé* dating from the second quarter of the fourteenth century, Paris Arsenal 5069, f. 153v (for the date, see Lord, "Three Manuscripts," 163). Here the figures are more clearly the three *lives;* e.g., the figure representing the contemplative life is male.

18. On it, see Reginald Hyatte, "The Manuscripts of the Prose Commentary (Fifteenth Century) on *Les échecs amoureux*," *Manuscripta*, 26 (1982): 25–26.

19. Trans. Leslie George Whitbread, *Fulgentius the Mythographer* (Columbus: Ohio State University Press, 1971), 65.

20. Ibid., 64.

21. Henry Bergen, ed., *The Troy Book*, by John Lydgate, 4 vols., Early English Text Society, ES 97, 103, 106, 126 (London: EETS, 1906–35), 4.32.

Index

University of Pennsylvania Press

MIDDLE AGES SERIES

Edward Peters, General Editor

Edward Peters, ed. *Christian Society and the Crusades, 1198–1229.* Sources in Translation, including The Capture of Damietta by Oliver of Paderborn. 1971

Edward Peters, ed. *The First Crusade: The Chronicle of Fulcher of Chartres and Other Source Materials.* 1971

Katherine Fischer Drew, trans. *The Burgundian Code: The Book of Constitutions or Law of Gundobad and Additional Enactments.* 1972

G. G. Coulton. *From St. Francis to Dante: Translations from the Chronicle of the Franciscan Salimbene (1221–1288).* 1972

Alan C. Kors and Edward Peters, eds. *Witchcraft in Europe, 1110–1700: A Documentary History.* 1972

Richard C. Dales. *The Scientific Achievement of the Middle Ages.* 1973

Katherine Fischer Drew, trans. *The Lombard Laws.* 1973

Henry Charles Lea. *The Ordeal.* Part III of Superstitition and Force. 1973

Henry Charles Lea. *Torture.* Part IV of Superstition and Force. 1973

Henry Charles Lea (Edward Peters, ed.). *The Duel and the Oath.* Parts I and II of Superstition and Force. 1974

Edwards Peters, ed. *Monks, Bishops, and Pagans: Christian Culture in Gaul and Italy, 500–700.* 1975

Jeanne Krochalis and Edward Peters, ed. and trans. *The World of Piers Plowman.* 1975

Julius Goebel, Jr. *Felony and Misdemeanor: A Study in the History of Criminal Law.* 1976

Susan Mosher Stuard, ed. *Women in Medieval Society.* 1976

James Muldoon, ed. *The Expansion of Europe: The First Phase.* 1977

Clifford Peterson. *Saint Erkenwald.* 1977

Robert Somerville and Kenneth Pennington, eds. *Law, Church, and Society: Essays in Honor of Stephan Kuttner.* 1977

Donald E. Queller. *The Fourth Crusade: The Conquest of Constantinople, 1201–1204.* 1977

Pierre Riché (Jo Ann McNamara, trans.). *Daily Life in the World of Charlemagne.* 1978

Charles R. Young. *The Royal Forests of Medieval England.* 1979

Edward Peters, ed. *Heresy and Authority in Medieval Europe.* 1980

Suzanne Fonay Wemple. *Women in Frankish Society: Marriage and the Cloister, 500–900.* 1981

R. G. Davies and J. H. Denton, eds. *The English Parliament in the Middle Ages.* 1981

Edward Peters. *The Magician, the Witch, and the Law.* 1982

Barbara H. Rosenwein. *Rhinoceros Bound: Cluny in the Tenth Century.* 1982

Steven D. Sargent, ed. and trans. *On the Threshold of Exact Science: Selected Writings of Anneliese Maier on Late Medieval Natural Philosophy.* 1982

Benedicta Ward. *Miracles and the Medieval Mind: Theory, Record, and Event, 1000–1215.* 1982

Harry Turtledove, trans. *The Chronicle of Theophanes: An English Translation of anni mundi 6095–6305 (A.D. 602–813).* 1982

Leonard Cantor, ed. *The English Medieval Landscape.* 1982

Charles T. Davis. *Dante's Italy and Other Essays.* 1984

George T. Dennis, trans. *Maurice's Strategikon: Handbook of Byzantine Military Strategy.* 1984

Thomas F. X. Noble. *The Republic of St. Peter: The Birth of the Papal State, 680–825.* 1984

Kenneth Pennington. *Pope and Bishops: The Papal Monarchy in the Twelfth and Thirteenth Centuries.* 1984

Patrick J. Geary. *Aristocracy in Provence: The Rhône Basin at the Dawn of the Carolingian Age.* 1985

C. Stephen Jaeger. *The Origins of Courtliness: Civilizing Trends and the Formation of Courtly Ideals, 939–1210.* 1985

J. N. Hillgarth, ed. *Christianity and Paganism, 350–750: The Conversion of Western Europe.* 1986

William Chester Jordan. *From Servitude to Freedom: Manumission in the Sénonais in the Thirteenth Century.* 1986

James William Brodman. *Ransoming Captives in Crusader Spain: The Order of Merced on the Christian-Islamic Frontier.* 1986

Frank Tobin. *Meister Eckhart: Thought and Language.* 1986

Daniel Bornstein, trans. *Dino Compagni's Chronicle of Florence.* 1986

James M. Powell. *Anatomy of a Crusade, 1213–1221.* 1986

Jonathan Riley-Smith. *The First Crusade and the Idea of Crusading.* 1986

Susan Mosher Stuard, ed. *Women in Medieval History and Historiography.* 1987

Avril Henry, ed. *The Mirour of Mans Saluacioune.* 1987

María Menocal. *The Arabic Role in Medieval Literary History.* 1987

Margaret J. Ehrhart. *The Judgment of the Trojan Prince Paris in Medieval Literature.* 1987

Betsy Bowden. *Chaucer Aloud: The Varieties of Textual Interpretation.* 1987

Michael Resler. *EREC by Hartmann von Aue.* 1987

A. J. Minnis. *Medieval Theory of Authorship.* 1987